Guilt Free Gourmet

FOOD THAT TASTES "TOO GOOD" TO BE "GOOD FOR YOU"

OVER 1,200 LOW FAT BUT "DELICIOUS" RECIPES

By

INTERNATIONAL YACHT CHEF

SAM MILES

Published by   WELLNESS PUBLISHING, INC.
                   1323 S.E. 17th St., Suite # 694
                   Ft. Lauderdale, Fl,   33316

Printed in the United States of America.

ISBN: 0-9641843-0-3

Editor: Melissa Becker
Food Editor: Barbara Lawrence
Copy Editors: Helen Mathias, Linda Mitchell
Artist: Andrew Wiltshire

Remember to consult your physician before starting any diet or exercise program!

This cookbook is a collection of recipes which have been gathered from various sources & adapted to meet the low-fat criteria. The data contained herein is true & complete to the best of our knowledge. All recommendations are made without any guarantees on the part of the author or publisher, who disclaim all liability in all liability in connection with the use of this data.

Fat contents are based on information found in the U. S. Department of Agriculture handbooks, The Fat Counter by Annete B. Natow, Ph.D., R.D. & Jo-Ann Heslin, M.A.,R.D., food manufacturers & labels.

This book is available to organizations for use as a Fund Raiser for Charities.

This book is dedicated to everyone who has struggled to find low-fat foods that taste so good you want (& can have) seconds or thirds, and...

To all the guests on the yachts who wanted me to hurry & write down all the recipes so they could have them....... here they are!

So, to you all, eat hardy, enjoy, experiment & have fun getting thinner every day!

Cindy!
Best of everything
except fat!

CHEF'S MOTTO: *Just because it's never been done (or you haven't done it), don't be afraid to try it.*
                  If it's been done to death, do it better or differently.

CONTENTS

I would like to give you a family recipe to transform into low fat &/or publish in your next book...

GUILT FREE GOURMET
BY REQUEST

Name of Recipe_____ Category_____ Serves_____

(I am listing the ingredients in the order that they are used)

_____   _____

_____   _____

_____   _____

_____   _____

_____   _____

_____   _____

_____   _____

_____

_____

_____

_____

_____

_____

Attach a second sheet if necessary.

I give you the rights to this recipe, to print, re-print, change or whatever is necessary, by mailing it to you.

Signature_____

NAME_____STREET_____APT/BOX_____

CITY_____STATE_____ZIP_____

Mail to:
Wellness Publishing, Inc., 1323 S.E. 17th St. #694, Ft. Lauderdale, Fl. 33316

We strive for perfection, so if you happen to find an error,
please let us know, so we can correct it in the next printing.

Helpful Tips

After spending most of my adult life dieting, I'd finally given up. And...

I LOST THE WEIGHT WITHOUT DIETING & it was great to be able to eat most of the foods I love so much, & eat as much of them as I wanted. (No fried foods—but then we can't have everything in life.)

So, when the guests would come on board the yachts, they couldn't wait to try my food just to see if it was as good as people had told them & if they could really eat all they wanted & still lose weight. My favorite compliment, which happened again & again, was when they would ask the stewardess, "Are you sure I can have this? You'd better ask Sam if this is for me or someone else." And they would be so amazed when I would come to the table & assure them they could have all they wanted.

GUILT FREE GOURMET is such a great way to eat, there's no worry about going 'off the diet' & thereby typically gaining back all the weight. Once you've reached your goal, you just naturally want to continue the low-fat way of eating. It's so easy & delicious!!!

Because it has finally been proven that it's not really the calories that count when it comes to putting on or taking off weight, but what's **in** those calories. If there is not much fat coming into the body, it's almost impossible to gain weight.

The less fat in your diet, the more freedom you have to indulge in those luscious, high-calorie foods we all seem to love. The problem comes from not knowing how much fat your body needs in a day and where your body gets it.

Magazine & newspaper articles, as well as food manufacturers, tend to confuse rather than explain what you should or should not be eating, what with the percent of fat factors & formulas. So, make it easy on yourself & your body....

KEEP IT SIMPLE & SWEET (& DELICIOUS, TOO)

It is recommended that women trying to lose weight stay near the 20 gram mark and men around 30 grams. This allows for what I call "floaters" (grams of fat that somehow sneak into your diet that you forget to count).

Children should not have fat suppressed from their main diet, but it might be a good idea to start cutting back on the fat in their snacks. Check with your doctor before starting any new diet plan.

A sample of the surprising fat content of some foods:

CHEDDAR CHEESE	1 OZ	9.4 GRAMS
EGG	1	5.6
OILS	1 T	13.6
MAYO	1 T	11.0
BUTTER	1 T	12.3
MARGARINE	1 T	12.0
AVOCADO	1	30.0
NUTS	1 OZ	15.0

So you see, it doesn't take much to exceed your daily goal if you don't know the fat content of the food. Now you will learn how to create imaginative meals that are low fat, but you must also become aware of the fat in the foods you buy.

CHECK THE LABELS on packaged foods. You'll be surprised at how much you can eat and still lose weight if the food contains little or no fat. But, you must be sure you're using LOW-FAT or 0-FAT ingredients.

There are LOW-FAT & 0-FAT foods on the market. Look for these & others:

FAT-FREE salad dressings, KRAFT FREE MIRACLE WHIP, FAT-FREE breads, PROMISE ULTRA, LAND O' LAKES NO-FAT sour cream & LIGHT & LIVELY and GUILT FREE sour cream & cottage cheese. Beware, some other brands of sour cream will separate when heated.

KRAFT PHILADELPHIA, HEALTHY CHOICE & ALPINE LACE FAT-FREE cream cheese.

HEALTHY CHOICE, ALPINE LACE, KRAFT, POLLY-0, BORDEN, SARGENTO, FRIGO Low-fat and Fat-Free cheeses, ALPINE LACE and WEIGHT WATCHER'S FAT-FREE PARMESAN, GUILT FREE NONFAT ICE CREAM & FROZEN YOGURTS, DREAM WHIP topping (the one you make from the package), Fat Free Cool Whip (frozen).

BUTTER BUDS, EGG BEATERS, OSCAR MAYER TURKEY BACON (1 gm per slice), HEALTHY CHOICE hot dogs, (1 gm ea), HEALTHY CHOICE ground beef (1 gm per ounce),

Cookies, cakes and snacks by ENTENMANN'S and JELL-O, KEEBLER FAT-FREE DEVIL'S FOOD COOKIES, NABISCO FAT- FREE SALTINES and SNACKWELL crackers & cookies, MR. SALTY FAT-FREE PRETZELS and SKINNY's various chips, PIONEER Non-Fat biscuit mix, BETTY CROCKER Fat-Free frostings and No-Yolks pasta.

BEWARE OF LOW-CHOLESTEROL FOODS, they may not be low-fat, just low in saturated fat, which is good for your health, but will still put weight on you.

EAT..EAT..EAT. Don't skimp on meals. Your body can't break down fat unless it has the proper vitamins, minerals and nutrients. If you don't feel like eating breakfast, have a LIQUADA (p 324) or a commercial nutritious drink..anything to get your metabolism going. I take a multivitamin with each meal.

Drink plenty of fluids every day, at least 8 glasses. Try to drink 1 about 10 minutes before each meal. Decaf coffee or tea after dinner is also good.. If possible, make lunch your big meal of the day; but if this is not possible, try to eat dinner earlier than you normally would. The later you eat, the less time your body has to burn off the fat & calories in that dinner.

Use Egg Beaters egg substitute whenever possible (add Butter Buds to give them a richer taste). When baking cakes or muffins, it's better to underbake. If it looks done to you, it's probably underdone and will be tough & chewy. Using cake flour will result in a more tender product.

When we use Fat-Free Miracle Whip, we add lemon juice, dry mustard, Louisiana Hot Sauce & Worcestershire Sauce to make it taste more like real mayonnaise. An even quicker fix is to drizzle a little juice from a jar of roasted, pickled, red bell peppers (usually found near the fresh pasta at better grocers).

Hershey's Chocolate Syrup & Cocoa have very little fat.

If you must use fats, use strong flavors—you'll need less to get the taste you want. Examples: Olive, Sesame or Walnut oil, Cheddar, Bleu or Parmesan cheese.

NEVER saute' onions, green peppers, etc. in oil or butter. Instead, simmer in other types of liquids, such as stocks or wine (or microwave).

Use a spray vegetable oil to coat pans. We find PAM regular and butter flavors work best as does the BERTOLLI olive oil spray.

If you exercise, do it **BEFORE BREAKFAST**. This will make your body burn fat for its fuel instead of calories. It's much easier for your body to burn calories than it is to burn up fat, and it's the fat you want to burn.

Have a LIQUADA (p 324) after your morning workout or throughout the day.

For creamed soups, use pureed, cooked potatoes to thicken instead of cream. CARNATION OR PET evaporated skim milk works well in some soups.

When making stock from canned broths, skim off the fat before using by dragging a paper towel across the top several times to remove fat. Or, keep several cans chilled (remember, vegetable too), so the fat is easier to remove.

The trick to making stock from cubes taste better is to always use vegetable cubes along with the chicken, beef, or ham cubes, etc. We use KNORR, as we think it gives the best flavor with a low-fat content.

When making marinades, leave out the oil, add a little water and shorten the time for marinating. (Without oil, the marinade will be absorbed more quickly.)

Eventually, skim milk is the only milk you should be using. It has less than 1/2 gram of fat per cup. 1% milk has 2.6, 2% has 4.7, whole milk has 8.0. Try using 2% for two or three weeks, then 1% for two or three weeks. This will make it easier to get used to the taste of skim milk.

Try low-fat buttermilk for salad dressings & baking.

Do not skip desserts if you are a dessert person. Depriving yourself is ridiculous when there are so many desserts that are low-fat or 0-fat. You will find that you actually enjoy staying on a low-fat program once you realize how easy it is and **HOW MUCH YOU GET TO EAT.**

In the following recipes, it is assumed that you will

ALWAYS REMOVE ALL SKIN AND FAT

FROM ANY MEAT REQUIRED.

THINK OF CALORIES AS LIGHT AS FEATHERS...

THINK OF FAT AS HEAVY ROCKS!!!

Hors D'oeuvres

&

Appetizers

Remember when we specify Kraft Fat-Free Miracle Whip, we suggest that you spice it up first before continuing with the recipe. Just add some dry mustard or deli stone ground mustard, a little fresh lemon juice, some Worcestershire Sauce and a little Louisiana Hot Sauce. (Kraft probably doesn't add these because the acidity would cause a much shorter shelf life, but they do bring out its flavor.)

SHERRIED, STUFFED ARTICHOKE BOTTOMS

 easy   SERVES 12   FAT = TR EA

2 C	MUSHROOMS, DICED	SIMMER THESE INGREDIENTS
1 C	ONIONS, DICED	UNTIL ALMOST DRY.
1 CL	GARLIC, MINCED (OPTIONAL)	
1/4 C	DRY SHERRY	
------	WATER IF NEEDED	
1 T	FRESH THYME	ADD THESE, MIX WELL AND
4 T	FRESH PARSLEY, CHOPPED	SPREAD ON THE BOTTOMS.
1/4 C	FAT-FREE MIRACLE WHIP	
1/2 C	NO-FAT SOUR CREAM &/OR CREAM CHEESE	
	SALT & PEPPER TO TASTE	
	DRY SHERRY (ENOUGH TO GET A STUFFING CONSISTENCY)	
2 CANS	ARTICHOKE BOTTOMS, QUARTERED	
3 T	PARMESAN CHEESE	SPRINKLE OVER.

Broil until golden brown and bubbly.

SPINACH STUFFED ARTICHOKE BOTTOMS

easy   SERVES 12   FAT = 1.5 GM EA

1/2 C	ONIONS, DICED	SIMMER THESE INGREDIENTS
3 CL	GARLIC, MINCED	UNTIL ALMOST DRY.
1/2 C	WATER	
10 OZ	FROZEN CHOPPED SPINACH, THAWED, DRAINED	ADD THESE, MIX WELL AND
1/4 t	NUTMEG	SPREAD ON THE BOTTOMS.
1/2 t	CAVENDER'S GREEK SEASONING	
3/4 C	NO-FAT SOUR CREAM	
2 CANS	ARTICHOKE BOTTOMS, HALVED OR QUARTERED	
2 OZ	PART-SKIM MOZZARELLA, GRATED	SPRINKLE OVER.

Bake at 375 until brown or bubbly on top.

You could substitute mushroom caps for the artichoke bottoms.

PICKLED BABY CARROTS

easy   SERVES 16   FAT = TR EA

2 C	WHITE WINE VINEGAR	BRING THESE INGREDIENTS TO
2 C	APPLE CIDER	A BOIL.
2 T	RED WINE OR RASPBERRY VINEGAR	
2 T	PICKLING SPICE	
1/2 t	DRIED DILL (OPTIONAL)	
1/4 C	BROWN SUGAR	ADD & SIMMER FOR 15 MIN.
2 LBS	BABY CARROTS, SCRAPED CLEAN	CHILL.

MUSHROOM PEPPER CAVIAR

20 OZ   FAT = TR EA

1 EA	GREEN, RED BELL PEPPER, MINCED	SIMMER THESE INGREDIENTS
1/2 C	ONIONS, MINCED	UNTIL ALMOST DRY.
4 T	WATER OR DRY SHERRY	
1 LB	MUSHROOMS, MINCED	
1/4 C	FAT-FREE CHICKEN STOCK	
2 T	BUTTER BUDS	
1/8 t	KNOX GELATIN (SPRINKLED OVER THE SHERRY)	
2 T	DRY SHERRY	LET SIT FOR 2 MINUTES.
1 T	FRESH PARSLEY, CHOPPED	COMBINE ALL INGREDIENTS.
1/4 t	CAVENDER'S GREEK SEASONING	SIMMER 5 MINUTES & COOL.
1/2 t	DRIED THYME	

Pack into small crocks, chill 8 hours. Serve as you would caviar.

CRAB CREAM-CHEESE BALLS

24 OZ   FAT = TR EA

1 LB	CRAB MEAT, PICKED CLEAN (OR IMITATION)	COMBINE ALL INGREDIENTS.
2 C	FAT-FREE CREAM CHEESE, SOFT	
4 T	PARMESAN CHEESE	SHAPE INTO 3 BALLS.
4 T	BUTTER BUDS (DISSOLVED IN THE HOT WATER)	
2 T	HOT WATER	
1	ONION, MINCED	
1 t	FRESH LEMON JUICE	
1 t	OLD BAY SEASONING	
1/2 t	WORCESTERSHIRE SAUCE	SPRINKLE WITH MORE OLD
------	FAT-FREE MIRACLE WHIP AS NEEDED	BAY SEASONING OR PAPRIKA
1 CL	GARLIC, MINCED (OPTIONAL)	& CHILL.

LEMON PEPPER CHEESE BALLS   16 OZ   FAT = TR EA

2 C	FAT-FREE CREAM CHEESE, SOFT	COMBINE THESE INGREDIENTS.
1 T	GARLIC, MINCED	
3 T	BUTTER BUDS (DISSOLVED IN THE HOT WATER)	SHAPE INTO 4 BALLS.
1 T	HOT WATER	
2 t	FRESH CHIVES, CHOPPED	ROLL IN LEMON PEPPER.
2 t	FRESH BASIL, CHOPPED	
2 t	DILL, MINCED (OPTIONAL)	
2 t	CARAWAY SEED, GROUND	CHILL.
------	LEMON PEPPER	

PARMESAN CHICKEN STRIPS   SERVES 16   FAT = 2 GM EA

1/2 C	EGG BEATERS	COMBINE THESE FOR DIPPING.
1/4 C	SKIM MILK	
1/2 C	FAT-FREE BREAD CRUMBS	COMBINE THESE TO DREDGE THE STRIPS, AFTER THEY HAVE BEEN DIPPED.
1/2 C	PARMESAN CHEESE	
1 t	DRIED BASIL	
1/2 t	DRIED THYME	
1/2 t	ONION POWDER	
1/4 t	SALT	
1/8 t	PEPPER	
2 LBS	CHICKEN BREAST STRIPS	DIP, DREDGE & PLACE ON A PAM SPRAYED PAN.

Spray strips with Pam, bake at 400 for 20 minutes or until done.

GINGER CHICKEN OR BEEF CUBES   SERVES 24   FAT = 1 GM EA

3 LBS	MEAT CUBES	BROWN IN A PAM-SPRAYED PAN, ADD VEGGIES AND SIMMER FOR 4 MINUTES.
1 C	ONION, SQUARES	
4 CL	GARLIC, MINCED	
4	RED & GREEN PEPPERS, IN SQUARES	THREAD ALL EXCEPT GINGER ON SKEWERS.
1 INCH	FRESH GINGER, PEELED, MINCED	
1/2 C	SOY SAUCE	COMBINE REMAINING ITEMS. SIMMER, BRUSH ON KABOBS AND BROIL UNTIL DONE.
2 T	WHITE WINE VINEGAR	
1/4 t	GROUND GINGER (OR TO TASTE)	

ORIENTAL CHICKEN

easy   SERVES 32   FAT = 1 GM EA

1 C	EGG BEATERS	WHISK THESE TO MAKE A LIGHT
1 C	FLOUR	BATTER.
1/2 C	LIGHT BEER	
1 T	BUTTER BUDS	
1 T	SOY SAUCE	
1 t	SALT	
		DIP IN BATTER, DRAIN AND PLACE
4 LBS	CHICKEN BREASTS, 1" CUBES	ON A PAM-SPRAYED PAN.

Spray pieces with Pam, bake at 400 for 15-20 minutes.

SAUCE

quick   5 CUPS   FAT = TR EA

28 OZ	CRUSHED PINEAPPLE	SIMMER THESE FOR 10 MINUTES.
2 t	GARLIC, MINCED	
1 C	BROWN SUGAR	
1 t	FRESH GINGER, PEELED, GRATED	
1/2 C	VINEGAR	
3/4 C	SOY SAUCE	COMBINE WELL & ADD.
6 T	CORNSTARCH	HEAT 5 MINUTES TO THICKEN.

Serve this sauce hot over chicken or use for dipping a dipping sauce.

SPICY CHICKEN STRIPS

easy   SERVES 4   FAT = 2 GM EA

8 OZ	NO-FAT SOUR CREAM	COMBINE AND CHILL THESE FOR
2 T	FRESH LEMON JUICE	1 HOUR.
2 T	BUTTER BUDS	
1/2 t	CHILI POWDER	ADD THE STRIPS.
1/2 t	GARLIC SALT	CHILL FOR 1 HOUR.
1/4 t	GROUND CUMIN	
1/4 t	OLD BAY SEASONING	
1/4 t	CAVENDER'S GREEK SEASONING	
		DREDGE STRIPS IN CHIPS, PLACE
16 OZ	CHICKEN BREAST STRIPS	ON A PAM-SPRAYED PAN.
2 C	CRUSHED HOMEMADE TORTILLA CHIPS	SPRAY PIECES WITH PAM.
		BAKE AT 375 FOR 20 MINUTES.

To make homemade chips, spray corn tortillas with Pam and bake at 350 for 8-10 minutes until just turning brown. Crack each into wedges.

BAKED EGGPLANT SALAD

SERVES 8   FAT = 3 GM EA

2	EGGPLANTS, CUBED, SALTED 30 MIN., DRAINED	
3 C	ONIONS, DICED	LAYER THESE IN A SPRAYED DISH
2 C	TOMATO SAUCE	& BAKE AT 375 FOR 30-40 MIN.
2 C	TOMATO PASTE	
1/2 C	GREEN OLIVES (OR BLACK), SLICED	
1/4 C	CAPERS, MINCED	SPRINKLE WITH PARMESAN.
2 T	BUTTER BUDS	SERVE HOT.

SPINACH CREPE BITES

48 PIECES   FAT = .5 GM EA

1 C	FLOUR	COMBINE AND CHILL THESE FOR
3/4 C	SKIM MILK	2 HOURS.
1/4 C	COOKED SPINACH, DRAINED, CHOPPED	
1/4 C	GREEN ONIONS, MINCED	
1/2 C	EGG BEATERS	
1/8 t	SALT	
1/8 t	GROUND NUTMEG	MAKE CREPES (p 120).
1 C	NO-FAT SOUR CREAM	COMBINE & SPREAD THESE ON
3/4 C	PART SKIM RICOTTA CHEESE	CREPES.
1/2 C	99% FAT-FREE HAM, MINCED	ROLL UP TIGHTLY & CHILL FOR 1
1/4 C	PARMESAN CHEESE	HOUR.
2 t	CAVENDER'S GREEK SEASONING	
2 T	FRESH PARSLEY, CHOPPED	SLICE IN 1/2" WIDTHS.
1 t	DRIED THYME	ARRANGE ON A TRAY.
1 CL	GARLIC, MINCED	

CARROT-STUFFED ENDIVE

48 PIECES   FAT = TR EA

8	BELGIAN ENDIVE	WASH & DRY EACH LEAF.
1 C	RADISHES, GRATED, DRIED	COMBINE REMAINING ITEMS.
2 C	CARROTS, GRATED, DRIED	
1/2 C	GREEN ONION, MINCED	PIPE OR SPOON A DAB ONTO THE
1/4 C	NO-FAT SOUR CREAM	BASE OF EACH ENDIVE LEAF.
1/4 C	FAT-FREE CREAM CHEESE	
1 t	DRIED DILL	
1 T	FRESH LEMON JUICE	ARRANGE IN A CIRCLE.
1/8 t	PEPPER OR LEMON PEPPER	
1/8 t	CINNAMON, OR NUTMEG (OPTIONAL)	

CHEESE-STUFFED ENDIVE

quick　24 PIECES　　　FAT = 1 GM EA

4 HDS	BELGIAN ENDIVE	WASH & DRY EACH LEAF.
1 C	FAT-FREE CREAM CHEESE	COMBINE & PIPE ONTO THE BASE
1/2 C	NO-FAT SOUR CREAM	OF EACH LEAF.
4 T	PARMESAN CHEESE	
1/2 OZ	GORGONZOLA OR BLEU CHEESE	
------	PAPRIKA	SPRINKLE OVER CHEESE.

Arrange in a circular pattern on a tray with a doily on it.

ITALIAN STUFFED CLAMS

24 PIECES... 48 PIECES　　　FAT = .5 GM EA

1 T	FRESH OREGANO, MINCED	SIMMER THESE UNTIL TENDER.
1 C	ONION, MINCED	
1 T	FRESH BASIL, MINCED	
1/4 t	OLD BAY SEASONING	
4 CL	GARLIC, MINCED	IF TOO DRY, ADD A LITTLE MORE
1/2 t	CAVENDER'S GREEK SEASONING	CLAM JUICE.
1 C	FAT-FREE BREAD CRUMBS	ADD REMAINDER & STUFF EACH
3/4 C	RESERVED CLAM JUICE (OR AS NEEDED)	SHELL.
2 T	FRESH LEMON JUICE	
4 T	FRESH PARSLEY, CHOPPED	SPRINKLE PARMESAN ON EACH.
1 C	FAT-FREE CREAM CHEESE	
24	LITTLE NECK CLAMS, CHOPPED (SAVE SHELLS)	
6 T	PARMESAN CHEESE	BAKE AT 375 UNTIL BUBBLY.

FRUIT KABOBS w VANILLA YOGURT SAUCE

 easy　24 SKEWERS　　　FAT = TR EA

1	PINEAPPLE, PEELED, CORED, CUBED	THREAD THE FRUIT CUBES ON
2 PTS	STRAWBERRIES, WASHED, HULLED	SMALL SKEWERS AND ARRANGE
1	HONEYDEW MELON, CUBED	ON A TRAY WITH BELOW DIP.
4	KIWI FRUITS, PEELED, QUARTERED	

VANILLA YOGURT SAUCE

2 CUPS　　　FAT = TR

ALL	JUICE FROM PREPARING ABOVE FRUITS	WHISK THESE & CHILL.
2 C	NON-FAT VANILLA YOGURT	
2 T	HONEY	
2 T	GRAND MARNIER	

MARINATED FISH FINGERS

24 PIECES   FAT = 1 GM EA

2 LBS	SOLE FILETS, FINGER-SIZE PIECES	
1/3 C	FAT-FREE CHICKEN STOCK	
4 T	FRESH LEMON JUICE	
2 T	FRESH PARSLEY, CHOPPED	
2 CL	GARLIC, MINCED	
1 t	DRIED ROSEMARY, GROUND	
1 t	DRY MUSTARD	
1 T	BUTTER BUDS	

COMBINE ALL IN A ZIPLOC BAG & CHILL FOR 1 HOUR.

BAKE ON A PAM-SPRAYED PAN AT 375 FOR 8-10 MINUTES.

SERVE WITH SAUCES BELOW.

TARTAR SAUCE

3 CUPS   FAT = TR EA

2 C	FAT-FREE MIRACLE WHIP
4 T	ONION, MINCED
3 T	SWEET RELISH
3 T	PIMENTO, DICED
2 T	FRESH LEMON JUICE
2 t	DIJON MUSTARD
2 t	FRESH BASIL, CHOPPED

COMBINE ALL INGREDIENTS.

CHILL.

CREOLE SAUCE

5 CUPS   FAT = TR EA

1	ONION, MINCED
1	GREEN BELL PEPPER, MINCED
1/2 C	MUSHROOMS, DICED
12	GREEN OLIVES, SLICED
4 T	FAT-FREE CHICKEN STOCK

SIMMER THESE UNTIL ALMOST DRY.

2 C	FAT-FREE BEEF STOCK
1 C	DRY WHITE WINE
3/4 C	TOMATO PASTE
1 t	CHILI POWDER
1 t	WORCESTERSHIRE SAUCE
	SALT & PEPPER TO TASTE

ADD & SIMMER 30 MINUTES.

SERVE HOT OR COLD.

LAMB KABOBS w GINGER MINT

36 SKEWERS   FAT = 1 GM EA

2 LBS	LEAN LAMB, THIN STRIPS
1 C	MINT JELLY
1 LB	BUTTON MUSHROOMS
2 LBS	ZUCCHINI, CUBED
3/4 C	RED WINE VINEGAR
1/2 C	CRYSTALLIZED GINGER, MINCED

MARINATE ALL FOR 6 HOURS.

THREAD ON SKEWERS & BAKE AT 400 FOR 10 MINUTES OR MORE, DEPENDING ON SIZE OF STRIPS.

SWEDISH MEATBALLS   48 PIECES   FAT = 1 GM EA

1/2 C	FAT-FREE CHICKEN STOCK	SIMMER UNTIL ALMOST DRY.
1 C	ONION, DICED	REMOVE FROM HEAT.
1 C	EGG BEATERS	ADD THESE, SHAPE INTO SMALL
2 C	SKIM MILK	BALLS & CHILL 1 HOUR.
1 C	FAT-FREE BREAD CRUMBS	
2 LBS	GROUND TURKEY BREASTS (HOMEMADE)	
	(PROCESS CHOP-CHOP IN PROCESSOR)	
1 C	YELLOW SQUASH, PEELED, CHOPPED FINE	
2 t	SALT	BROWN IN A PAM-SPRAYED PAN.
1/2 t	DILL	REMOVE & PLACE IN A SPRAYED
1/2 t	ALLSPICE	DISH.
1/2 t	PEPPER	
	MORE FAT-FREE BREAD CRUMBS IF NEEDED	
------	NUTMEG	
------	CARDAMOM	
6 T	FLOUR	PUREE THESE & SIMMER 10 MIN.
2 C	FAT-FREE BEEF STOCK	POUR OVER MEATBALLS.
1 C	NO-FAT SOUR CREAM	
1 t	DILL (OPTIONAL)	BAKE AT 350 FOR 30 MINUTES.
		GARNISH WITH DILL SPRIGS.

ITALIAN STUFFED MUSHROOMS   36 PIECES   FAT = TR EA

36	MUSHROOMS, CLEANED (REMOVE & CHOP STEMS)	
1	ONION, MINCED	ADD THESE TO THE STEMS.
2 CL	GARLIC, MINCED	
1/2 C	FAT-FREE BREAD CRUMBS	
1/4 C	FRESH PARSLEY, CHOPPED	STUFF THE MUSHROOMS.
1/4 C	FAT-FREE ITALIAN DRESSING (MORE IF NECESSARY)	
2 T	FAT-FREE MIRACLE WHIP	BROIL UNTIL BUBBLY.
2 T	DRIED ITALIAN HERBS (OR TO TASTE)	
6 T	PARMESAN CHEESE	

SEAFOOD STUFFED MUSHROOMS 48 PIECES FAT = TR EA

48	MUSHROOMS, CLEANED (REMOVE STEMS)	
1 T	FRESH LEMON JUICE	COMBINE THESE.
12 OZ	ARTIFICIAL CRAB, MINCED	
1 t	CAVENDER'S GREEK SEASONING	
1/4 C	NO-FAT SOUR CREAM	
1/4 C	FAT-FREE MIRACLE WHIP	
1/4 t	OLD BAY SEASONING	
1 t	FRESH OREGANO	ADJUST SEASONINGS TO TASTE &
1/2 C	ONIONS, MINCED	STUFF MUSHROOMS.
1 CL	GARLIC, MINCED	
6 T	PARMESAN CHEESE	
2 T	FAT-FREE BREAD CRUMBS, MORE IF NECESSARY	
1 LGE	SLICE SWISS CHEESE, CUT IN SQUARES	PLACE ON EACH MUSHROOM.
------	CAVENDER'S GREEK SEASONING	SPRINKLE OVER CHEESE & BROIL UNTIL BUBBLY.

PECAN STUFFED MUSHROOMS 50 PIECES FAT = 1 GM EA

3 LBS	MUSHROOMS, CLEANED (REMOVE STEMS)	
1/4 C	PECANS, CHOPPED	COMBINE THESE.
1/4 C	CANNED WATER CHESTNUTS, MINCED, DRIED	
1/4 C	FRESH PARSLEY, CHOPPED	
1 CL	GARLIC, MINCED	
1/2 C	NO-FAT SOUR CREAM	
1/2 C	FAT-FREE CREAM CHEESE	STUFF MUSHROOMS & SPRAY w
1/2 C	FAT-FREE BREAD CRUMBS, MORE IF NEC.	WITH PAM BUTTER SPRAY.
1/4 C	FAT-FREE SALTINES, CRUSHED	
2 T	BUTTER BUDS (MIX WITH 1 T HOT WATER)	
1/4 t EA	SALT, PEPPER	
1/4 t	DRIED THYME	BAKE AT 375 FOR 15 MINUTES.

WINE SAUTEED MUSHROOMS SERVES 16 FAT = TR EA

2 LBS	MUSHROOMS, CLEANED	SIMMER THESE UNTIL TENDER.
2	RED ONIONS, DICED	
1 C	DRY WHITE WINE	
2 CL	GARLIC, MINCED	
2 T	SOY SAUCE	ADD THESE INGREDIENTS.
1/4 t	CAYENNE OR OLD BAY SEASONING	
1 T	FRESH LEMON JUICE	HEAT & SERVE.

RED WINE MUSHROOMS

easy   SERVES 16   FAT = TR EA

1 C	RED WINE
1/2 C	RED WINE VINEGAR
1/2 C	WATER
1/2 C	ONION, MINCED
2 T	SUGAR
2 T	FRESH PARSLEY, CHOPPED
2 T	GREEN PEPPER, MINCED
1/2 t	DRIED BASIL, CRUSHED
2 CL	GARLIC, MINCED
1/4 t	SALT
2 LBS	MUSHROOMS, CLEANED, TRIMMED

COMBINE ALL & BOIL.

SIMMER 2 MINUTES.

CHILL 2 HOURS.

MARINATED MUSHROOMS

easy   SERVES 8   FAT = TR EA

1 C	KNORR BEEF STOCK (OR WHITE WINE)
2	LEMONS, JUICED
1	BAY LEAF
2 T	BUTTER BUDS
2 CL	GARLIC, MINCED
1/2 t	SALT
1/2 t	FRESH OREGANO, CHOPPED
1/4 t	PEPPER OR OLD BAY SEASONING
1 LB	SMALL MUSHROOMS

COMBINE ALL THE INGREDIENTS EXCEPT THE MUSHROOMS.

BRING TO A BOIL & POUR OVER THE MUSHROOMS.

CHILL, REMOVE BAY LEAF.

You might like to add a little red wine vinegar for a stronger taste.

PHYLLO OYSTER PUFFS

24 PIECES   FAT = 1 GM EA

1/2 C	COTTAGE CREAM (p 392)
4 OZ	LOW-FAT FETA, CRUMBLED
3	GREEN ONIONS, MINCED
1 BNCH	FRESH PARSLEY, CHOPPED
2 OZ	EGG BEATERS
ZEST OF 1	LEMON, MINCED
1/2 t	CAVENDER'S GREEK SEASONING
12	SHEETS PHYLLO, SPRAYED
24	OYSTERS, DRIED WELL

COMBINE THESE.

FOLD EACH SPRAYED SHEET OF PHYLLO IN HALF. CUT THESE IN HALF & SPRAY AGAIN.

PLACE A DAB OF CHEESE MIX ON EACH & TOP WITH AN OYSTER.

PLACE MORE CHEESE MIX ON TOP & FOLD UP LIKE A FLAG.
(p 397)

Bake at 400 for 15-20 minutes or until golden.

MINIATURE QUICHE

easy

16 QUICHE   FAT = 1 GM EA

3/4 C	EGG BEATERS	
1/4 C	FLOUR	
1/2 t	BAKING POWDER	
1/4 t	SALT	
1 C	COTTAGE CREAM (p 392)	
3 OZ	LOW-FAT CHEDDAR, SHREDDED	
1/3 C	GREEN ONION, MINCED	
1/2 t	LOUISIANA HOT SAUCE	
	FAT-FREE BREAD CRUMBS	

MIX ALL, EXCEPT THE BREAD CRUMBS.

SPRAY MINI QUICHE PANS. PRESS CRUMBS INTO BOTTOMS.

FILL WITH BATTER AND BAKE AT 350 FOR 20 MINUTES. COOL 15 MINUTES.

MINI CRAB MEAT-ARTICHOKE QUICHE

32 QUICHE   FAT = 1 GM EA

1 C	EGG BEATERS
1 C	FAT-FREE COTTAGE CHEESE
1/3 C	FLOUR
2 OZ	LOW-FAT JACK CHEESE, GRATED
3/4 t	BAKING POWDER
2 OZ	PARMESAN CHEESE
1/4 t	SALT
1/2 C	ONION, DICED
2 CL	GARLIC, CHOPPED
1/4 t	OLD BAY SEASONING
1/3 C	FAT-FREE BREAD CRUMBS

PUREE THESE INGREDIENTS.

1/3 C	FRESH PARSLEY, STEMS REMOVED
8 OZ	CRAB, PICKED CLEAN
4 JARS	MARINATED ARTICHOKE HEARTS, DRAINED, TRIMMED WELL

ADD THESE AND PROCESS CHOP-CHOP.

Spray mini quiche pan with Pam, press bottoms with bread crumbs. Fill and bake at 350 for 25 minutes. Cool 15 minutes.

STEAMED SHRIMP

easy

SERVES 8   FAT = 2.5 GM EA

1 C	WATER
1 C	WHITE WINE
2	BAY LEAVES

COMBINE IN A LARGE POT WITH A RACK IN THE BOTTOM & BRING TO A BOIL.

3 T	OLD BAY SEASONING
1 T	SALT
5 LBS	SHRIMP, UNPEELED

TOSS THESE TOGETHER AND ADD TO ABOVE FOR 4 MINUTES. REMOVE FROM HEAT & LET SIT COVERED FOR 30 MINUTES.

SHRIMP PETALS

32 PETALS   FAT = TR EA

1/4 C	FAT-FREE MIRACLE WHIP	COMBINE THESE WELL.
4 OZ	FAT-FREE CREAM CHEESE, SOFT	
2 CL	GARLIC, MINCED	
4 T	PARMESAN CHEESE	ADJUST SEASONINGS TO YOUR
2 T	ONION, MINCED	TASTE.
1/2 t	FRESH LEMON JUICE	
1/4 t	CAVENDER'S GREEK SEASONING	PLACE A SMALL DAB ON THE
------	CAYENNE PEPPER TO TASTE	BASE OF EACH OF THE PETALS.
	DRY SHERRY (OPTIONAL)	
12 OZ	COOKED TINY SALAD SHRIMP, RINSED	ARRANGE ON A DOILY COVERED TRAY IN A CIRCULAR PATTERN
2	COOKED ARTICHOKE, SEPARATED, DIPPED IN COLD ORANGE JUICE & DRIED	AROUND A PINK CARNATION.

ROSEMARY MARINATED SHRIMP

36 SHRIMP   FAT = TR EA

1 C	BOTTLED CLAM JUICE	COMBINE AND BOIL THESE FOR 3
1 C	WORCESTERSHIRE SAUCE	MINUTES.
4 t	GARLIC, MINCED	
4 t	GROUND ROSEMARY	
2 t EA	SALT & PEPPER	COOL BY ADDING ICE.
2 t	FRESH THYME, MINCED	
1 t	OLD BAY SEASONING	
1 t	CELERY SALT	
36	LARGE SHRIMP, PEELED & DEVEINED	ADD TO ABOVE & MARINATE IN
1/4 C	FRESH PARSLEY, CHOPPED	A ZIPLOC BAG FOR 3 HOURS.

Grill, bake or broil, basting with marinade.

ANGELS ON BAREBACK

quick

32 ANGELS   FAT = TR EA

1 LB	COOKED TURKEY BREASTS, IN CUBES	TOSS THE MEAT WITH LIQUID
6 DROPS	LIQUID SMOKE (OR TO TASTE)	SMOKE.
1 LB	RED AND/OR GREEN SEEDLESS GRAPES	
2 CANS	WHOLE WATER CHESTNUTS	

Thread grape, chestnut, turkey cube on fancy toothpick. Stand upright. You can change this to Oriental Angels by substituting Soy Sauce or Teriyaki Sauce for the Liquid Smoke.

TURKEY YAKITORI

easy   16 SKEWERS   FAT = TR EA

1/2 C	RICE WINE	COMBINE AND BOIL THESE FOR 3 MINUTES.
1/2 C	SAUTERNE WINE	
1/2 C	SOY SAUCE	
1/4 C	DRY SHERRY (OR LEMON JUICE)	
1/4 C	BROWN SUGAR	COOL.
3 CL	GARLIC, MINCED	
1 T	FRESH GINGER, PEELED, GRATED (ONLY FRESH WILL DO)	
2	BELL PEPPER (1" PIECES)	
8	GREEN ONIONS (1" PIECES)	ADD TURKEY & MARINATE IN A ZIPLOC BAG FOR 4 HOURS.
	CRUSHED RED PEPPER FLAKES (OPTIONAL)	
2 LBS	TURKEY BREASTS, THIN STRIPS	THREAD ON 4" SKEWERS. BASTE WHILE BROILING 4 MINUTES ON EACH SIDE.

OTHER EASY FAT-FREE MARINADES FOR TURKEY ARE:

I

1/2 C EA	DRY & SWEET VERMOUTH	COMBINE THESE WITH THE MEAT & MARINATE FOR 4 HOURS.
1/2 C	SOY SAUCE	
4 T	FRESH LEMON JUICE	
3 CL	GARLIC, MINCED	THREAD ON 4" SKEWERS.
1 t	GROUND GINGER	
1 t	CRUSHED RED PEPPER FLAKES	BASTE WHILE BROILING UNTIL DONE.

easy

II

2 CANS	GREEN CHILIES, DICED	PUREE THESE & BOIL 1 MINUTE.
1/2 C	FRESH LIME JUICE	
1/4 C	HONEY	
8 CL	GARLIC, MINCED	REMOVE FROM HEAT & ADD THE CILANTRO.
1	JALAPENO PEPPER, MINCED	
1/2 t	CORNSTARCH	
		ADD YOUR MEAT AND MARINATE
2 T	FRESH CILANTRO, MINCED	FOR 2 HOURS.

easy

III

1 C	SOY SAUCE	PUREE ALL INGREDIENTS.
1/2 C	MOCK OIL (p 395)	
1/4 C	RICE WINE VINEGAR	ADD YOUR MEAT AND MARINATE
1/4 C	ASIAN CHILI PASTE	FOR 2 HOURS.
2 T	FRESH GINGER, PEELED, MINCED	

easy

Chips, Dips & Spreads

HOMEMADE PITA CHIPS

 quick   32 WEDGES   FAT = TR EA

1 PKG	FAT-FREE PITA BREAD, SPLIT OPEN AND CUT IN WEDGES OR CIRCLES	
		SPRAY WITH PAM BUTTER OR
2 t	GARLIC POWDER	PAM OLIVE OIL.
1 t	DRIED OREGANO	
1 t	GROUND CUMIN	COMBINE & SPRINKLE OVER.
1 t	PAPRIKA	
1/2 t	CAYENNE PEPPER	BAKE AT 350 FOR 8 TO 10 MIN.
1/2 t	SALT	COOL.

Experiment with various seasonings listed below or just bake plain with salt.

TORTILLA CHIPS

 quick   80 WEDGES   FAT = TR EA

1 PKG	FAT-FREE TORTILLAS (CORN OR FLOUR)	SPRAY EACH WITH PAM.
------	SALT TO TASTE	
	ANY FAVORITE SEASONINGS (OPTIONAL)	SPRINKLE ON EACH.

Bake at 350 for 8-10 minutes until golden brown. Cool. Crack into wedges.

WONTON CHIPS OR BAGEL CHIPS

quick   FAT = TR EA

1 PKG	WONTON WRAPS, CUT DIAGONALLY (OR EGG ROLL WRAPS, QUARTERED)	
OR		
1 PKG	FAT-FREE BAGELS, SLICED AS THIN AS POSSIBLE	

Spray with Pam Butter or Olive Oil Spray, season & bake at 375 for 8 minutes.

TRY THESE SEASONINGS ON YOUR CHIPS:

CREOLE SEASONING (p 21)	CAJUN SEASONING (p 21)
CINNAMON & SUGAR (OR EQUAL)	JERK SEASONING (p 21)
LEMON PEPPER & ITALIAN HERBS	FAT-FREE PARMESAN CHEESE
CAVENDER'S GREEK SEASONING	McCORMICK SALAD SEASONING
EVERGLADES SEASONING	GARLIC SALT & BASIL

CAJUN SEASONING
quick   1 1/2 CUPS   FAT = TR EA

	RECIPE I	OR		**RECIPE II**
1/4 C	SALT		1/2 C	HUNGARIAN PAPRIKA
1/4 C	HUNGARIAN PAPRIKA		1/4 C	GARLIC POWDER
3 T	ONION POWDER		1/4 C	BLACK PEPPER
3 T	GARLIC POWDER		1/4 C	CAYENNE PEPPER
3 T EA	WHITE, BLACK & CAYENNE PEPPER		2 T EA	OREGANO, THYME
3 T EA	DRIED OREGANO, THYME		1 T EA	CUMIN, OR GR BAY LEAF
	BLENDERIZE THESE.	OR		BLENDERIZE THESE.

CALIFORNIAN SEASONING
quick   4 CUPS   FAT = TR EA

2 C	TOASTED ONION FLAKES	3 T EA	CUMIN, ALLSPICE
3 T EA	DRIED OREGANO, PARSLEY, THYME	3 T	GARLIC POWDER
3 T EA	BLACK, CAYENNE PEPPER	3 T EA	GR CLOVES, SALT
3 T EA	GROUND CELERY SEED, BAY LEAF	1 T	MACE
	BLENDERIZE ALL.		

CREOLE SEASONING
quick   2 CUPS   FAT = TR EA

1/3 C EA	BLACK & CAYENNE PEPPER & PAPRIKA	3 T EA	DRY OREGANO, THYME
1/4 C EA	SALT, GRANULATED GARLIC	1 T	GR CELERY SEED
1/4 C	GRANULATED ONION	1 t	OLD BAY SEASONING
	BLENDERIZE ALL.		

CREOLE MEAT SEASONING
quick   3 CUPS   FAT = TR EA

1 C EA	SALT, GRANULATED GARLIC	1/4 C	GROUND CUMIN
1/2 C EA	BLACK, CAYENNE PEPPER	1 T	GROUND CELERY SEED
	BLENDERIZE ALL.		

JERK SEASONING
quick   1 CUP   FAT = TR EA

	RECIPE I	OR		**RECIPE II**
1/2 C EA	THYME, SUGAR, GRANULATED ONION		1/2 C	ONION FLAKES
1/4 C	PAPRIKA		1/2 C	ONION POWDER
2 T EA	DR OREGANO, SALT		5 T EA	THYME, SALT
2 t EA	CINNAMON, NUTMEG		5 T EA	SUGAR, DR CHIVES
2 t EA	CUMIN, CHILI POWDER		3 T EA	BLACK, CAYENNE P.
2 t EA	BLACK, CAYENNE PEPPER		2 T	ALLSPICE
			1 T EA	NUTMEG, CINNAMON
	BLENDERIZE THESE.	OR		BLENDERIZE THESE.

GARAM MASALA

quick 1 CUP FAT = TR

1/2 C	CARDAMOM SEEDS		4 STKS	CINNAMON, CRUSHED
3 T EA	CUMIN SEEDS, CLOVES, PEPPERCORNS		1 T	GRATED NUTMEG
	BLENDERIZE ALL VERY WELL.			

CHEF'S SALT

quick 1 CUP FAT = TR

1/2 C	SALT		1/4 C	WHITE PEPPER
1/4 C	SPANISH PAPRIKA		2 T	CELERY SEED
1/4 C	GARLIC POWDER	BLENDERIZE ALL.		

HERBED SALT

quick 1 CUP FAT = TR

1/4 C	DRIED OREGANO		2 T	CELERY SEED
2 T	DRIED THYME		2 T	COARSE SALT
2 T	DRIED MARJORAM		2 T	PEPPERCORNS
2 T	GARLIC POWDER	BLENDERIZE ALL.		

PORK SEASONING

quick 1 CUP FAT = TR

3/4 C	DRIED GRATED ORANGE PEEL		2 t	CAVENDER'S SEASONING
2 T EA	ONION POWDER, GROUND CUMIN		1 t	CR RED PEPPER FLAKES
1 T	SALT		1 t	GROUND GINGER
	BLENDERIZE ALL.			

TOAST POINTS OR CUPS

quick FAT = TR

Cut crusts from fat-free bread. Spray with Pam Butter Spray. Either leave square or cut into 3" circles and press into Pam-sprayed muffin cups.

You could also cut the bread in smaller circles and press into mini muffin pans, or cut into triangles and place on rack.

Bake at 375 until golden. The cups can be filled with any number of goodies.

HOMEMADE CROUTONS

easy FAT = TR EA

2 LOAVES	FAT-FREE BREAD, CUBED	SPRAY LIGHTLY.
------	PAM BUTTER OR OLIVE OIL SPRAY	
1/4 C	PARMESAN (1/2 REGULAR, 1/2 FAT-FREE)	SPRINKLE OVER AND BAKE AT 350
------	CAVENDER'S GREEK SEASONING	UNTIL GOLDEN BROWN.

PEPPERCORN PATE w MADEIRA

22 OZ   FAT = .5 GM EA

4 T	BUTTER BUDS	SIMMER THESE UNTIL ALMOST
1/2 C	WATER	DRY.
1	LARGE BERMUDA ONION, CHOPPED	
2 CL	GARLIC, CHOPPED	
1 LB	COOKED TURKEY BREASTS, DICED	ADD THESE AND PUREE.
1/2 C	EGG BEATERS, COOKED, DICED	
1 T	FRESH TARRAGON (OR 1 t DRIED)	
1 t	SALT	
1 t	DRIED THYME	PACK INTO SMALL RAMEKINS,
1/2 t	GROUND BLACK PEPPER	LINED WITH PLASTIC WRAP.
1/4 t	CAYENNE PEPPER	
1/4 t	GROUND CLOVES	TOP WITH CRACKED BLACK OR
1/4 t	GROUND ALLSPICE	GREEN PEPPERCORNS.
1/4 C	MADEIRA WINE	CHILL 6 HOURS.

Unmold & allow to stand at room temperature before serving.

CHICKEN PATE

12 MOLDS   FAT − 5 GM EA

1 1/2 LBS	CHICKEN BREAST CUBES	PUREE THESE INGREDIENTS.
1	ONION, CHOPPED	
1 CL	GARLIC, SLICED	
1/2 LB	PORK, LEAN CENTER CUT, CUBED	(YOU MUST TOTALLY REMOVE
1/4 C	EGG BEATERS	ALL TRACES OF FAT FROM BOTH
1/3 C	FLOUR	MEATS)
2 T	BUTTER BUDS	
2 t	SALT	
1/2 t	ALLSPICE	
1/2 t	CRUSHED PINK OR GREEN PEPPERCORNS	ADD THESE & STIR WELL.
1/2 C	BRANDY	
1/2 C	SKIM MILK (MORE IF NECESSARY)	

Pack in small crocks or mini loaf pans. Place a bay leaf on top of each. Place in baking pan containing 1" hot water. Bake at 300 for 110 minutes.

Chill 12 hours. Unmold, clean mold, return pate to mold, spoon on aspic. Chill until aspic is set. Unmold to serve.

ASPIC:

1 CUP   FAT = TR

1 PKG	KNOX GELATIN (SPRINKLED OVER THE BRANDY)	LET SIT FOR 2 MIN. & HEAT TO
1 C	FAT-FREE BEEF STOCK	DISSOLVE.
2 T	BRANDY OR DRY SHERRY	COOL UNTIL SYRUPY AND SPOON
		OVER PATE

SHRIMP PATE w DILL   8 MOLDS   FAT = 1.5 GM EA

1	ONION, MINCED	BOIL THESE FOR 5 MINUTES.
1	CELERY STALK, MINCED	
4 C	WATER	
4 T	WHITE WINE	
1/4 t	SALT	
1	BOUQUET GARNI (FRESH THYME, FRESH PARSLEY & BAY LEAF)	
2 LBS	SHRIMP	ADD SHRIMP, SIMMER FOR 3 MIN. DRAIN & REMOVE THE BOUQUET.
3 T	BUTTER BUDS	ADD THESE AND PROCESS CHOP-
1/2	LEMON, JUICED	CHOP IN FOOD PROCESSOR.
2 T	DRY SHERRY OR DRY RED WINE	
1 t	DILL, CHOPPED	LINE SMALL CROCKS w PLASTIC
1/2 t	LOUISIANA HOT SAUCE	WRAP, FILL & CHILL 4 HOURS.
1/4 t	NUTMEG	
1/4 t	WHITE PEPPER	INVERT & REMOVE PLASTIC.

CRAB COCKTAIL SPREAD   SERVES 12   FAT = 3 GM EA

1 LB	FAT-FREE CREAM CHEESE, SOFT	LINE 8" PAN w PLASTIC WRAP.
1/2 t	OLD BAY SEASONING	PACK IN THE CHEESE MIXTURE &
2 T	FRESH LEMON JUICE	CHILL 2 HOURS.
------	FAT-FREE MIRACLE WHIP(IF NEEDED FOR CONSISTENCY)	INVERT & REMOVE PLASTIC.
1 C	HEINZ COCKTAIL SAUCE	COMBINE THESE & SPREAD OVER
1 C	COOKED SALAD SHRIMP	THE CHEESE.
1/3 C	GREEN ONION. MINCED	
1/3 C	GREEN BELL PEPPERS, MINCED	
1/4 C	BLACK OLIVES, SLICED	
1 LB	CRAB MEAT, PICKED CLEAN (OR IMITATION)	
4 T	PARMESAN CHEESE	SPRINKLE OVER TOP.

Serve with sliced French Bread, slightly toasted if desired.

You could also make Pita Chips (p 20), and use as crackers.

VEGETABLE PATE   SERVES 12   FAT = TR EA

2 LBS	SPINACH, COOKED, DRAINED, CHOPPED	PUREE THESE TO CREATE THE
1 C	EGG BEATERS	SPINACH LAYERS.
1 t EA	CAVENDER'S GREEK SEASONING, BUTTER BUDS	
1/2 t	NUTMEG	SET ASIDE.
1/4 t	OLD BAY SEASONING	

6	TOMATOES, PEELED, SEEDED, CHOPPED	COMBINE AND SIMMER THESE
1	ONION, MINCED	UNTIL ALMOST DRY.
2 CL	GARLIC, MINCED	
1/4 t	SALT	
		ADD THESE TO TOMATO MIX
1 C	EGG BEATERS	TO FINISH THE TOMATO LAYER
1 T	BASIL, CHOPPED	& SET ASIDE.

6	LEEKS, CHOPPED, BLANCHED 3 MIN.	SIMMER 8 MINUTES OR UNTIL
1 C	SKIM MILK	ALMOST DRY. COOL.
1 C	EGG BEATERS	ADD THESE TO THE LEEK MIX
1/2 t EA	SALT, DRIED THYME	TO FINISH THE LEEK LAYER.

Layer 1/2 spinach in sprayed loaf pan, then all of tomatoes, all of leek, then the remaining spinach. Cover with Pam-sprayed foil, bake at 350 for 2 hours in pan with 1" water. Let sit 15 minutes. Serve hot with Bechamel Sauce or cold with Dijon Mayo.

DIJON MAYO   *quick* 3/4 CUPS   FAT = TR

1/2 C	FAT-FREE MIRACLE WHIP	
1/4 C	NO-FAT SOUR CREAM	COMBINE THESE & CHILL FOR 1
2 t	DIJON MUSTARD (OR TO TASTE)	HOUR.
1 t	GARLIC, MINCED	
1/2 t EA	FRESH LEMON JUICE, BRANDY	SALT & PEPPER TO TASTE.

BECHAMEL SAUCE   *easy* 3 CUPS   FAT = TR EA

2 T	ONION, MINCED	
1/4 C	BUTTER BUDS (OR TO TASTE)	SIMMER THESE UNTIL TENDER.
1/4 C	FAT-FREE CHICKEN STOCK	
2 C	SCALDED SKIM MILK AS NEEDED	ADD THESE & SIMMER FOR 2
1/4 t EA	SALT & WHITE PEPPER	MIN. REMOVE FROM HEAT &
		STRAIN.
1/2 C	COLD SKIM MILK	COMBINE WELL & ADD.
2 T	CORNSTARCH, SLIGHTLY ROUNDED	HEAT TO THICKEN.
------	FRESH PARSLEY, MINCED (OPTIONAL)	
------	NUTMEG (OPTIONAL-BE CAREFUL, NOT TOO MUCH)	THIN w SKIM MILK IF NEEDED.

HOT CRAB MEAT CURRY   SERVES 8   FAT = 1 GM EA

1 C	FAT-FREE CREAM CHEESE, SOFT	COMBINE ALL INGREDIENTS.
1/4 C	NO-FAT SOUR CREAM	
1	ONION, MINCED	
1 t	FRESH LEMON JUICE	
1 t	WORCESTERSHIRE SAUCE	HEAT THROUGH UNTIL BUBBLY,
1 t	CURRY POWDER	EITHER IN A SAUCEPAN OR IN A
1 C	CRAB MEAT, PICKED CLEAN	CASSEROLE IN THE OVEN.
------	SALT & PEPPER TO TASTE	
1/4 C	RED BELL PEPPER, MINCED	
1 CL	GARLIC, MINCED (OPTIONAL)	
2 T	PARMESAN CHEESE (OPTIONAL—MIX IN OR SPRINKLE OVER TOP)	

(ADDS 4 GM FAT)

Serve with Toast Triangles or Pita Chips (p 20).
You could also spread this on Wheat Bread, cut into pretty shapes & broil.

CRAB DIP   SERVES 12   FAT = TR EA

1 C	NO-FAT SOUR CREAM	BLEND THESE INGREDIENTS.
1/4 C	FAT-FREE MIRACLE WHIP	
1 T	CAPERS, SLIGHTLY CRUSHED	
1/2 C	RED, GREEN & YELLOW PEPPERS, MINCED	FOLD IN THE CRAB LAST.
1 CL	GARLIC, MINCED	SALT & PEPPER TO TASTE.
1 T	FRESH LEMON JUICE	
1 T	ONION, MINCED	CHILL 2 HOURS TO BLEND THE FLAVORS.
2 C	CRAB, PICKED CLEAN AND CHOPPED	

If you add   2   T   Parmesan, the fat content would only change to 2/3 GM each.

GARLIC CRAB DIP   3 CUPS   FAT = TR EA

1 C	NO-FAT SOUR CREAM	BLEND THESE INGREDIENTS.
1/4 C	FAT-FREE MIRACLE WHIP	
3 CL	GARLIC, MINCED	
1 T	GREEN ONION, MINCED	FOLD IN THE CRAB LAST.
1 t	CHILI SAUCE	
1 t	WORCESTERSHIRE SAUCE	SALT & PEPPER TO TASTE.
1 t	FRESH LEMON JUICE (OR TO TASTE)	
1/2 t	LOUISIANA HOT SAUCE	
12	WATER CHESTNUTS, MINCED	CHILL 2 HOURS TO BLEND THE FLAVORS.
2 C	CRAB, PICKED CLEAN AND CHOPPED	

SEAFOOD DIP

26 OZ   FAT = 1 GM EA

8 OZ	FAT-FREE CREAM CHEESE
8 OZ	SMOKED OYSTER, TROUT OR SALMON
1 C	NO-FAT SOUR CREAM
8	GREEN ONIONS, MINCED
2 T	FAT-FREE MIRACLE WHIP
1 T	DILL, CHOPPED (OPTIONAL)
	SALT & PEPPER TO TASTE

RINSE THE SMOKED ITEM WELL TO REMOVE EXCESS OIL. PAT DRY.

COMBINE ALL INGREDIENTS AND CHILL FOR 1 HOUR.

SHRIMP DIP

2 1/2 CUPS   FAT = TR EA

1/4 C	HEINZ KETCHUP
8 OZ	FAT-FREE CREAM CHEESE
3 DROPS	WORCESTERSHIRE SAUCE
1/2 C	FAT-FREE MIRACLE WHIP
1/4 C	NO-FAT SOUR CREAM
1/4 C	ONION, MINCED
1/2 t	OLD BAY SEASONING
------	FRESH LEMON JUICE TO TASTE
------	HORSERADISH (OPTIONAL)

WHISK THESE INGREDIENTS.

8 OZ	COOKED SALAD SHRIMP, RINSED

FOLD IN & CHILL.

Great for Pita Chips (p 20), or vegetables.

CLAM PESTO SAUCE (ALSO GREAT FOR PASTA)

3 CUPS   FAT = TR EA

36	CLAMS
3 C	FISH STOCK (OR BOTTLED CLAM BROTH)
24	DRIED RED CHILIES, DICED
1/2 C	CHICK PEAS, COOKED OR CANNED
10 CL	GARLIC, ROASTED
1 C	FRESH PARSLEY, CHOPPED
3 T	FRESH OREGANO, CHOPPED
1	LIME, ZESTED, MINCED
1/4 C	FRESH LIME JUICE
	FRESH CILANTRO LEAVES FOR GARNISH

COOK UNTIL SHELLS OPEN. REMOVE CLAMS, STRAIN BROTH & REDUCE 1/2.

PUREE THESE.

ADD CLAMS AND PROCESS WITH A CHOP-CHOP MOTION.

PESTO SAUCE

easy

24 TABLESPOONS   FAT = 1.5 GM EA

2 C	FRESH BASIL, WASHED
1 C	FRESH SPINACH, WASHED
1/4 C	FAT-FREE PARMESAN CHEESE
1/4 C	PARMESAN CHEESE
1/4 C	PINE NUTS OR ALMONDS
1/4 C	MOCK OIL (p 395)
4 CL	GARLIC, SLICED (OR TO TASTE)

PUREE ALL INGREDIENTS.

SALT TO TASTE.

ADJUST CONSISTENCY w WATER
OR FAT-FREE PARMESAN.

SPICY SWEET & SOUR DIPPING SAUCE

quick

2 1/2 C   FAT = TR EA

1 C	BALSAMIC VINEGAR
1 C	SOY SAUCE
4 T	SUGAR
4 T	CILANTRO, MINCED
2 T	CRUSH RED PEPPER FLAKES (OR TO TASTE)
1 T	FRESH GINGER, PEELED, MINCED

PUREE ALL INGREDIENTS.

SALT & PEPPER TO TASTE.

TROPICAL DIPPING SAUCE

5 CUPS   FAT = TR EA

3	RED ONIONS, DICED
2	RED BELL PEPPER, DICED
1 1/2 C	WATER
1/2 C	FRESH LINE JUICE
1/2 C	MOCK OIL (p 395)
1/3 C	RED WINE VINEGAR
1/4 C	CILANTRO, MINCED
4 CL	GARLIC, DICED (OR TO TASTE)
1	JALAPENO PEPPER, MINCED
2 t	DRIED THYME

BOIL THESE INGREDIENTS 1 MIN.

PUREE.

SALT & PEPPER TO TASTE.

YOGURT SAUCE

quick

3 CUPS   FAT = TR EA

	I	OR		II
2 C	NON-FAT YOGURT		2 C	NON-FAT YOGURT
1 C	CUCUMBER, PEELED, SEEDED, DICED		1 C	CUCUMBER, P, S & DICED
1 C	FRESH CILANTRO, CHOPPED		1/4 C	DRY WHITE WINE
2 T	FRESH LIME JUICE		1 CL	GARLIC, MINCED
1 t	CAVENDAR'S GREEK SEASONING		1 T	DILL, MINCED
	SALT & PEPPER TO TASTE			SALT & PEPPER TO TASTE

OPTIONS: MINCED RADISHES, GREEN ONIONS, FRESH
PARSLEY, MINT OR CORIANDER LEAVES

DO NOT ADD BOTH CORIANDER
AND MINT.

First Courses

CEVICHE

easy   SERVES 6   FAT = 1 GM EA

1 LB	WHITE FISH (LOW IN FAT), CUBES	MARINATE THESE A MINIMUM
1 C	FRESH LEMON JUICE	OF 4 HOURS IN A GLASS DISH.
1 C	FRESH LIME JUICE	DRAIN.
2	ONIONS, DICED	ADD THESE & CHILL 2 HOURS.
1	JALAPENO PEPPER, SEEDED & MINCED	
2 C	TOMATOES, PEELED, SEEDED, CHOPPED	
1 C	CANNED GREEN CHILIES, CHOPPED	
2 T	FRESH OREGANO, CHOPPED	
1 T	FRESH CILANTRO OR PARSLEY, CHOPPED	SALT & PEPPER TO TASTE.

Serve on a bed of lettuce or in a tomato shell or both.

SCALLOP CEVICHE

easy   SERVES 6   FAT = 1 GM EA

1 LB	BAY SCALLOPS, CLEANED	MARINATE THESE A MINIMUM
1 C EA	FRESH LEMON AND LIME JUICE	OF 4 HOURS IN A GLASS DISH. DRAIN.
1 EA	GREEN, RED BELL PEPPER, DICED	ADD THESE & CHILL 2 HOURS.
6	GREEN ONIONS, DICED	
2 T	FRESH CILANTRO OR PARSLEY, CHOPPED	
1/2 t	OLD BAY SEASONING	
2 DROPS	LOUISIANA HOT SAUCE (OR TO TASTE)	
1 t	HORSERADISH IF DESIRED	SALT & PEPPER TO TASTE.

Serve on a bed of lettuce with twirling lime slices.

CRAB CASSOULETS

SERVES 6   FAT = 4 GM EA

8 OZ	FAT-FREE CREAM CHEESE	COMBINE THESE.
1 C	NO-FAT SOUR CREAM	
1 t	FRESH LEMON JUICE	FOLD IN THE CRAB LAST.
1/2 C	GREEN ONIONS, MINCED	
1 T	DRY MUSTARD	THIN w SKIM MILK IF NEEDED.
2 t	OLD BAY SEASONING	
2 OZ	PART SKIM MOZZARELLA, GRATED	SPOON INTO SPRAYED GRATIN DISHES.
2 LB	CRAB MEAT, PICKED CLEAN	
1/4 C	PARMESAN CHEESE	SPRINKLE OVER TOPS.

Bake at 325 for 25 minutes. Broil if necessary to brown.

CHICKEN SATE w PEANUT SAUCE

SERVES 12   FAT = 4 GM EA
(Including Sauce)

24 OZ	CHICKEN BREASTS, IN THIN STRIPS	
1/2 C	FAT-FREE CHICKEN STOCK	COMBINE & CHILL FOR 4 HOURS.
1/2 C	SOY SAUCE	
2 T	CURRY POWDER	
2 t	SUGAR	THREAD ON SOAKED, WOODEN
3 CL	GARLIC, MINCED	SKEWERS SMALLER THAN PLATE TO BE USED.

PEANUT SAUCE

1/2 C	CHICKEN STOCK	PUREE THESE INGREDIENTS.
2 T	FRESH CILANTRO, OR PARSLEY, CHOPPED	
1/4 C	HEALTH VALLEY PEANUT BUTTER OR DRY ROASTED PEANUTS, GROUND	
1/4 C	SOY SAUCE	HEAT TO WARM AND BRUSH ON
2 T	BALSAMIC VINEGAR	THE CHICKEN.
2 T	HONEY	
1 t	GARLIC, MINCED	
1/4 t	OLD BAY SEASONING	
2	CUCUMBERS, GROOVED & SLICED RICE WINE VINEGAR JUST TO COVER	PLACE IN 6 TINY RAMEKINS. COVER WITH THE VINEGAR.

Broil skewered chicken 4 minutes each side. Place 3 or 4 on each plate with the ramekin of cucumbers. Drizzle extra sauce over skewers.

STEAMED CLAMS

SERVES 12   FAT = TR EA

1 C	WATER	COMBINE & HEAT THESE.
1 C	WHITE WINE	
1 t	OLD BAY SEASONING	ADD CLAMS, COVER & COOK FOR
2 T	BUTTER BUDS	12 MINUTES OR UNTIL SHELLS
1/4 C	FRESH PARSLEY, MINCED	OPEN.
2 T	GARLIC, MINCED	
4	GREEN ONIONS, MINCED	SERVE 3 TINY BOWLS OF SAUCES
72	CHERRYSTONE CLAMS, SCRUBBED	BELOW TO EACH PERSON FOR DIPPING.

(1) RED WINE VINEGAR   (2) STRAINED CLAM BROTH   (3) BUTTER BUDS MIXED IN HOT WATER
Fresh lemon juice &/or Garlic Powder could be added to Butter Buds.

You can get a different taste by substituting 2 cans of beer, Celery Salt, Tabasco and Bay Leaves for the water, wine & Old Bay Seasoning.

STUFFED CLAMS

SERVES 12   FAT = TR EA

36	SMALL CLAMS, STEAMED, CHOPPED (SAVE THE SHELLS)	STRAIN THE BROTH.
3/4 C	FAT-FREE CHICKEN STOCK	SIMMER THESE UNTIL ALMOST
1 C	RED BELL PEPPER, DICED	DRY. REMOVE FROM HEAT.
4 CL	GARLIC, MINCED	
1	ONION, MINCED	
3/4 C	FRESH PARSLEY, CHOPPED	ADD THESE ALONG WITH THE
1 1/2 C	FAT-FREE BREAD CRUMBS	CHOPPED CLAMS.
2 T	FRESH LEMON JUICE	
1 1/2 t	DRIED BASIL	
1/2 t	OLD BAY SEASONING	SPOON INTO CLEAN SHELLS.
	CLAM JUICE (ENOUGH TO MOISTEN)	
1 T	FRESH PARSLEY, CHOPPED	COMBINE & SPRINKLE OVER THE
5 T	PARMESAN CHEESE	CLAMS.

Bake at 400 for 8-10 minutes or until bubbly.

CURRIED OYSTERS

SERVES 6   FAT = 2 GM EA
(Including Sauce)

BASE

5	CARROTS, GRATED, COOKED WELL, DRAINED	
1 T	TARRAGON VINEGAR	PUREE THESE WELL AND SPOON
2 T	BUTTER BUDS	INTO THE DEEP SIDE OF OYSTER
1/2 t	EQUAL	SHELLS.
24	OYSTERS (SAVE 24 DEEP SHELLS)	PLACE ONE ON EACH BASE.

SAUCE

1/2 C	ONIONS, MINCED	SIMMER THESE UNTIL ALMOST
1/2 C	FAT-FREE CHICKEN STOCK	DRY.
2 t	CURRY POWDER (OR TO TASTE)	ADD THESE & BRING TO A BOIL.
1 C	OYSTER LIQUID	REMOVE FROM HEAT.
1/2 C	SKIM MILK	
2 T	BUTTER BUDS	
2 T	ARROWROOT OR CORNSTARCH	COMBINE WELL, WHISK IN AND
1/2 C	SKIM MILK (+ or - FOR CONSISTENCY)	HEAT TO THICKEN.

Spoon sauce over oysters, Bake at 400 for 10 minutes until bubbly. (You could substitute artichoke bottoms for the shells if necessary)

CRAB IMPERIAL

SERVES 6   FAT = 2 GM EA

1/2 C	GREEN ONION, MINCED	COMBINE AND SIMMER THESE
1/2 C	GREEN PEPPER, MINCED	UNTIL TENDER.
1/4 C	CELERY, MINCED	
1/2 C	FAT-FREE CHICKEN STOCK (MORE IF NEEDED)	
3/4 C	PIMENTO, CHOPPED	ADD THESE INGREDIENTS.
1 T	FRESH PARSLEY, CHOPPED	
1/4 t	OLD BAY SEASONING	
1/2 t	DIJON MUSTARD	
------	LOUISIANA HOT SAUCE	
------	CAYENNE PEPPER	
1/4 C	FAT-FREE MIRACLE WHIP	
2 T	NO-FAT SOUR CREAM	FOLD IN THE CRAB AND THE EGG
1 T	BUTTER BUDS	BEATERS AND SPOON INTO 6
		SPRAYED GRATIN DISHES.
1/2 C	EGG BEATERS	
1 LB	CRAB MEAT, PICKED CLEAN	
	PAM BUTTER SPRAY	COMBINE BREAD CRUMBS AND
	FAT-FREE BREAD CRUMBS	PARMESAN & SPRINKLE ON EA.
2 T	PARMESAN CHEESE	

Bake at 375 for 15 minutes. You may need to broil briefly to brown the tops.

CHINESE EGG ROLL SALAD

SERVES 12   FAT = 1 GM EA

2 CL	GARLIC, MINCED	PUREE THESE INGREDIENTS FOR
1 t	DRIED MINT	THE DRESSING.
6	LEMONS, JUICED	
3/4 C	WATER	HEAT TO THICKEN.
5 T	SOY SAUCE	
3 T	OYSTER SAUCE (AVAILABLE IN MOST STORES)	
1/4 t	OLD BAY SEASONING	
2 T	SUGAR	
1 T	CORNSTARCH	
2 LBS	COOKED SHRIMP, CHOPPED	COMBINE AND TOSS THESE WITH
1 LB	BEAN SPROUTS	SOME OF THE DRESSING.
4	BELGIAN ENDIVE, SHREDDED	ROLL UP IN BLANCHED ROMAINE
4 LGE	CARROTS, SHREDDED	LEAVES.
24	ROMAINE LEAVES, BLANCHED	SPOON FILLING ONTO LEAVES &
		ROLL UP.

Drizzle remaining dressing over rolls, sprinkle with Sesame Seeds.

SPRINGTIME EGG ROLLS

12 EGG ROLLS   FAT = 1 GM EA

1 LB	TURKEY BREASTS, MINCED	BROWN IN A PAM-SPRAYED
1	ONION, DICED	PAN.
2 CL	GARLIC, MINCED	
1/4 C	DRIED MUSHROOMS, SOAKED 30 MIN.	DISCARD STEMS, SLICE AND
1 C	FAT-FREE CHICKEN STOCK	ADD THESE.
4	GREEN ONIONS, SLICED	
3	CARROTS, SHREDDED	SIMMER UNTIL TENDER.
1/2 C	CABBAGE, SHREDDED (OR BEAN THREADS)	
1/4 C	EGG BEATERS	COMBINE & ADD THESE.
1/4 C	SOY SAUCE	
2 T	DRY SHERRY	SIMMER JUST TO THICKEN.
1 T	FRESH GINGER, PEELED, GRATED	!!!DO NOT OVER COOK!!!
1 T	ARROWROOT	COOL.
1 T	OYSTER SAUCE (OPTIONAL)	

Roll up in blanched lettuce or Romaine leaves.

Serve with Hot Mustard Sauce and/or Sweet & Sour Sauce.

HOT MUSTARD SAUCE

quick   1 CUP   FAT = TR EA

1/2 C	DRY MUSTARD	MIX WELL.
1/4 C	RICE VINEGAR	
1/4 C	BOILING WATER (OR AS NEEDED)	
3 T	BUTTER BUDS	
------	SUGAR TO TASTE	

SWEET & SOUR SAUCE

quick   2 1/2 CUPS   FAT = TR EA

1 1/2 C	FAT-FREE CHICKEN STOCK	
1/2 C	LIGHT BROWN SUGAR	COMBINE ALL INGREDIENTS &
1/2 C	RICE WINE VINEGAR	HEAT TO THICKEN.
1/4 C	SOY SAUCE	
3 T	CORNSTARCH	
2 T	LEMON JUICE OR FROZEN PINEAPPLE CONCENTRATE	
1 t	GARLIC POWDER	
1 t	GROUND GINGER	
1 T	PIMENTO, MINCED	
------	5 SPICE POWDER	
------	RED CURRANT JELLY TO TASTE	

OLD BAY SEAFOOD MOUSSE   SERVES 12   FAT = TR EA

1 PKG	KNOX GELATIN (SPRINKLED OVER THE WATER)	LET SIT FOR 2 MINUTES.
1/4 C	WATER	
1 C	TOMATO SAUCE	BRING THESE INGREDIENTS TO A
1/2 C	V8 JUICE OR WATER	BOIL.
1/2 t	DILL, CHOPPED	
1/4 C	ONION, MINCED	
1/4 C	CELERY, MINCED	REMOVE FROM HEAT.
1/4 C	GREEN PEPPER, MINCED	
1 C	FAT-FREE MIRACLE WHIP	ADD REMAINING INGREDIENTS.
16 OZ	FAT-FREE CREAM CHEESE	
1 LB	CRAB OR SHRIMP, COOKED, MINCED	
1 t	OLD BAY SEASONING (OR TO TASTE)	POUR INTO MOLDS LINED WITH
	FRESH PARSLEY & LEMON FOR GARNISHES	PLASTIC WRAP & CHILL.

ESCARGOT CROUSTADES   SERVES 8   FAT = 1 GM EA

24	2" CIRCLES OF FAT-FREE BREAD	PRESS INTO PAM- SPRAYED MINI QUICHE PANS & TOAST.
24	ESCARGOT, RINSED, DRY	PLACE 1 IN EACH.
1/2 C	DRY WHITE WINE	COMBINE THESE AND HEAT TO
1/2 C	RICH FAT-FREE CHICKEN STOCK	REDUCE BY 1/2.
1/2 C	ONIONS, MINCED	
8 CL	GARLIC, MINCED	REMOVE BAY LEAVES.
1/4 C	BUTTER BUDS	
1 t	FRESH THYME, MINCED	REMOVE FROM HEAT.
2	BAY LEAVES	
1 1/2 C	SKIM MILK	COMBINE WELL, WHISK IN AND
2 T	ARROWROOT OR CORNSTARCH	HEAT TO THICKEN.
	SALT & PEPPER	
		ADD TOMATOES & HEAT 1 MIN.
1 C	TOMATOES, PEELED, SEEDED & CHOPPED	SPOON SAUCE ON EACH.
4 T	FRESH BASIL, MINCED	SPRINKLE WITH BASIL.
		BROIL UNTIL BUBBLY.

MOUSSELINE OF SCALLOPS & SALMON

SERVES 6   FAT = 7 GM EA
(Including Sauce)

1 LB	SCALLOPS (COLD)	
------ EA	SALT, PEPPER, NUTMEG	PUREE THESE.
1/4 C	EGG BEATERS (COLD)	
2 T	BUTTER BUDS	
1/2 C	EVAPORATED SKIM MILK (ICE COLD)	ADD AS NEEDED FOR A MOUSSE-
	OR MORE	LIKE CONSISTENCY.

Spoon this mixture into 6 or 8 Pam-sprayed ramekins 3/4 full.

1/2 LB	SALMON (COLD)	PUREE THESE.
2 T	FRESH PARSLEY, CHOPPED	
1/2 C	EGG BEATERS (COLD)	
2 T	BUTTER BUDS	
1 DROP	RED FOOD COLORING	
		ADD AS NEEDED TO GET A STIFF
1/4 C	EVAPORATED SKIM MILK (COLD) OR AS NEEDED	MOUSSE-LIKE CONSISTENCY.

Place this mixture in a piping bag & pipe into the center of the scallop mixture in the ramekins. (Stop squeezing before removing from scallop mix). You want the final result to appear to be a Salmon 'YOLK' surrounded by the 'WHITE' of the scallop mixture.

Place ramekins in a waterbath, cover lightly with foil & bake in a preheated oven at 325 for 30 minutes or until knife inserted comes out clean. Serve on beds of blanched spinach. Serve w SALMON MOUSSELINE SAUCE.

SALMON MOUSSELINE SAUCE

quick   5 CUPS   FAT = TR EA

1 C	ONIONS, MINCED	COMBINE & REDUCE THESE BY
2 C	WHITE WINE	1/2. REMOVE FROM HEAT.
1/2 C	RED WINE VINEGAR	
2 C	EVAPORATED SKIM MILK	COMBINE WELL & WHISK INTO
3 T	CORNSTARCH, SLIGHTLY ROUNDED	ABOVE.
3 T	BUTTER BUDS	
1/2 t	OLD BAY SEASONING (OR TO TASTE)	HEAT TO THICKEN.
1/2 t	SAFFRON POWDER (OR TO TASTE)	

SAFFRON STEAMED MUSSELS

SERVES 12   FAT = 2 GM EA

It is worth the extra effort to soak the mussels in water with cornmeal in it for 2 hours. This helps them to spit out the sand inside.

72	MUSSELS, CLEANED	COVER & BOIL THESE UNTIL ALL
4 C	DRY WHITE WINE	OF THE SHELLS ARE OPEN.
2 CL	GARLIC, MINCED	REMOVE & STRAIN THE BROTH THROUGH WET CHEESE CLOTH.
5	GREEN ONIONS, CHOPPED	
1/2 C	FRESH PARSLEY, CHOPPED	
2 T	CELERY, MINCED	ADD THESE TO THE BROTH AND
1 T	FRESH LEMON JUICE	REDUCE BY 1/2.
1/4 t	OLD BAY SEASONING	
1/4 t	GROUND PEPPER	
6 CL	GARLIC, MINCED	
6	FRESH TARRAGON LEAVES, MINCED	
1 t	TURMERIC	
2 C	TOMATO CONCASSE (p 396)	ADD THESE AND SIMMER FOR 2
1 t	SAFFRON STRANDS	MINUTES. PLACE MUSSELS IN A
	FRESH BASIL, MINCED	FLAT SOUP BOWL & POUR SAUCE
	BOTTLED CLAM JUICE (TO TASTE)	OVER.

Serve with Fat-Free Sourdough or French Bread so that you can soak up all of the goodness of the broth.

OYSTER CASSOULET

easy   SERVES 8   FAT = 6 GM EA

1 1/2 C	MARINATED ARTICHOKE HEARTS, DRAINED, TRIMMED WELL	
1 C	PICKLED RED BELL PEPPERS	CHOP THESE & BRING TO A FULL
1 C	SKIM MILK	BOIL.
1/2 C	OYSTER LIQUID	
1 C	FAT-FREE BREAD CRUMBS	ADD THESE, STIRRING WELL.
1 C	PARMESAN CHEESE	
1/4 C	BUTTER BUDS	PLACE 3 T OF MIX IN EACH OF 8 SPRAYED RAMEKINS.
32	OYSTERS	PLACE 4 IN EACH & COVER WITH REMAINING MIXTURE.

Bake at 350 for 20 minutes.

If you use 1/2 regular Parmesan & 1/2 Fat Free, then FAT = 4 GM EA.

BAKED OYSTERS

easy   SERVES 6   FAT = 4 GM EA

1/2 C	FAT-FREE MIRACLE WHIP	COMBINE THESE & SPOON OVER
1/4 C	NO-FAT SOUR CREAM	EACH OYSTER.
1/2 C	GREEN ONIONS, MINCED	
3 CL	GARLIC, MINCED	
1 T	BUTTER BUDS	
1 T	FRESH LEMON JUICE	
1 T	WORCESTERSHIRE SAUCE	
3 T	FRESH PARSLEY, CHOPPED	
2 T	DRIED ITALIAN HERBS	
		SPRINKLE CHEESE OVER.
1/4 C	PARMESAN CHEESE	
		BAKE AT 450 UNTIL THE OYSTERS
36	OYSTERS ON THEIR HALF SHELL	PLUMP AND EDGES CURL.

If you don't have oyster shells, try using artichoke bottoms.

OYSTERS BIENVILLE

SERVES 8   FAT = 4 GM EA

2 BNCH	GREEN ONION, CHOPPED FINE	SIMMER THESE UNTIL ALMOST
1 C	FAT-FREE CHICKEN STOCK	DRY.
2 CL	GARLIC, MINCED	
1 LB	SHRIMP, CHOPPED FINE	ADD THESE AND SIMMER FOR 3
1 C	MUSHROOMS, CHOPPED	MINUTES.
1/4 C	DRY WHITE WINE OR DRY SHERRY	SET ASIDE.
3 C	FAT-FREE CHICKEN STOCK	
1 C	EVAPORATED SKIM MILK	COMBINE THESE AND HEAT TO
1/4 C	BUTTER BUDS	THICKEN.
1/4 C	ARROWROOT OR CORNSTARCH	REMOVE FROM HEAT.
3/4 C	EGG BEATERS	TEMPER THESE WITH THE HOT
1 T	DRIED ITALIAN HERBS	MILK MIXTURE & ADD TO THE
1 T	PAPRIKA	SHRIMP MIXTURE.
	OYSTER LIQUID	USE TO THIN IF NECESSARY.
------	SALT & PEPPER	SEASON TO TASTE.
32	OYSTERS	SPRAY 8 RAMEKINS AND FILL 1/2
3 OZ	LOW-FAT SHARP CHEDDAR, SHREDDED	FULL WITH THE SAUCE.

Place 4 oysters in each and top with more sauce. Sprinkle with Cheddar Cheese and bake at 400 for 20 minutes or more, until golden brown.

SPICY OYSTER RAMEKINS

SERVES 8   FAT = 2 GM EA

1/2 C	ONIONS, DICED	SIMMER THESE UNTIL THEY ARE
1/2 C	GREEN PEPPER, DICED	ALMOST TENDER.
3 CL	GARLIC, MINCED	
1/2 C	LIQUID FROM OYSTERS, STRAINED	
2 T	BUTTER BUDS	
6 OZ	TOMATO PASTE	ADD THESE AND SIMMER FOR 5
3/4 C	TOMATO SAUCE	MINUTES.
1/2 C	TOMATO CONCASSE (p 396)	
2 T	FRESH LEMON JUICE	
1 T	BROWN SUGAR	REMOVE FROM HEAT.
1/4 t	LOUISIANA HOT SAUCE OR OLD BAY SEASONING	
2 PTS	OYSTERS, RINSED, DRAINED	ADD & SPOON INTO 6 SPRAYED RAMEKINS.
3 T	FRESH PARSLEY, CHOPPED	
2 T	PARMESAN CHEESE (OPTIONAL-ADDS 4 GM FAT)	COMBINE & SPRINKLE OVER THE
	FAT-FREE BREAD CRUMBS (OPTIONAL)	TOPS.

Broil until bubbly and golden brown.
Serve with Toast Points (p 22) and Egg Beaters that have been scrambled & minced.

SHRIMP REMOULADE

SERVES 6   FAT = TR EA

1 C	FAT-FREE MIRACLE WHIP	COMBINE THESE & CHILL.
1 C	NO-FAT SOUR CREAM	
1 T	DRY MUSTARD (OR TO TASTE)	
1 T	BUTTER BUDS	
1 T	FRESH LEMON JUICE	
1 T	RED WINE VINEGAR	
1 T	HORSERADISH (OPTIONAL)	ARRANGE COOKED SHRIMP ON
1 t	PAPRIKA	BEDS OF LETTUCE.
------	LOUISIANA HOT SAUCE	
4	GREEN ONIONS, SLICED THIN	
1/4 C	TOMATO PASTE	POUR THE SAUCE OVER.
3 T	CAPERS, DRAINED, MINCED	
1/4 C	FRESH PARSLEY, CHOPPED	
3 CL	GARLIC, MINCED	
1 T	SWEET PICKLE RELISH (OPTIONAL)	
		GARNISH WITH THE PIMENTO.
36	SHRIMP, CLEANED, COOKED & COOLED	
1/4 C	PIMENTO, DICED	

Place lemon twirls & halved Cherry Tomatoes on edge of plate.

CRAB SALAD   SERVES 4   FAT = 2 GM EA

1/4 C	NO-FAT SOUR CREAM	COMBINE THESE & CHILL.
1/4 C	FAT-FREE MIRACLE WHIP	
2 T	ONION, MINCED	
1 T	BUTTER BUDS	
1 T	FRESH LEMON JUICE	
1 T	FRESH TARRAGON, MINCED (OPTIONAL)	
1 t	DRY MUSTARD	
1 CL	GARLIC, MINCED	
1 t	CHILI POWDER (OR TO TASTE)	
1	GREEN PEPPER, DICED	
1 C	MARINATED ARTICHOKE HEARTS, DRAINED, TRIMMED WELL & DICED	
1/2 C	CELERY, MINCED	
1/2 C	GREEN ONIONS, SLICED	
1/2 C	EGG BEATERS, FRIED, SCRAMBLED & DICED	
------	CAVENDER'S GREEK SEASONING TO TASTE	
1 LB	CRAB, PICKED CLEAN (OR IMITATION)	FOLD IN GENTLY AND SERVE ON
	CHERRY TOMATOES, HALVED	BEDS OF LETTUCE.

Garnish with Cherry Tomatoes & lime wedges.

SALMON PASTA   *quick*   SERVES 6   FAT = 5 GM EA

2 C	RED ONIONS, SLICED & QUARTERED	SIMMER THESE UNTIL ALMOST
2 C	FISH STOCK (OR BOTTLED CLAM JUICE)	TENDER.
1/4 C	BUTTER BUDS	
1 C	RED BELL PEPPER, SLICED VERY THIN	ADD & SIMMER 2 MINUTES.
2 C	SALMON, IN STRIPS	ADD & SIMMER 2 MORE MIN.
1/2 C	GREEN ONIONS, SLICED	
1/2 C	LOW-FAT FETA CHEESE, CRUMBLED	STIR IN & ADD AS MUCH OF THE
1/2 C	FAT-FREE BREAD CRUMBS (FINE) AS NEEDED	CRUMBS AS NEEDED TO THICKEN
------	SALT & PEPPER TO TASTE	THE SAUCE.
6 C	COOKED NO-YOLKS NOODLES	TOSS WITH THE SAUCE.

You might like to surround the pasta with Red Pepper Coulis (p 261) and dot with tiny capers. Place a wedge of lemon on the side.

SHIITAKE MUSHROOMS   SERVES 8   FAT = TR EA

3 C	SHIITAKE MUSHROOMS (SOAKED IN HOT WATER 30 MINUTES)	
	DISCARD STEMS & QUARTER THE MUSHROOMS.	
1 C	BURGUNDY WINE	
1 C	FAT-FREE CHICKEN STOCK	
2 C	RED ONIONS, SLICED THIN & QUARTERED	
2 CL	GARLIC, MINCED	COMBINE ALL INGREDIENTS AND
6 T	SOY SAUCE	SIMMER FOR 45 MINUTES.
1/4 C	BUTTER BUDS	
3 T	BROWN SUGAR	REMOVE FROM HEAT.
1 T	CHILI POWDER	
1 t	CRUSHED CORIANDER	
------	SALT & PEPPER TO TASTE	
6 T	SKIM MILK	COMBINE WELL, WHISK IN AND
2 T	CORNSTARCH	HEAT TO THICKEN.
6	TOAST CUPS (p 22)	LAY TOAST CUPS ON THEIR SIDE.
		SPOON SAUCE AROUND.

Partially fill with the mushrooms & garnish with Egg Beaters that have been scrambled & minced.

WILD WONTONS   SERVES 8   FAT = TR EA

3 C	VARIETY OF WILD MUSHROOMS, CHOPPED	FRY IN SPRAYED PAN UNTIL THE
1 C	ONIONS, DICED	MOISTURE IS ALMOST GONE.
1/4 C	GARLIC, MINCED (OR TO TASTE)	
2 t	ITALIAN HERBS	COOL.
		PLACE 1 t FILLING ON EACH.
40	WONTON SKINS	MOISTEN 2 SIDES & FOLD INTO A
		TRIANGLE & SEAL.
		WRAP AROUND A FINGER & SEAL
		POINTS. BOIL 3 MINUTES.
1 EA	RED, YELLOW, GREEN PEPPERS, JULIENNED	BLANCH THESE & DRAIN.
2 OZ EA	SHIITAKE, MORELLE, CREMINI MUSHROOMS	ON 8 PLATES, CREATE BEDS FOR
		THE WONTONS.
1 C	MUSHROOM SAUCE, STRAINED (p 259)	
1 T	DRY SHERRY	HEAT HESE AND DRIZZLE OVER
1 t	SOY SAUCE	THE WONTONS.
2 OZ	FRESH ENOKI MUSHROOMS	PLACE ON EACH SERVING.

ARTICHOKE PASTA

SERVES 8   FAT = 4 GM EA

3 C	MARINATED ARTICHOKES, DRAINED, TRIMMED WELL & DICED	
1 C	FAT-FREE MIRACLE WHIP	
1 C	NO-FAT SOUR CREAM	COMBINE AND HEAT THROUGH
8 OZ	MUSHROOMS, SLICED	UNTIL HOT.
4 OZ	PICKLED RED BELL PEPPERS, DICED	
1/2 C	PARMESAN CHEESE	
1/2 C	FAT-FREE PARMESAN CHEESE	
1 t	FRESH LEMON JUICE	
------	SALT & PEPPER TO TASTE	COOK PASTA AND TOSS WITH
------	SKIM MILK TO THIN IF NECESSARY	1/2 OF THE SAUCE.
		DIVIDE AMONG 8 PLATES AND
1 LB	SPINACH LINGUINE	TOP WITH REST OF THE SAUCE.

BROILED EGGPLANT ROLLS

SERVES 4   FAT = 3 GM EA

8 SLICES	EGGPLANT, 1/3" x 6", SALTED, DRAINED 20 MIN., RINSED & PATTED DRY.	
		BROIL 3 MINUTES EACH SIDE.
8 T	SOFT LOW-FAT GOAT CHEESE	
8 T	FAT-FREE PARMESAN CHEESE	COMBINE AND SPREAD ON EACH
1 CL	GARLIC, MINCED WELL	SLICE OF EGGPLANT.
3	TOMATOES, PEELED SEEDED & CHOPPED (SAVE 8 T TO SPRINKLE LATER)	SPRINKLE OVER EACH AND ROLL UP.
1/4 C	FRESH PARSLEY, MINCED	SPRINKLE PARMESAN OVER.
4 T	PARMESAN CHEESE	BROIL TO BROWN SLIGHTLY. PLACE 2 ON EACH PLATE.
8 T	CHOPPED TOMATOES FROM ABOVE	SPRINKLE WITH TOMATOES.

ASPARAGUS VINAIGRETTE

SERVES 8   FAT = TR EA

42	ASPARAGUS SPEARS, TOUGH ENDS DISCARDED	SIMMER 4 MINUTES AND SHOCK
3 C	BOILING WATER	IN ICE WATER FOR 2 MINUTES.
1 C	FAT-FREE ITALIAN VINAIGRETTE (p 107)	TOSS TOGETHER & LET SIT FOR
2 T	PICKLED RED BELL PEPPERS, MINCED	20 MINUTES.
		PLACE 5 SPEARS FAN-LIKE, ON A
8 t	PICKLED RED BELL PEPPERS, MINCED	PLATE, WITH A TEASPOON OF PEPPERS AT THE BASE OF EACH.

Soups

Remember two things when making soups:

1)
If you're not making your stock from scratch (and believe me, you don't always have to), be sure to use KNORR Vegetable Bouillon Cubes along with the Chicken, Beef, Ham or Fish Cubes. This gives the stock more depth and "from scratch" taste.

If you want to use canned broth (I think Swanson's is the best), be sure to de-fat first by dragging a paper towel across the top several times to remove the fat, (or chill the can & scoop off the fat),then, heat & dissolve a KNORR Vegetable Cube, to add that extra depth of flavor (or add a can of skimmed vegetable broth). If you have room in the refrigerator, keep several cans chilled to make removing fat even easier.

2)
Instead of using cream to thicken soups, use either evaporated skim milk or well-cooked potatoes, pureed with Butter Buds & skim milk. You want the potatoes to be the consistency of heavy whipping cream. If you don't cook them enough or puree them enough, you'll end up with lumpy or grainy soup.

Also remember that most soups freeze well. We've found two good ways:

The easiest seems to be in small Ziploc Freezer Bags. Be sure to press out all excess air & label. Place flat in freezer until frozen; then they will stack well.

Or, you can fill serving size plastic containers or cups almost full & freeze. Add water to the top of each container & freeze again. This protects the soup from freezer burn.

So make big batches, freeze & thaw for homemade soup without any fuss.

CARIBBEAN AVOCADO SOUP

easy   SERVES 8   FAT = 4 GM EA

1	AVOCADO, PEELED, SEED REMOVED	PUREE ALL INGREDIENTS.
1 C	WATERCRESS	
4 C	FAT-FREE CHICKEN STOCK	
2 C	EVAPORATED SKIM MILK	SALT & WHITE PEPPER TO TASTE.
1/4 C	WHITE RUM	
1 t	CURRY POWDER (OR TO TASTE)	CHILL FOR 1 HOUR.
1	LIME, JUICED	
1 T	BUTTER BUDS	
1/2 t	CAVENDER'S GREEK SEASONING	
2 C	(OR AS NEEDED) PUREED COOKED POTATOES TO THICKEN.	

To serve, float a very thin slice of papaya or mango in each bowl.

MR. MAC'S FAVORITE CARROT SOUP

easy   SERVES 8   FAT = TR EA

12	CARROTS, PEELED & DICED	SIMMER ALL INGREDIENTS 'TIL COMPLETELY COOKED.
2	POTATOES, PEELED & DICED	
3	KNORR CHICKEN BOUILLON CUBES	
1	KNORR VEGGIE BOUILLON CUBE	PUREE AND ADJUST THICKNESS WITH SKIM MILK.
	WATER TO COVER	

COLD & CREAMY CUCUMBER SOUP

SERVES 12   FAT = 1 GM EA

2	CUCUMBERS, PEELED, SEEDED, CHOPPED	
2	CUCUMBERS, UNPEELED, SEEDED, CHOPPED	PUREE ALL INGREDIENTS OR...
6 C	1% BUTTERMILK	
2 C	NO-FAT SOUR CREAM	PROCESS CHOP-CHOP IF YOU LIKE IT CHUNKY.
1/2 C	FRESH PARSLEY, STEMS REMOVED	
1/4 C	FRESH DILL (OPTIONAL)	
1 T	BUTTER BUDS	
2 t	SALT	CHILL FOR 2 HOURS.
------	LOUISIANA HOT SAUCE	
12	DABS OF MORE SOUR CREAM	FLOAT A DAB ON EACH BOWL.
12	TINY DILL SPRIGS	STAND ONE UP IN EACH DAB.

CREAMY GAZPACHO

SERVES 10   FAT = .5 GM EA

8	GREEN ONIONS, CHOPPED	
2	GREEN PEPPER, CHOPPED	
2	CUCUMBERS, PEELED, SEEDED, CHUNKS	
2	TOMATOES, PEELED, SEEDED, DICED	
2 C	TOMATO OR V8 JUICE	
3 C	1% BUTTERMILK	
1 t	WORCESTERSHIRE SAUCE	
------	LOUISIANA HOT SAUCE	

PROCESS THESE WITH A CHOP-CHOP MOTION TO THE DESIRED CONSISTENCY.

ADD THESE AND CHILL.

GARNISH EA BOWL WITH DICED GREEN PEPPER.

GAZPACHO

SERVES 8   FAT = TR EA

2	TOMATOES, PEELED, SEEDED, MINCED
2 CL	GARLIC, MINCED
4	GREEN ONIONS, MINCED
1	CELERY STALK, MINCED
1	CUCUMBER, PEELED, SEEDED & MINCED
1	GREEN PEPPER, MINCED
2 T	FRESH BASIL, MINCED
2 T	FRESH PARSLEY, MINCED
2 T	FRESH LEMON JUICE
1/2 t	CAVENDER'S GREEK SEASONING
1/4 t	OLD BAY SEASONING
1 QT	TOMATO OR V8 JUICE
1/2 C	WHITE WINE (OPTIONAL)
1/2 C	EGG BEATERS, SCRAMBLED DRY & DICED

COMBINE THESE INGREDIENTS.

CHILL.

FOR A SMOOTHER CONSISTENCY YOU COULD PUREE 1/2 OF THIS MIXTURE.

ADD SALT, PEPPER AND GARLIC POWDER TO TASTE.

SPRINKLE FOR GARNISH.

Some might like just a splash of red wine vinegar &/or a drop or two of Tabasco. Or, for a change, try adding bottled clam broth & sprinkle with tiny shrimp.

CREAM PEA SOUP (HOT OR COLD)

quick

SERVES 10   FAT = TR EA

7 C	FROZEN PETITE PEAS
3 C	FAT-FREE CHICKEN STOCK
1 t	SUGAR
4	GREEN ONIONS, MINCED
2 T	BUTTER BUDS
2 C	EVAPORATED SKIM MILK
2 OZ	99% FAT-FREE TURKEY HAM, MINCED

COMBINE THESE & SIMMER FOR 20 MINUTES.
PUREE, ADD HAM & CHILL.

GARNISH w LIME ZEST ON DABS OF FAT-FREE SOUR CREAM.

PEAR & LEEK SOUP (HOT OR COLD)

easy   SERVES 10   FAT = TR EA

3 C	FAT-FREE CHICKEN STOCK	SIMMER THESE FOR 20 MINUTES.
3 C	LEEKS, WASHED WELL, CHOPPED	
6-8	PEARS, PEELED & CHOPPED	ADD AND SIMMER FOR 10 MORE
1 t	GROUND SAVORY	MINUTES.
2 T	BUTTER BUDS	
	WHITE PEPPER TO TASTE	
3 C	FAT-FREE CHICKEN STOCK	
1 T	FRESH LEMON JUICE	ADD AND PUREE.

Garnish with pear slices sprinkled with Bleu Cheese crumbles.

WATERCRESS VICHYSSOISE

easy   SERVES 10   FAT = TR EA

4	LEEKS, WASHED WELL, CHOPPED	COMBINE & SIMMER FOR 30 MIN.
1	ONION, CHOPPED	
5	POTATOES, PEELED & DICED	
4 C	FAT-FREE CHICKEN STOCK	
2 T	BUTTER BUDS	
2 BNCH	WATERCRESS, WASHED	ADD & SIMMER FOR 5 MORE MIN.
		PUREE, COOL & THEN BLEND IN
1 C	EVAPORATED SKIM MILK	THE REST.
1/2 t	CAVENDER'S GREEK SEASONING	
	SALT & WHITE PEPPER TO TASTE	CHILL.

Float individual watercress leaves on each bowl.

CHILLED ZUCCHINI SOUP

easy   SERVES 10   FAT = .5 GM EA

2 LBS	ZUCCHINI, SEEDED & SLICED	SIMMER THESE FOR 30 MINUTES.
2	ONIONS, SLICED	
2 CL	GARLIC, SLICED	PUREE.
1 T	CURRY POWDER (MORE OR LESS TO YOUR TASTE)	
2 C	FAT-FREE CHICKEN STOCK	
2 T	BUTTER BUDS	
2 t	GROUND CUMIN	ADD THESE & SALT & PEPPER TO
3 C	1% BUTTERMILK	TASTE. CHILL.

Sprinkle Paprika on a swirl of No-Fat Sour Cream.

JERUSALEM ARTICHOKE SOUP

SERVES 12   FAT = TR EA

3 LBS	ARTICHOKES, PEELED, SLICED	SIMMER UNTIL VERY, VERY
4	ONIONS, SLICED	TENDER.
3	POTATOES, PEELED, CUBED	
4 C	FAT-FREE CHICKEN STOCK	
2	PEACHES, PEELED, SLICED	ADD THESE AND SIMMER FOR
4 C	SKIM MILK	5 MORE MINUTES.
------	SUGAR TO TASTE	
2 T	BUTTER BUDS	PUREE WELL.
	SALT & WHITE PEPPER TO TASTE	

Garnish with julienned strips of pimento & peaches.

CREAM OF ASPARAGUS (HOT OR COLD)

easy   SERVES 10   FAT = TR EA

2 LBS	ASPARAGUS (TOUGH ENDS BROKEN OFF), DICED	SIMMER UNTIL VERY, VERY
	(SAVE 10 TIPS FOR GARNISH)	TENDER.
1	ONION, DICED	(DO NOT COVER)
2	POTATOES, PEELED & DICED	
6 C	WATER (OR AS NEEDED)	PUREE IN BATCHES.
4	KNORR CHICKEN BOUILLON CUBES	
1 t	BUTTER BUDS	
------	SKIM MILK (AS NEEDED)	ADD TO ADJUST CONSISTENCY.
10 t	NO-FAT SOUR CREAM	LAY ON EACH SERVING.
10	BLANCHED ASPARAGUS TIPS	PLACE ON SOUR CREAM.

CREAM OF VEGGIE SOUP

FAT = TR EA

Make as above, substituting broccoli, carrots or any vegetable you like.

BEEF CONSOMME'

SERVES 6   FAT = TR EA

4 C	FAT-FREE BEEF STOCK	SIMMER THESE FOR 7 MINUTES.
1	CINNAMON STICK, 1 INCH	
1 C	BOILING WATER	
1 C	RED WINE	REMOVE CINNAMON STICK.
1/2 t	CAVENDER'S GREEK SEASONING	SEASON TO TASTE.
1/4 t	GROUND PEPPER	STRAIN THROUGH LAYERS OF
------	CAYENNE PEPPER	WET CHEESE CLOTH.
2	EGG WHITES, BEATEN STIFF, NOT DRY	FLOAT A DAB OF WHITES ON EA
	FRESH CHIVES, CHOPPED	SERVING.
		SPRINKLE WITH CHIVES.

BLACK BEAN SOUP

SERVES 10   FAT = 2 GM EA

2 C	BLACK BEANS, SOAKED OVERNIGHT	DRAIN.
6 C	NEW WATER	ADD & SIMMER 1 HOUR.
2	KNORR HAM BOUILLON CUBES	
1	KNORR VEGGIE BOUILLON CUBE	
2 C	99% FAT-FREE TURKEY HAM, MINCED	ADD AND SIMMER ANOTHER 30
3 CL	GARLIC, MINCED (OR MORE)	MINUTES OR UNTIL DONE.
2	BELL PEPPERS, CHOPPED	
3 C	ONIONS, CHOPPED	ADD WATER AS NEEDED.
1	BAY LEAF (REMEMBER TO REMOVE)	
------	SALT & PEPPER TO TASTE	PUREE PARTS OF THIS TO GET THE THICKNESS YOU LIKE.
OPTIONS:	CUMIN &/OR CHILI POWDER	

Garnish with diced Canadian Bacon (TRIMMED WELL) & Lemon Spirals. Serve with white rice & raw onions & a splash of port or sherry.

BLACK EYED PEA SOUP

SERVES 10   FAT = 1 GM EA

1 LB	BLACK EYED PEAS, SOAKED OVERNIGHT	DRAIN.
6 C	NEW WATER	ADD & SIMMER 1 HOUR.
2	KNORR HAM OR BEEF BOUILLON CUBES	
1	KNORR VEGGIE OR CHICKEN BOUILLON	
2 C	99% FAT-FREE HAM OR TURKEY HAM	
3 C	ONIONS, MINCED	PUREE PART OF THIS TO THICKEN AS DESIRED.
------	SALT & PEPPER TO TASTE	

ITALIAN VEGETABLE BEAN SOUP   SERVES 12   FAT = 1 GM EA

1 C	DRY WHITE PEA BEANS (BOIL, LET SIT 1 HR)	DRAIN.
10 C	NEW WATER	ADD & SIMMER FOR 30 MINUTES.
6 OZ	CANADIAN BACON, TRIMMED & DICED	ADD THESE & SIMMER 1 HOUR.
3	TOMATOES, CHOPPED	
2 C	CABBAGE, SHREDDED	
1/2 C	RED WINE	
4 CL	GARLIC, MINCED	
2 T	FRESH BASIL, MINCED	
2	ONIONS, DICED	
2	CARROTS, DICED	
2	POTATOES, DICED	
1	ZUCCHINI, DICED	
2	KNORR BEEF BOUILLON CUBES	
1	CHICKEN BOUILLON CUBE	
1	VEGGIE BOUILLON CUBE	
1/4 C	LONG GRAIN RICE	ADD THESE & SIMMER 20 MIN.
2 T	FRESH PARSLEY, CHOPPED	
1/4 C	PARMESAN CHEESE	SPRINKLE OVER EACH.

You might like to add a little cooked pasta, such as Bow Ties, Penne, etc. to each bowl before serving.

NAVY BEAN SOUP   *easy*   SERVES 16   FAT = 1 GM EA

1 LB	NAVY BEANS, SOAKED OVERNIGHT, DRAINED, RINSED	
4	KNORR HAM BOUILLON CUBES	
1 C	99% FAT-FREE TURKEY HAM, DICED	
8 C	NEW WATER (MORE IF NEEDED)	COMBINE ALL INGREDIENTS AND
2 C	DRY WHITE WINE (OPTIONAL)	SIMMER 1 TO 2 HOURS.
2 C	ONIONS, DICED	
2 C	CARROTS, GRATED (OPTIONAL)	
1 C	GREEN BELL PEPPER, DICED (OPTIONAL)	
------	PEPPER TO TASTE	

You might like to puree some of this to thicken.

EASY BRUNSWICK STEW

SERVES 20   FAT = 1 GM EA

2 C	DICED CARROTS, COOKED (OR CANNED)	COMBINE ALL INGREDIENTS EXCEPT
2 C	DICED POTATOES, COOKED (OR CANNED)	THE CHICKEN.
16 OZ CAN	CORN, INCLUDING LIQUID	
16 OZ CAN	CREAMED CORN	SIMMER FOR 1 HOUR.
14 OZ CAN	PETITE PEAS, INCLUDING LIQUID	
8 OZ CAN	OKRA, RINSED, CRUSHED	ADD SHREDDED CHICKEN DURING
64 OZ CAN	PUREED TOMATOES	LAST 15 MINUTES.
32 OZ CAN	CRUSHED TOMATOES	
4	KNORR CHICKEN BOUILLON CUBES (OR MORE)	SALT & PEPPER TO TASTE.
1	KNORR BEEF BOUILLON CUBES	
1 C	WATER (OR MORE) DE-FATTED FROM COOKING THE CHICKEN	
	TOMATO PASTE IF NEEDED	
6	CHICKEN BREASTS, COOKED & SHREDDED	

I know you'll think it's crazy, but this stew is just not the same if you dice the chicken instead of shredding it.

CAULIFLOWER CHEESE SOUP

SERVES 18   FAT = 2 GM EA

2 HEADS	CAULIFLOWER, DICED	COMBINE & SIMMER THESE FOR 45
4	CARROTS, DICED	MINUTES.
2	POTATOES, DICED	
2	ONIONS, DICED	
8 C	WATER (OR MORE)	PUREE IN BATCHES.
3	KNORR CHICKEN BOUILLON CUBES	
2	KNORR VEGGIE BOUILLON CUBES	
1/2 t	FRESH THYME, MINCED	ADD THESE & SIMMER 5 MINUTES.
1/2 t	CAVENDER'S GREEK SEASONING	
1/4 t	FRESH TARRAGON, MINCED (OR TO TASTE)	
4 C	SKIM MILK OR EVAPORATED SKIM MILK	
1 C	DRY WHITE WINE (OPTIONAL)	SALT & PEPPER TO TASTE.
10 T	PARMESAN CHEESE	SPRINKLE OVER EACH BOWL.
2 C	TINY CAULIFLOWER FLORETS, COOKED	

Garnish with swirls of Yellow Pepper Coulis (made as Red Pepper Coulis, but substituting yellow peppers, p 261).

CORIANDER CARROT SOUP

 easy   SERVES 10   FAT = TR EA

2 LBS	CARROTS, PEELED, DICED	COMBINE & SIMMER THESE
1	ONION, PEELED, DICED	INGREDIENTS FOR 45 MIN.
1	POTATO, PEELED, DICED	
1 1/2 t	GROUND CORIANDER	PUREE IN BATCHES.
2 C	FAT-FREE CHICKEN STOCK	
1 T	BUTTER BUDS	
------	PEPPER & CORIANDER TO TASTE	ADD ENOUGH MILK FOR THE
2 C	CHICKEN STOCK (OR EVAPORATED SKIM MILK)	CORRECT CONSISTENCY.

Garnish with fresh Coriander & Chives floating on a dab of No-Fat Sour Cream.

CURRIED CARROT & LEEK SOUP (HOT OR COLD)

easy   SERVES 12   FAT = TR EA

4	LEEKS, WASHED WELL, DICED	COMBINE & SIMMER THESE
12	CARROTS, SLICED	INGREDIENTS FOR 45 MIN.
2	POTATOES, DICED	
1	PARSNIP, PEELED & DICED	
1 T	CURRY POWDER (MORE OR LESS TO TASTE)	
1 t	GROUND CUMIN	
1/4 t	NUTMEG, GRATED	PUREE IN BATCHES.
5 C	FAT-FREE CHICKEN STOCK	
2/3 C	FRESH ORANGE JUICE	
2 C	REGULAR OR EVAPORATED SKIM MILK	ADD FOR CONSISTENCY.

Garnish with Garlic Croutons or chopped apples & raisins.

This soup, paired with cold & creamy cucumber soup, make a very tasty designer soup (p 54).

SECRET CLAM CHOWDER   SERVES 10   FAT = 3 GM EA

80	LITTLE NECK CLAMS, STEAMED	SET CLAMS ASIDE AND STRAIN BROTH THROUGH WET CHEESE CLOTH.
6	POTATOES, DICED, COOKED	
3	ONIONS, DICED, COOKED	
	WATER FROM ABOVE TO MAKE 5 CUPS	
2	KNORR FISH BOUILLON CUBES	ADD REST OF INGREDIENTS TO BROTH & SIMMER 5 MINUTES.
2	KNORR VEGGIE BOUILLON CUBES	
2 C	EVAPORATED SKIM MILK	
2 T	BUTTER BUDS	
2 C	SEA SCALLOPS, PUREED	
1/2 t	CAVENDER'S GREEK SEASONING	
1/4 t	OLD BAY SEASONING (OR TO TASTE)	
1/4 t	CELERY SALT (OPTIONAL)	
		ADD PARSLEY IN LAST 5 MIN. RETURN CLAMS & SERVE.
2 T	FRESH PARSLEY	

MANHATTAN CLAM CHOWDER   SERVES 12   FAT= 2 GM EA

Prepare as above substituting tomato puree & tomato sauce for the milk & the water and add:

1 C	GREEN PEPPERS, DICED & STEAMED
1 C	RED BELL PEPPERS, DICED & STEAMED
1/2 C	CELERY, MINCED & STEAMED
2 CL	GARLIC, MINCED
------	SWEET FRESH BASIL, OREGANO, THYME TO TASTE.
1	BAY LEAF (REMEMBER TO REMOVE)
------	PAPRIKA
	ADDITIONAL OLD BAY SEASONING TO TASTE

SPECIAL CORN CHOWDER   *easy*   SERVES 12   FAT = 1 GM EA

2	CELERY STALKS, MINCED	COMBINE AND SIMMER THESE INGREDIENTS UNTIL DONE.
2	POTATOES, MINCED	
2	ONIONS, MINCED	
4 C	FAT-FREE CHICKEN STOCK	
1 LB	FROZEN CORN	ADD AND SIMMER 5 MINUTES. (DO NOT BOIL)
2 C	EVAPORATED SKIM MILK	
1 T	BUTTER BUDS	
8 OZ	LOBSTER OR IMITATION CRAB MEAT, CHOPPED	

For a creamier consistency, puree 1/3 of this soup before adding lobster.

WHITE CORN CHOWDER

easy   SERVES 10   FAT = TR EA

2 CL	GARLIC, MINCED	SIMMER THESE UNTIL TENDER.
4	SHALLOTS, MINCED	
1/2	JALAPENO PEPPER, SEEDED, MINCED	
3	POTATOES, PEELED, CUBED	
4 C	FAT-FREE CHICKEN STOCK	
4 C	WHITE KERNELS	ADD & SIMMER 5 MINUTES.
		PUREE 1/3 TO THICKEN.
2 C	FAT-FREE CHICKEN STOCK (MORE IF NECESSARY)	

Garnish with fresh Cilantro.

CRAB BISQUE

SERVES 8   FAT = 2 GM EA

1	ONION, DICED	SIMMER THESE FOR 45 MINUTES
2	POTATOES, PEELED, CUBED	& PUREE.
1 C	FAT-FREE FISH STOCK	
2 T	BUTTER BUDS	
6	SCALLIONS, SLICED, STEAMED	ADD THESE & SIMMER 5 MORE
3 C	EVAPORATED SKIM MILK (OR AS NEEDED)	MINUTES.
1/2 t	PAPRIKA	
1/2 t	MACE	
1 LB	CRAB MEAT, PICKED (OR IMITATION)	ADD THESE & SERVE.
2 T	FRESH PARSLEY, CHOPPED	
------	PEPPER & LOUISIANA HOT SAUCE TO TASTE	

If using imitation crab meat, be sure to shred it.

You might like to add **'ONE'** of the following optional seasonings just before serving: Old Bay, Dry Mustard, Garlic Powder, Cayenne, Fresh Lemon Juice, Sherry, Drambuie, Irish Mist or Liquid Smoke.

If you would like to make this more like a stew, just add a touch each of saffron and Worcestershire Sauce along with the following:

2	CHOPPED BELL PEPPERS, STEAMED
1 C	POTATOES, DICED, COOKED
1 C	CREAMED CORN
1 C	WHITE WINE
2 C	TOMATOES, PEELED & DICED

DESIGNER SOUP

This is simply two or more soups poured simultaneously into a bowl with a divider(s) in the middle to keep the colors from blending. This can be done with a variety of cream soups to create different themes: Eclipse (black bean, potato), Tropical Sunset (cold blueberry (2 shades), July 4th (cold blueberry, strawberry, honeydew melon or pear).

To make the divider, cut styrofoam or a paper plate to fit the contour of the bowl. Experiment and have fun. To make pastel soups, add evaporated skim milk.

The shapes can be 1/2 & 1/2, fan shaped, eclipse, sunset, Ying & Yang etc.

FRUIT SOUPS

Puree the fruit & thin with fat-free chicken stock, a compatible juice, or evaporated skim milk, depending on the color you are trying to create. A touch of lemon or lime juice adds a nice crispness.

PORT & STARBOARD SOUP

PORT SIDE   MAKE V8 SOUP (p 64).

STARBOARD SIDE   MAKE CREAM OF VEGGIE SOUP USING BROCCOLI (p 47).

Place divider down center of bowl (you'll need someone to hold this divider for you) and pour the two soups simultaneously, red on left, green on right. Remove the divider, wipe off and repeat with remaining bowls.

EASY LENTIL SOUP

easy   SERVES 10   FAT = TR EA

1 LB	LENTILS, PICKED & RINSED	SIMMER THESE FOR 1 HOUR.
8 C	NEW WATER	
4	ONIONS, DICED	ADD THESE & SIMMER 30
8	CARROTS, DICED	MINUTES OR UNTIL DONE.
4	KNORR CHICKEN CUBES	
1	KNORR HAM OR BEEF CUBE	
4 STRIPS	TURKEY BACON, FRIED & DICED	ADD WATER AS NECESSARY.

FULL & RICH MINESTRONE

SERVES 12   FAT = 1 GM EA

4	POTATOES, DICED	SIMMER THESE FOR 1 HOUR.
4	CARROTS, GRATED	
3	ONIONS, CHOPPED	
4 C	FAT-FREE BEEF STOCK	
20 OZ	CANNED CRUSHED TOMATOES	
3 C	KIDNEY BEANS, COOKED	
4 CL	GARLIC, MINCED	
4 SL	CANADIAN BACON, TRIMMED WELL, IN SHORT JULIENNE STRIPS	
2 t	GROUND FENNEL (OR TO TASTE)	
2 C	COOKED NO-YOLKS PASTA	ADD THESE AND SIMMER FOR 2
4 C	SPINACH CHIFFONADE	MINUTES.
1/4 C	FRESH PARSLEY, CHOPPED	
1/2 t	FRESH OREGANO, CHOPPED	ADD CRUSHED TOMATOES &/OR
1/2 t	FRESH BASIL, CHOPPED	STOCK AS NEEDED.

Serve w Parmesan Cheese, Italian Salad (p 114) & Fat-Free Italian Bread.
(Remember to add 2 GM Fat for each tablespoon of Parmesan used)

ATLANTIC MUSHROOM SOUP

quick   SERVES 8   FAT = TR EA

2 C	RED ONIONS, DICED	SIMMER THESE FOR 15 MINUTES.
2 C	FAT-FREE BEEF OR CHICKEN STOCK	
2 T	BUTTER BUDS	
2 LBS	MUSHROOMS, DICED	ADD & SIMMER FOR 10 MIN.
2 C	CLAM JUICE	
1 C	EVAPORATED SKIM MILK	ADD DURING LAST 5 MINUTES.
2 C	BABY SHRIMP	

You may like to add a dash of Worcestershire, fresh lemon juice or dry sherry.
You could also thicken with pureed potatoes for a creamier soup.

Pre-soak mushrooms when you are using dried mushrooms. Discard the stems, strain the water & use as part of the chicken stock.

WILD MUSHROOM SOUP SERVES 10   FAT = TR EA

4	ONIONS, DICED	SIMMER THESE UNTIL DONE.
2 LBS	SHIITAKE OR CHANTERELLES, DICED	
8 C	FAT-FREE CHICKEN STOCK	PUREE 1/2.
2 C	COOKED, PUREED POTATOES	
2	LEMONS, ZEST ONLY, MINCED	
1/4 C	BUTTER BUDS	

You might like to add a little Worcestershire Sauce or dry sherry.

CREAM OF MUSHROOM w BRANDY   SERVES 12   FAT = 1 GM EA

1 C	ONIONS, MINCED	SIMMER THESE FOR 30 MINUTES.
4 CL	GARLIC, MINCED	
4 C	FAT-FREE CHICKEN STOCK	PUREE.
2	POTATOES, PEELED & DICED	
1/4 C	BUTTER BUDS	
6 C	MUSHROOMS, SLICED	SIMMER THESE TOGETHER 15
2 C	FAT-FREE CHICKEN STOCK	MINUTES & ADD TO ABOVE.
1/4 C	BRANDY	ADD THESE AS NEEDED.
------	NUTMEG, GRATED	
4 C	EVAPORATED SKIM MILK	SALT & PEPPER TO TASTE.

WILD MUSHROOM & BARLEY SOUP   SERVES 8   FAT = TR EA

1 LB	MUSHROOMS, CHOPPED	SIMMER THESE UNTIL DONE.
7 OZ	SHIITAKE MUSHROOMS, SLICED	
4 C	FAT-FREE CHICKEN STOCK	
2	RED ONION, THINLY SLICED & QUARTERED	
2 CL	GARLIC, MINCED	
1 C	COOKED BARLEY	
1 T	FRESH LEMON JUICE	ADD THESE & SIMMER 5 MIN.
1/4 C	FRESH PARSLEY, CHOPPED	
2 T	MADEIRA WINE OR SHERRY	
1 1/2 C	EVAPORATED SKIM MILK	

OKRA STEW

SERVES 6   FAT = TR EA

1 LB	OKRA, SLICED, BLANCHED 10 MIN., RINSED	SIMMER THESE FOR 2 MINUTES.
2	ONIONS, DICED, STEAMED	
1	CELERY STALK, MINCED	
2 C	FAT-FREE CHICKEN STOCK	
2 CL	GARLIC, MINCED	
1/2 t	GROUND CUMIN	
4	TOMATOES, PEELED, CHOPPED	
1/2 t	CAVENDER'S GREEK SEASONING	
------	SALT & PEPPER TO TASTE	
	EVAPORATED SKIM MILK TO ADJUST CONSISTENCY	

CREAMED ONION SOUP

easy   SERVES 12   FAT = 2 GM EA

8	ONIONS, CHOPPED	SIMMER THESE UNTIL THEY ARE VERY TENDER.
3 C	FAT-FREE CHICKEN STOCK	
2	POTATOES, PEELED, DICED	
2 T	BUTTER BUDS	PUREE. (OR PUREE 1/2)
1	RED ONION, DICED, STEAMED	ADD & SIMMER 10 MINUTES.
5 C	EVAPORATED SKIM MILK	
1/4 C	LOW-FAT GRATED CHEDDAR	SPRINKLE ON EACH BOWL AND
------	WORCESTERSHIRE SAUCE (OPTIONAL)	BROIL TO MELT.

OYSTER NOODLE SOUP

easy   SERVES 12   FAT = 4 GM EA

1 C	CELERY, MINCED	SIMMER THESE UNTIL DONE.
2 C	ONIONS, DICED	
2 CL	GARLIC, CRUSHED	
2 C	BOTTLED CLAM JUICE & JUICE FROM OYSTERS (STRAINED)	
2 C	FAT-FREE CHICKEN STOCK	
1/2	LEMON, ZEST ONLY, MINCED	
2 T	BUTTER BUDS	
2 T	FRESH PARSLEY, CHOPPED	ADD THESE AND SIMMER FOR 5 MINUTES.
1 C	DRY WHITE WINE	
1 T	SOY SAUCE	
2-3 DROPS	LOUISIANA HOT SAUCE	
2 QT	OYSTERS	ADD OYSTERS & SIMMER UNTIL EDGES START TO CURL.
12 OZ	COOKED NO-YOLKS NOODLES	PLACE IN EACH BOWL AND FILL WITH HOT SOUP.

OYSTER STEW

easy   SERVES 8   FAT = 2 GM EA

2 C	FAT-FREE CHICKEN STOCK	SIMMER THESE UNTIL DONE.
1/2 C	ONIONS, DICED	
1/2 C	CARROTS, DICED	
1/2 C	SHREDDED POTATOES	
1/4 C	CELERY, MINCED	
3 C	EVAPORATED SKIM MILK	ADD THESE & SIMMER UNTIL
1/2 C	MUSHROOMS, CHOPPED	SHROOMS ARE TENDER.
1/2 C	DRY SHERRY WINE (OPTIONAL)	
2 T	BUTTER BUDS	
1/8 t	OLD BAY SEASONING	
1 PT	OYSTERS (STRAIN LIQUID & ADD ALSO)	ADD AND SIMMER UNTIL THE
	PEPPER TO TASTE	EDGES START TO CURL.
1-2 C	PUREED COOKED POTATOES	
	(AS NEEDED FOR CONSISTENCY)	

RED PEPPER SOUP

easy   SERVES 8   FAT = TR EA

6	RED BELL PEPPERS, DICED	SIMMER THESE UNTIL DONE.
2	ONIONS, DICED	
1	CARROT, DICED	
2	POTATOES, DICED	
4 CL	GARLIC, MINCED	PUREE WELL.
4 C	WATER (OR MORE)	
3	KNORR CHICKEN BOUILLON CUBES	
2	KNORR VEGGIE BOUILLON CUBES	
1/2 t	CAVENDER'S GREEK SEASONING	ADD SEASONINGS TO TASTE AND
1/4 t	OLD BAY SEASONING	ADJUST CONSISTENCY.
1 t	GROUND CUMIN	
1/2 C	DRY SHERRY (OPTIONAL)	
2 C	TOMATO OR V8 JUICE (AS NEEDED FOR CONSISTENCY)	

YELLOW PEPPER SOUP

easy   SERVES 8   FAT = TR EA

8	YELLOW BELL PEPPERS, DICED	
2	ONIONS, DICED	SIMMER THESE UNTIL DONE.
2 CL	GARLIC, DICED	
2	POTATOES, PEELED & CUBED	
5 C	FAT-FREE CHICKEN STOCK	PUREE AND USE THE STOCK TO
	(OR AS NEEDED)	ADJUST THE CONSISTENCY.
------	CAYENNE, SALT & PEPPER TO TASTE	ADD TO TASTE.

POTATO CHOWDER

 SERVES 10   FAT = 1 GM EA

2	ONIONS, DICED	SIMMER THESE UNTIL VERY
6	POTATOES, DICED	TENDER & PUREE HALF.
5 C	FAT-FREE CHICKEN STOCK	
4 SL	CANADIAN BACON, TRIMMED & DICED	ADD THESE & SIMMER 5 MIN.
1 C	SKIM MILK	
1 C	EVAPORATED SKIM MILK (OR AS NEEDED)	
2 T	BUTTER BUDS	
1/2 t	CAVENDER'S GREEK SEASONING	SALT & PEPPER TO TASTE.

Thicken with pureed potatoes if necessary. Garnish with a sprinkling of chopped chives, corn or baby shrimp.

MR. MAC'S FAVORITE POTATO SOUP

 SERVES 10   FAT – TR EA

8	POTATOES, PEELED & DICED	SIMMER ALL OF THESE WITHOUT
4	ONIONS, PEELED & DICED	STIRRING FOR 45 MINUTES.
3	KNORR CHICKEN BOUILLON CUBES	
2	KNORR VEGGIE BOUILLON CUBES	MASH SLIGHTLY AND ADD SKIM
	WATER TO COVER WELL	MILK AS NEEDED.
12	GREEN ONIONS, GREEN PART ONLY, SLICED	ADD DURING LAST 5 MINUTES.

SWEET POTATO SOUP

 SERVES 12   FAT = TR EA

2 CL	GARLIC, CRUSHED	SIMMER THESE UNTIL DONE.
1	CELERY STALK, MINCED	
2	ONION, DICED	
5 C	FAT-FREE CHICKEN STOCK	
40 OZ	CANNED SWEET POTATOES	ADD & PUREE IN BATCHES.
2 T	BUTTER BUDS	
------	CINNAMON TO TASTE	
------	NUTMEG, GRATED	
------	ALLSPICE	
2 T	MAPLE SYRUP	SALT & PEPPER TO TASTE.
1 C	EVAPORATED SKIM MILK	ADJUST CONSISTENCY TO YOUR
2 C	FAT-FREE CHICKEN STOCK	TASTE.

Float a dab of No-Fat Sour Cream on each serving & sprinkle with red currants (or you could substitute golden raisins).

RUM PUMPKIN SOUP

quick   SERVES 6   FAT = 1 GM EA

3 C	COOKED PUMPKIN	SIMMER THESE 20 MINUTES.
3 C	FAT-FREE CHICKEN STOCK	
2 T	BUTTER BUDS	
2 C	EVAPORATED SKIM MILK	ADD & SIMMER 5 MINUTES.
2 T	DARK RUM (OR TO TASTE)	
------	CINNAMON TO TASTE	ADJUST THICKNESS IF NEEDED
------	SALT & PEPPER TO TASTE	w PUREED, COOKED POTATOES.

Sweeten No-Fat Sour Cream or Non-Fat Vanilla Yogurt with brown sugar. Float a dab on each bowl & sprinkle with minced orange zest or minced peaches.

You can do this same soup with butternut or acorn squash instead of pumpkin.

SEAFOOD BOUNTY

SERVES 18   FAT = 1 GM EA

6 C	FAT-FREE CHICKEN STOCK	SIMMER THESE FOR 30 MINUTES.
16 OZ	CANNED WHOLE TOMATOES, CHOPPED	
2 C	ONIONS, CHOPPED	
5 C	POTATOES, PEELED & CUBED	
2 C	CARROTS, DICED	
2	KNORR FISH BOUILLON CUBES	
1	KNORR VEGGIE BOUILLON CUBE	
1/2 t	OLD BAY SEASONING (OR TO TASTE)	
2 T	BUTTER BUDS	
1 LB	CRAB MEAT, CLEANED (OR IMITATION)	ADD THESE & HEAT THROUGH.
8 OZ	TINY SHRIMP	
8 OZ	BABY CLAMS	
4 OZ	PIMENTO, DICED	

If using imitation crab meat, be sure to shred it. Garnish with a little extra chipped pimento or grated carrot.

SAFFRON SEAFOOD SOUP

SERVES 12   FAT = 2 GM EA

1/2 C	FENNEL, JULIENNED	SIMMER THESE UNTIL DONE.
1/2 C	CARROTS, JULIENNED	
1/2 C	LEEK, JULIENNED	
1/4 C	CELERY, MINCED	
1 C	FAT-FREE CHICKEN STOCK	
36	MUSSELS, SCRUBBED & DE-BEARDED	ARRANGE IN A SHALLOW PAN.
24	LITTLE CLAMS IN SHELL, SCRUBBED WELL	
24	LARGE SHRIMP, PEELED & DEVEINED	
1 t	SAFFRON	COMBINE THESE WITH VEGGIES
6 C	FISH STOCK	& POUR OVER MUSSELS.
1 LB	LOW-FAT WHITE FISH, IN 2 OZ PIECES	
1 t	TURMERIC	COVER AND SIMMER UNTIL THE
------	FRESH PARSLEY & PAPRIKA	SHELLS OPEN.

Serve in flat bowl with lots of Fat-Free Sourdough Bread (or over rice).

SEAFOOD GUMBO

SERVES 16   FAT = 1 GM EA

3 C	ONIONS, DICED	SIMMER THESE UNTIL ALMOST
1 EA	RED, YELLOW & GREEN PEPPER, DICED	TENDER.
1/2 C	CELERY, MINCED	
1 T	WORCESTERSHIRE SAUCE	
1 t	LOUISIANA HOT SAUCE (OR TO TASTE)	
2 C	DRY WHITE WINE	
2 QT	WATER	
4 CL	GARLIC, MINCED	
4	KNORR FISH BOUILLON CUBES	
3	KNORR VEGGIE BOUILLON CUBES	
1 T	LEMON ZEST, MINCED	
1 CAN	OKRA, RINSED & SLIGHTLY CRUSHED	
1/4 C	FRESH PARSLEY, CHOPPED	ADD THESE AND SIMMER UNTIL
2 C	OYSTERS (STRAIN JUICE & ADD)	SEAFOOD IS DONE.
10	CRAB CLAWS, MEAT ONLY	
1 LB	FISH CUBES	
1 LB	SHRIMP, CLEANED, HALVED LENGTHWISE IF LARGE	

If you would like to change the character of this great soup, just add either pureed cooked potatoes & skim milk or canned crushed tomatoes and Italian Herbs.

CAJUN SHRIMP CHOWDER   SERVES 12   FAT = TR EA

3 EA	RED, GREEN BELL PEPPERS, DICED	SIMMER THESE UNTIL TENDER.
2	CELERY STALKS, MINCED	
2	ONIONS, DICED	
1	POTATO, PEELED, MINCED	
6 CL	GARLIC, MINCED	
32 OZ	CANNED CRUSHED TOMATOES	
1 C	RED WINE	
1 C	BOTTLED CLAM BROTH	
1 t	OLD BAY SEASONING	
1/2 t	CAYENNE PEPPER (OR TO TASTE)	
		ADD SHRIMP AND SIMMER FOR 5
3 LBS	SHRIMP, CLEANED, HALVED IF LARGE	MINUTES.
------	SALT & PEPPER	ADJUST SEASONING.

You can thicken, by adding cooked potatoes pureed with Butter Buds & skim milk.

SHRIMP AND WHITE BEAN SOUP   SERVES 10   FAT = TR EA

2	ONIONS, DICED	SIMMER THESE UNTIL TENDER.
1 C	GREEN PEPPERS, DICED	
1 T	LEMON ZEST, MINCED	
3 C	FISH STOCK OR CLAM JUICE	
1	CARROT, SHREDDED	
2 C	DRY WHITE WINE	ADD & SIMMER FOR 5 MINUTES.
1 CAN	WHITE BEANS, RINSED	
1 CAN	OKRA, RINSED, SLIGHTLY CRUSHED	
2 T	WORCESTERSHIRE SAUCE	
4 CL	GARLIC, CRUSHED	
1 t	CAVENDER'S GREEK SEASONING	
1 LB	SHRIMP, CLEANED, HALVED IF LARGE	ADD AND SIMMER FOR 5 MORE
3 T	FRESH PARSLEY, CHOPPED	MINUTES.
------	LOUISIANA HOT SAUCE TO TASTE	

Garnish with skin of yellow squash, julienned.

TOMATO BASIL SOUP HOT OR COLD

SERVES 10   FAT = TR EA

10	TOMATOES, PEELED, SEEDED & DICED	SIMMER THESE FOR 30 MINUTES.
2	CELERY STALKS, MINCED	
10	FRESH BASIL LEAVES, CHOPPED	
2	ONIONS, DICED	
1	LEMON, JUICED	
5 C	FAT-FREE CHICKEN STOCK	REMOVE THE BAY LEAF BEFORE
2	BAY LEAVES	CONTINUING.
1/4 C	TOMATO PASTE	ADD THESE & PUREE.
2 T	BUTTER BUDS	
1 T	SUGAR	
10	FRESH BASIL LEAVES, CHOPPED	ADD & SEASON TO TASTE.
------	SALT & PEPPER	
------	GROUND GINGER	SIMMER 5 MINUTES.
------	ALLSPICE	
------	WORCESTERSHIRE SAUCE	
ZEST OF 1	LEMON, MINCED	

Garnish with julienned basil.

TURTLE SOUP

SERVES 16   FAT = 2 GM EA

1 LB	TURTLE MEAT, DICED	SIMMER THESE UNCOVERED FOR
3 QT	WATER	2 HOURS.
4 CL	GARLIC, CRUSHED	
1	BAY LEAF	SKIM OFF THE TOP.
1 t	FRESH LEMON JUICE (MORE LATER IF NEEDED)	
4 C	FAT-FREE CHICKEN STOCK, AS NEEDED	
2 C	ONION, DICED	ADD THESE AND SIMMER FOR 45
2	CELERY STALKS, MINCED	45 MINUTES.
6 T	TOMATO PASTE	
2 T	BUTTER BUDS	
1 t	SUGAR	REMOVE BAY LEAF.
1-2 C	PUREED COOKED POTATOES	ADJUST THICKNESS AS YOU LIKE
------	CAVENDER'S GREEK SEASONING	& SEASON TO TASTE.
6 T	DRY SHERRY	ADD DURING LAST 5 MINUTES.

Garnish with Egg Beaters, scrambled dry & diced.

TWIRLING EGG SOUP

quick   SERVES 10   FAT = TR EA

1/2 C	EGG BEATERS	COMBINE, FRY AS 2 CREPES AND
1	GREEN ONION, MINCED FINE (GREEN ONLY)	ROLL EACH UP TIGHTLY.
		COOL. SLICE IN 1/8" WIDTHS.
10 C	WATER	
1	GREEN ONION, SLICED THIN (WHITE ONLY)	BOIL THESE.
4	KNORR CHICKEN BOUILLON CUBES	PLACE 'EGG TWIRLS' IN EACH
3	KNORR VEGGIE BOUILLON CUBES	BOWL.

Gently pour stock over and sprinkle with more green onion slices.

V8 SOUP   (HOT OR COLD)

quick   SERVES 8   FAT = TR EA

20 OZ	V8 JUICE	COMBINE & PUREE THESE.
12 OZ JAR	PICKLED RED BELL PEPPERS, DRAINED	
1 C	PUREED COOKED POTATOES	
24 OZ	V8 JUICE	ADD & HEAT THROUGH.
1 t	CAVENDER'S GREEK SEASONING	SALT & PEPPER TO TASTE.

Add more pureed cooked potatoes if you like it thicker.

WHITE VEAL STEW

SERVES 12   FAT = 5 GM EA

3 LBS	VEAL CUBES, TRIMMED, BROWNED IN PAM	SIMMER THESE FOR 30 MINUTES.
3 CL	GARLIC, MINCED	
2	ONIONS, DICED	
1 T	DILL (OPTIONAL)	
4 C	FAT-FREE CHICKEN STOCK	
3	CARROTS, JULIENNED	ADD THESE AND SIMMER FOR 10
2	LEEKS, WASHED WELL, JULIENNED	MINUTES.
2	POTATOES, JULIENNED	
2 T	BUTTER BUDS	
2 C	PUREED POTATOES	ADD THESE .
1/4 t	NUTMEG	ADJUST CONSISTENCY TO YOUR
	SKIM MILK AS NECESSARY	TASTES.

EASY VEGETABLE SOUP

SERVES 16   FAT = TR EA

5	CARROTS, SHREDDED IN PROCESSOR	SIMMER THESE FOR 45 MINUTES.
4	CELERY STALKS, MINCED	
2	ONIONS, MINCED	
1 C	FROZEN CORN	
1 C	DICED POTATOES	
1 C	GREEN BEANS, SLICED 1/4" WIDTHS	
5 C	FAT-FREE CHICKEN STOCK (MORE IF NECESSARY)	
24 OZ	CANNED CRUSHED TOMATOES	
1 t	DRIED OREGANO	ADD DURING LAST 5 MINUTES.
------	SALT & PEPPER TO TASTE	

For a little more Italian flavor, add 1 t each: Ground Fennel, Italian Herbs & Cavender's Greek Seasoning.

VEGGIE NOODLE SOUP

SERVES 12   FAT = TR EA

2	CARROTS, JULIENNED	SIMMER THESE UNTIL DONE.
2	ONIONS, JULIENNED	
1/2 t	GARLIC POWDER	
1/2 t	DRIED THYME	
2 T	BUTTER BUDS	
8 C	FAT-FREE CHICKEN STOCK	
1	YELLOW SQUASH, JULIENNED	ADD DURING LAST 2 MINUTES.
1	ZUCCHINI, JULIENNED	
4 C	NO-YOLKS NOODLES, COOKED	PLACE SOME IN EACH BOWL &
------	SALT & PEPPER TO TASTE	FILL WITH HOT SOUP.

ITALIAN BREAD SOUP

SERVES 6   FAT = 2 GM EA

8 SL	FAT-FREE ITALIAN BREAD, SPRAYED w PAM	
------	GARLIC SALT, TO SPRINKLE ON BREAD	BAKE AT 350 FOR 15 MINUTES.
2 C	FAT-FREE CHICKEN STOCK	SIMMER THESE FOR 20 MINUTES
16 OZ	CANNED TOMATOES, CHOPPED, w JUICE	IN DUTCH OVEN.
2	ONIONS, SLICED, QUARTERED	
3	CARROTS, SLICED	
1	CELERY STALK, SLICED	
1 CL	GARLIC, MINCED (OR TO TASTE)	
16 OZ	CANNED KIDNEY BEANS, RINSED, DRAINED	ADD THESE AND SIMMER FOR 5
1	ZUCCHINI OR SQUASH, SLICED	MINUTES.
1	RED BELL PEPPER, DICED	
1/2 t	DRIED GROUND ROSEMARY	
5 C	CHOPPED GREENS (ESCAROLE, ROMAINE, SPINACH, ETC.)	
------	SALT & PEPPER TO TASTE	ADD, TOP WITH BREAD CRUMBS
3 T	PARMESAN CHEESE	& BAKE 30 MINUTES.

TORTILLA SOUP

SERVES 6   FAT = 2 GM EA

2 LBS	TOMATOES, PEELED, SEEDED, CHOPPED	PUREE THESE.
6 CL	GARLIC, CRUSHED	
1	ONION, DICED	
2 T	TOMATO PASTE	
2 T	FRESH CILANTRO	
1 T	GROUND CUMIN	
1 t	FRESH OREGANO	
1 t	CHILI POWDER (OR TO TASTE)	
1	JALAPENO, MINCED (OPTIONAL)	
4 OZ CAN	DICED GREEN CHILIES	COMBINE THESE WITH ABOVE &
6 C	FAT-FREE CHICKEN STOCK	& SIMMER FOR 30 MINUTES.
2	BAY LEAVES (OPTIONAL-REMEMBER TO REMOVE)	
56	CORN TORTILLA CHIPS (p 20), CRUSHED	ADD HALF & SIMMER 5 MINUTES.
------	NO-FAT SOUR CREAM	GARNISH WITH SOUR CREAM &
		CRUSHED CHIPS.
OPTIONS:	TEQUILA, COOKED CHICKEN CUBES, LIME JUICE, WORCESTERSHIRE SAUCE	

Salads

AMBROSIA STARTER

SERVES 8   FAT = TR EA

4	ORANGES, PEELED, SECTIONED	COMBINE AND MARINATE THESE
1	GRAPEFRUIT, PEELED, SECTIONED	FOR 4 HOURS.
1	RED APPLE, SLICED IN CRESCENTS	
2 C	SEEDLESS RED & GREEN GRAPES	
1 C	PINEAPPLE CHUNKS WITH JUICE	
1/2 C	ORANGE JUICE	DIVIDE AMONG 8 PLATES LINED
1/4 C	GRAND MARNIER	WITH LETTUCE.
1 t	COCONUT FLAVORING	
------	ORANGE ZEST	SPRINKLE OVER EACH.

Try serving in a red wine glasses with lettuce chiffonade in the bottom.

APRICOT SALAD

easy   SERVES 8   FAT = TR EA

1 C	WARM BRANDY FOR SOAKING APRICOTS	
12 OZ	DRIED APRICOTS, SOAKED 20 MINUTES, DRAINED & SLICED	
1 C	APPLE JUICE	
1 C	DATES, SLICED	COMBINE AND SERVE ON BEDS
1 C	GOLDEN PLUMP RAISINS	OF SHREDDED SALAD GREENS.
4	BANANAS, SLICED (TOSSED IN ORANGE JUICE)	
3 T	ORANGE ZEST, MINCED	SPRINKLE OVER EACH.

ITALIAN BEAN SALAD

SERVES 8   FAT = 1 GM EA

2 C	DRY WHITE BEANS, SOAKED OVERNIGHT, DRAINED	
2 C	RED ONIONS, SLICED, QUARTERED	SIMMER THESE FOR 90 MINUTES.
4 C	NEW WATER	
2	KNORR CHICKEN BOUILLON CUBES	DRAIN & COOL.
------	SALT & FRESH GROUND PEPPER	
1 C	FAT-FREE ITALIAN DRESSING	TOSS WITH REMAINING ITEMS.
1/4 C	FRESH PARSLEY, CHOPPED	
1 C	PICKLED RED BELL PEPPERS, CHOPPED	CHILL.
1 LB	MUSHROOMS, QUARTERED	
1/4 C	DRIED ITALIAN HERBS	
2 T	PARMESAN CHEESE	
2 T	PICKLED CHERRY PEPPERS, CHOPPED	
------	JUICE FROM BELL & CHERRY PEPPERS	SALT & PEPPER TO TASTE.

Serve on beds of Red Leaf lettuce.

BROCCOLI & MUSHROOM SALAD

 SERVES 12 FAT = TR EA

1 C	NO-FAT SOUR CREAM	PUREE THESE.
1/2 C	FAT-FREE MIRACLE WHIP	
3 CL	GARLIC, MINCED	
1/2 C	ONIONS, MINCED	
1 T	BUTTER BUDS	
1 t	WORCESTERSHIRE SAUCE	
1 t	FRESH LEMON JUICE	
2 T	FRESH PARSLEY, CHOPPED	
------	DRY WHITE WINE (ENOUGH FOR CONSISTENCY)	ADD AMOUNT DESIRED.
2 LBS	BROCCOLI FLORETS, STEAMED 4 MIN.	TOSS ALL TOGETHER AND CHILL
2 C	MUSHROOMS, SLICED	FOR 4 HOURS.
2 C	CHERRY TOMATOES, HALVED	
2	RED ONION, SLICED THIN & QUARTERED	
1 CAN	SLICED WATER CHESTNUTS, DRAINED	SALT & PEPPER TO TASTE.

GINGER GREEN BEAN SALAD

 SERVES 8 FAT = TR EA

2 LBS	GREEN BEANS, BLANCHED 5 MIN., SHOCKED	COMBINE ALL INGREDIENTS.
1 T	FRESH GINGER, PEELED, MINCED	
2 T	DRY MUSTARD	SALT & PEPPER TO TASTE.
2 T	WATER	
1 T	WHITE VINEGAR	CHILL.
1 T	SOY SAUCE	
1 t	SUGAR	SERVE AT ROOM TEMPERATURE.

MARINATED GREEN BEAN SALAD

easy SERVES 12 FAT = TR EA

2 LBS	BEANS, TRIMMED, BLANCHED 5 MIN., DRAINED	
2 C	TOMATO SAUCE	COMBINE ALL INGREDIENTS AND
2 C	CHERRY TOMATOES, HALVED	CHILL OVERNIGHT.
1 C	ONION, DICED	
1 t	CINNAMON	
1/4 t	NUTMEG, GRATED	
1/2 t	CAVENDER'S GREEK SEASONING	
------	RED WINE VINEGAR TO TASTE	

CAESAR SALAD

 SERVES 8   FAT = 3 GM EA

2 HDS	ROMAINE LETTUCE, WASHED, CHILLED, TORN	TOSS THESE & DIVIDE AMONG 8
1 C	PEPPERIDGE FARM CAESAR CROUTONS	PLATES.
1/2	RED ONION, SLICED THIN, QUARTERED	
3/4 C	CAESAR DRESSING (p 94)	
1/2 C	EGG BEATERS, SCRAMBLED, DICED	SPRINKLE THESE ON TOP OF THE
1/4 C	PARMESAN CHEESE	SALADS.

Try Homemade Croutons for the perfect touch—they're easy (p 20).

Try using 1/2 regular Parmesan & 1/2 Fat-Free Parmesan.

CARROT SALAD

 SERVES 6   FAT = TR EA

1 LB	CARROTS, GRATED	COMBINE ALL & SALT TO TASTE.
1/2 C	RAISINS, SOAKED & DRAINED	
1/2 C	FAT-FREE MIRACLE WHIP	
1/2 C	APPLESAUCE OR CRUSHED PINEAPPLE	
1 T	BUTTER BUDS	
1 t	NUTMEG, GRATED	
1 t	SUGAR (OR TO TASTE)	

You can change this dish by adding curry & No-Fat Sour Cream.

CAULIFLOWER SALAD

easy SERVES 8   FAT = 1 GM EA

1/2 C	FAT-FREE MIRACLE WHIP	COMBINE THESE.
1/2 C	NO-FAT SOUR CREAM	
2 T	FRESH LEMON JUICE	
1 T	WORCESTERSHIRE SAUCE	
1 T	BUTTER BUDS	
2 HDS	CAULIFLOWER, FLORETS	COOK 6 MINUTES.
1/4 C	CAPERS, DRAINED, MINCED	TOSS ALL INGREDIENTS & CHILL
1/4 C	BUTTER BUDS	4 HOURS.
16	PIMENTO STUFFED OLIVES, SLICED	SPRINKLE OVER EACH.

FOUR BEAN CHICKEN SALAD

 easy　　　SERVES 12　　　FAT = 2 GM EA

1 C	FAT-FREE ITALIAN DRESSING	COMBINE ALL INGREDIENTS AND CHILL.
2 T	DIJON MUSTARD	
1/4 C	NO-FAT SOUR CREAM	
1 T	DRIED ITALIAN HERBS	
1 CAN	GREEN BEANS, DRAINED	
1 CAN	WAXED BEANS, DRAINED	
1 CAN	KIDNEY BEANS, RINSED	
2 CANS	CHICK PEAS, DRAINED	
1 LB	COOKED CHICKEN BREAST CUBES	
1	RED ONION, THINLY SLICED & QUARTERED	
1/2 C	PICKLED RED BELL PEPPER, SLICES	

DILLED CHICKEN SALAD

 easy　　　SERVES 12　　　FAT = 2 GM EA

1 C	NO-FAT SOUR CREAM	COMBINE THESE FOR DRESSING.
2 T	DILL, CHOPPED	
2 T	SOY SAUCE	
8 DROPS	LOUISIANA HOT SAUCE (OPTIONAL)	
2 LBS	COOKED CHICKEN BREAST CUBES	TOSS THESE WITH DRESSING & CHILL 1 HOUR.
2 C	WATER CHESTNUTS, SLICED	
2 C	BROCCOLI FLORETS, BLANCHED 5 MIN & SHOCKED	
2 C	WATER CHESTNUTS, SLICED	
10	GREEN ONIONS, SLICED	
1 C	HALVED SEEDLESS GRAPES	SERVE WITH CANTALOUPE BALLS

CHICKEN & FETA SALAD

easy　　　SERVES 12　　　FAT = 2 GM EA

2 T	FRESH BASIL, CHOPPED	PUREE THESE FOR DRESSING.
1/2 PKG	EQUAL (OR TO TASTE)	
2 CL	GARLIC, MINCED	
1/3 C	NO-FAT SOUR CREAM	
2 T	FRESH LEMON JUICE	
2 T	WHITE WINE VINEGAR	
1 T	DIJON MUSTARD	
2 LBS	COOKED CHICKEN BREAST CUBES	COMBINE & TOSS THESE WITH THE DRESSING.
1/2 C	CUCUMBER, DICED	
5	RADISHES, MINCED	
2 C	MUSHROOMS, QUARTERED	SERVE ON BEDS OF SPINACH.
4	GREEN ONIONS, SLICED	
2 OZ	FETA CHEESE, CRUMBLED	SPRINKLE OVER EACH.

CHICKEN & FRUIT COLESLAW

 SERVES 14   FAT = 1 GM EA

1/2 C	FAT-FREE MIRACLE WHIP		COMBINE THESE WELL.
1/4 C	NO-FAT SOUR CREAM (OR MORE)		
2 T	FRESH LEMON JUICE		
2 T	HONEY		SALT & PEPPER TO TASTE.
1 T	BUTTER BUDS		
1 t	POPPY SEEDS		
1 3/4 LBS	COOKED CHICKEN BREAST CUBES		ADD ABOVE TO THESE & TOSS.
2 C	CABBAGE, SHREDDED		
2 C	RED APPLE CHUNKS		
2 C	RED GRAPE HALVES		
1/4 C	CELERY, MINCED		CHILL 1 HOUR.

PINEAPPLE CHICKEN SALAD

 SERVES 14   FAT = 2 GM EA

1/4 C	BROWN SUGAR		PUREE THESE ADDING OIL LAST.
1/2 C	PINEAPPLE LIQUID FROM BELOW		
1/4 C	BALSAMIC VINEGAR		
1/2 C	FAT-FREE MIRACLE WHIP		
2 t	WALNUT OIL		
2 C	COOKED ORZO, COLD		TOSS THESE WITH DRESSING &
2 LBS	COOKED CHICKEN BREAST CUBES		SERVE IN QUARTERED PINEAPPLE
2 C	SEEDLESS RED GRAPE HALVES		SHELLS.
1 C	CELERY, MINCED		
1/2 C	ONION, DICED		INSERT PINEAPPLE LEAVES FOR
2 C	PINEAPPLE CHUNKS		GARNISH.
2 C	MANDARIN ORANGE SECTIONS		

CHICKEN LENTIL SALAD

SERVES 8   FAT = 3 GM EA

1 C	LENTILS, COVER WITH WATER		COOK UNTIL TENDER, DRAIN & COOL.
16	CHERRY TOMATOES, HALVED		ADD THE REST OF INGREDIENTS
4 C	COOKED CHICKEN BREAST CUBES		& CHILL.
1	ONION, DICED & BLANCHED		
1/4 C	FRESH LEMON JUICE (OR TO TASTE)		
1/4 C	FRESH PARSLEY, CHOPPED		
2 CL	GARLIC, MINCED		
1 t	PAPRIKA		
1/2 t	CAYENNE PEPPER		
1/2 t	TURMERIC		

SLICED CHICKEN SALAD   SERVES 12   FAT = 2 GM EA

1/2 C	KETCHUP	PUREE THESE FOR THE SAUCE.
1/4 C	NO-FAT SOUR CREAM	CHILL.
1 OZ	BLEU CHEESE, CRUMBLED	
1/2 C	BROWN SUGAR	
1/2 C	VINEGAR	
1/3 C	FAT-FREE CHICKEN STOCK	
4 CL	GARLIC, CRUSHED	
1/2 t	CAVENDER'S GREEK SEASONING	
2 LBS	CHICKEN BREASTS	POACH BREASTS IN THESE UNTIL
2/3 C	WATER	JUST DONE.
1/2 C	WORCESTERSHIRE SAUCE	DRAIN, DICE & TOSS WITH 1/2 OF
		ABOVE. CHILL.
	RED & ICEBERG LETTUCE	
8	RADISHES, SLICED	ARRANGE ON 12 COLD PLATES &
1	CUCUMBER, SLICED	TOP WITH THE SLICED BREASTS.
2	TOMATOES, SMALL WEDGES	
1/2	RED ONION, SLICED & QUARTERED	
16	CARROT CURLS	SPOON ON REMAINING SAUCE.
1	GREEN BELL PEPPER, SLICED	
1	RED BELL PEPPER, SLICED	

SWEET & SOUR CHICKEN SALAD   _easy_   SERVES 8   FAT = 2 GM EA

1/4 C	SUGAR	HEAT THESE FOR 4 MINUTES.
1 T	CORNSTARCH	
1/2 C	KETCHUP	
3 T	VINEGAR	
2 T	PINEAPPLE JUICE	
2 T	SOY SAUCE	
1/2 C	WATER	
1 t	FRESH GINGER, PEELED, GRATED	
2	CARROTS, SLICED VERY THIN	
1	GREEN PEPPER, SLICED THIN	
1/2	RED ONION, SLICED THIN	ADD CHICKEN AND COOK FOR 5
		MINUTES.
2 LBS	CHICKEN BREASTS, IN STRIPS	ADD THE REST AND SIMMER FOR
1 LB	MUSHROOMS, SLICED	3 MINUTES.
1 C	PINEAPPLE CHUNKS	
6 C	COOKED RICE (OPTIONAL)	SERVE ON BEDS OF SPINACH AND
		GARNISH WITH CHERRY TOMATO
		HALVES.

PRETTY PEPPER COLESLAW

 easy   SERVES 16   FAT = TR EA

1/2 C	NO-FAT SOUR CREAM	COMBINE THESE WELL.
1/2 C	FAT-FREE MIRACLE WHIP	
3 CL	GARLIC, MINCED	
1 t	DRY MUSTARD	SALT & PEPPER TO TASTE.
1/2 t	CHILI POWDER	
1/4 t	OLD BAY SEASONING	
1 t	SUGAR	
------	SKIM MILK, AS NEEDED	
4 C EA	RED & WHITE CABBAGE, SHREDDED	TOSS THESE WITH ABOVE.
8	GREEN ONIONS, CHOPPED	
4	CARROTS, SHREDDED	
1	RED BELL PEPPER, DICED	
1	YELLOW BELL PEPPER, DICED	CHILL 2 HOURS.
1	GREEN BELL PEPPER, DICED	
4 T	FRESH BASIL, CHOPPED	

CORN SALAD

easy   SERVES 12   FAT = 2 GM EA
(Without Parmesan, Fat = Tr Ea)

1/2 C	FAT-FREE MIRACLE WHIP	
1/2 C	NO-FAT SOUR CREAM	COMBINE THESE.
1 t	SUGAR	
1 t	PAPRIKA	
1/4 t	OLD BAY SEASONING (OPTIONAL)	
3	CARROTS, GRATED	ADD THESE & TOSS.
3	APPLES, GRATED	
24 OZ	FROZEN CORN, THAWED	
1 T	FRESH LEMON JUICE	
1 t	SUGAR	SALT & PEPPER TO TASTE.
2	RED BELL PEPPERS, DICED	CHILL.
1/2 C	PARMESAN CHEESE (OPTIONAL—ADDS 16 GM FAT)	

Serve on bed of lettuce.   Garnish with red pepper strips.

COUSCOUS SALAD

easy SERVES 8 FAT = TR EA

2 C	COUSCOUS	COMBINE, COVER AND REMOVE
2 C	BOILING FAT-FREE STOCK	FROM HEAT.
3 T	FRESH LEMON JUICE	SET ASIDE FOR 5 MINUTES.
3 T	LEMON ZEST, MINCED	COOL & FLUFF WITH FORK.
3	TOMATOES, PEELED, SEEDED, DICED	ADD THESE.
1/4 C	FRESH PARSLEY, CHOPPED	CHILL FOR 2 HOURS.
1/4 C	MINT, CHOPPED (OPTIONAL)	
2	GREEN ONIONS, SLICED THIN	SALT & PEPPER TO TASTE.
1	ENGLISH CUKE, QUARTERED, SLICED	

CUCUMBER SPINACH SALAD

easy SERVES 12 FAT = TR EA

2	ENGLISH CUKES, CHOPPED	COMBINE & CHILL THESE FOR 1
4	GREEN ONION, CHOPPED	HOUR.
1 t	CAVENDER'S GREEK SEASONING	
3 CL	GARLIC, MINCED	DRAIN.
1/2 t	GROUND CUMIN	
1/4 t	OLD BAY SEASONING	
1 C	NO-FAT SOUR CREAM	ADD, TOSS WELL AND SERVE ON
		THE SPINACH.
4 C	SPINACH LEAVES, TORN IN PIECES	
1/2 t	PAPRIKA	SPRINKLE OVER.

STUFFED CUCUMBER SALAD

SERVES 12 FAT = TR EA

2	CUCUMBERS, GROOVED AND CORED	
1 C	FAT-FREE CREAM CHEESE	COMBINE THESE WELL.
2 T	FAT-FREE MIRACLE WHIP	
2 T	FRESH PARSLEY, CHOPPED	
2 t	PAPRIKA	SALT & PEPPER TO TASTE.
1/2 C	YELLOW BELL PEPPER, MINCED	
4	GREEN ONIONS, MINCED	STUFF THE CUCUMBERS & CHILL
3 t	CAVENDAR'S GREEK SEASONING	OVERNIGHT.
1 C	FAT-FREE ITALIAN DRESSING	COMBINE & DIVIDE AMONG 12
1 t	SUGAR (OR TO TASTE)	LETTUCE-LINED PLATES.
1/2 t	DRY MUSTARD (OR TO TASTE)	
1/2 t	CURRY (OR MORE—OPTIONAL)	SLICE CUKES IN 1/2" WIDTHS &
6 C	CARROTS, GRATED	DIVIDE AMONG THE 12 SALADS.
1 C	SOAKED RAISINS, DRAINED	

ORIENTAL SALAD

SERVES 12   FAT = 1 GM EA

3 C	COOKED NO-YOLKS NOODLES	
2 C	NO-FAT SOUR CREAM	TOSS THESE & DIVIDE AMONG 12
2 t	SUGAR	COLD SALAD PLATES.
2 T	SOY SAUCE	
2 t	GARLIC, MINCED	
1 t	PAPRIKA	
1/2 t	OLD BAY SEASONING (OPTIONAL)	

24 OZ	BABY CORN ON THE COB	ARRANGE THESE ON NOODLES.
1	CUCUMBER, JULIENNED	
1	CELERY STALK, JULIENNED	
2	CARROTS, JULIENNED	
2	BELL PEPPERS, JULIENNED	
24 OZ	CHICKEN, COOKED, JULIENNED	
4	EGG BEATER CREPES, JULIENNED	(EGG BEATERS FRIED LIKE CREPES)
1	GREEN ONION, JULIENNED	
2	APPLES, JULIENNED	
1 C	MANDARIN ORANGE SECTIONS	
4 t	FRESH LEMON JUICE	

DRESSING

2 CUPS   FAT = TR EA

2	GREEN ONION, SLICED	PUREE THESE & DRIZZLE OVER.
4 CL	GARLIC, SLICED	
1/2 C	SOY SAUCE	
1 T	FRESH GINGER, PEELED, GRATED	
2 t	CRUSHED RED PEPPER FLAKES	
1/2 C	HONEY (OR TO TASTE)	
1/4 C	FAT-FREE MIRACLE WHIP	YOU'LL HAVE DRESSING LEFT
1 C	RED WINE VINEGAR	OVER BUT IT'S GREAT TO HAVE
		ON HAND.

OYSTER & ARTICHOKE SALAD

SERVES 6   FAT = 4 GM EA

------	MIXED GREENS	PLACE THESE ON 6 COLD PLATES.
12 LGE	ARTICHOKE HEARTS, COOKED, CUBED	
6 DZ	OYSTERS, STEAMED, COOLED	
4	GREEN ONIONS, SLICED	
1 BNCH	FLAT PARSLEY, MINCED	

DRESSING

1 C	FAT-FREE ITALIAN DRESSING	PUREE THESE & DRIZZLE OVER.
3 T	BUTTER BUDS	
3 T	BALSAMIC VINEGAR	
2 CL	GARLIC (OR MORE), MINCED	

SMOKED TROUT SALAD

quick   SERVES 10   FAT = 4 GM EA

4	CUKES, SCORED, SLICED 1/4"
60	CANTALOUPE BALLS
2 LBS	SMOKED TROUT, RINSED, DRIED, SLICED
2	SCALLIONS, SLICED

ARRANGE ON 10 COLD LETTUCE-LINED PLATES.

DRESSING

1/2 C	NON-FAT YOGURT
1/2 C	NO-FAT SOUR CREAM
3 T	RICE WINE VINEGAR
1 BNCH	FRESH CHIVES, MINCED
1 t	SUGAR (OR TO TASTE)
4	SCALLIONS, SLICED

WHISK THESE TOGETHER.

SALT & PEPPER TO TASTE.

DRIZZLE OVER.

SOLE & BEET SALAD

SERVES 6   FAT = 1 GM EA

1/4 C	RICE WINE VINEGAR
1 t	SUGAR
2 T	WATER
1/2 t	OLD BAY SEASONING
1 LB	SOLE OR FLOUNDER, COOKED, CUBED
1 1/2 C	POTATOES, COOKED, CUBED
2	APPLES, CUBED
1/2 C	ONION, DICED
1/2 C	DILL PICKLE, DICED (OPTIONAL)
1/2 C	NO-FAT SOUR CREAM

COMBINE AND CHILL THESE FOR 30 MINUTES.

SALT & PEPPER TO TASTE.

1 1/2 C	BEETS, COOKED, PEELED, CUBED
1/2 C	JICAMA OR CHINESE RADISH, JULIENNED
1/2 C	EGG BEATERS, SCRAMBLED & MINCED

ADD BEETS, TOSS AND SERVE ON BEDS OF RADICCHIO.
SPRINKLE THESE ON EACH.

MR. MAC'S FAVORITE TUNA SALAD

   3 CUPS   FAT = 1 GM EA

12 OZ	TUNA, PACKED IN WATER, DRAINED, FLAKED
3/4 C	FAT-FREE MIRACLE WHIP
2	CELERY STALKS, MINCED
1	ONION, DICED
2 T	SWEET RELISH (OR TO TASTE)
1 t	MUSTARD

MIX ALL INGREDIENTS & CHILL FOR 2 HOURS.

SALT & PEPPER TO TASTE.

TEX MEX TUNA SALAD

SERVES 6   FAT = 1 GM EA

1 LB	TUNA, COOKED, CUBED	COMBINE & SERVE ON BEDS OF ROMAINE LETTUCE.
1/4 C	FRESH LIME JUICE	
1	JALAPENO PEPPER, MINCED	
2	CUCUMBERS, CUBED	
2 C	FRESH CILANTRO LEAVES, MINCED	GARNISH WITH LIME WEDGES &
	SALT & PEPPER	SALSA.

Try surrounding with Homemade Tortilla Chips (p 20).

TUNA CABBAGE SALAD

SERVES 4   FAT = 1 GM EA

12 OZ	FRESH TUNA, IN STRIPS	FRY IN A HOT, SPRAYED PAN.
4 DROPS	WALNUT FLAVORING	REMOVE & KEEP WARM.
4	GREEN ONIONS, MINCED	ADD & SIMMER 5 MINUTES.
1/2	RED CABBAGE, SHREDDED	SALT & PEPPER & PLACE IN THE
1/4 C	RICE WINE VINEGAR	CENTER OF A PLATTER.
4 DROPS	WALNUT FLAVORING	
2	SHALLOTS, MINCED	ADD & SIMMER 5 MINUTES.
1/2	CABBAGE, SHREDDED	PLACE AROUND THE EDGE OF
1/4 C	RICE WINE VINEGAR	THE RED CABBAGE.
2 DROPS	WALNUT FLAVORING	
------	SALT & PEPPER	ARRANGE TUNA ON TOP.
3	GREEN ONIONS, SLICED	SPRINKLE OVER TUNA.

GINGERED TUNA SALAD

SERVES 4   FAT = 1 GM EA

6 T	SOY SAUCE	HEAT THESE UNTIL TUNA IS JUST DONE.
6 T	PINEAPPLE JUICE	
1 t	SUGAR (OR TO TASTE)	REMOVE TUNA & KEEP WARM.
12 OZ	FRESH TUNA CHUNKS	
3 T	FRESH GINGER, PEELED, MINCED	REMOVE PAN FROM HEAT.
1/4 t	CRUSHED RED PEPPER FLAKES	
2 CL	GARLIC, MINCED	
4	GREEN ONIONS, SLICED	
1/2 C	COLD WATER	COMBINE THESE WELL, WHISK IN
2 t	CORNSTARCH	& HEAT TO THICKEN.
4	PLATES OF GREENS, CUKES & RADISHES	PLACE TUNA ON THESE & SPOON SAUCE OVER.

MANGO SWORDFISH SALAD

easy   SERVES 8   FAT = 4 GM EA

8	4 OZ SWORDFISH STEAKS	COMBINE ALL & CHILL 1 HOUR.
4	MANGOES, PEELED, PUREED	
4	SCALLIONS, SLICED	
ZEST OF 2	LIMES, MINCED	THEN GRILL & SLICE.
1/4 C	FRESH LIME JUICE	
2 t	FRESH GINGER, PEELED, MINCED	ARRANGE SLICES ON PLATES OF
1	JALAPENO PEPPER, SEEDED, MINCED	MIXED SALAD GREENS.
4 CL	GARLIC, MINCED	
------	SALT & PEPPER	GARNISH WITH SLICES OF FRESH
		MANGO.

FISH & CARROT SALAD

easy   SERVES 6   FAT = 1 GM EA

3 C	COD OR FLOUNDER, COOKED, CUBED	COMBINE THESE.
1/4 C	FRESH LEMON JUICE (OR TO TASTE)	
1 t	DIJON MUSTARD	
2 CL	GARLIC	CHILL 30 MINUTES.
------	SALT & PEPPER	
4	CARROTS, GRATED	TOSS THESE & DIVIDE AMONG 6
2 HDS	BELGIAN ENDIVE, CHOPPED	COLD, LETTUCE-LINED PLATES.
2	GREEN ONIONS, SLICED	
1	TOMATO, DICED	
1/2 C	FRESH TARRAGON, CHOPPED	
2 T	CAPERS, DRAINED, MINCED	PLACE THE FISH ON TOP.
3	PLUM TOMATOES, SLICED	GARNISH

SOLE BUFFET RING

quick   SERVES 12   FAT = 2 GM EA

4 EA	ORANGES, LIMES, PEELED & SLICED	ALTERNATE THESE SLICES IN A
2	ONIONS, SLICED IN RINGS	LARGE CIRCLE.
3	GREEN PEPPERS, SLICED IN RINGS	
12	4 OZ SOLE FILLETS	SPRAY FISH WITH PAM BUTTER.
------	PAPRIKA	SPRINKLE WITH SEASONINGS &
2 CL	GARLIC, MINCED	BROIL 10 MINUTES PER INCH OF
4 T	ORANGE & LIME ZEST, MINCED	THICKNESS.
1 T	BUTTER BUDS	
------	SALT & PEPPER	LAY FISH ON ONIONS & PEPPERS.
1 C	ORANGE JUICE	COMBINE & DRIZZLE OVER THE
2 T	LIME JUICE	FISH.
1/2 t	LOUISIANA HOT SAUCE	

COCONUT CEVICHE   SERVES 8   FAT = 1 GM EA

1 LB	RED SNAPPER FILLETS IN SMALL CUBES	COMBINE & CHILL THESE FOR 4 HOURS.
1	LIME, ZESTED, MINCED	
1 C	ONION, DICED	
1	GREEN PEPPER, DICED	
1	RED BELL PEPPER, DICED	
1 C	FRESH LIME JUICE	
2 T	COCONUT FLAVORING	
1/4 t	CAVENDER'S GREEK SEASONING	
------	CRUSHED RED PEPPER FLAKES	
------	FRESH PARSLEY, MINCED	
1	MANGO, DICED	ADD, TOSS & FILL THE PAPAYAS.
4	RIPE PAPAYAS, HALVED, SEEDS REMOVED	
2	GREEN ONIONS, SLICED	SPRINKLE OVER EACH.

SALMON & SPINACH SALAD   SERVES 8   FAT = 2 GM EA

2 BNCHS	GREEN ONIONS, SLICED	MARINATE THESE FOR 30 MIN.
2 T	SALT	
6 T	RICE WINE VINEGAR	
2 T	SUGAR	
1/2 C	NO-FAT SOUR CREAM	COMBINE AND TOSS WITH THE ONIONS.
3 T	FRESH LIME JUICE	
1 LB	SMOKED SALMON, SLICED IN THIN STRIPS	
1 C	TOMATOES, DICED	
8 C	SPINACH LEAVES, WASHED	DIVIDE AMONG 8 COLD PLATES & TOP THE ABOVE.

SCALLOP & MUSHROOM SALAD   (quick)   SERVES 4   FAT = 1 GM EA

4 C	SPINACH LEAVES, WASHED	TOSS THESE & DIVIDE AMONG 4 SALAD PLATES.
2 C	MUSHROOMS, SLICED	
2 T	NO-FAT SOUR CREAM	
2 T	FRESH LEMON JUICE	
1/2 t	CAVENDER'S GREEK SEASONING	
16 LGE	SEA SCALLOPS, SLICED HORIZONTALLY	PAT SCALLOPS DRY, SPRAY WITH OLIVE OIL SPRAY & BAKE AT 375 FOR 2 MINUTES EACH SIDE OR UNTIL DONE.
1/2 t	OLD BAY SEASONING	
2 C	TOMATO CONCASSE (p 396)	PLACE ON TOP OF SALADS.
2	GREEN ONIONS, SLICED	SPRINKLE OVER SCALLOPS.

TURKEY CHEESE SALAD

easy   SERVES 12   FAT = 3 GM EA

2 LBS	TURKEY BREASTS, IN STRIPS	COMBINE & CHILL 12 HOURS.
1/2 C	WATER	
4 CL	GARLIC, MINCED	SALT & PEPPER TO TASTE.
1 t	GROUND ROSEMARY	
16	CRUSHED JUNIPER BERRIES	STIR-FRY BRIEFLY.
8 BNCHS	LAMB'S LETTUCE	DIVIDE AMONG 12 COLD PLATES
2 HDS EA	BIBB LETTUCE, RADICCHIO	& TOP WITH THE TURKEY STRIPS.
1 HD	CURLY ENDIVE	

DRESSING

6 OZ	LOW-FAT GOAT CHEESE	PUREE THESE.
3/4 C	SKIM MILK (OR MORE AS NEEDED)	
1	LEMON, JUICED	SALT & PEPPER TO TASTE.
2 t	CAVENDER'S GREEK SEASONING	
1 CL	GARLIC, MINCED	DRIZZLE OVER EACH.

TURKEY CURRY SALAD

easy   SERVES 6   FAT = 1 GM EA

2	APPLES, JULIENNED, SPRINKLED WITH ORANGE JUICE	
1 LB	TURKEY BREASTS, COOKED, CUT IN STRIPS	TOSS THESE TOGETHER.
1 C	MANGO, JULIENNED (OR CHUTNEY)	
1/2 C	FAT-FREE MIRACLE WHIP	COMBINE & TOSS WITH ABOVE.
1/2 C	NO-FAT SOUR CREAM	
	SKIM MILK TO THIN	
1 T	CURRY POWDER (OR TO TASTE)	
2 t	RAISINS OR CURRANTS	SPRINKLE OVER EACH.

TURKEY SALAD

easy   5 CUPS   FAT = 3 GM EA

| 4 C | TURKEY BREASTS, COOKED, CUBED | COMBINE THESE WITH THE |
| 1 C | CELERY, DICED | DRESSING & CHILL. |

DRESSING

1 C	FAT-FREE MIRACLE WHIP	WHISK THESE TOGETHER AND
1 T	FRENCH'S MUSTARD (OR TO TASTE)	USE JUST ENOUGH MILK TO GET
1 T	SUGAR (OR TO TASTE)	THE CONSISTENCY YOU LIKE.
1 T	SKIM MILK (OR AS NEEDED)	
------	SALT & PEPPER	

MEAT SALAD

 SERVES 6   FAT = 1 GM EA

16 OZ	TURKEY BREASTS, FLATTENED SLIGHTLY	COMBINE & MARINATE 1 HOUR.
1/4 C	WORCESTERSHIRE SAUCE	
1/4 C	WATER	SIMMER UNTIL DONE & SLICE.
1/2 C	RICE WINE (OR RED WINE) VINEGAR	
1 T EA	GARLIC POWDER	
1 T	ONION POWDER	
1 T	FRESH BASIL, CHOPPED	
1 T	BUTTER BUDS	
2 t	CELERY SALT	
1 t	PEPPER	
2	COOKED POTATOES, CUBED	ARRANGE ON THE GREENS AND
2	ZUCCHINI CUBES, BLANCHED	TOP WITH THE MEAT.
8	MUSHROOMS, QUARTERED	DRIZZLE HOT MARINADE OVER.
8	CHERRY TOMATOES, HALVED	
6	PLATES OF SALAD GREENS	

CURRIED MEAT SALAD

 SERVES 6   FAT = 1 GM EA

1/2 C	FAT-FREE MIRACLE WHIP	COMBINE THESE.
1/2 C	NO-FAT SOUR CREAM	
1/4 C	RED ONIONS, MINCED	
1/4 C	CURRY POWDER (OR TO TASTE)	
2 t	FRESH GINGER, PEELED, GRATED	
1 t	SOY SAUCE	
1 t	COCONUT FLAVORING	
2 C	COOKED TURKEY BREASTS, DICED	ADD THESE & TOSS.
1 C	RAISINS, SOAKED 15 MINUTES	
1 C	CANNED CHICK PEAS, DRAINED	
1/2 C	GREEN ONIONS, SLICED	

You can add rice, apples, oranges, bananas or almost anything.

PAELLA SALAD

SERVES 8   FAT = 4 GM EA
(Including Dressing)

4 OZ	SMOKED MUSSELS, RINSED & DRAINED	ARRANGE IN THE BOTTOM OF A
1 C	SHRIMP, PEELED, DEVEINED, COOKED	SPRAYED RICE RING.
8	BLACK OLIVES, SLICED	

4 OZ	SMOKED MUSSELS, ALSO RINSED & DRAINED	
1 C	SHRIMP, ALSO, PEELED, DEVEINED, COOKED	
1	RED BELL PEPPER, DICED	TOSS THESE WITH JUST ENOUGH
1	GREEN BELL PEPPER, DICED	DRESSING TO HOLD TOGETHER.
2	HEADS CHICORY, DICED	
1	ONION, DICED	
2 SM CANS	MANDARIN ORANGES, CHOPPED	
2 C	TURKEY BREASTS, COOKED, DICED	PRESS IN RING & CHILL.
4 C	COOKED RICE	

UNMOLD & DRIZZLE REMAINING
DRESSING OVER.

DRESSING

1 CUP   FAT = TR EA

2 CL	GARLIC, MINCED	WHISK THESE TOGETHER.
1/2 C	FAT-FREE MIRACLE WHIP	
1/2 C	NO-FAT SOUR CREAM	
2 t	FRESH LEMON JUICE	
	SKIM MILK AS NEEDED	

CHINESE TURKEY SALAD

easy

SERVES 12   FAT = 2 GM EA

1/4 C	RED CURRANT JELLY	MARINATE THESE FOR 6 HOURS.
1/4 C	DRY SHERRY	SPREAD MORE JELLY ON TURKEY
1/4 C	SOY SAUCE	& POUR MARINADE AROUND.
1 CL	GARLIC, MINCED	
1 t	5 SPICE POWDER	BAKE AT 325 FOR 30 MINUTES OR
2 LBS	TURKEY BREASTS	UNTIL DONE. COOL.

6 C	ASPARAGUS PIECES, BLANCHED 1 MIN.	COMBINE & CHILL THESE.
3 C	COOKED POTATOES (CUT TO MATCH ASPARAGUS)	
1/4 C	SOY SAUCE	ARRANGE ON 12 COLD PLATES OF
1/4 C	FAT-FREE BEEF STOCK	SPINACH OR LETTUCE.
1/4 C	SUGAR	
------	LOUISIANA HOT SAUCE TO TASTE	TOP WITH SMALL SLICES OF THE
		TURKEY.

1 T	SESAME SEEDS	SPRINKLE OVER SALADS.

HOT & SPICY POTATO SALAD

easy   SERVES 12   FAT = 1 GM EA

2/3 C	FAT-FREE MIRACLE WHIP	PUREE THESE INGREDIENTS.
1/2 C	NO-FAT SOUR CREAM	
1/4 C	DRY SHERRY	
1/4 C	CIDER VINEGAR (OR BALSAMIC)	
1 T	GORGONZOLA OR BLEU CHEESE	
1 T	WORCESTERSHIRE SAUCE	
1 t	CAVENDER'S GREEK SEASONING	
1/2 t	DRY MUSTARD	
16	RED POTATOES w SKINS, COOKED, SLICED	TOSS THESE WITH ABOVE.
2 LBS	GREEN BEANS, SLICED DIAGONALLY, STEAMED 4 MIN.	
1	JICAMA OR CHINESE RADISH, JULIENNED	
16	GREEN OR BLACK OLIVES, SLICED	
12	GREEN ONIONS, SLICED	
------	SALT & PEPPER TO TASTE	
3/4 C	EGG BEATERS, SCRAMBLED & MINCED	SPRINKLE ON EACH SERVING.
3 OZ	PIMENTO, DICED	

MOROCCAN RICE SALAD

SERVES 10   FAT = TR EA

2 C	BROWN RICE (COOKED IN FAT-FREE CHICKEN STOCK)	
1 C	RAISINS, SOAKED, DRAINED	
3	GREEN ONIONS, SLICED	COMBINE THESE.
1 C	FRESH BEAN SPROUTS, CHOPPED	
1	GREEN PEPPER, DICED	
1	CELERY STALK, DICED	
2 T	FRESH PARSLEY, CHOPPED	
1/4 C	TAMARI SAUCE (SEE BELOW)	
1/4 C	FRESH ORANGE JUICE	PUREE THESE & ADD TO ABOVE.
1/2 C	MOCK OIL (p 395)	
2 T	DRY SHERRY	
1	LIME, JUICED	
1 CL	GARLIC, MINCED	CHILL 2 HOURS.
1 t	FRESH GINGER, PEELED, GRATED	

TAMARI SAUCE

3/4 CUPS   FAT = TR EA

1/2 C	MOCK OIL (p 395)	SIMMER FOR 10 MINUTES.
2 CL	GARLIC, MINCED	
1/4 C	SOY SAUCE	COOL.
2 T	TAMARIND PULP	
1 t	SUGAR (OR TO TASTE)	

RICE RING SALAD

 SERVES 10   FAT = TR EA

1 C	PINEAPPLE CHUNKS w LIQUID	LINE A RICE RING WITH PLASTIC
1/2 C	FAT-FREE MIRACLE WHIP	WRAP & SPRAY WITH PAM.
1/2 C	NO-FAT SOUR CREAM	
1/2 C	GREEN PEPPER, DICED	COMBINE ALL & FILL RING.
1/2 C	GREEN ONION, SLICED	
1 LB	COOKED TURKEY BREASTS, OR 99% FAT-FREE HAM, DICED	
4 C	RICE, (COOKED IN FAT-FREE CHICKEN STOCK)	
1 T	SOY SAUCE	
1 t	MUSTARD	CHILL 2 HOURS.
1/2 t	SALT	

You might like to decorate the ring by placing flowers or petals cut out of pickled red bell peppers on the sprayed plastic wrap before filling.

SEAFOOD SALAD

 SERVES 8   FAT = TR EA

8 OZ	BAY SCALLOPS, COOKED	COMBINE ALL INGREDIENTS.
8 OZ	SHRIMP, PEELED, DEVEINED, COOKED	
1 LB	IMITATION CRAB, SHREDDED	CHILL 2 HOURS.
1/4 t	OLD BAY SEASONING	
1/2 C	FAT-FREE MIRACLE WHIP	SERVE ON WASHED SPINACH.
1	LEMON, JUICED	
1/2 C	NO-FAT SOUR CREAM	
6	SCALLIONS, SLICED	
6	PIMENTOS, SLICED	
1 t	GARLIC POWDER	

CURRIED SEAFOOD SALAD

 SERVES 10   FAT = 1 GM EA

1 LB	SHRIMP, PEELED, DEVEIN	TOSS THESE WITH THE DRESSING
1 LB	IMITATION CRAB, SHREDDED	BELOW.
1 C	PINEAPPLE CHUNKS, DRAINED, CHOPPED SLIGHTLY	
1/2 C	RAISINS, SOAKED IN PINEAPPLE JUICE, DRAINED	
1/2 C	MANDARIN ORANGE SECTIONS, DRAINED	
1/2 C	WATER CHESTNUTS, SLICED, DRAINED	SERVE ON BEDS OF LETTUCE.
1/2 C	GREEN ONION, SLICED	
1/2 C	GINGER JELLY	COMBINE THESE.
1/2 C	FAT-FREE MIRACLE WHIP	
1/2 C	NO-FAT SOUR CREAM	SALT & PEPPER TO TASTE.
1 T	CURRY POWDER (OR TO TASTE)	
	FRESH LEMON JUICE, AS NEEDED	

SHRIMP SALAD

 easy   SERVES 8   FAT = 1 GM EA

2 LBS	SHRIMP, PEELED, CLEANED, COOKED
6	GREEN ONIONS, SLICED THIN
1/2 C	CELERY, THINLY SLICED
1 T	KETCHUP
2 T	GARLIC, MINCED
1/4 C	NO-FAT SOUR CREAM
1/2 C	FAT-FREE MIRACLE WHIP
	SKIM MILK, IF NEEDED FOR CONSISTENCY
1 T	SOY SAUCE OR SHERRY (OPTIONAL)
1/2 C	EGG BEATERS, SCRAMBLED, DICED
------	CHOPPED PIMENTO

COMBINE ALL INGREDIENTS AND CHILL 2 HOURS.

SERVE ON BEDS OF LETTUCE. SURROUND WITH CUCUMBER SLICES AND TOMATO WEDGES.

SPRINKLE OVER EACH.

SHRIMP SALAD w GRAPES

 easy   SERVES 8   FAT = 1 GM EA

3/4 C	CELERY, FINELY CHOPPED
8	SCALLIONS, FINELY CHOPPED
1 t	CELERY SALT (OR TO TASTE)
1/4 t	OLD BAY SEASONING
3/4 C	NO-FAT SOUR CREAM
3/4 C	FAT-FREE MIRACLE WHIP
1 C EA	SEEDLESS RED & GREEN GRAPES, HALVED
1 T	CAPERS, CHOPPED (OPTIONAL)
2 LBS	SHRIMP, COOKED w OLD BAY SEASONING, COOLED

COMBINE ALL INGREDIENTS. SALT & PEPPER TO TASTE.

SERVE ON BEDS OF GREENS.

GARNISH WITH LITTLE BALLS OF CANTALOUPE & MELON.

For extra spiciness, you could add Worcestershire Sauce, Pick-A-Pepper, Cayenne, etc.

SHRIMP & CUCUMBER SALAD

easy   SERVES 4   FAT = 1 GM EA

1 LB	SHRIMP, CLEANED, COOKED
1	CUCUMBER, SLICED
8	CHERRY TOMATOES, HALVED
1/2 C	EGG BEATERS, SCRAMBLED, DICED
1/4 C	FRESH LEMON JUICE (OR TO TASTE)
1/2 C	FAT-FREE ITALIAN DRESSING
1/4 C	NO-FAT SOUR CREAM
1 t	SUGAR (OR TO TASTE)
1/2 C	SOY SAUCE

COMBINE ALL INGREDIENTS AND CHILL.

GARNISH WITH FRESH DILL AND PIMENTO STRIPS.

STEAK SALAD

easy   SERVES 8   FAT = 2 GM EA

1/4 C	SOY SAUCE	MARINATE THESE FOR 12 HOURS.
3 CL	GARLIC, MINCED	
1/4 t	PEPPER	
1 LB	TENDERLOIN STEAK, TRIMMED WELL (OR ROUND)	FRY IN A PAM-SPRAYED PAN TO DESIRED DONENESS & SLICE.
10	RED POTATOES, BOILED w SKINS, CUBED	TOSS THESE WITH SOME OF THE
1	RED ONION, JULIENNED	DRESSING BELOW AND ARRANGE
1	RED BELL PEPPER, JULIENNED	ON LETTUCE LINED PLATES.
1 C	FROZEN PEAS, BLANCHED	
1/4 C	FRESH PARSLEY, CHOPPED	ARRANGE STEAK OVER EACH.

DRESSING

easy   16 OZ   FAT = TR EA

1/4 C	RED WINE OR BALSAMIC VINEGAR	PUREE THESE INGREDIENTS.
1/4 C	FAT-FREE ITALIAN DRESSING	
2 CL	GARLIC, MINCED	SALT & PEPPER TO TASTE.
1 T	DIJON MUSTARD	
1 T	FRESH LEMON JUICE	
1 T	SUGAR	
2 t	WORCESTERSHIRE SAUCE	
2 t	FRESH TARRAGON, CHOPPED	
2 t	FRESH BASIL, CHOPPED	
2 t	FRESH OREGANO, CHOPPED	(YOU MIGHT WANT TO MAKE A
1 C	MOCK OIL, OR AS NEEDED (p 395)	DOUBLE BATCH OF THIS)

MEGA VEGGIE SALAD

SERVES 16   FAT = TR EA

2 C	BROCCOLI FLORETS, BLANCHED 4 MIN & SHOCKED	
2 C	MUSHROOMS, HALVED	TOSS ALL INGREDIENTS WITH
1 C	BABY CARROTS, SLICED THIN	THE DRESSING.
1 C	CAULIFLOWER FLORETS, BLANCHED 4 MIN & SHOCKED	
1/2 C	YELLOW SQUASH, DICED	
1/2 C	ZUCCHINI, DICED	CHILL.
1/2 C	GREEN ONIONS, SLICED	
1/2 C	ALFALFA SPROUTS	
1/2 C	RAISINS, SOAKED IN APPLE JUICE, DRAINED	
8 OZ	ALPINE LACE FREE N' LEAN MOZZARELLA CHEESE CUBES (OR TRY A SPICY LOW-FAT CHEESE)	
2 C	APPLES, DICED & DIPPED IN ORANGE JUICE	
1/2 C	DRESSING FROM "STEAK SALAD" ABOVE (OR USE A FAT-FREE ITALIAN)	

TARRAGON VEGETABLE SALAD

easy   SERVES 12   FAT = TR EA

2	CARROTS, CLEANED, SLICED DIAGONALLY	COMBINE & SIMMER THESE FOR
1 C	FAT-FREE CHICKEN STOCK	10 MINUTES.
		DRAIN & COOL.
2 PKG	FROZEN SNOW PEAS	
16	CHERRY TOMATOES, HALVED	ADD THESE & TOSS.
1	CUCUMBER, GROOVED & SLICED	
1/2 C	FAT-FREE ITALIAN DRESSING	
1/4 C	TARRAGON VINEGAR	CHILL OVERNIGHT.
1/4 C	FAT-FREE MIRACLE WHIP	
1 t	FRESH TARRAGON, CHOPPED	
2 CL	GARLIC, MINCED	

WINTER SALAD

quick   FAT = TR

2 C	FAT-FREE ITALIAN DRESSING	COMBINE AND DRIZZLE OVER
1/2 C	FAT-FREE MIRACLE WHIP	SPINACH AND YOUR CHOICE OF
2 T	BROWN SUGAR	INGREDIENTS.
2 CL	GARLIC, MINCED	
2 t	POPPY SEEDS	

YOUR CHOICE OF:

GRAPES	PINEAPPLE CHUNKS	APRICOTS	MANDARIN ORANGE SECTIONS
DATES	RED ONIONS, DICED	BANANAS	APPLES, DICED AND TOSSED IN
			ORANGE JUICE

ZUCCHINI CAPER SALAD

easy   SERVES 10   FAT = TR EA

4	ZUCCHINI, DICED	COMBINE THESE.
1	RED ONION, DICED	
1	RED BELL PEPPER, DICED	
1	YELLOW BELL PEPPER, DICED	
5 T	CAPERS, CRUSHED SLIGHTLY	
1 T	FRESH PARSLEY, CHOPPED	
1/4 C	FAT-FREE ITALIAN DRESSING	COMBINE & TOSS THESE WITH
1/4 C	FAT-FREE MIRACLE WHIP	THE ABOVE.
1 T	FRESH LEMON JUICE	
1/2 t	SUGAR	
1/2 t	DRY MUSTARD	SERVE ON BEDS OF LETTUCE.
------	SALT & PEPPER TO TASTE	

CHRISTMAS SALAD   SERVES 6   FAT = TR EA

2 LBS	BEETS, COOKED & SLICED	LINE A PLATE WITH RED & GREEN
4 C	BRUSSELS SPROUTS, COOKED, CUT IN HALF	LEAF LETTUCE, BELGAIN ENDIVE
4	NAVEL ORANGES, PEELED & SLICED	WATERCRESS & RADICCHIO.
3	RED OR PINK GRAPEFRUIT, PEELED & SLICED	
1	RED ONION, THINLY SLICED & SEPARATED	PLACE VEGGIES AND FRUIT IN A
		PRETTY PATTERN.
1/2 C	MOCK OIL, OR AS NEEDED (p 395)	
1/3 C	RED WINE VINEGAR	
3 T	FRESH TARRAGON, OR ROSEMARY OR PARSLEY	PUREE THESE INGREDIENTS.
2 T	DIJON MUSTARD	
1 T	BALSAMIC VINEGAR	SALT & PEPPER TO TASTE.
3	SUN-DRIED TOMATOES, BLANCHED & MINCED	
1 CL	GARLIC	DRIZZLE OVER.

COBB SALAD   SERVES 4   FAT = 5 GM EA

8 C	MIXED SALAD GREENS	DIVIDE GREENS AMONG 4 COLD
3	CHICKEN BREASTS, COOKED, DICED	SALAD PLATES.
3	TOMATOES, DICED	
1 1/2 C	EGG BEATERS, SCRAMBLED & DICED	ARRANGE THESE IN ROWS ON THE
1 1/2	RED ONION, DICED	GREENS.
4 SL	OSCAR MAYER BACON, FRIED, DICED	
1 1/2 C	MARINATED ARTICHOKE HEARTS, DRAINED, TRIMMED WELL, DICED	
1 C	FAT-FREE VINAIGRETTE (p 106-110)	DRIZZLE OVER & THEN TOP
4 T	ROQUEFORT OR BLEU CHEESE, CRUMBLED	EACH WITH CHEESE.

POPPY ZUCCHINI SALAD   *easy*   SERVES 12   FAT = .5 GM EA

1/2 C	FAT-FREE MIRACLE WHIP	WHISK THESE INGREDIENTS.
1/2 C	RED WINE VINEGAR	
1/4 C	DRIED ITALIAN OR SPAGHETTI SEASONING	
1 T	POPPY SEEDS	
------	SALT & PEPPER TO TASTE	
------	SKIM MILK FOR CONSISTENCY	
3	ZUCCHINI, DICED	TOSS THESE WITH ABOVE &
2	ONIONS, DICED	CHILL 2 HOURS.
1 PT	CHERRY TOMATOES, HALVED OR QUARTERED	

CONFETTI SALAD

 SERVES 4 FAT = TR EA

1 C	CORN, FROZEN, BLANCHED	COMBINE THESE AND TOSS WITH
1 C	CUCUMBER, DICED	THE SAUCE.
1 C	BLACK BEANS, COOKED, RINSED (CANNED ARE OK)	
4	RADISHES, SLICED THINLY	
1/3 C EA	RED, YELLOW, GREEN BELL PEPPER, DICED	
1/2	RED ONION, SLICED THINLY & QUARTERED	
2 C	NON-FAT LIME YOGURT	WHISK THESE TOGETHER.
1/4 C	FRESH CILANTRO, MINCED	
2 T	FRESH LIME JUICE	SALT & PEPPER TO TASTE.
1 CL	GARLIC, MINCED TO A PASTE	

MUSHROOM SALAD

 SERVES 4 FAT = TR EA

1 LB	MUSHROOMS, SLICED	COMBINE THESE.
1	RED ONION, SLICED THINLY & QUARTERED	
4 OZ JAR	PICKLED RED BELL PEPPERS, DICED	
1	GREEN BELL PEPPER, DICED	
1/2 C	MOCK OIL (p 395)	PUREE THESE AND TOSS WITH
1/4 C	BALSAMIC VINEGAR OR FRESH LEMON JUICE	ABOVE.
1 T	FRESH BASIL OR OREGANO OR THYME MINCED	
------	SALT & PEPPER TO TASTE	CHILL 8 HOURS
1 t	DIJON MUSTARD (OPTIONAL)	

You could add thinly sliced zucchini, carrots or other favorite veggie.

WALDORF SALAD

quick SERVES 8 FAT = TR EA

1/2 C	FAT-FREE MIRACLE WHIP	COMBINE THESE AND CHILL 2
2	RED APPLES, CUBED	HOURS.
1/4 C	RAISINS	
1/4 C	CELERY, MINCED	TOSS AND SERVE ON BEDS OF
1/4 C	RED ONIONS, MINCED	LETTUCE.
1/2 t	HONEY	
1/4 t	WALNUT FLAVORING (OR TO TASTE)	ADD COOKED CHICKEN & / OR
1/8 t	DRY MUSTARD	PASTA IF YOU LIKE.

Dressings

EASY BLEU CHEESE DRESSING

quick   16 OZ   FAT = 1 GM EA

1 C	1% BUTTERMILK	
1 C	NO-FAT SOUR CREAM	
2 OZ	BLEU CHEESE, CRUMBLED	
1 T	BUTTER BUDS	
------	GARLIC POWDER TO TASTE	

WHISK ALL INGREDIENTS.

SALT & PEPPER TO TASTE.

BLEU CHEESE DRESSING

quick   18 OZ   FAT = 1 GM EA

1 C	FAT-FREE MIRACLE WHIP
1/2 C	NO-FAT SOUR CREAM
1/2 C	1% BUTTERMILK
1 T	STEAK SAUCE
1 T	BUTTER BUDS
1 T	DRIED ITALIAN SEASONING
1 T	FRESH PARSLEY, CHOPPED
7 DROPS	LOUISIANA HOT SAUCE
1 CL	GARLIC, MINCED
2 OZ	BLEU CHEESE

PUREE THESE INGREDIENTS.

SALT & PEPPER TO TASTE.

ADD BLEU CHEESE & PROCESS
CHOP-CHOP.

SHERRY BLEU CHEESE DRESSING

quick   16 OZ   FAT = 1 GM EA

1 C	FAT-FREE MIRACLE WHIP
1 C	NO-FAT SOUR CREAM
2 T	DRY SHERRY
1 T	BUTTER BUDS
1 t	WORCESTERSHIRE SAUCE
1/2 t	DRY MUSTARD
1/2 t	GARLIC POWDER
1/2 t	CAVENDER'S GREEK SEASONING
1/2 t	EVERGLADES SEASONING
2 OZ	BLEU CHEESE, MINCED

PUREE THESE INGREDIENTS.

SALT & PEPPER TO TASTE.

BLEND IN WELL.

BURGUNDY DRESSING

quick   32 OZ   FAT = TR EA

2 C	MOCK OIL (p 395)
2 C	BURGUNDY WINE
2 T	HONEY (OR TO TASTE)
2 T	BUTTER BUDS
1 T	FRESH PARSLEY, MINCED
2 CL	GARLIC, MINCED

PUREE ALL INGREDIENTS.

SALT & PEPPER TO TASTE.

BUTTERMILK DRESSING

16 OZ   FAT = TR EA

1 C	1% BUTTERMILK	PUREE ALL INGREDIENTS.
1/2 C	NO-FAT SOUR CREAM	
1/2 C	FAT-FREE MIRACLE WHIP	
1/4 C	FRESH PARSLEY, CHOPPED	
1 T	BUTTER BUDS	
2 t	EVERGLADES SEASONING	
1/2 t	ONION POWDER	
1/4 t	GARLIC POWDER	SALT & PEPPER TO TASTE.
1/4 t	CAVENDER'S GREEK SEASONING	

BASIL BUTTERMILK DRESSING

16 OZ   FAT = TR EA

2 C	FRESH BASIL LEAVES	PUREE ALL INGREDIENTS.
1 C	1% BUTTERMILK	
1/2 C	NO-FAT SOUR CREAM	
1/4 C	FAT-FREE MIRACLE WHIP	
2	GREEN ONIONS, SLICED	
1 T	BUTTER BUDS	
1 T	FRESH LEMON JUICE	
1 t	CAVENDER'S GREEK SEASONING	
1 t	EVERGLADES SEASONING	
------	SALT & PEPPER TO TASTE	

CHAMPAGNE DRESSING

quick

24 OZ   FAT = TR EA

1/2 C	EGG BEATERS	PUREE ALL INGREDIENTS.
1/2 C	CHAMPAGNE VINEGAR	
1 T	DIJON MUSTARD	
1 T	BUTTER BUDS	
2 C	MOCK OIL (p 395)	SALT & PEPPER TO TASTE.

CAESAR DRESSING I

  20 OZ   FAT = 1 GM EA

2 CL	GARLIC, MINCED	PUREE ALL INGREDIENTS.
1/4 C	EGG BEATERS	
6	GREEN OLIVES	
1/4 C	BALSAMIC VINEGAR (OR RED OR WHITE WINE VINEGAR)	
2 T	DIJON MUSTARD (OR TO TASTE)	
1 T	FRESH LEMON JUICE	
1 T	BUTTER BUDS	
1 t	CAVENDER'S GREEK SEASONING	SALT & PEPPER TO TASTE.
2 C	MOCK OIL (p 395) OR NO-FAT SOUR CREAM	
1/2 C	PARMESAN CHEESE	

OPTIONS: WORCESTERSHIRE, LOUISIANA HOT SAUCE, WHITE TUNA IN WATER, DRAINED.

CAESAR DRESSING II

quick   12 OZ   FAT = 2 GM EA

1 CL	GARLIC, MINCED (OR TO TASTE)	PUREE ALL INGREDIENTS.
1/4 C	FRESH LEMON JUICE	
1/2 C	PARMESAN CHEESE	
1/4 C	NO-FAT SOUR CREAM	
1 T	DIJON MUSTARD (OR TO TASTE)	
1 T	BUTTER BUDS	
1 t	WORCESTERSHIRE SAUCE	SALT & PEPPER TO TASTE.
1 C	MOCK OIL (p 395 MADE w CHICKEN STOCK)	

COLORADO DRESSING

quick   16 OZ   FAT = TR EA

1/2 C	RED WINE VINEGAR	PUREE ALL INGREDIENTS.
1 1/2 C	NO-FAT SOUR CREAM	
2 CL	GARLIC, CRUSHED	
1 T	DIJON MUSTARD	
1 T	BUTTER BUDS	
2 t	SUGAR	
2 t	WORCESTERSHIRE SAUCE	
2 t	DRIED TARRAGON	
1 t	DRIED BASIL	
1 t	DRIED OREGANO	
1/2 t	CAVENDER'S GREEK SEASONING	SALT & PEPPER TO TASTE.
1/2	LEMON, JUICED	

COTTAGE CHEESE DRESSING

 12 OZ FAT = TR EA

1 C	FAT-FREE COTTAGE CHEESE
1/4 C	FAT-FREE MIRACLE WHIP
1/2 C	SUGAR
1 T	BUTTER BUDS
1 t	DRY MUSTARD
1/4 t	SALT
4 t	HORSERADISH
1 T	RED WINE VINEGAR
1 T	FRESH LEMON JUICE
1 T	EVERGLADES SEASONING

PUREE ALL INGREDIENTS.

SALT & PEPPER TO TASTE.

CLASSIC CREAM DRESSING

 10 OZ FAT = TR EA

1/2 C	EVAPORATED SKIM MILK
1/2 C	NO-FAT SOUR CREAM
1/4 C	BALSAMIC OR TARRAGON VINEGAR
1 T	BUTTER BUDS
2 t	GARLIC, MINCED
2 t	FRESH PARSLEY, CHOPPED
2 t	FRESH ROSEMARY, CHOPPED
1 t	DIJON MUSTARD
1 t	FRESH LEMON JUICE
1/2 t	DRY MUSTARD
1/4 t	SUGAR

PUREE ALL INGREDIENTS.

SALT & PEPPER TO TASTE.

CUCUMBER DRESSING

quick 32 OZ FAT = TR EA

2 C	CUCUMBERS, PEELED & SEEDED
1 C	NO-FAT SOUR CREAM
1/2 C	FAR FREE MIRACLE WHIP
1/2 C	FAT-FREE PLAIN YOGURT
1 T	FRESH DILL (OR TO TASTE)
2 T	ONION, DICED
1 T	BUTTER BUDS
1 t	FRESH LEMON JUICE
1/2 t	CAVENDER'S GREEK SEASONING
------	SUGAR OR EQUAL TO TASTE

PUREE ALL INGREDIENTS.

SALT & PEPPER TO TASTE.

CREAMY DILL

  8 OZ   FAT = TR EA

1/2 C	NO-FAT SOUR CREAM	PUREE ALL INGREDIENTS.
1/2 C	1% BUTTERMILK	
1 T	SUGAR	
2 T	FRESH DILL (OR TO TASTE)	
1 T	BUTTER BUDS	
1 T	ONION, MINCED	
1 T	GARLIC, MINCED	
------	CAVENDER'S GREEK SEASONING	SALT & PEPPER TO TASTE.
------	FRESH LEMON JUICE TO TASTE	

CREAMY SOY FRENCH DRESSING

  16 OZ   FAT = TR EA

1 C	MOCK OIL (p 395)	PUREE ALL INGREDIENTS.
1/2 C	RED WINE VINEGAR	
1/4 C	FAT-FREE MIRACLE WHIP	
1/4 C	NO-FAT SOUR CREAM	
2 T	HEINZ CHILI SAUCE	
2 T	DIJON MUSTARD	
2 T	SOY SAUCE (OR TO TASTE)	SALT & PEPPER TO TASTE.
1 T	BUTTER BUDS	
1/4 t	FRESH GINGER, PEELED, MINCED (OPTIONAL)	

SPICY FRENCH DRESSING   I OR II

quick 20 OZ   FAT = TR EA

I			II		
1 C	MOCK OIL (p 395)		2 C	MOCK OIL (p 395)	
1/2 C	HEINZ CHILI SAUCE		2 T	HEINZ CHILI SAUCE	
1/3 C	FAT-FREE MIRACLE WHIP		1/3 C	NO-FAT SOUR CREAM	
1/3 C	HONEY		1 T	SUGAR	
1/3 C	BALSAMIC VINEGAR		2/3 C	RED WINE VINEGAR	
1 T	BUTTER BUDS		2 CL	GARLIC, CRUSHED	
1 t	CAVENDER'S GREEK SEASONING		1 t	PAPRIKA	
1/2 t	PICK A PEPPER SAUCE (OPTIONAL)		1 T	WORCESTERSHIRE	
1/2 t	PAPRIKA		2 T	FRESH LEMON JUICE	
------	CELERY SALT TO TASTE		1 T	MUSTARD	
------	ONION POWDER TO TASTE		1 T	BUTTER BUDS	
------	SALT & PEPPER TO TASTE		------	HOT SAUCE (OPT)	
------	GARLIC POWDER TO TASTE		------	SALT & PEPPER TO TASTE	
	BLENDERIZE THESE.	OR		BLENDERIZE THESE.	

CREAMY GARLIC

16 OZ   FAT = TR EA

1 C	FAT-FREE CREAM CHEESE, SOFTENED	PUREE ALL INGREDIENTS.
1 C	NO-FAT SOUR CREAM	
1 T	DIJON MUSTARD	
ZEST OF 1	LEMON, MINCED	
1/4 t	CAYENNE PEPPER	
1/4 C	FRESH PARSLEY, CHOPPED	
2 T	BUTTER BUDS	
5 CL	GARLIC, CRUSHED (OR TO TASTE)	SALT & PEPPER TO TASTE.
1/4 t	CAVENDER'S GREEK SEASONING	

GARLIC OREGANO

24 OZ   FAT = TR EA

2 C	MOCK OIL (p 395)	PUREE ALL INGREDIENTS.
1 C	WHITE WINE VINEGAR	
8 CL	GARLIC, CRUSHED	
1/2 C	FRESH OREGANO, STEMS REMOVED	SALT & PEPPER TO TASTE.
1 T	BUTTER BUDS	
1 t	DRY MUSTARD	

GREEN GODDESS

16 OZ   FAT = TR EA

1/2 C	FRESH PARSLEY, STEMS REMOVED	PUREE ALL INGREDIENTS.
1/2 C	FRESH CHIVES, CHOPPED	
1/2 C	NO-FAT SOUR CREAM	
1/2 C	FAT-FREE MIRACLE WHIP	
6	GREEN ONIONS, SLICED	
3 T	TARRAGON VINEGAR	SALT & PEPPER TO TASTE.
2 T	BUTTER BUDS	
1 CL	GARLIC, MINCED	

CREAMY HERB DRESSING I

20 OZ   FAT = TR EA

1/2	ONION, DICED	PUREE ALL INGREDIENTS.
1	JALAPENO PEPPER, SEEDED, DICED	
1/4 C	FRESH DILL, STEMS REMOVED	
1/4 C	FRESH PARSLEY, STEMS REMOVED	
2 T	FRESH THYME, STEMS REMOVED	
1/2 C	SHERRY VINEGAR	
1 1/2 C	NO-FAT SOUR CREAM	
1/2 C	FAT-FREE MIRACLE WHIP OR CREAM CHEESE	SALT & PEPPER TO TASTE.
2 T	BUTTER BUDS	
2 t	CAVENDER'S GREEK SEASONING	

CREAMY HERB DRESSING II

quick   32 OZ   FAT = TR EA

1 C	1% BUTTERMILK
1 1/2 C	NO-FAT SOUR CREAM
1/2 C	ONION, CHOPPED
1/2 C	GREEN PEPPER, CHOPPED
1/4 C	FRESH CILANTRO
1/4 C	WATERCRESS
1/4 C	WHITE WINE
1 T	BUTTER BUDS
1 t	FRESH OREGANO, STEMS REMOVED
1 t	FRESH DILL (OPTIONAL)

PUREE ALL INGREDIENTS.

CAVENDER'S GREEK SEASONING & SALT & PEPPER TO TASTE.

HONEY DIJON DRESSING

quick   16 OZ   FAT = TR EA

1 C	NO-FAT SOUR CREAM
1/2 C	DIJON MUSTARD
1/2 C	HONEY (OR TO TASTE)
3 T	RED WINE VINEGAR
1 T	BUTTER BUDS

PUREE THESE & ADD HONEY TO TASTE.

HONEY LIME DRESSING

     32 OZ   FAT = TR EA

ZEST OF 2	LIMES, MINCED
2/3 C	HONEY
2/3 C	FRESH LIME JUICE
1 t	MUSTARD
1 t	PAPRIKA
1 C	NO-FAT SOUR CREAM
1/2 C	FAT-FREE MIRACLE WHIP
1 C	MOCK OIL (p 395)
1 T	BUTTER BUDS
------	LOUISIANA HOT SAUCE TO TASTE

PUREE ALL INGREDIENTS.

SALT & PEPPER TO TASTE.

HONEY NUT DRESSING

quick   32 OZ   FAT = TR EA

2 C	MOCK OIL (p 395)
2/3 C	RED WINE VINEGAR
2/3 C	HONEY
1/2 C	SUGAR
2 T	FRESH LEMON JUICE
2 T	PINEAPPLE JUICE
1 T	BUTTER BUDS
2 t	DRY MUSTARD
2 t	CELERY SALT
2 t	PECAN OR WALNUT FLAVORING

PUREE ALL INGREDIENTS.

SALT & PEPPER TO TASTE.

HONEY ORANGE DRESSING

 24 OZ   FAT = TR EA

2 C	NO-FAT SOUR CREAM	PUREE ALL INGREDIENTS.
1 SM CAN	MANDARIN ORANGE SECTIONS	
1/4 C	RED WINE VINEGAR	
1/4 C	ONION, DICED	
1/4 C	DIJON MUSTARD	
2 T	FRESH PARSLEY, STEMS REMOVED	
2 T	BUTTER BUDS	
3 T	HONEY	

HOT HONEY VINEGAR DRESSING

 12 OZ   FAT = TR EA

1/2 C	RED WINE VINEGAR	COMBINE & HEAT.
1 C	MOCK OIL (p 395 MADE WITH STOCK)	
1 T	DIJON MUSTARD (OR TO TASTE)	
3 T	BROWN SUGAR (OR TO TASTE)	
1 T	BUTTER BUDS	
------	FRESH HERBS OF YOUR CHOICE (OPTIONAL)	

EASY CREAMY ITALIAN DRESSING

 18 OZ   FAT = TR EA

1 1/2 C	COMMERCIAL FAT-FREE ITALIAN DRESSING	PUREE ALL INGREDIENTS.
1/2 C	NO-FAT SOUR CREAM	
2 T	PARMESAN CHEESE	
1 T	BUTTER BUDS	
8	GREEN, PIMENTO STUFFED OLIVES & JUICE FOR CONSISTENCY	
1 1/2 T	FRESH OREGANO OR ITALIAN HERBS	

CREAMY ITALIAN DRESSING

20 OZ   FAT = TR EA

1 1/2 C	NO-FAT SOUR CREAM	PUREE ALL INGREDIENTS.
1/2 C	RED WINE VINEGAR	
1/4 C	WHITE WINE (OPTIONAL)	
1/4 C	ONION, DICED	
2 CL	GARLIC, CRUSHED	
2 T	FRESH PARSLEY, STEMS REMOVED	
1 T	DRIED ITALIAN HERBS	
1 T	BUTTER BUDS	
1/2 T	FRESH BASIL, STEMS REMOVED	
1/4 t	GROUND FENNEL	SALT & PEPPER TO TASTE.
1/4 t	CAVENDER'S GREEK SEASONING	

FRENCH ITALIAN DRESSING   *quick*   24 OZ   FAT = TR EA

2 C	MOCK OIL (p 395 MADE WITH STOCK)	PUREE ALL INGREDIENTS.
1 C	WHITE WINE VINEGAR (OR TO TASTE)	
1/2 C	SUGAR	
1 T	DIJON MUSTARD	
1 T	MARJORAM	
1 T	FRESH BASIL, STEMS REMOVED	
1 T	BUTTER BUDS	
1 t	CAVENDER'S GREEK SEASONING	
1 t	DRIED ITALIAN HERBS	SALT & PEPPER TO TASTE.
4 CL	GARLIC, CRUSHED	

HOT JUNIPER DRESSING   32 OZ   FAT = TR EA

3 C	FAT-FREE CHICKEN STOCK	SIMMER ALL INGREDIENTS FOR
1 C	ONIONS, SHREDDED	30 MINUTES.
1/2 C	CARROTS, SHREDDED	
16	JUNIPER BERRIES	
2 SPRIGS	FRESH THYME	
1	SMALL BAY LEAF	REMOVE BAY LEAF & PUREE.
2	TOMATOES, PEELED, SEEDED & CHOPPED	SALT & PEPPER TO TASTE.

CREAMY LEMON DRESSING   *quick*   32 OZ   FAT = TR EA

3 C	MOCK OIL (p 395)	PUREE ALL INGREDIENTS.
1/2 C	FRESH LEMON JUICE (OR TO TASTE)	
1 C	NO-FAT SOUR CREAM	
2 T	DIJON MUSTARD	
6	GREEN ONIONS, SLICED	
3 T	FRESH TARRAGON, STEMS REMOVED	
3 T	TARRAGON VINEGAR	
2 T	BUTTER BUDS	
1/2 t	LEMON PEPPER	SALT & PEPPER TO TASTE.
1/2 t	CAVENDER'S GREEK SEASONING	

LEMON YOGURT DRESSING   *quick*   8 OZ   FAT = TR EA

1 C	NON-FAT YOGURT	WHISK ALL INGREDIENTS.
2	LEMONS, JUICED	
1/4 C	NON-FAT MILK POWDER	
1 T	BUTTER BUDS	
1/2 t	LEMON PEPPER	SALT & PEPPER TO TASTE.
1 t	SUGAR OR EQUAL (OR TO TASTE)	

Trying different fruit yogurt provides a nice change.

MANDARIN DRESSING 24 OZ FAT = TR EA

1/2 C	RICE WINE VINEGAR (OR TO TASTE)	PUREE ALL INGREDIENTS.
2 T	SOY SAUCE	
1 1/2 C	FROZEN PINEAPPLE JUICE CONCENTRATE	
4 t	FRESH GINGER, PEELED, MINCED	
3 CL	GARLIC, CRUSHED	
1 T	BUTTER BUDS	
1/4 t	CRUSHED RED PEPPER FLAKES (OR TO TASTE)	
1 C	NO-FAT SOUR CREAM	

Works well as a marinade substituting sherry for the Mock Oil.

MANGO-CHUTNEY DRESSING 12 OZ FAT = TR EA

1 1/2 C	NO-FAT SOUR CREAM	WHISK ALL INGREDIENTS.
1	MANGO, CHOPPED (IF AVAILABLE)	
1/4 C	MANGO CHUTNEY (MORE IF NOT USING FRESH)	
2 T	BUTTER BUDS	
2 t	TURMERIC OR POPPY SEEDS	
	ADD MANDARIN JUICE OR SKIM MILK TO CORRECT CONSISTENCY	

This is good over carrots, cucumbers, etc.

MUSTARD & HERB DRESSING 20 OZ FAT = TR EA

1/2 C	QUARK (SEE BELOW)	PUREE ALL INGREDIENTS.
1/2 C	NO-FAT SOUR CREAM	
6 T	TARRAGON VINEGAR	
1/4 C	DIJON MUSTARD (OR TO TASTE)	
2 T	BUTTER BUDS	
1/2 C	SOY SAUCE	
3 T	FRESH HERBS (CHERVIL, CHIVES, BASIL, ETC.)	SALT & PEPPER TO TASTE.
1/2 C	MOCK OIL, OR AS NEEDED (p 395)	

QUARK FAT = TR

4 C	SKIM MILK	BOIL, ADD JUICE, & COOL.
1/2	LEMON, JUICED	BOIL, COOL, & STRAIN.

MUSTARD-DILL DRESSING

 quick   28 OZ   FAT = TR EA

1/2 C	DIJON MUSTARD
1/2 C	NO-FAT SOUR CREAM
1/2 C	CIDER OR WHITE WINE VINEGAR
1 T	DRIED TARRAGON
1 T	DRIED DILL
2 C	MOCK OIL, (p 395)
1/4 C	PARMESAN CHEESE
2 T	BUTTER BUDS
1 t	CAVENDER'S GREEK SEASONING

PUREE ALL INGREDIENTS.

SALT & PEPPER TO TASTE.

POPPY SEED   I OR II

quick   12 OZ   FAT = TR EA

I

1 C	MOCK OIL (p 395)
1/3 C	HONEY
1/4 C	RED WINE VINEGAR
2 T	POPPY SEEDS
2 T	BUTTER BUDS
1 T	ONION, MINCED
1 T	DIJON MUSTARD

II

1/2 C	ORANGE JUICE
1 C	NO-FAT SOUR CREAM
3 T	HONEY
2 T	BUTTER BUDS
1 T	POPPY SEEDS

POPPY SEED   III OR IV

quick   20 OZ   FAT = TR EA

III

1 C	MOCK OIL (p 395)
3/4 C	SUGAR
3/4 C	RED WINE VINEGAR
3 T	POPPY SEEDS
2 T	BUTTER BUDS
1 t	ORANGE JUICE
1 t	DRY MUSTARD
1/2 t	ONION POWDER
1/2 t	CAVENDER'S GREEK SEASONING

IV

1 C	NO-FAT SOUR CREAM
1/2 C	RED WINE VINEGAR
6 T	HONEY
2 T	ITALIAN SEASONING
2 T	BUTTER BUDS
1 T	POPPY SEEDS
	SALT & PEPPER TT
1 C	MANGOES, DICED (OPTIONAL)

You can make any of the Poppy Seed Dressings creamier by adding either Fat-Free: Sour Cream, Cream Cheese, Miracle Whip or Vanilla Yogurt.

SOUR CREAM DRESSING   32 OZ   FAT = TR EA

1 C	NO-FAT SOUR CREAM	PUREE ALL INGREDIENTS.
1 C	FAT-FREE MIRACLE WHIP	
1 C	FAT-FREE COTTAGE CHEESE	
3/4 C	RED WINE VINEGAR (OR TO TASTE)	
1/4 C	1 % BUTTERMILK	
2 T	BUTTER BUDS	
4 t	FRESH PARSLEY, STEMS REMOVED	
1 t	DRY MUSTARD	
1/4 C	SUGAR (OR TO TASTE)	SALT & PEPPER TO TASTE.
4 CL	GARLIC, MINCED	

STILTON DRESSING   38 OZ   FAT = .5 GM EA

2 C	NO-FAT SOUR CREAM	PUREE THESE INGREDIENTS.
1/2 C	1% BUTTERMILK	
1/2 C	FAT-FREE CREAM CHEESE	
2 T	NON-FAT MILK POWDER	
2 T	DRY SHERRY	
2 T	BUTTER BUDS	
1 C	1 % BUTTERMILK (AS NEEDED FOR CONSISTENCY)	
4 t	FRESH LEMON JUICE (OR TO TASTE)	SALT & PEPPER TO TASTE.
2 t	STRONG MUSTARD	
		ADD CHEESE & PROCESS CHOP-CHOP.
2 OZ	STILTON CHEESE	

ROQUEFORT DRESSING   20 OZ   FAT = 1 GM EA

1 C	NO-FAT SOUR CREAM	PUREE THESE INGREDIENTS.
1 1/2 C	1 % BUTTERMILK	
2 T	BUTTER BUDS	
1 T	TARRAGON VINEGAR	
1 t	FRESH LEMON JUICE	
1 t	WORCESTERSHIRE SAUCE	
1 t	CAVENDER'S GREEK SEASONING	SALT & PEPPER TO TASTE.
1/2 t	GARLIC POWDER	
1/2 t	ONION SALT	
------	LOUISIANA HOT SAUCE TO TASTE	
		ADD CHEESE & PROCESS CHOP-CHOP.
2 OZ	ROQUEFORT, CRUMBLED	

SWEET & SOUR DRESSING

16 OZ   FAT = TR EA

1 C	MOCK OIL (p 395)
1/2 C	VINEGAR
1 C	BROWN SUGAR
1 T	ONION, MINCED
1 t	CELERY SALT
1 t	DRY MUSTARD
1 t	PAPRIKA

PUREE ALL INGREDIENTS.

GOOD HOT OR COLD.

ITALIAN SWEET & SOUR DRESSING

24 OZ   FAT = TR EA

1 C	RED WINE VINEGAR
2 C	MOCK OIL (p 395)
1/2 C	SUGAR
4 CL	GARLIC, CRUSHED
2 t	DRIED ITALIAN HERBS
2 t	CELERY SALT
2 t	DRY MUSTARD
2 t	WORCESTERSHIRE SAUCE
1 t	GROUND FENNEL
1/2 t	LOUISIANA HOT SAUCE

PUREE ALL INGREDIENTS.

SALT & PEPPER TO TASTE.

TEX MEX DRESSING

16 OZ   FAT = TR EA

1 C	PICANTE SALSA
1 C	NO-FAT SOUR CREAM
3 T	RED WINE VINEGAR
3 T	ONIONS, DICED
2 T	FRESH CILANTRO, CHOPPED
1	TOMATO, PEELED, SEEDED, CHOPPED
1	JALAPENO PEPPER, SEEDED, MINCED
1 T	FRESH LEMON JUICE
1 t	SUGAR OR EQUAL (OR TO TASTE)

WHISK ALL INGREDIENTS.

GREEN TOMATO DRESSING

20 OZ   FAT = TR EA

1 C	NO-FAT SOUR CREAM
6 T	WINE VINEGAR (OR TO TASTE)
12	GREEN TOMATOES, PEELED, SEEDED
1/4 C	NON-FAT MILK POWDER
1/4 t	CAVENDER'S GREEK SEASONING

PROCESS ALL INGREDIENTS IN A CHOP-CHOP MOTION.

SALT & PEPPER TO TASTE.

TOMATO HERB

40 OZ   FAT = TR EA

1 C	V8 JUICE	PUREE ALL INGREDIENTS.
1/2 C	1% BUTTERMILK	
2 C	MOCK OIL (p 395)	
2	TOMATOES, PEELED, SEEDED	
1/2 C	RED WINE VINEGAR	
2 CL	GARLIC, CRUSHED	
1	ONION, DICED	
2 T	FRESH BASIL, STEMS REMOVED	
2 T	FRESH PARSLEY, STEMS REMOVED	
2 T	FRESH OREGANO, STEMS REMOVED	
2 T	CHERVIL, CHOPPED	SALT & PEPPER TO TASTE.
1 t	DILL (OPTIONAL)	
1/2 t	CAVENDER'S GREEK SEASONING	

TOMATO FRENCH DRESSING

20 OZ   FAT = TR EA

1 C	MOCK OIL (p 395)	PUREE ALL INGREDIENTS.
1/2 C	KETCHUP	
1/2 C	BALSAMIC VINEGAR	
1/2 C	SUGAR	
2 T	DIJON MUSTARD	
2 T	ONION, DICED	
1 t	WORCESTERSHIRE SAUCE	
1 t	CAVENDER'S GREEK SEASONING	
1/4 t	OLD BAY SEASONING	
2 CL	GARLIC, CRUSHED	SALT & PEPPER TO TASTE.
1/4 t	GROUND CLOVES	

TOMATO PEPPER DRESSING

32 OZ   FAT = TR EA

4	PICKLED RED BELL PEPPERS, CHOPPED	PUREE ALL INGREDIENTS.
1 C	TOMATO CONCASSE (p 396)	
1 C	MOCK OIL (p 395)	
1/2 C	ONION, CHOPPED	
1/4 C	BALSAMIC OR RED WINE VINEGAR	
1/4 C	1% BUTTERMILK	
1 T	FRESH BASIL, STEMS REMOVED	
2 t	DIJON MUSTARD	SALT & PEPPER TO TASTE.
1/4 t	CAVENDER'S GREEK SEASONING	

SUN-DRIED TOMATO DRESSING
quick   28 OZ   FAT = TR EA

1 C	FAT-FREE MIRACLE WHIP OR SOUR CREAM	PUREE ALL INGREDIENTS.
1/2 C	SKIM MILK (OR MORE FOR CONSISTENCY)	
3/4 C	RED WINE OR BALSAMIC VINEGAR	
24	SUN-DRIED TOMATOES—POACHED IN WATER (NO OIL)	
2 T	PARMESAN CHEESE	
1 T	BUTTER BUDS	
8	GREEK OR CALAMATA OLIVES, PITTED	SALT & PEPPER TO TASTE.
------	BRINE FROM OLIVES FOR THINNING	

1000 ISLAND DRESSING
quick   16 OZ   FAT = TR EA

1/2 C	HEINZ CHILI SAUCE	WHISK ALL INGREDIENTS.
1/2 C	FAT-FREE MIRACLE WHIP	
1/2 C	NO-FAT SOUR CREAM	
3 T	SWEET RELISH	
2 T	CAPERS, MINCED	
1 T	FRESH PARSLEY, STEMS REMOVED	
1 T	PIMENTO, DICED	
1 T	HONEY	
1 T	BUTTER BUDS	
1/2 t	FRESH LEMON JUICE	SALT & PEPPER TO TASTE.
1/4 t	ONION, MINCED	

VINAIGRETTE I
quick   36 OZ   FAT = TR EA

3 C	MOCK OIL (p 395)	PUREE ALL INGREDIENTS.
1 C	BALSAMIC VINEGAR (OR TO TASTE)	
1/2 C	SOY SAUCE	
1/4 C	FRESH OREGANO, STEMS REMOVED	SALT & PEPPER TO TASTE.
1/4 C	FRESH BASIL, STEMS REMOVED	
2 T	DIJON MUSTARD (OR TO TASTE)	
2 T	BUTTER BUDS	
3 CL	GARLIC, CRUSHED	PAPRIKA—OPTIONAL.

VINAIGRETTE II
quick   14 OZ   FAT = TR EA

1 C	MOCK OIL (p 395)	PUREE ALL INGREDIENTS.
1/2 C	RED WINE VINEGAR	
2 T	FRESH LEMON JUICE	
2 T	DIJON MUSTARD	
1 T	HONEY	
1 T	FRESH PARSLEY, STEMS REMOVED	
1 T	BUTTER BUDS	
4 CL	GARLIC, CRUSHED	SALT & PEPPER TO TASTE.
1 t	WORCESTERSHIRE SAUCE	

HERB VINAIGRETTE

20 OZ   FAT = TR EA

2 C	MOCK OIL (p 395)	PUREE ALL INGREDIENTS.
1/2 C	SHERRY VINEGAR (OR TO TASTE)	
3 T	DIJON MUSTARD (OR TO TASTE)	
3 T	FRESH PARSLEY, STEMS REMOVED	
3 T	DRIED ITALIAN HERBS	
4 CL	GARLIC, CRUSHED	SALT & PEPPER TO TASTE.
	FRESH LEMON JUICE TO TASTE	

ITALIAN VINAIGRETTE I

20 OZ   FAT = TR EA

2 C	MOCK OIL (p 395)	PUREE ALL INGREDIENTS.
1/2 C	RED WINE VINEGAR	
1/2 C	FRESH LEMON JUICE	
3 T	ONIONS, CHOPPED	
3 T	SUGAR	
1/4 C	FRESH BASIL, STEMS REMOVED	
1 T	DRIED ITALIAN HERBS	SALT & PEPPER TO TASTE.
1 t	CAVENDER'S GREEK SEASONING	
1/4 t	GROUND FENNEL	

You can add chopped tomatoes & artichokes & serve over chicken..

ITALIAN VINAIGRETTE II

24 OZ   FAT = TR EA

2 C	MOCK OIL (p 395)	PUREE ALL INGREDIENTS.
1/2 C	TARRAGON VINEGAR (OR TO TASTE)	
3 T	PARMESAN CHEESE	
6	OLIVES	
2	GREEN ONIONS, DICED	
1/4 C	FRESH PARSLEY, STEMS REMOVED	
2 T	FRESH BASIL, STEMS REMOVED	
1 T	FRESH OREGANO, STEMS REMOVED	
1 T	SUGAR	
1 T	FRESH LEMON JUICE	
4 CL	GARLIC, CRUSHED	SALT & PEPPER TO TASTE.
1 t	CAVENDER'S GREEK SEASONING	

MUSTARD VINAIGRETTE

 12 OZ   FAT = TR EA

3 T	DIJON MUSTARD	PUREE ALL INGREDIENTS.
2 C	RED WINE VINEGAR	
2 C	MOCK OIL (p 395)	
4	GREEN ONIONS, SLICED	
3 T	FRESH THYME, STEMS REMOVED	SALT & PEPPER TO TASTE.
2 T	DRIED ITALIAN HERBS	

Try experimenting with different mustards, such as: Mesquite, Stone Ground, Honey, Creole, etc.

WARM MUSTARD VINAIGRETTE

 16 OZ   FAT = TR EA

1 C	MOCK OIL (p 395)	PUREE ALL INGREDIENTS
1/2 C	BALSAMIC VINEGAR (OR TO TASTE)	& HEAT.
1/2	ONION, DICED	
1/4 C	DIJON MUSTARD (OR TO TASTE)	
2 CL	GARLIC, CRUSHED	SALT & PEPPER TO TASTE.
2 T	BROWN SUGAR (OR TO TASTE)	

ONION PARSLEY VINAIGRETTE

 18 OZ   FAT = TR EA

1 C	MOCK OIL (p 395)	PUREE ALL INGREDIENTS.
2	ONIONS, CHOPPED	
1/2 C	FRESH PARSLEY, STEMS REMOVED	
1/4 C	WHITE WINE VINEGAR	
1 T	DRY MUSTARD	
1/2 t	CAVENDER'S GREEK SEASONING	SALT & PEPPER TO TASTE.
------	EQUAL TO TASTE	

ORANGE VINAIGRETTE

 32 OZ   FAT = TR EA

2 C	MOCK OIL (p 395)	PUREE ALL INGREDIENTS.
1/2 C	RED WINE VINEGAR (OR TO TASTE)	
11 OZ CAN	MANDARIN ORANGES, DRAINED	
1	ONION, CHOPPED	
1/2 C	HEINZ CHILI SAUCE	
2	LEMONS, JUICED	
1 T	PAPRIKA	SALT & PEPPER TO TASTE.
1 t	SUGAR OR EQUAL (OR TO TASTE)	

SHERRY VINAIGRETTE

 20 OZ   FAT = 1 GM EA

2 C	MOCK OIL (p 395)
1/2 C	SHERRY VINEGAR
1 T	DIJON MUSTARD (OR TO TASTE)
1 T	WALNUT FLAVORING
2 T	FRESH LEMON JUICE
2 T	PINEAPPLE JUICE
1 OZ	WALNUTS, MINCED

PUREE ALL INGREDIENTS
EXCEPT WALNUTS.

SPICY VINAIGRETTE

 24 OZ   FAT = TR EA

2 C	MOCK OIL (p 395)
1/2 C	RED WINE VINEGAR (OR TO TASTE)
1/2 C	FRESH ORANGE JUICE (OR TO TASTE)
1 T	HONEY (OR MORE)
4 CL	GARLIC, CRUSHED
2 t	CHILI POWDER
2 t	DRY MUSTARD
1 t	DRIED ITALIAN HERBS
1/2 t	CAVENDER'S GREEK SEASONING
1/4 t	OLD BAY SEASONING
1/4 t	LEMON PEPPER

PUREE ALL INGREDIENTS.

SALT & PEPPER TO TASTE.

FRENCH TARRAGON VINAIGRETTE

 20 OZ   FAT = TR EA

2 C	MOCK OIL (p 395)
1/2 C	TARRAGON VINEGAR
4 CL	GARLIC, CRUSHED
1	ONION, DICED
1/4 C	FRESH TARRAGON, STEMS REMOVED
1 T	WORCESTERSHIRE SAUCE
1 T	DIJON MUSTARD
1 t	PAPRIKA
1 t	CELERY SALT

PUREE ALL INGREDIENTS.

SALT & PEPPER TO TASTE.

WARM PORT VINAIGRETTE

  24 OZ   FAT = TR EA

2 C	MOCK OIL (p 395)	PUREE ALL & HEAT.
3/4 C	PORT WINE	
1/4 C	BALSAMIC OR RED WINE VINEGAR	
1/2	ONION, DICED	
3 T	HONEY	
3 T	FRESH LEMON JUICE	

WALNUT DRESSING

14 OZ   FAT = 1 GM EA

1 T	WALNUT OIL	PUREE ALL INGREDIENTS.
2 T	WALNUT FLAVORING	
1 C	MOCK OIL (p 395)	
1/3 C	SHERRY VINEGAR	
2 T	MOLASSES	
1 t	DRY MUSTARD	
1 t	PAPRIKA	SALT & PEPPER TO TASTE.
1/4 t	LOUISIANA HOT SAUCE	

YOGURT DRESSING

20 OZ   FAT = TR EA

1 C	NON-FAT YOGURT	WHISK ALL INGREDIENTS.
1/4 C	NON-FAT MILK POWDER	
2 T	SOY SAUCE	
2 T	WINE VINEGAR	
2 T	ONION, MINCED	
2 T	GARLIC, MINCED	
1 t	FRESH PARSLEY, MINCED	
1 t	FRESH BASIL, MINCED	
1 t	FRESH DILL (OPTIONAL)	SALT & PEPPER TO TASTE.
1 t	STRONG MUSTARD (OR TO TASTE)	

Experiment with different flavors of yogurt.

Luncheon Ideas

BEET MOLDS

12 MOLDS   FAT = TR EA

1 PKG	KNOX GELATIN (SPRINKLED ON THE SHERRY)	LET SIT FOR 2 MINUTES.
1/4 C	DRY SHERRY	
1 C	FAT-FREE CHICKEN STOCK	ADD THESE INGREDIENTS.
2/3 C	SUGAR	
1/2 C	FRESH LEMON JUICE	HEAT TO DISSOLVE.
2 T	HORSERADISH	
1 T	RED WINE VINEGAR	COOL UNTIL SLIGHTLY THICK.
1/4 t	SALT	
1/4 t	CELERY SALT	
3 DROPS	LOUISIANA HOT SAUCE	
1 C	CABBAGE, SHREDDED & MINCED	STEAM THESE FOR 20 MINUTES
2	CARROTS, SHREDDED	& COOL.
3 CANS	BEETS, SHREDDED	COMBINE ALL INGREDIENTS.

Fill 12 small molds. Chill 8 hours. Unmold and serve on beds of lettuce.

DILLY CUCUMBERS & ONIONS

easy   SERVES 6   FAT = TR EA

2	ENGLISH CUCUMBERS, 1/4" SLICES	COMBINE ALL INGREDIENTS.
2	RED ONIONS, SLICED THIN, QUARTERED	
1 C	WHITE WINE OR CIDER VINEGAR	
1/2 C	WATER	
4 t	SUGAR OR EQUAL (OR TO TASTE)	SALT & PEPPER TO TASTE.
2 T	FRESH DILL, CHOPPED	CHILL 2 HOURS.

Or you could drain the cucumbers & add   1 C   No-Fat Sour Cream or Yogurt.

ORIENTAL CUCUMBERS

easy   SERVES 8   FAT = TR EA

4	ENGLISH CUCUMBERS, 1/4" SLICES	COMBINE & CHILL.
1 C	RICE WINE VINEGAR	
1 T	SUGAR OR EQUAL (OR TO TASTE)	
6 T	SOY SAUCE	
2 t	FRESH GINGER, PEELED, GRATED	
1/2 t	LOUISIANA HOT SAUCE	

CHEESY CRAB RAMEKINS

easy   SERVES 4   FAT = 3 GM EA

1/2 C	FAT-FREE CHICKEN OR CLAM BROTH	COMBINE AND HEAT THESE.
3 T	BUTTER BUDS	
1/2 t	OLD BAY SEASONING	
3/4 C	SKIM MILK (MIX WELL WITH ARROWROOT)	ADD THESE OFF THE HEAT.
1 T	ARROWROOT (MORE FOR THICKER SAUCE)	RETURN TO HEAT & THICKEN.
1 LB	CRAB MEAT, PICKED CLEAN	COMBINE & FOLD IN THESE.
1 C	ALPINE LACE FAT-FREE CHEDDAR, SHREDDED	
4	GREEN ONIONS, SLICED THIN	
1 T	FRESH LEMON JUICE	
3 T	PARMESAN CHEESE	FILL SPRAYED RAMEKINS.
1 t	WORCESTERSHIRE SAUCE	
1 t	DRY MUSTARD	
3 T	FAT-FREE BREAD CRUMBS	COMBINE & SPRINKLE ON EACH.
3 T	FRESH PARSLEY, MINCED	SPRAY WITH PAM BUTTER.
2 t	PAPRIKA	
		BAKE AT 375 FOR 20 MINUTES.

EGGPLANT COUSCOUS

SERVES 12   FAT = TR EA

2 C	COUSCOUS	COMBINE AND REMOVE FROM
2 C	BOILING CHICKEN STOCK	HEAT, COVER & SET ASIDE FOR
1 T	TURMERIC (MORE IF YOU LIKE)	5 MINUTES.
1 t	SAFFRON	
1/4 C EA	RED & GREEN BELL PEPPER, DICED, BLANCHED	
1/4 C	EGGPLANT CUBES, BLANCHED	
1/4 C	CARROTS, DICED, BLANCHED	KEEP THESE VEGGIES HOT.
1/4 C	ZUCCHINI CUBES, BLANCHED	
4 CL	GARLIC, MINCED	SIMMER THESE FOR THE SAUCE,
1 C	ONION, DICED	THEN COMBINE WITH ALL OF
1 C	FRESH CILANTRO, MINCED	ABOVE.
4 C	TOMATOES, PEELED, SEEDED, DICED	
1 C	RAISINS	
1 C	CHICK PEAS	
2 t	DRIED CORIANDER	
2 t	FRESH THYME, CHOPPED	
2 t	GROUND CUMIN	SALT & PEPPER TO TASTE.
1 t	SUGAR OR EQUAL (OR TO TASTE)	
1/4 C	HARRISSA OR TOMATO PASTE	

EGGPLANT CAPONATA   SERVES 14   FAT = 2 GM EA

1/2 C	BALSAMIC VINEGAR	PUREE THESE INGREDIENTS.
1 C	MOCK OIL (p 395)	
3	EGGPLANTS, CUBED, SALTED 30 MIN., BLOT DRY WITH PAPER TOWELS	
1 C	CELERY, MINCED	COMBINE ALL INGREDIENTS &
1 C	ONIONS, DICED	CHILL FOR 2 HOURS OR MORE.
6 CL	GARLIC, MINCED	
56 OZ	CANNED PLUM TOMATOES, DRAINED & CHOPPED	
2 T	SUGAR	
2 T	TOMATO PASTE	
15	BLACK OLIVES, SLICED	
15	GREEN OLIVES, SLICED	
1/4 C	CAPERS, DRAINED, SLIGHTLY CRUSHED	

ITALIAN SALAD   *easy*   SERVES 8   FAT = 2 GM EA

3 BNCH	ROMAINE, CLEANED & CHOPPED	TOSS ALL THE INGREDIENTS.
1 PT	CHERRY TOMATOES, HALVED	YOU MIGHT LIKE TO SERVE OVER
1 PT	MUSHROOMS, HALVED	ADDITIONAL ROMAINE.
1 C	PICKLED RED BELL PEPPERS, CHOPPED	
2 JARS	MARINATED ARTICHOKE HEARTS, DRAINED, TRIMMED WELL, CHOPPED	
1 C	PICKLED CHERRY PEPPERS, QUARTERED	ADD SOME OF THE JUICE OF THE
1 JAR	PEPPERONCINI PEPPERS, QUARTERED	VARIOUS PEPPERS.
1 EA	RED, YELLOW, GREEN BELL PEPPER, CHOPPED	
16	CALAMATA OLIVES	SPRINKLE PARMESAN OVER AND
1/4 C	PARMESAN CHEESE	SERVE w GARLIC BREAD (p 341).
OPTIONS:	SLICED PEPPERONI, JULIENNED (REMEMBER TO ADJUST FAT COUNT)	

BAKED CLAMS   SERVES 8   FAT = 2 GM EA

4 C	SKIM MILK	COMBINE THESE IN A SPRAYED
1 1/2 C	EGG BEATERS	10" x 13" DISH.
7 C	FAT-FREE BREAD CRUMBS	SALT & PEPPER TO TASTE.
1/4 C	BUTTER BUDS	
1 C	ONION, MINCED	LET SIT 30 MINUTES.
1/2 C	GREEN PEPPER, MINCED	
1 T	WORCESTERSHIRE SAUCE	BAKE AT 350 FOR 30 MINUTES.
2 t	OLD BAY SEASONING	
4 CANS	10 OZ EA, BABY CLAMS w LIQUID (STRAINED)	
4 C	CHERRYSTONE CLAMS	

PASTA PRIMAVERA

 easy   SERVES 10   FAT = 1 GM EA

1/4 C	FAT-FREE CHICKEN STOCK	SIMMER THESE FOR 6 MINUTES.
1	RED ONION, DICED	
1/2 C	FRESH OR FROZEN PEAS	COOL & DRAIN.
4	CARROTS, JULIENNED	
2	ZUCCHINI, JULIENNED	
1/2 C	DRY WHITE WINE	
1 C	NO-FAT SOUR CREAM	COMBINE THESE AND TOSS WITH
1 LB	ROTINI PASTA, COOKED, COOLED	ABOVE.
1/4 C	FRESH PARSLEY, CHOPPED	
2	TOMATOES, PEELED, SEEDED, DICED	
2 CL	GARLIC, MINCED	DIVIDE AMONG 8 PLATES LINED
1 T	WHITE WINE	WITH LETTUCE.
1 T EA	FRESH OREGANO, BASIL	
1 T	FRESH LEMON JUICE (OR TO TASTE)	
1/4 C	PARMESAN CHEESE	SPRINKLE OVER.

Garnish with 4 black olive slices on each plate. Try adding shrimp, Fat-Free Cheese, broccoli or broccoflower.

There are so many varieties of potato salads, I'm just going to give a few dressings here, along with various options. So, pick the dressing you like and then select your favorite ingredients, for your very own style of potato salad.

Mix & match...have fun with it. But remember to make the dressing spicier than you might normally like, because you'll be adding a lot of very bland potatoes.

AMERICAN POTATO SALAD DRESSING

 quick   10 OZ   FAT = TR EA

1 C	FAT-FREE SOUR CREAM OR MIRACLE WHIP	BLEND ALL INGREDIENTS.
1/4 C	MUSTARD (OR TO TASTE)	
2 T	CIDER VINEGAR (OR TO TASTE)	
------	SKIM MILK AS NEEDED	SALT & PEPPER TO TASTE.
------	SUGAR TO TASTE	

CHEESY POTATO SALAD DRESSING

quick   16 OZ   FAT = 1 GM EA

1 1/2 C	NO-FAT SOUR CREAM	PUREE ALL INGREDIENTS.
1/4 C	DRY SHERRY	
1/4 C	BALSAMIC OR RED WINE VINEGAR	
2 OZ	GORGONZOLA OR BLEU CHEESE	
1/2 t	WORCESTERSHIRE SAUCE	SALT & PEPPER TO TASTE.
1/4 t	DRY MUSTARD (OR TO TASTE)	

HOT GERMAN POTATO SALAD DRESSING

  8 OZ   FAT = TR EA

1/2 C	WATER	COMBINE & THEN HEAT.
1 T	FLOUR	
1 T	BUTTER BUDS	
1/2 C	CIDER VINEGAR (OR TO TASTE)	ADD & SIMMER TO THICKEN.
1 T	BROWN SUGAR	
1 t	STONE GROUND MUSTARD (OPTIONAL)	SALT & PEPPER TO TASTE.

So once you've chosen the salad dressing you like, go ahead & pick the ingredients that will compliment your family's favorites.

Just add cooked potatoes, celery, onions, red & green bell peppers and 3 or 4 of the following choices:

OPTIONS: CAPERS, CUCUMBERS, ORANGE ZEST, MUSHROOMS, WATERCRESS, OLIVE SLICES, TURKEY HAM, ASPARAGUS, GREEN BEAN SLICES, CARROTS, PICKLES, PIMENTO

SPICES: PARSLEY, TARRAGON, BASIL, THYME, MINT, DILL, MINCED GARLIC
GARNISHES: CHERRY TOMATO HALVES, SCRAMBLED EGG BEATERS, MINCED, PAPRIKA

CRUSTLESS CRAB QUICHE SUPREME

  SERVES 6   FAT = 5 GM EA

1/2 C	EGG BEATERS	COMBINE THESE & POUR INTO A
1 1/2 C	CRAB MEAT, PICKED CLEAN (OR IMITATION)	SPRAYED 10" DISH.
2 C	MUSHROOMS, SLICED	
8 OZ	LOW-FAT MOZZARELLA, SHREDDED	
2 C	EGG BEATERS	PUREE THESE & POUR OVER.
1 C	NO-FAT SOUR CREAM	
1 C	FAT-FREE COTTAGE CHEESE	
1/2 C	PARMESAN CHEESE	BAKE AT 325 FOR 45 MINUTES.
2 T	BUTTER BUDS	
------	SALT & PEPPER & OLD BAY SEASONING	

PHYLLO PIE CRUST

quick   1 CRUST   FAT = 3 GM

Spray a sheet of Phyllo with Pam Butter Spray, lay another on top, repeat until you have 4 sheets. Place in pie plate, bringing edges up high, trim. This makes a delicately "ragged" crust.

ARTICHOKE QUICHE

 quick   SERVES 6   FAT = 4 GM EA

1/4 C	FAT-FREE CHICKEN STOCK	SIMMER THESE UNTIL ALMOST DRY.
1	ONION, MINCED	
2 CL	GARLIC, MINCED	

1 1/2 C	EGG BEATERS	COMBINE ALL INGREDIENTS AND PLACE IN PHYLLO CRUST (p 116).
1 1/2 C	FAT-FREE COTTAGE CHEESE, PUREED	
1 C	NO-FAT SOUR CREAM	
1 1/2 C	MARINATED ARTICHOKE HEARTS, DRAINED, TRIMMED WELL, DICED	
1/2 C	PARMESAN CHEESE	
1/4 C	FRESH PARSLEY, MINCED	BAKE AT 325 FOR 45 MINUTES OR UNTIL KNIFE COMES OUT CLEAN.
2 T	BUTTER BUDS	
1/4 t	FRESH BASIL, MINCED	
1/4 t	CAVENDER'S GREEK SEASONING	

SEAFOOD QUICHE

 easy   SERVES 6   FAT = 2 GM EA

6	GREEN ONIONS, MINCED	COMBINE & SIMMER THESE FOR 3 MINUTES.
1 C	SHRIMP, DICED	
1 C	SEA SCALLOPS OR IMITATION CRAB, DICED	
1/4 C	CLAM BROTH	REMOVE FROM HEAT.
2 T	MADEIRA WINE	

1 1/2 C	EGG BEATERS	COMBINE & ADD TO ABOVE.
1 C	NON-FAT COTTAGE CHEESE, PUREED	
1 C	FAT-FREE CREAM CHEESE	POUR INTO A PHYLLO CRUST. (p 116)
1/4 C	PARMESAN CHEESE	
1/2 t	CAVENDER'S GREEK SEASONING	BAKE AT 325 FOR 40 MINUTES OR UNTIL KNIFE COMES CLEAN.

SPINACH QUICHE

 easy   SERVES 6   FAT = 3 GM EA

1	RED ONION, MINCED	SIMMER UNTIL ALMOST DRY.
1/4 C	FAT-FREE CHICKEN STOCK	

1 C	NON-FAT COTTAGE CHEESE, PUREED	COMBINE & POUR IN A PHYLLO CRUST (p 116).
10 OZ	FROZEN SPINACH, DRAINED WELL, CHOPPED	
1 C	NO-FAT SOUR CREAM	
1/2 C	PARMESAN CHEESE	
2 C	EGG BEATERS	BAKE AT 325 FOR 40 MINUTES OR UNTIL KNIFE COMES CLEAN.
2 T	BUTTER BUDS	
1/2 t	CAVENDER'S GREEK SEASONING	

ARTICHOKE FRITTATA SERVES 6 FAT = 2 GM EA

1 C	ONIONS, DICED	FRY IN A PAM-SPRAYED OVEN-PROOF PAN FOR 6 MINUTES.
1/2 LB	MUSHROOMS, SLICED	
1 C	POTATOES, SHREDDED	
10 OZ	FROZEN SPINACH, DRAINED WELL, CHOPPED	ADD THESE & BAKE AT 350 FOR 45 MINUTES OR UNTIL FIRM.
2 C	EGG BEATERS	
1/4 C	PARMESAN CHEESE	
2 C	MARINATED ARTICHOKE HEARTS, DRAINED, TRIMMED WELL & DICED	
2 T	BUTTER BUDS	
------	SALT & PEPPER	

SEAFOOD FRITTATA SERVES 6 FAT = TR EA

1 C	POTATOES, SHREDDED	FRY IN A PAM-SPRAYED OVEN-PROOF PAN FOR 6 MINUTES.
1 C	ONIONS, DICED	
1 C	FROZEN SHRIMP, COOKED, CHOPPED	ADD THESE TO HEAT THROUGH.
1 C	CRAB MEAT (OR SHREDDED SEA LEGS)	
3 T	DRY SHERRY	
2 T	FRESH CHIVES, CHOPPED	
2 T	BUTTER BUDS	
2 C	EGG BEATERS	ADD THESE & BAKE AT 350 FOR 45 MINUTES OR UNTIL FIRM.
------	SALT, PEPPER, DRIED TARRAGON	
------	LOUISIANA HOT SAUCE	

Sprinkle with fresh parsley & paprika.

HAM FRITTATA *quick* SERVES 6 FAT = 2 GM EA

2	ONIONS, DICED	FRY IN A PAM-SPRAYED OVEN-PROOF PAN FOR 6 MINUTES.
4	POTATOES, SHREDDED	
6 SL	CANADIAN BACON, TRIMMED WELL, JULIENNED	
2 C	EGG BEATERS	ADD THESE & BAKE AT 350 FOR 45 MINUTES OR UNTIL FIRM.
2 T	BUTTER BUDS	
------	SALT & PEPPER	
		BROIL TO PUFF SLIGHTLY.

ITALIAN BAKED EGGS SERVES 4   FAT = 2 GM EA

4	TOMATOES, SCOOPED OUT, SALT & PEPPERED	
------	DRIED ITALIAN HERBS, SPRINKLED INSIDE	
1/2 C EA	GREEN PEPPERS, RED ONIONS, MINCED	SIMMER THESE UNTIL DRY.
1/2 C	MUSHROOMS, DICED	
1/4 C	FAT-FREE CHICKEN STOCK	
1 C	DRIED FAT-FREE BREAD CUBES	ADD TO ABOVE & SPOON INTO
2 C	EGG BEATERS	TOMATOES.
1/4 C	PARMESAN CHEESE	BAKE AT 375 FOR 20 MINUTES OR
1 T	FRESH BASIL, MINCED	UNTIL DONE.

PINEAPPLE BENEDICT SERVES 6   FAT = 3 GM EA

12 SL	CANADIAN BACON, TRIMMED	HEAT THESE & PUT ON TOASTED
12 SL	PINEAPPLE	ENGLISH MUFFINS.
6	BANANAS, QUARTERED (OPTIONAL)	
1/3 C	BROWN SUGAR	KEEP WARM.
6	ENGLISH MUFFINS, SPLIT & TOASTED	
3 C	EGG BEATERS, SALT & PEPPER	FRY, SCRAMBLE & PLACE ON THE
2 T	BUTTER BUDS	ABOVE.

Heat equal parts of No-Fat Sour Cream, Non-Fat Vanilla Yogurt & Pineapple Juice for a quick sauce.

MEDITERRANEAN BOUILLABAISSE   SERVES 10   FAT = 1 GM EA

56 OZ	CANNED TOMATOES, CHOPPED	SIMMER THESE 45 MINUTES.
4 C	FISH STOCK OR CLAM BROTH	
6 CL	GARLIC, MINCED	
2	ONIONS, DICED	
4	POTATOES, DICED	
1 C	CORN	
3 T	TOMATO PASTE	
1 T EA	FRESH BASIL, THYME, MINCED	SALT & PEPPER & CAYENNE TO
2	BAY LEAVES (REMEMBER TO REMOVE)	TASTE.
1/4 t	CRUSHED RED PEPPER FLAKES	
2 LBS	FISH CUBES	ADD THESE FOR 10 MINUTES OR
4 C	ZUCCHINI, DICED	UNTIL SHELLS OPEN.
1 C	DRY WHITE WINE	
20 EA	MUSSELS, CHERRYSTONE CLAMS, SCRUBBED	SERVE OVER RICE WITH LEMON
1/4 C	FRESH PARSLEY, MINCED	WEDGES.

CREPES

24 CREPES   FAT = TR EA

1/2 C	EGG BEATERS	
2 C	CAKE FLOUR	
2 C	SKIM MILK (OR AS NEEDED)	
1 t	BAKING SODA	
2 T	BUTTER BUDS	
1 t	BUTTER, MELTED	

BLENDERIZE & LET SIT FOR 30 MINUTES.

POUR A SMALL AMOUNT INTO A SPRAYED PAN, SWIRL TO COVER THE BOTTOM, BROWN & FLIP, OVER, BROWN & REMOVE.

SWEET CREPES

Make as above & add:

3 T	SUGAR
1 T	REAL VANILLA EXTRACT

OPTION: 2 T LIQUEUR

SAVORY CREPES

12 CREPES   FAT = TR EA

1/2 C	EGG BEATERS
1/8 t	SALT
1 C	BEER
1 C	FLOUR
2 T	BUTTER BUDS
------	SKIM MILK IF NEEDED TO THIN

WHISK THESE TOGETHER & LET SIT FOR 5 MINUTES.

CURRIED CHICKEN CREPES

16 CREPES   FAT = 1 GM EA

6 C	COOKED TURKEY OR CHICKEN BREASTS
1 C	COOKED ONION SLICES
1 T	CURRY POWDER
1/2 C	RAISINS, SOAKED 30 MIN. & DRAINED (OPTIONAL)

SHRED MEAT, COMBINE & SPOON ONTO 16 CREPES---DO NOT ROLL UP YET.

2 1/4 C	FAT-FREE CHICKEN STOCK
1 T	BUTTER BUDS
1	ONION, MINCED
1	APPLE, CHOPPED
2	CARROTS, GRATED

SIMMER THESE FOR 5 MINUTES.

1 C	SKIM MILK (OR MORE)
2 T	FLOUR
2 T	CURRY POWDER
------	SUGAR
3 T	ORANGE JUICE

PUREE THESE & ADD TO ABOVE. SIMMER 10 MIN. TO THICKEN.

SPOON 3 T ON EACH CREPE & ROLL UP.

Place in a sprayed dish, pour extra sauce over & bake at 350 for 20 minutes.

CREPES FLORENTINE

16 CREPES   FAT = 2 GM EA
(Including Sauce)

1/2 C	FAT-FREE CHICKEN STOCK	
2	ONIONS, DICED	SIMMER THESE FOR 5 MINUTES.
2 CL	GARLIC, MINCED	
1	RED BELL PEPPER, DICED	
1 LB	MUSHROOMS, SLICED	

10 OZ	FROZEN SPINACH, SQUEEZED DRY, CHOPPED	ADD THESE & DIVIDE AMONG 16
3 C	COOKED TURKEY BREASTS, DICED	CREPES (p 122).
3/4 C	NO-FAT SOUR CREAM	
1/4 C	DRY SHERRY	ROLL UP, COVER WITH SAUCE &
1/2 t	CAVENDER'S GREEK SEASONING	BAKE AT 350 FOR 15 MINUTES.

SAUCE

3 C	FAT-FREE CHICKEN STOCK	HEAT THESE TO BOILING.
1 C	DRY SHERRY	
2 T	BUTTER BUDS	REMOVE FROM HEAT.

1 C	SKIM MILK	COMBINE WELL, WHISK INTO
4 T	CORNSTARCH	ABOVE & HEAT TO THICKEN.
2 T	BUTTER BUDS	

1/2 C	PARMESAN CHEESE	STIR IN & POUR OVER CREPES.

SEAFOOD CREPES I

16 CREPES   FAT – 2 GM EA
(Including Sauce)

1/4 C	FAT-FREE CHICKEN STOCK	
1 BCH	GREEN ONION, SLICED	SIMMER THESE FOR 5 MINUTES.
1/2 t	CAVENDER'S GREEK SEASONING	

8 OZ	FAT-FREE CREAM CHEESE	ADD THESE & STIR WELL.
1 C	NO-FAT SOUR CREAM	
1/2 C	DRY SHERRY	SPOON ONTO THE CREPES (p 122),
1 C	SHRIMP, COOKED, DICED	ROLL UP & PLACE IN A SPRAYED
1 C	BAY SCALLOPS, COOKED, DICED	DISH.
1 C	IMITATION CRAB, SHREDDED	BAKE AT 350 FOR 15 MINUTES.
		SPOON SAUCE OVER EACH.

SAUCE

1 C	SKIM MILK	PUREE & HEAT TO THICKEN.
2 T	BUTTER BUDS	
2 T	FLOUR	
1/4 t	CAVENDER'S GREEK SEASONING	SALT & PEPPER TO TASTE.
1/2 t	DRY MUSTARD	

1/4 C	PARMESAN CHEESE	ADD JUST BEFORE SERVING.

SEAFOOD CREPES II

SERVES 12   FAT = 2 GM EA

2 LBS	FLOUNDER FILLET CHUNKS	POACH SEAFOOD SEPARATELY IN
8 OZ	SHRIMP, PEELED & DEVEINED, CHUNKS	OLD BAY & MILK UNTIL DONE.
8 OZ	BAY SCALLOPS	
2 C	SKIM MILK	REMOVE SEAFOOD, KEEP WARM.
1 t	OLD BAY SEASONING	
1 C	MUSHROOMS, SLICED	ADD & SIMMER FOR 3 MINUTES.
4	GREEN ONIONS, SLICED	
2 CL	GARLIC, MINCED	
1 C	CANNED CHICK PEAS	
1/4 C	DRY WHITE WINE	PUREE & ADD TO ABOVE.
1 T	CORNSTARCH	
1/4 C	DRY WHITE WINE	ADD THESE & RETURN SEAFOOD
3	TOMATOES, PEELED, CHOPPED	TO PAN.
1/2 t	OLD BAY SEASONING (OR TO TASTE)	
1 t	CAVENDER'S GREEK SEASONING (OR TO TASTE)	
		FILL & ROLL CREPES. POUR ANY
24	CREPES (SEE BELOW)	EXTRA SAUCE OVER CREPES & BROIL.

CREPES

easy   24 CREPES   FAT = TR EA

1/2 C	EGG BEATERS	PUREE & LET SIT FOR 30 MIN.
1 C	FLOUR	
1 C	SKIM MILK (OR AS NEEDED)	
2 T	BUTTER BUDS	POUR AND SWIRL A SMALL
1 t	CANOLA OIL	AMOUNT INTO A SPRAYED, HOT PAN.
24	DILL SPRIGS	LAY A SPRIG ON TOP, FLIP & FRY THE OTHER SIDE.

This will decorate the outside of each crepe.

Remember, crepes freeze well & they're great to have on hand. Keep them in a box so their edges don't get broken.

SMOKED SCALLOPS   SERVES 4   FAT = 2 GM EA

1 LB	SEA SCALLOPS	MARINATE THESE FOR 30 MIN.
1/2 C	SOY SAUCE	
8 DROPS	LOUISIANA HOT SAUCE (OR MORE)	SIMMER UNTIL OPAQUE, REMOVE
2 T	FRESH LEMON JUICE	FROM PAN & KEEP WARM.
2 DROPS	LIQUID SMOKE	
1	ONION, MINCED	ADD THESE & REDUCE BY 1/2.
1 C	REISLING WINE	
2 DROPS	LIQUID SMOKE (OR TO TASTE)	
2 T	BUTTER BUDS	
3 T	SAFFRON	ADD TO THE ONION MIXTURE &
2 C	EVAPORATED SKIM MILK	REDUCE BY 1/2 AGAIN.
1 OZ	CANADIAN BACON, TRIMMED WELL, JULIENNED	
1/4 C	NO-FAT SOUR CREAM	SERVE UNDER THE SCALLOPS.
1 C	CHANTERELLES, SLICED (OTHER MUSHROOMS ARE OK)	
1/4 C	RED WINE (OPTIONAL)	

SEAFOOD FAJITAS   12 FAJITAS   FAT = 2 GM EA

1 C	FAT-FREE CHICKEN OR SEAFOOD STOCK	SIMMER THESE FOR 3 MINUTES.
1 EA	GREEN & RED BELL PEPPERS, JULIENNED	
2	ONION, HALVED & SLICED	
1 T	GARLIC, MINCED	TOSS THESE , ADD TO ABOVE &
1 T	CORNSTARCH	HEAT JUST UNTIL SHRIMP TURN
1	LEMON, JUICED	PINK.
1 t	OLD BAY SEASONING	
1 t	GROUND CUMIN (OR TO TASTE)	SALT & PEPPER TO TASTE.
1 LB	SHRIMP, PEELED & DEVEINED	
1 LB	IMITATION CRAB MEAT, SHREDDED	ADD JUST BEFORE SERVING.

Serve in heated Fat-Free Tortillas, with shredded lettuce, diced tomato, diced onion, Low-Fat Cheddar, Fat-Free Sour Cream & sliced black olives (Not Too Many).

SEAFOOD SPINACH FETTUCINE

easy   SERVES 8   FAT = 2 GM EA

1 LB	BAY SCALLOPS, CLEANED, COOKED	COMBINE THESE.
1 LB	SHRIMP, PEELED, DEVEINED, COOKED	
1 1/2 LBS	SPINACH FETTUCINE, COOKED	
8	TOMATOES, PEELED, SEEDED, CHOPPED	
8	GREEN ONIONS, SLICED	
1 C	FAT-FREE MIRACLE WHIP	COMBINE THESE & TOSS WITH
1 C	NO-FAT SOUR CREAM	ABOVE.
1	LEMON, JUICED (OR TO TASTE)	
4 T	FRESH PARSLEY, CHOPPED	
1 t	DRY MUSTARD	
1 t	WORCESTERSHIRE SAUCE	SALT & PEPPER TO TASTE.
1/4 t	OLD BAY SEASONING (OR TO TASTE)	
6 CL	GARLIC, MINCED	
	SKIM MILK AS NEEDED	CHILL 2 HOURS.

SAKE-SAKE SOLE

easy   SERVES 6   FAT = 1 GM EA

2 LB	SOLE OR FLOUNDER FILLETS, IN CUBES	TOSS FISH IN SALT, CHILL 3 HRS.
3 T	SALT	& RINSE.
		THREAD ON SKEWERS.
1/2 C	SAKE	COMBINE, BRUSH ON KABOBS
1/4 C	EGG BEATERS	& BROIL 3 MINUTES EACH SIDE.
1/4 t	OLD BAY SEASONING	

FISH IN BLACK BEAN SAUCE

 quick   SERVES 8   FAT = 1 GM EA

1 C	FISH STOCK	SIMMER THESE INGREDIENTS.
1/2 C	BLACK BEANS, COOKED OR CANNED, MASHED	
1/4 C	SOY SAUCE	
1/4 C	SWEET RICE WINE	
4 CL	GARLIC, MINCED	
2 T	FRESH GINGER, PEELED, MINCED	
1 T	CHILI PASTE	
		ADD FISH & ONIONS, COVER &
8	WHITE, LEAN, FISH FILLETS	POACH 10 MINUTES PER INCH
8	GREEN ONIONS, SLICED	OR UNTIL FISH IS FLAKY.

Seafood

A lot of people think, if they eat fish, they're automatically being "good". Unfortunately, this is not always true. (Check fat contents on the following pages). But it's not only the fat "in" the fish that hurts, it's also how it is prepared.

Remember....you can substitute a leaner type of fish in most of these recipes. Cold water fish tend to be higher in fat content. Before serving, remove all skin and darker colored meat. This is where a lot of the fat is found.

To give you an idea of the fish you should be using in your menus, I've included a list of various seafoods in order of fat content.

FISH	FAT PER 3.5 OZ	FISH	FAT PER 3.5 OZ
ABALONE	.3	BASS, SEA	2.0
BASS, WHITE SEA	.5	FRESH WATER	2.6
CRAPPIE, WHITE	.8	STRIPED	2.7
CRAYFISH, FRESH	.5	BUTTERFISH, GULF	2.9
CROAKER, WHITE	.8	CRAB	2.0
FLOUNDER	.5	HALIBUT	2.0
PICKEREL	.5	MACKEREL, KING	2.0
PIKE, BLUE	.9	MONKFISH	2.0
SHRIMP	.8	MUSKIE	2.5
TUSKFISH	.5	MUSSELS	2.2
		OYSTERS, PACIFIC	2.0
BASS, BLACK	1.2	PERCH, ATLANTIC	2.0
CLAMS	1.0	ROCKFISH	2.0
COD	1.0	TROUT, BROOK	2.1
CRAWFISH	1.0		
CUSK	1.0	ALLIGATOR	3.0
CUTTLEFISH	1.0	BLUEFISH	3.3
		CATFISH	3.1
DOLPHIN	1.0	CROAKER, ATLANTIC	3.2
FLATFISH	1.0	KINGFISH	3.0
GROUPER	1.0	PERCH, WHITE	3.9
HADDOCK	1.0	SNAIL	3.0
HAKE	1.0	WHALE	3.0
		WOLFISH	3.0
LOBSTER	1.0		
OCTOPUS	1.0	BUFFALO FISH	4.2
ORANGE ROUGHY	1.0	CARP	4.2
PERCH, FRESH WATER	1.0	OYSTERS, EASTERN	4.0
PIKE, NORTHERN	1.0	SALMON, CHUM	4.0
WALLEYE	1.2	PINK	4.0
POLLOCK	1.0	SWORDFISH	4.0
		TROUT, SEA	4.0
SCALLOPS	1.0	TUNA, BLUEFIN	4.1
SNAPPER	1.0		
SOLE	1.0	DRUM	5.0
TUNA, YELLOWFIN	1.0	MACKEREL, SPANISH	5.0
TURTLE	1.0	JACK	5.6
WHITING	1.0	SALMON, COHO	6.0
		YELLOWTAIL	6.0

FISH	FAT PER 3.5 OZ
ALBACORE	7.5
MACKEREL, PACIFIC	7.3
SALMON, ATLANTIC	7.0
SARDINES	8.6
BUTTERFISH	9.0
POMPANO	9.5
SALMON, SOCKEYE	9.0
BUTTERFISH, NORTH	10.2
HERRING,ATLANTIC	10.0
SALMON, CHINOOK	11.0
TROUT, RAINBOW	11.4
MACKEREL, ATLANTIC	12.0
EEL	13.0
DOGFISH	15.0
HALIBUT, GREENLAND	15.0
HERRING,PACIFIC	15.0
SABLEFISH	17.0
TROUT, LAKE	19.9

BRANDY BUTTER SAUCE   4 OZ.   FAT = TR EA
(For grilling warm water lobster, catfish or almost any seafood)

4 T	HOT WATER	COMBINE ALL
4 T	BUTTER BUDS	
4 T	BRANDY	BRUSH ON WHILE GRILLING

CITRUS BRANDY SAUCE   4 OZ.   FAT = TR EA

1 T	FRESH LEMON JUICE (or orange, or pineapple), to taste	COMBINE ALL
4 T	HOT WATER	
4 T	BUTTER BUDS	BRUSH ON WHILE
4 T	BRANDY	GRILLING.

QUICK BUTTER CREAM SAUCE   4 OZ   FAT = TR EA

4 T	BUTTER BUDS	COMBINE ALL
4 T	HOT WATER	
4 T	POWDERED SKIM MILK	BRUSH ON WHILE
4 T	FAT FREE SOUR CREAM	GRILLING

LEMON BUTTER CREAM SAUCE   4 OZ   FAT = TR EA

Make QUICK BUTTER CREAM SAUCE above and add   1 T   FRESH LEMON JUICE (or to taste)

DILLY BUTTER CREAM SAUCE   4 OZ   FAT = TR EA

Make QUICK BUTTER CREAM SAUCE above and add 1 T FRESH MINCED DILL (or to taste)
This is also good using LEMON BUTTER CREAM SAUCE as a base. You
can also use TARRAGON or another of your favorite herbs.

CITRUS MAYO   8 OZ   FAT = TR EA

3/4 C	FAT FREE MIRACLE WHIP	COMBINE & SPREAD
1/4 C	FROZEN ORANGE JUICE CONCENTRATE (or lemon)	ON FISH SANDWICHES

This also makes a good dressing for fruit salad if you thin it a little with skim milk.

LOUISIANA ALLIGATOR

 easy   SERVES 8   FAT = 6 GM EA

1 C	FAT-FREE CHICKEN STOCK	COMBINE ALL INGREDIENTS AND
2 EA	ONION, BELL PEPPER, DICED	SIMMER FOR 45 MINUTES.
4 CL	GARLIC, MINCED	
2 C	CELERY, DICED	
4	TOMATOES, CHOPPED	LOUISIANA HOT SAUCE TO TASTE
1/2 C	WHITE WINE	
2 T	FRESH LEMON JUICE	SALT & PEPPER TO TASTE.
2 T	WORCESTERSHIRE SAUCE	
2 T	BUTTER BUDS	ADD SUGAR IF NEEDED.
1 t	PICK-A-PEPPER SAUCE	
1/2 t	GROUND CLOVES	
1/4 t	OLD BAY SEASONING	
4	BAY LEAVES (REMOVE BEFORE SERVING)	SERVE OVER RICE.
3 LBS	ALLIGATOR MEAT CHUNKS (OR TURKEY BREASTS)	

BLACK BASS w BALSAMIC SOUR CREAM

 quick   SERVES 4   FAT = 2 GM EA
(Including Sauce)

4	6 OZ SEA BASS FILLETS, S & P	SPRAY WITH PAM OLIVE OIL AND GRILL OR BROIL.

BALSAMIC SOUR CREAM

2 CUPS   FAT = TR EA

1 1/4 C	NO-FAT SOUR CREAM	COMBINE, SIMMER & WHISK FOR
2 T EA	FLOUR, BUTTER BUDS	3 MINUTES.
2 T	NON-FAT MILK POWDER	
1/2 C	BALSAMIC VINEGAR	SERVE OVER FISH.

WHOLE BAKED BASS

 easy   SERVES 8   FAT = 1 GM EA

4	LEMONS, SLICED	PLACE IN A SPRAYED DISH.
5 LBS	WHITE SEA BASS, CLEANED, S & P	LAY ON LEMON SLICES.
3	LEMONS, JUICED	SPRINKLE OVER ALL.
6 T	FAT-FREE MIRACLE WHIP	COMBINE & SPREAD OVER FISH.
1/4 C	NO-FAT SOUR CREAM	
1 T	FRESH LEMON JUICE	
1	RED ONION, MINCED	
1 C	FAT-FREE BREAD CRUMBS	COMBINE & SPRINKLE OVER. SPRAY AND BAKE AT 400 FOR 45
1/4 C	DRIED THYME OR ITALIAN HERBS	MINUTES OR UNTIL DONE.

BAKED BASS

easy   SERVES 10   FAT = 4 GM EA

5 LBS	WHITE SEA BASS, CLEANED	COMBINE THESE & BRUSH INSIDE
1/4 C	HEINZ CHILI SAUCE	& OUT.
1/4 C	FAT-FREE MIRACLE WHIP	
2	LEMONS, SLICED	PLACE IN A SPRAYED DISH, ADD
1	ONION, SLICED	ONIONS & TOP WITH THE FISH.
2	LEMONS, SLICED	LAY ON TOP OF THE FISH.
1	ONION, SLICED	SPRINKLE REMAINING OVER THE
1/4 C	FRESH PARSLEY, CHOPPED	LEMONS & BAKE AT 400 FOR 45
------	OLD BAY SEASONING	MINUTES OR UNTIL DONE.

BAKED BLUEFISH

easy   SERVES 8   FAT = 7 GM EA

Using flounder would cut the fat to 1 GM EA

3 LBS	FILLETS, RINSED, S & P	LAY IN A SPRAYED DISH & TOP
2	ONIONS, SLICED THIN	WITH REMAINING INGREDIENTS.
1	CELERY STALK, SLICED THIN	
1	RED BELL PEPPER, SLICED THIN	
1	GREEN PEPPER, SLICED THIN	COVER & BAKE AT 325 FOR 30-40
4 CL	GARLIC, MINCED	MIN. OR UNTIL FLAKY TO FORK.
16 OZ	TOMATO SAUCE	
24 OZ	CANNED WHOLE TOMATOES, CHOPPED	
2 T	DRIED ITALIAN HERBS	

BROILED CLAMS

quick   SERVES 8   FAT = 2 GM EA

4 DZ	SMALL CLAMS, OPENED, SHELL TOPS DISCARDED	
1/2 C	HOT WATER	COMBINE & SPRINKLE ON EACH.
1/2 C	BUTTER BUDS, DISSOLVED IN ABOVE WATER	
2 T	CAVENDER'S GREEK SEASONING	BROIL FOR 1 MINUTE OR UNTIL
2 T	WORCESTERSHIRE SAUCE	DONE.

CRAB BOIL

6 DOZEN FAT = TR EA

6 QTS	WATER
2 C	WHITE WINE
1 C	SALT
16 CL	GARLIC, CRUSHED
2	CARROTS, DICED
1/4 C	PICKLING SPICE
2 t	DILL
1 T	OLD BAY SEASONING
1 t	ALLSPICE
1 t	GROUND CLOVES
1 t	CURRY POWDER
6 DZ	CRABS

BRING ALL TO A BOIL EXCEPT CRABS.

ADD CRABS AND SIMMER UNTIL SHELLS TURN RED.

REMOVE CRABS.

EASTERN SHORE BROILED CRAB CAKES

SERVES 6 FAT = 3 GM EA

12	2" TOASTED BREAD CIRCLES
1 C	SOFT, FAT-FREE BREAD CUBES
1/4 C	SKIM MILK
2 LBS	CRAB MEAT, PICKED CLEAN
4	GREEN ONIONS, MINCED
1/2 C	EGG BEATERS
1/2 C	FAT-FREE MIRACLE WHIP (+ IF NEEDED TO BIND)
1/4 C	RED BELL PEPPER, FINELY MINCED (OPTIONAL)
2 T	BUTTER BUDS
2 T	FRESH PARSLEY, MINCED
1 T	BAKING POWDER
2 t	DRY MUSTARD
1 t	WORCESTERSHIRE SAUCE
1/4 t	OLD BAY SEASONING
1/4 t	CAVENDER'S GREEK SEASONING
1/2 t EA	SALT & PEPPER

PLACE ON A SPRAYED PAN.

TOSS THESE AND LET SIT FOR 5 MINUTES.

COMBINE & ADD TO ABOVE.

SPOON ONTO TOASTED BREAD CIRCLES.

SPRINKLE WITH PAPRIKA AND BROIL ON THE MIDDLE RACK UNTIL BUBBLY.

CURRIED SCALLOP CRAB CAKES w SHERRY TOMATO SAUCE SERVES 6 FAT = 1.5 GM EA

6	2" TOASTED BREAD CIRCLES	PLACE ON A SPRAYED PAN.
6 OZ	SCALLOPS	PUREE THESE INGREDIENTS.
1/4 C	EGG BEATERS	
2 T	CREAM SHERRY	
1 T	DIJON MUSTARD	
1 T	BUTTER BUDS	
1 T	FAT-FREE MIRACLE WHIP	
2 CL	GARLIC, SLICED	FOLD IN THE CRAB AND SPOON
1 t	CURRY POWDER (OR TO TASTE)	ONTO TOASTED CIRCLES AND BROIL ON THE MIDDLE RACK 'TIL
1 LB	CRAB MEAT, PICKED CLEAN	BUBBLY.

SHERRY TOMATO SAUCE 3 CUPS FAT = TR EA

1	ONION, MINCED	
3 CL	GARLIC, MINCED	COMBINE & SIMMER 30 MINUTES.
1/2 C	FAT-FREE CHICKEN STOCK	
2 C	TOMATOES, PEELED, SEEDED & CHOPPED	
1/4 C	WHITE WINE	
1/4 C	BUTTER BUDS	
1/2 C	CREAM SHERRY	ADD & SIMMER 5 MINUTES.
2 T	SHERRY VINEGAR	SALT & PEPPER TO TASTE.
1 t	CRUSHED RED PEPPER FLAKES	SERVE WITH THE CRAB CAKES.

ORIENTAL CRAB CAKES SERVES 6 FAT = 1.5 GM EA
(Including Sauce)

12	2" TOASTED BREAD CIRCLES	PLACE ON A SPRAYED PAN.
1 LB	CRAB MEAT, PICKED CLEAN	COMBINE THESE AND PLACE ON
1/2 LB	TURKEY BREASTS, COOKED, PUREED	THE CIRCLES.
1/2 C	FAT-FREE BREAD CUBES	
4	GREEN ONION, MINCED	
2 T	FAT-FREE MIRACLE WHIP	
1 t	OLD BAY SEASONING	BROIL UNTIL BUBBLY.
1/2 C	EGG BEATERS	

ORIENTAL SAUCE 5 CUPS FAT = TR EA

3 C	FAT-FREE CHICKEN STOCK	COMBINE & HEAT THESE.
1/4 C	KETCHUP	
1 C	BROWN SUGAR	REMOVE FROM HEAT.
1 C	SHERRY VINEGAR	COMBINE WELL, WHISK IN AND
1/4 C	SOY SAUCE	HEAT TO THICKEN.
1/4 C	CORNSTARCH	SERVE WITH THE CRAB CAKES.

CRAB IMPERIAL

SERVES 6   FAT = 2 GM EA
(Including Sauce)

1 1/2 LBS	CRAB MEAT, PICKED CLEAN	
1 T	FRESH LEMON JUICE	TOSS THESE & CHILL.
1 C	SKIM MILK	SIMMER THESE 'TIL THICKENED.
3 T	FLOUR	
3 T	BUTTER BUDS	
1 t	CORNSTARCH	REMOVE FROM HEAT.
1/2 C	EGG BEATERS	COMBINE THESE WELL.
1/2 C	CREAM SHERRY	
1/4 C	PIMENTOS, DICED	TOSS WITH ALL OF THE ABOVE.
1/2 C	GREEN PEPPERS, DICED, BLANCHED	
1/2 C	ONIONS, MINCED, BLANCHED	
1 T	WORCESTERSHIRE SAUCE	
2 T	FRESH PARSLEY, CHOPPED	
1 T	CAPERS, MINCED (OPTIONAL)	SPRAY 6 GRATIN DISHES WITH
1 t	DIJON MUSTARD	PAM BUTTER SPRAY.
1/2 t	CAVENDER'S GREEK SEASONING	
1/2 t	CELERY SALT	FILL WITH MIXTURE.
1/2 t	PEPPER OR OLD BAY SEASONING	

IMPERIAL SAUCE

3/4 C	NO-FAT SOUR CREAM	BLEND THESE & SPREAD ON THE
1/4 C	PARMESAN CHEESE	TOP OF EACH DISH.
1/4 C	EGG BEATERS	
2 T	BUTTER BUDS	
1/2 t	OLD BAY SEASONING	
1/2 t	FRESH LEMON JUICE (OR TO TASTE)	BAKE AT 450 FOR 12 MINUTES.

CRAB SOUFFLE

SERVES 4   FAT = 2 GM EA

2 C	CRAB IMPERIAL (RECIPE ABOVE)	SPOON INTO 4 PAM-SPRAYED RAMEKINS.
2 T	FLOUR	
3 T	BUTTER BUDS	SIMMER THESE 'TIL THICKENED.
1/4 C	SKIM MILK	
2 t	DIJON MUSTARD	
1/4 t	PICK-A-PEPPER SAUCE	
------	OLD BAY SEASONING	REMOVE FROM HEAT.
1/4 t	ALLSPICE	
		COMBINE AND FOLD INTO THE FLOUR MIXTURE.
1/2 C	EGG BEATERS	
2 T	PARMESAN CHEESE	SPOON THIS OVER THE CRAB &
4	EGG WHITES, BEATEN STIFF, NOT DRY	SPRINKLE WITH 1 T PARMESAN. BAKE AT 375 FOR 30 MINUTES.

STEAMED CRABS

quick   2 DOZEN CRABS   FAT = TR EA

2 C	WATER	COMBINE IN A LARGE POT WITH RACK IN THE BOTTOM.
2 C	VINEGAR	
2 DZ	LARGE CRABS	SPRINKLE SEASONINGS ON EACH LAYER OF CRABS AS THEY GO INTO THE POT.
1/4 C	OLD BAY SEASONING	
2 T	CAVENDER'S GREEK SEASONING	

Cover & steam 20 minutes or until shells turn red.

BROILED CATFISH

quick   SERVES 8   FAT = 7 GM EA

------	OLD BAY SEASONING	SPRINKLE OVER THE FISH AND SET ASIDE IN A SPRAYED DISH.
8	6 OZ FILLETS, RINSED & DRIED	
2	ONIONS, DICED	SIMMER THESE FOR 4 MINUTES.
12 CL	GARLIC, MINCED	
1/2 C	FRESH THYME, CHOPPED	
1 C	FRESH OREGANO, CHOPPED	
1 C	FLAT PARSLEY, CHOPPED	POUR OVER FISH & BAKE AT 400 FOR 10 MINUTES.
1 C	FAT-FREE CHICKEN STOCK	
1/4 C	FAT-FREE BREAD CRUMBS	COMBINE & SPRINKLE OVER. BROIL 3-5 MINUTES MORE, OR 'TIL BROWN & FLAKY TO FORK
1/4 C	PARMESAN CHEESE	

CATFISH PARMESAN

 quick   SERVES 8   FAT = 8 GM EA

1/2 C	EGG BEATERS	COMBINE FOR DIPPING THE FISH & SET ASIDE.
2 T	SKIM MILK	
1/2 C	PARMESAN CHEESE	COMBINE FOR DREDGING FISH & SET ASIDE.
1/4 C	FLOUR	
1/4 C	FAT-FREE BREAD CRUMBS	
1 t	PAPRIKA	
8	6 OZ FILLETS, RINSED & DRIED	SALT & PEPPER.

Dip fish in egg mix & dredge in flour mix. Place in sprayed dish, spray with Pam again & bake at 400 for 10-15 minutes or until flaky to fork.

You might like to drizzle dry vermouth & lemon juice around fish.

COD CREOLE

easy   SERVES 6   FAT = 2 GM EA

2	LEMONS, SLICED	PLACE IN A SPRAYED DISH AND
6	6 OZ FILLETS, RINSED, DRIED, S & P	TOP WITH FISH.
1/4 C	NO-FAT SOUR CREAM	COMBINE AND SPREAD ON THE
2 T	BUTTER BUDS	FISH.
1 T	FRESH LEMON JUICE	
1/4 t	OLD BAY SEASONING	
1	GREEN PEPPER, SLICED THIN	LAYER THESE INGREDIENTS ON
1	TOMATO, SLICED THIN	THE FISH.
1	ONION, SLICED THIN	BAKE AT 375 FOR 30 MINUTES OR
1 T	DRIED ITALIAN HERBS	UNTIL FLAKY TO FORK.

BAKED COD

easy   SERVES 6   FAT = 4 GM EA

6	6 OZ FILLETS, RINSED, DRIED, S & P	
1 t	SAGE	SPRINKLE THESE OVER FISH.
1/4 t	OLD BAY SEASONING	
1 C	FAT-FREE SWISS CHEESE, GRATED	COMBINE & SPREAD OVER FISH.
1 C	NO-FAT SOUR CREAM	BAKE AT 350 FOR 25 MINUTES OR
1/4 C	PARMESAN CHEESE	UNTIL FLAKY TO FORK.

COD w SAFFRON SAUCE

quick   SERVES 6   FAT = 2 GM EA

1 C	FAT-FREE FISH STOCK (OR CHICKEN)	
6 T	FRESH LEMON JUICE	PUREE THESE AND POUR INTO A
6 T	FRESH PARSLEY, CHOPPED	LARGE FRY PAN.
2 T	FLOUR	
2 t	CORNSTARCH	
2 t	SAFFRON	
1 t	TURMERIC	
1 t	CAVENDER'S GREEK SEASONING	
4 CL	GARLIC, SLICED	
1	ONION, MINCED	ADD & SIMMER 3 MINUTES.
1	GREEN PEPPER, MINCED	
1	TOMATO, CHOPPED	
		ADD FISH, COVER & POACH FOR
6	6 OZ FILLETS, RINSED	5 MINUTES. TURN & SIMMER 3
		MORE OR UNTIL FLAKY TO FORK.

GINGER COD

SERVES 8   FAT = 2 GM EA

8	6 OZ FILLETS, SALT & LEMON PEPPER
------	PAPRIKA

PLACE IN A SPRAYED DISH AND SPRINKLE WITH PAPRIKA.

1 C	SKIM MILK
1 C	CRUSHED PINEAPPLE
1/4 C	PINEAPPLE JUICE
2 T	FRESH GINGER, PEELED, GRATED
ZEST OF 1	LEMON, MINCED
1 T	CORNSTARCH
1 t	SUGAR

COMBINE & HEAT TO THICKEN.

POUR OVER FISH & BAKE AT 375 UNTIL FLAKY TO FORK.
(10 MIN PER INCH OF THICKNESS)

SWEET & SOUR COD

SERVES 8   FAT = 2 GM EA

2 C	SUGAR SYRUP (p 393)
2/3 C	RED WINE VINEGAR
1/4 C	STRAWBERRIES
1/2 t	SALT
2 T	CORNSTARCH

PUREE & HEAT TO THICKEN.

8	6 OZ FILLETS, RINSED

ADD FISH & POACH UNTIL FLAKY TO FORK.

HERBED COD or SNAPPER

SERVES 8   FAT = 2 GM EA

8	6 OZ FILLETS, RINSED, DRIED, S & P

2 T	FRESH GINGER, PEELED, CHOPPED
1 C	FRESH ROSEMARY, STEMS REMOVED
2 T	FRESH THYME, STEMS REMOVED

MINCE IN A FOOD PROCESSOR & SPRINKLE ON FISH.

PLACE IN A SPRAYED DISH.

1 C	FAT-FREE CHICKEN STOCK
1 C	DRY WHITE WINE
1/4 C	DRY SHERRY

ADD THESE & SPRAY WITH PAM. BAKE AT 375 (10 MIN. PER INCH OF THICKNESS).

COD w TOMATOES

SERVES 2   FAT = 2 GM EA

2	6 OZ FILLETS, RINSED, S & P	PLACE IN A SPRAYED DISH.
1/2 C	EVAPORATED SKIM MILK	COMBINE & POUR THESE OVER
1/2 C	DRY WHITE WINE	THE FISH.
2 C	TOMATOES, PEELED & CHOPPED	
1 T	FRESH LEMON JUICE	
1 T	CORNSTARCH	BAKE AT 400 FOR 25 MINUTES OR
1/2 t	CAVENDER'S GREEK SEASONING	UNTIL FLAKY TO FORK.

BAKED COD

SERVES 2   FAT = 2 GM EA

1/2 C	NO-FAT SOUR CREAM OR MIRACLE WHIP	COMBINE THESE TO DIP FISH.
1/4 C	FRESH LEMON JUICE	
2 t	WORCESTERSHIRE SAUCE	
1 C	FAT-FREE BREAD CRUMBS	COMBINE THESE TO DREDGE THE
3 T	BUTTER BUDS	FISH.
2	6 OZ FILLETS, RINSED, DRIED, S & P	

Dip fish, then dredge & bake at 350 for 20 minutes or until flaky to fork.

MEDITERRANEAN COD

SERVES 8   FAT = 2 GM EA

4 C	FAT-FREE CHICKEN STOCK	SIMMER THESE FOR 4 MINUTES.
2 LBS	ONIONS, SLICED	
2 T	WHITE WINE VINEGAR	
1 t	CAPERS, MINCED	
1/2 t	ALLSPICE	
1/2 t	SAFFRON	
1/2 t	GROUND CUMIN	ADD FISH, COVER AND POACH 10
1/4 t	CINNAMON	10 MINUTES OR UNTIL FLAKY TO
1/4 t	GROUND CLOVES	FORK.
8	6 OZ FILLETS, RINSED, S & P.	

BROILED DOLPHIN

SERVES 6   FAT = 2 GM EA

6	6 OZ FILLETS, RINSED, DRIED, S & P
1/4 C	NO-FAT SOUR CREAM
1/4 C	FAT-FREE MIRACLE WHIP
1/4 C	FRESH ORANGE JUICE
2 T	ORANGE ZEST, MINCED

COMBINE & SPREAD THESE OVER FISH.
BAKE AT 400 UNTIL FLAKY.
(10 MIN PER INCH OF THICKNESS)
BROIL TO BROWN SLIGHTLY.

GRILLED DOLPHIN

SERVES 8   FAT = 2 GM EA

8	6 OZ FILLETS, RINSED
1 C	ORANGE JUICE
1/2 C	WATER
1/4 C	FRESH LIME JUICE
2 CL	GARLIC, MINCED
------	SALT & PEPPER

MARINATE ALL IN A ZIPLOC BAG FOR 2 HOURS.

GRILL OR BROIL UNTIL FLAKY TO FORK.

This marinade also works well for scallop kabobs.

COCONUT DOLPHIN

SERVES 8   FAT = 2 GM EA

8	6 OZ FILLETS, RINSED, DRIED, S & P

PLACE IN A SPRAYED DISH.

2 C	SKIM MILK
2 T	CORNSTARCH
2 T	PINEAPPLE JUICE
1 T	COCONUT FLAVORING (OR TO TASTE)

COMBINE AND ADD THESE.
SPRAY FISH & BAKE AT 375 FOR 20 MINUTES OR UNTIL FLAKY TO FORK.

Garnish with sliced pineapple or sprinkle with crushed pineapple.

ORIENTAL DOLPHIN FLORENTINE

SERVES 8   FAT = 2 GM EA

2 LBS	SPINACH, WASHED
2 T	SOY SAUCE
2 T	RICE WINE VINEGAR

TOSS THESE AND STEAM FOR 30 SECONDS.

8	6 OZ FILLETS, RINSED
1/2 C	SOY SAUCE
1/2 C	FRESH ORANGE JUICE
1/4 C	FRESH GINGER, PEELED, GRATED

SIMMER THESE FOR 10 MINUTES PER INCH OF THICKNESS.

SERVE ON THE SPINACH.

DOLPHIN or SCALLOPS GRATIN

SERVES 8   FAT = 2.5 GM EA

1 C	SKIM MILK	SIMMER THESE TO THICKEN.
1/4 C	FRESH LEMON JUICE	
1/4 C	BUTTER BUDS	SALT & PEPPER TO TASTE.
1 T	CORNSTARCH	
1 t	DRY SHERRY	
5 CL	GARLIC, MINCED	
1/2 C	FRESH PARSLEY, MINCED	ADD FISH & POUR IN 8 SPRAYED GRATIN DISHES.
3 LBS	FISH CUBES OR BAY SCALLOPS	SPRINKLE REMAINING ITEMS ON
3/4 C	FAT-FREE BREAD CRUMBS	THE TOPS.
2 T	FRESH LEMON JUICE	SPRAY AND BAKE AT 400 FOR 12
2 T	PARMESAN CHEESE	MINUTES.

OVEN FRIED FLOUNDER

SERVES 8   FAT = 3 GM EA

1/2 C	EGG BEATERS	COMBINE THESE TO DIP FISH.
3/4 C	FROZEN PINEAPPLE JUICE CONCENTRATE	
1 t	LOUISIANA HOT SAUCE	
25	FAT-FREE SALTINE CRACKERS, CRUSHED	COMBINE THESE TO DREDGE THE
1/2 C	PARMESAN CHEESE	FISH.
8	6 OZ FILLETS, RINSED, DRIED, S & P	

Dip fish, then dredge. Spray fillets with Pam Butter Spray. Bake at 400 for 20 minutes or until fish is flaky to fork.

BAKED FLOUNDER

SERVES 6   FAT = 1 GM EA

2	LEMONS, SLICED	PLACE UNDER FISH IN SPRAYED
6	6 OZ FILLETS, RINSED, S & P	DISH.
1/4 C	WHITE WINE	COMBINE & POUR THESE OVER
2 T	FRESH LEMON JUICE	FISH.
1/2 t	SALT	
6	GREEN ONIONS, SLICED	
1	ONION, DICED	BAKE AT 350 FOR 20 MINUTES OR
1	TOMATO, PEELED, SEEDED, CHOPPED	UNTIL FLAKY TO FORK.
1/4 C	FRESH PARSLEY, MINCED	
1/2 t	FRESH THYME, MINCED	

CHILI FLOUNDER

SERVES 6   FAT = 1 GM EA

6	6 OZ FILLETS, RINSED, DRIED, S & P	SPRINKLE OVER FISH, BAKE AT
1 t	CHILI POWDER	400 FOR 6 MINUTES & TURN.
1/2 C	HEINZ CHILI SAUCE	COMBINE & SPREAD THESE OVER
1/4 C	NO-FAT SOUR CREAM	THE FISH.
1/4 C	SOY SAUCE	
1 T	FRESH LEMON JUICE	BROIL 4 MORE MINUTES OR 'TIL
		FLAKY TO FORK.

FLOUNDER w LEMON MUSTARD SAUCE

SERVES 6   FAT = 1 GM EA

6	6 OZ FILLETS, RINSED	SIMMER THESE 8 MINUTES AND
1 C	DRY WHITE WINE	REMOVE FROM HEAT.
2 T	DIJON MUSTARD	
2 T	FRESH LEMON JUICE	
1/2 C	SKIM MILK	COMBINE WELL, WHISK IN AND
1/2 T	CORNSTARCH	HEAT TO THICKEN.
		SALT & PEPPER TO TASTE.

Remove fish when done & pour sauce over. Garnish with lemon spirals.

PUFFY FLOUNDER

SERVES 4   FAT = 1 GM EA

4	6 OZ FILLETS, RINSED, DRIED, S & P	SPRINKLE & BAKE AT 400 FOR 8
------	OLD BAY SEASONING	MINUTES.
6	EGG WHITES, BEATEN TO STIFF, NOT DRY	COMBINE & SPREAD OVER FISH.
1 C	NO-FAT SOUR CREAM	
2 T	FRESH PARSLEY, CHOPPED	BAKE AGAIN UNTIL GOLDEN.
2 T	BUTTER BUDS	(APPROXIMATELY 3-5 MINUTES)
1	LEMON, JUICED	
------	SALT	

FLOUNDER ON BEDS OF SPINACH

 SERVES 8   FAT = 1 GM EA

1/2 C	FAT-FREE FISH STOCK	SIMMER THESE 10 MINUTES.
1 C	DRY WHITE WINE	
4	ONIONS, SLICED	
1 LB	MUSHROOMS, SLICED	
2 T	BUTTER BUDS	
1/2 t	OLD BAY SEASONING	
		ADD FISH, COVER & POACH FOR
8	6 OZ FILLETS, RINSED	5 MINUTES EA SIDE & REMOVE.
1 C	FAT-FREE SOUR CREAM	WHISK INTO SAUCE. S & P TO TASTE.
3 LBS	SPINACH, WASHED, STEMMED	
1/4 C	FRESH LEMON JUICE	TOSS & STEAM 30 SECONDS.
1/4 t	CAVENDER'S GREEK SEASONING	SERVE UNDER FISH.

ITALIAN BAKED FISH

 SERVES 8   FAT = 2 GM EA

4	ONIONS, SLICED	LAY IN A PAM-SPRAYED DISH.
4	TOMATOES, PEELED, SLICED	
1 C	FAT-FREE BREAD CRUMBS	SPRINKLE OVER THE TOMATOES
1 t	DRIED ITALIAN HERBS	& ONIONS.
8	6 OZ FILLETS, RINSED, DRIED, S & P	PLACE ON TOP OF VEGGIES AND SPRAY WITH PAM BUTTER.
1 C	PORT OR SHERRY	COMBINE & POUR ON FISH.
3 T	FRESH LEMON JUICE	
3 T	TOMATO PASTE	
1/4 C	PARMESAN CHEESE	SPRINKLE OVER & BAKE AT 400
------	PAPRIKA	10 MINUTES OR UNTIL FLAKY TO FORK.

SURF ROLLS   SERVES 8   FAT = 2 GM EA

8	6 OZ FILLETS, RINSED, DRIED, S & P	SEASON FISH WITH OLD BAY, PUT
1 t	OLD BAY SEASONING	2 SHRIMP ON EACH & ROLL UP.
16	SHRIMP, CLEANED & COOKED	

Place in a sprayed dish, seam side down & spray with Pam Butter. Bake at 375 for 25 minutes or until flaky to fork.

1 C	SKIM MILK	SIMMER THESE TO THICKEN.
1 C	CLAM BROTH	
1/4 t	OLD BAY SEASONING	SALT & PEPPER TO TASTE.
2 T	CORNSTARCH	
2 T	WHITE WINE	SPOON OVER THE FISH.
------	LOUISIANA HOT SAUCE TO TASTE	SPRINKLE WITH PAPRIKA.

STUFFED FLOUNDER   SERVES 6   FAT = 2 GM EA

1 C	FAT-FREE CHICKEN STOCK	SIMMER THESE FOR 5 MINUTES.
1/2 C	CELERY, DICED	
1 C	ONION, DICED	COOL.
6 CL	GARLIC, MINCED	
2 LBS	SHRIMP, COOKED, CHOPPED	ADD THESE, STUFF THE FILLETS
1/2 LB	CRAB MEAT (OR IMITATION), SHREDDED	& ROLL UP.
2	FAT-FREE HAMBURGER BUNS (p 342), MINCED	
1/2 C	EGG BEATERS	
1/2 C	GREEN ONIONS, SLICED THIN	PLACE SEAM SIDE DOWN IN A
1/2 C	FRESH PARSLEY, CHOPPED	SPRAYED DISH AND BRUSH WITH
1/2 C	FAT-FREE SALTINE CRACKER CRUMBS	MORE EGG BEATERS.
------	SALT & CAYENNE PEPPER TO TASTE	
		BAKE AT 375 FOR 25 MINUTES OR
12	4 OZ FILLETS, RINSED, DRIED, S & P	UNTIL FLAKY TO FORK.

FLOUNDER & CRAB STACKS

 SERVES 4   FAT = 3 GM EA

8	4 OZ FILLETS, RINSED, DRIED, S & P	

8 OZ	CRAB MEAT, PICKED CLEAN	COMBINE & SPREAD THESE ON 4
1/2	GREEN PEPPER, DICED, BLANCHED	FILLETS.
1/2	ONION, DICED, BLANCHED	
1/2 C	EGG BEATERS	TOP WITH REMAINING FILLETS,
2 T	NO-FAT SOUR CREAM	(CREATING 4 STACKS).
1/2 t	DRY MUSTARD	
1/2 t	WORCESTERSHIRE SAUCE	

2 T	NO-FAT SOUR CREAM	COMBINE & SPREAD ON TOPS OF
2 t	FRESH LEMON JUICE	THE STACKS.
3 T	PARMESAN CHEESE	SPRAY WITH PAM BUTTER.
2 T	BUTTER BUDS	BAKE AT 375 FOR 25 MINUTES OR
1/2 t	DRIED ITALIAN HERBS	UNTIL FLAKY TO FORK.
1/4 t	OLD BAY SEASONING	

FLOUNDER VERONIQUE

 SERVES 4   FAT = 2 GM EA

2 C	DRY WHITE WINE	SIMMER THESE FOR 3 MINUTES.
1	RED ONION, MINCED	
1/4 C	BUTTER BUDS	

4	6 OZ FILLETS, RINSED	ADD FISH & SIMMER 8 MINUTES.
		REMOVE TO A BROILING PAN.

1 C	SKIM MILK	COMBINE WELL, WHISK IN AND
1/4 C	NO-FAT SOUR CREAM	HEAT TO THICKEN.
2 T	CORNSTARCH	
1 t	SUGAR	

2 C	SEEDLESS GRAPES, HALVED	FOLD INTO ABOVE, S & P AND
2 T	PARMESAN CHEESE	SPOON OVER THE FISH.
		BROIL UNTIL GOLDEN.

GRILLED HERBED GROUPER

easy   SERVES 4   FAT = 2 GM EA

4	6 OZ FILLETS, RINSED	MARINATE THESE FOR 1 HOUR.
1/2 C	CLAM BROTH	
1 T	FRESH LEMON JUICE	SALT & PEPPER.
1/2	ONION, MINCED	
2 CL	GARLIC, CRUSHED	GRILL OR BROIL UNTIL FISH
2 T	FRESH OREGANO, MINCED	IS FLAKY TO FORK.
3 T	FRESH LEMON JUICE	ADD THESE TO THE MARINADE &
3 T	BUTTER BUDS	SIMMER 5 MINUTES.
3 T	BLACK OLIVES, MINCED	
2 T	DRIED ITALIAN HERBS	SERVE WITH FISH.
2 T	FRESH BASIL, CHOPPED	

SPICED GROUPER or SNAPPER

easy   SERVES 8   FAT = 2 GM EA

8	6 OZ FILLETS, RINSED	MARINATE THESE FOR 6 HOURS.
6 CL	GARLIC, MINCED	
1 T	CRUSHED RED PEPPER FLAKES	
1/2 t	OLD BAY SEASONING	DISCARD MARINADE.
1/2 t	FRESH THYME, MINCED	
1/2 t	DRIED SAGE	SALT & PEPPER & BUTTER BUDS.
1 C	WHITE WINE VINEGAR	
1 C	CLAM BROTH	GRILL OR BROIL UNTIL FISH IS
		FLAKY TO FORK.

BROILED HADDOCK

quick   SERVES 6   FAT = 2 GM EA

6	6 OZ FILLETS, RINSED, DRIED, S & P	PLACE IN A SPRAYED DISH. BROIL 5 MINUTES.
1/2 C	NO-FAT SOUR CREAM	
1/4 C	FAT-FREE MIRACLE WHIP	COMBINE & SPREAD THESE OVER
1/4 C	BUTTER BUDS	THE FISH.
2 T	LEMON JUICE, OR WINE OR VINEGAR	
2 T	FRESH PARSLEY, CHOPPED	BROIL 5 MIN. OR UNTIL FLAKY TO FORK.

POACHED HADDOCK

quick   SERVES 4   FAT = 2 GM EA

2 C	CLAM BROTH OR WINE OR A COMBINATION	COMBINE & HEAT.
1 1/2 T	OLD BAY SEASONING	
1 T	FRESH LEMON JUICE	
1 t	CAVENDER'S GREEK SEASONING	ADD THE FISH, COVER & POACH
4	6 OZ FILLETS, RINSED	10 MINUTES OR UNTIL DONE.

HADDOCK w MUSTARD SAUCE

quick   SERVES 8   FAT = 2 GM EA

8	6 OZ FILLETS, RINSED, DRIED, S & P	PLACE IN A SPRAYED DISH.
4	ONIONS, SLICED THIN	LAY ON THE FISH.
2 C	NO-FAT SOUR CREAM	COMBINE & SPREAD THESE OVER
1/2 C	WHOLE GRAIN MUSTARD	OVER THE FISH.
1/4 C	BUTTER BUDS (DISSOLVED IN THE WATER	COVER AND BAKE AT 350 FOR 20
1/4 C	HOT WATER	MINUTES OR UNTIL FLAKY.
1/4 t	OLD BAY SEASONING	
------	WHITE WINE (OPTIONAL)	

HADDOCK w CUCUMBER SAUCE

quick   SERVES 8   FAT = 2 GM EA

1 C	STRONG FISH STOCK (OR MORE)	COMBINE & SIMMER THESE FOR
3 C	NO-FAT SOUR CREAM	5 MINUTES.
1/4 C	BUTTER BUDS	
6	CUCUMBERS, PEELED, GRATED	
		ADD FISH, COVER & POACH FOR
8	6 OZ FILLETS, RINSED, S & P	10 MINUTES OR UNTIL FLAKY.

BAKED HALIBUT

easy   SERVES 4   FAT = 4 GM EA

4	6 OZ STEAKS, RINSED, DRIED, S & P	PLACE IN A SPRAYED DISH.
1/4 C	NO-FAT SOUR CREAM	COMBINE & SPREAD THESE ON
2 T	BUTTER BUDS (DISSOLVED IN THE WATER)	THE FISH.
2 T	HOT WATER	
1 T	FRESH LEMON JUICE	
1 T	WORCESTERSHIRE SAUCE	
3	GREEN ONIONS, SLICED	BAKE AT 375 FOR 20-25 MINUTES
2 T	FRESH PARSLEY, CHOPPED	OR UNTIL FLAKY.

BAKED HALIBUT w ONIONS

easy   SERVES 6   FAT = 4 GM EA

6	6 OZ STEAKS, RINSED, S & P	PLACE LEMON & ONIONS UNDER
3	ONIONS, SLICED THIN	& OVER THE FISH.
3	LEMONS, SLICED THIN	
1/2 C	EVAPORATED SKIM MILK	COMBINE, POUR OVER FISH AND
1/4 C	FAT-FREE MIRACLE WHIP	BAKE AT 350 FOR 25-30 MINUTES
1/4 C	NO-FAT SOUR CREAM	OR UNTIL FLAKY.
1 T	LEMON ZEST, MINCED	
	GARNISH WITH LEMON WEDGES	

LOBSTER, SHRIMP & SCALLOP NEWBURG   SERVES 10   FAT = 2 GM EA

18 OZ	LOBSTER, SHELLED, STEAMED 4 MINUTES & SLICED IN CIRCLES (SAVE SHELLS)	
18 OZ	SHRIMP, CLEANED, STEAMED 4 MINUTES & SLICED HORIZONTALLY (SAVE SHELLS)	
18 OZ	SEA SCALLOPS, CLEANED, STEAMED 2 MINUTES	
ALL	LOBSTER & SHRIMP SHELLS FROM ABOVE	CHOP & SIMMER THESE FOR 30
2 C	FAT FREE FISH STOCK	MINUTES.
2 OZ	BRANDY	ADD THESE TO THE SHELLS.
1/2	ONION, MINCED	SIMMER FOR 15 MINUTES.
2 T	TOMATO PASTE	
80 OZ	FISH STOCK	ADD, REDUCE BY HALF & STRAIN THROUGH LAYERS OF CHEESE-CLOTH.
1 1/2 C	SKIM MILK	COMBINE THESE, ADD TO ABOVE
1/4 C	ARROWROOT OR CORNSTARCH	HEAT TO THICKEN.
1/4 C	BUTTER BUDS	ADD SEAFOOD TO SAUCE AND
2 OZ	DRY SACK SHERRY	SERVE IN A RING OF RICE.

BROILED OYSTERS w LEMON SAUCE   SERVES 4   FAT = 4 GM EA
(Including Sauce)

24	OYSTERS, DRAINED	PLACE EA IN THE BOTTOM OF A SHELL OR ARTICHOKE BOTTOM.
1 C	FAT-FREE BREAD CRUMBS	
2 T	BUTTER BUDS	COMBINE THESE & PLACE A DAB
1 T	FRESH THYME, OREGANO, MINCED	ON TOP OF EACH OYSTER.
1 T	GREEN ONIONS, MINCED	
1 T	FRESH PARSLEY, MINCED	
1 T	DRIED MARJORAM	
1/2 C	ONIONS, MINCED	SPRINKLE ONIONS OVER & BROIL FOR 2 MINUTES.

Spoon sauce (below) onto oysters & broil again until done.

LEMON SAUCE   3 CUPS   FAT = TR EA

1 C	DRY WHITE WINE	SIMMER THESE TO THICKEN.
1 C	SKIM MILK	
1/4 C	BUTTER BUDS	REMOVE FROM HEAT.
2 T	CORNSTARCH	TEMPER WITH EGG BEATERS &
1/4 C	FRESH LEMON JUICE	RETURN TO HEAT TO THICKEN.
	OYSTER JUICE, AS NEEDED	

!!!DO NOT OVER COOK!!!

1/2 C	EGG BEATERS	SALT & PEPPER TO TASTE.

SALMON & ASPARAGUS SAUCE

easy   SERVES 6   FAT = 8 GM EA
(Including Sauce)

12	3 OZ FILLETS (PINK OR CHUM)	WRAP AROUND ASPARAGUS AND
18	ASPARAGUS SPEARS, BLANCHED	SECURE WITH A PICK.
1 C	WHITE WINE	POACH FISH ROLLS UNTIL FLAKY.
1 C	FISH STOCK	
1	ONION, MINCED	REMOVE & KEEP WARM.

Serve Asparagus Sauce under fish. Sprinkle with more concasse if you like.

ASPARAGUS SAUCE

5 CUPS   FAT = TR EA

2 C	FAT-FREE CHICKEN STOCK	COOK THESE UNTIL VERY WELL
2 C	ASPARAGUS, SLICED THINLY	DONE & PUREE.
1 T	FRESH LEMON JUICE	ADD CONCASSE & SIMMER FOR 2
		MINUTES.
1 C	TOMATO CONCASSE (p 396)	

BAKED SCALLOPS w ORANGE SAUCE

 SERVES 6   FAT = 2.5 GM EA

1 LB	SEA SCALLOPS, CLEANED, DRIED	PLACE IN A SPRAYED DISH.
2 SM CANS	MANDARIN ORANGE SECTIONS (SAVE JUICE)	SPRAY THEM & BAKE AT 450 FOR 6 MINUTES.
1 LB	BAY SCALLOPS, CLEANED, DRIED	ADD THESE & SPRAY AGAIN.
1 t	CAVENDER'S GREEK SEASONING	SPRINKLE OVER & BAKE AT 400 FOR 4 MINUTES.

ORANGE SAUCE

1 1/2 CUPS   FAT = TR EA

1 C	NO-FAT SOUR CREAM	HEAT THESE & SPOON ON EACH PLATE.
1/2 C	MANDARIN ORANGES, CHOPPED	
2 T	BUTTER BUDS	
------	JUICE FROM MANDARINS AS NEEDED	PLACE THE SCALLOPS ON TOP.

SCALLOP KABOBS

 SERVES 4   FAT = 3.5 GM EA

2 LBS	SEA SCALLOPS, CLEANED, DRIED	THREAD ALL ALTERNATELY ON SKEWERS AND BRUSH WITH THE BUTTER MIXTURE.
1 LB	CARROTS, SLICED 1/2", STEAMED	
1 LB	ZUCCHINI, SLICED 1/2", STEAMED	GRILL OR BROIL.
1/4 C	HOT WATER	
1/4 C	BUTTER BUDS	COMBINE FOR THE BUTTER MIX.
1 t	CAVENDAR'S GREEK SEASONING	
1 T	GARLIC, MINCED	
2 T	PARMESAN CHEESE (OPTIONAL)	GRILL ONLY UNTIL OPAQUE.

TERIYAKI SCALLOP KABOBS

 SERVES 6   FAT = 2.5 GM EA

3 LBS	SEA SCALLOPS, CLEANED, DRIED	MARINATE FOR 2 HOURS.
2	RED ONION, QUARTERED, BLANCHED	
4	RED & GREEN PEPPERS, IN SQUARES	ALTERNATE ON SKEWERS &
1	GREEN ZUCCHINI, SLICED 1/2"	GRILL OR BROIL JUST UNTIL
1	YELLOW SQUASH, SLICED 1/2"	SCALLOPS ARE OPAQUE.
16	CHERRY TOMATOES	
2 C	SOY SAUCE	
1 C	DRY SHERRY	
1/4 C	BROWN SUGAR	BOIL MARINADE & BRUSH ON
6 CL	GARLIC, MINCED	WHILE GRILLING.
2 T	FRESH GINGER, PEELED, GRATED	
4 DROPS	LOUISIANA HOT SAUCE (OR TO TASTE)	SERVE ON BEDS OF RICE.

If you'd like to serve with pasta, thicken marinade with No-Fat Sour Cream & heat.

SEAFOOD KABOBS w VARIOUS SAUCES

SERVES 8   FAT = 2 GM EA

8 OZ	COD CUBES	COMBINE & CHILL THESE FOR 20 MINUTES.
8 OZ	HADDOCK CUBES	
8	CRAWFISH, SHELLED, DEVEINED	
16	SHRIMP, PEELED & DEVEINED	THREAD ON SKEWERS & BRUSH WITH BRANDY.
16	CLAMS, SHUCKED	
32 PC	VEGGIES OF YOUR CHOICE, BLANCHED	
1/4 C	HOT BRANDY	
1/4 C	BUTTER BUDS (DISSOLVED IN THE BRANDY)	GRILL OR BROIL.
1 t	OLD BAY SEASONING	
1 t	CAVENDER'S GREEK SEASONING	SERVE ON RICE OR PASTA.

VEGGIE CHOICES: ONIONS, RED & GREEN BELL PEPPERS, ZUCCHINI, MUSHROOMS
EGGPLANT, COOKED CARROTS, CHERRY TOMATOES, SQUASH

BASIL SAUCE

4 CUPS   FAT = 3 GM EA

2 C	FAT-FREE CHICKEN STOCK	HEAT THESE TO THICKEN.
1/4 C	BUTTER BUDS	
2 T	CORNSTARCH	REMOVE FROM HEAT. SLOWLY WHISK IN THE EGG BEATERS & HEAT JUST TO THICKEN.
1/4 C	BALSAMIC VINEGAR	
1/4 C	FRESH LEMON JUICE	
1 T	LEMON ZEST, MINCED	

!!!DO NOT OVER COOK!!!

3/4 C	EGG BEATERS (AS NEEDED)	FOLD IN BASIL AND TOSS WITH PASTA.
2 C	FRESH BASIL, CHOPPED	
1/4 C	PARMESAN (OPTIONAL-ADDS 8 GM FAT)	

FAJITA SAUCE

3 CUPS   FAT = TR EA

Make Basil Sauce, but omit the basil & Parmesan Cheese. Add these items:

1	JALAPENO PEPPER, MINCED
1 C	FRESH CILANTRO, CHOPPED
2 T	GROUND CORIANDER SEEDS

ROSEMARY SAUCE

3 CUPS   FAT = TR EA

Make Basil Sauce, but omit the basil & Parmesan Cheese. Add these items:

1 C	FRESH ROSEMARY, MINCED EXTREMELY FINE OR BLENDERIZED
1 C	FRESH OREGANO, CHOPPED
ZEST OF 2	ORANGES, MINCED

LOBSTER w CHAMPAGNE SAUCE

quick   SERVES 6   FAT = 2 GM EA
(Including Sauce)

6	1/2 LB MAIN LOBSTER TAILS	BOIL 5 MINUTES & CUT IN HALF.
	PAM BUTTER SPRAY	LOOSEN MEAT AND BRUSH WITH
6 T	BRANDY	BRANDY. BROIL 3 MINUTES OR
		UNTIL DONE.

CHAMPAGNE SAUCE

3 CUPS   FAT = TR EA

2 C	CHAMPAGNE	SIMMER THESE TO THICKEN.
1 C	SKIM MILK	
1/4 C	BUTTER BUDS	THIN WITH MORE SKIM MILK IF
3 T	ARROWROOT OR CORNSTARCH	NECESSARY.
1	RED ONION, MINCED FINE	
1	BOUQUET GARNI (4 SPRIGS PARSLEY, 1 BAY LEAF & 1 SPRIG THYME)	
------	SALT & PEPPER TO TASTE	REMOVE BOUQUET.

Spoon sauce onto plates. Place tails on sauce. Garnish w green seedless grapes & celery leaves.

STUFFED LOBSTER

SERVES 8   FAT = 3 GM EA

4	LOBSTER TAILS, BOILED 4 MIN.	CUT IN HALF & REMOVE MEAT.
8 OZ	SHRIMP, PEELED, DEVEINED, COOKED	DICE ALL SEAFOOD.
8 OZ	CRAB MEAT, PICKED CLEAN	
1	ONION, MINCED	COMBINE & ADD TO ABOVE.
1/2 C	CELERY, MINCED	
1/2 C	EGG BEATERS	
3	LOW-FAT HAMBURGER BUNS, MINCED & SOAKED IN SKIM MILK	
1/4 C	PIMENTO, CHOPPED	STUFF THE 8 HALF SHELLS AND
2 T	FRESH PARSLEY, CHOPPED	BAKE AT 325 FOR 20 MINUTES,
1 t	OLD BAY SEASONING	BASTING FREQUENTLY.
------	SALT & PEPPER	
1/2 C	DRY SHERRY	COMBINE FOR BASTING.
1/4 C	BUTTER BUDS	
1 T	FRESH LEMON JUICE	

LOBSTER NEWBURG

 easy   SERVES 4   FAT = 2 GM EA

2 T	BUTTER BUDS	SIMMER THESE TO THICKEN.
2 T	CORNSTARCH	(NOT TOO THICK)
2 C	SKIM MILK (MORE IF NECESSARY)	
3 T	DRY SHERRY	REMOVE FROM HEAT.
4 C	LOBSTER MEAT, COOKED, DICED	ADD THESE AND POUR INTO 4
1 LB	MUSHROOMS, SLICED, COOKED	SPRAYED GRATIN DISHES.
1/2 C	RED BELL PEPPER, MINCED, STEAMED	
1/4 C	EGG BEATERS	
2 T	FRESH PARSLEY, CHOPPED	BROIL UNTIL BUBBLY.
2 T	PARMESAN (OPTIONAL—ADDS 4 GM FAT)	SPRINKLE OVER EACH BEFORE BROILING, IF USING.

SEAFOOD CASSEROLE

easy   SERVES 4   FAT = 2 GM EA

1 1/2 C	WHITE WINE	SIMMER THESE FOR 5 MINUTES
1 LB	SEA SCALLOPS, CLEANED & HALVED	& SPOON THE SEAFOOD INTO A
1 LB	SHRIMP, PEELED & DEVEINED & TAILED	SPRAYED CASSEROLE.
1 t	SALT	
1/2 LB	MUSHROOMS, SLICED	ADD THESE TO LIQUID LEFT IN
1/2 C	RED ONION, MINCED	PAN & SIMMER FOR 5 MINUTES.
2 T	BUTTER BUDS	SPOON INTO CASSEROLE.
1/2 C	EVAPORATED SKIM MILK	PUREE, ADD TO LIQUID & HEAT
3 T	FLOUR	TO THICKEN.
		POUR ALL INTO CASSEROLE.

You can refrigerate for tomorrow's dinner, or top & cook now.

1 C	FAT-FREE BREAD CRUMBS	COMBINE AND SPRINKLE OVER
1/4 C	BUTTER BUDS (DISSOLVED IN MILK BELOW)	THE TOP.
1/4 C	HOT SKIM MILK	
2 T	FRESH PARSLEY, CHOPPED	BAKE AT 375 FOR 25 MINUTES.

BASIC FISH PAPILLOTE

Papillotes are made with sprayed foil, parchment or Phyllo (4 sprayed layers, stacked).

Each should be cut in the shape of a heart & sprayed with Pam Butter or Bertolli Olive Oil Spray. Individual portions of fish are placed on one side & then various herbs & other ingredients are added. The other side is then folded over, creating what looks like a lumpy half of a heart. Starting from the top of the heart, fold edges to seal, in about 1/2" folds, overlapping each fold until you reach the bottom of the heart. Fold this tip under. If using Phyllo, spray with Pam Butter or Bertolli Olive Oil Spray.

These are baked at 400 or 450 for approximately 10 minutes per inch of thickness of fish & extra ingredients.

If using parchment or phyllo, slit tops & serve surrounded by accompaniments.

If using foil, open and remove contents to plates & serve.

This style is not just a unique way of serving but helps retain the moisture of the fish.

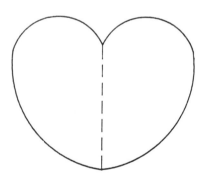

PLACE FISH ON RIGHT
SIDE AND FOLD
LEFT SIDE OVER

MAKE 1/2' FOLDS
AROUND EDGE

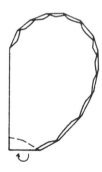

FOLD TIP UNDER

HADDOCK PAPILLOTE

SERVES 8   FAT = 2 GM EA

8	6 OZ FILLETS, RINSED, DRIED, S & P
6	POTATOES, JULIENNED, BLANCHED
1 T	BUTTER BUDS
4	TOMATOES, CHOPPED
2	RED ONIONS, DICED
2	GREEN PEPPERS, JULIENNED
1/4 C	FRESH OREGANO, CHOPPED
1/4 C	FRESH THYME, CHOPPED

LAY ON SPRAYED HEARTS.
TOP WITH REMAINING ITEMS.

SPRAY WITH PAM BUTTER SPRAY
& FOLD AS ON p 152.
BAKE AT 450 FOR 10 MIN. PER
INCH THICKNESS OF PACKAGE.

HALIBUT PAPILLOTE

SERVES 8   FAT = 4 GM EA

8	6 OZ FILLETS, RINSED, DRIED, S & P
2	CUCUMBERS, JULIENNED
4	CARROTS, JULIENNED, BLANCHED
2 LBS	ASPARAGUS TIPS, BLANCHED
4	GREEN ONIONS, SLICED THIN
1/2 C	FRESH TARRAGON LEAVES
------	CAVENDER'S GREEK SEASONING

LAY ON SPRAYED HEARTS.
TOP WITH REMAINING ITEMS.
SPRAY & FOLD AS ON p 152.

BAKE AT 450 FOR 10 MIN. PER
INCH THICKNESS OF PACKAGE.

WHITE SEA BASS PAPILLOTE

SERVES 8   FAT = 1 GM EA

8	6 OZ FILLETS, RINSED, DRIED, S & P
1 T	CHILI POWDER
2	ONIONS, SLICED THIN
2	CARROTS JULIENNED, BLANCHED
1	ZUCCHINI, JULIENNED
1 T	FRESH GINGER, PEELED, MINCED
1 T	SOY SAUCE

LAY ON SPRAYED HEARTS.
SPRINKLE OVER FISH.
TOP WITH REMAINING ITEMS.
SPRAY & FOLD AS ON p 152.

BAKE AT 450 FOR 10 MIN. PER
INCH THICKNESS OF PACKAGE.

BLUEFISH PAPILLOTE

SERVES 4   FAT = 7 GM EA

1	ZUCCHINI, SLICED THIN LENGTHWISE
4	6 OZ FILLETS, RINSED, DRIED, S & P
1	RED BELL PEPPER, JULIENNED
1	GREEN BELL PEPPER, JULIENNED
1 C	TOMATO CONCASSE (p 396)
4 CL	GARLIC, MINCED
1 T	DRIED ITALIAN HERBS
1 C	WHITE CORN KERNELS
1/4 C	NO-FAT SOUR CREAM

LAY ON SPRAYED HEARTS.
PLACE ON ZUCCHINI & TOP WITH
REMAINING INGREDIENTS.

SPRAY & FOLD AS ON p 152.
BAKE AT 400 FOR 10 MIN. PER
INCH OF THE THICKNESS OF THE
PACKAGE.

FLOUNDER PAPILLOTE

SERVES 4   FAT = 2 GM EA

1	ONION, SLICED THIN
4	6 OZ FILLETS, RINSED, DRIED, S & P
1	ZUCCHINI, SLICED THIN
1/2 C	FRESH BASIL, MINCED
1/4 C	DRY WHITE WINE
1/4 C	NO-FAT SOUR CREAM
1/4 C	TOMATO CONCASSE (p 396)

LAY ON SPRAYED HEARTS. PLACE ON THE ONIONS AND TOP WITH THESE.

SPRAY & FOLD AS ON p 152 AND BAKE AT 400 FOR 10 MINUTES PER INCH OF THICKNESS OF THE PACKAGE.

SEAFOOD PAPILLOTE

SERVES 8   FAT = 2 GM EA

8	4 OZ FLOUNDER, RINSED, DRIED, S & P
8	SHRIMP, CLEANED, SPLIT LENGTHWISE
8	BAY SCALLOPS, CLEANED
8	PACIFIC OYSTERS
16	SNOW PEAS, BLANCHED
8	MUSHROOMS, SLICED
1 T	FRESH GINGER, PEELED, MINCED
2 T	DRY SHERRY
2 T	SOY SAUCE

LAY ON SPRAYED HEARTS & TOP WITH THESE INGREDIENTS.

SPRAY & FOLD AS ON p 152 AND BAKE AT 450 FOR 10 MINUTES PER INCH OF THICKNESS OF THE PACKAGE.

TUNA PAPILLOTE

SERVES 8   FAT = 2 GM EA

8	6 OZ FILLETS, RINSED, DRIED, S & P
1 EA	RED & GREEN BELL PEPPER, JULIENNED
2	ONIONS, SLICED THIN
1	CELERY STALK, SLICED THIN
2 C	TOMATO CONCASSE (p 396)
4 CL	GARLIC, MINCED
1/4 C	LOUISIANA HOT SAUCE
2 T	WORCESTERSHIRE SAUCE
1 T	FRESH OREGANO
1 t	OLD BAY SEASONING
8 SL	LEMON, WITHOUT PEEL & SEEDS

LAY ON SPRAYED HEARTS & TOP WITH THESE INGREDIENTS.

SPRAY & FOLD AS ON p 152 AND BAKE AT 450 FOR 10 MINUTES PER INCH OF THICKNESS OF THE PACKAGE.

BROILED ORANGE ROUGHY

SERVES 4   FAT = 2 GM EA

4	6 OZ FILLETS, RINSED, DRIED, S & P
------	OLD BAY SEASONING
2	LEMONS, JUICED
4 DROPS	LIQUID SMOKE (OR TO TASTE)
1 T	BUTTER BUDS (DISSOLVED IN A LITTLE HOT WATER)

COMBINE ALL INGREDIENTS AND SPRINKLE OVER FISH. BROIL UNTIL FISH IS FLAKY TO FORK.

CURRIED ORANGE ROUGHY

SERVES 8   FAT = 2 GM EA

3/4 C	NO-FAT SOUR CREAM	COMBINE AND COAT FISH WITH
1/2 C	FAT-FREE MIRACLE WHIP	THESE INGREDIENTS.
1 T	FRESH LEMON JUICE	
1 T	LOUISIANA HOT SAUCE	
1 T	CURRY POWDER (OR TO TASTE)	
1 T	GARLIC, MINCED	
2 t	WORCESTERSHIRE SAUCE	
2 t	CREOLE MUSTARD (OR STONE GROUND)	
8	6 OZ FILLETS, RINSED, DRIED, S & P	
2 C	FAT-FREE SALTINE CRACKERS, CRUSHED	COMBINE AND SPRINKLE OVER.
2 T	BUTTER BUDS	BAKE AT 400 FOR 20 MINUTES
		OR UNTIL FLAKY TO FORK.

ITALIAN ORANGE ROUGHY

SERVES 6   FAT = 2 GM EA

6	6 OZ FILLETS, RINSED, S & P	SIMMER THESE UNTIL ALMOST
1/2 C	WHITE ZINFANDEL WINE	DONE. (8-10 MIN.)
2 T	FRESH LEMON JUICE	
2 T	BUTTER BUDS	
1	ONION, MINCED	
1/4 C	FRESH OREGANO, CHOPPED	
1/2 t	GROUND FENNEL SEEDS	
1 T	BUTTER BUDS	SPRINKLE THESE OVER THE FISH
1 LB	MUSHROOMS, SLICED	& BAKE AT 350 FOR 4 MINUTES
3 T	SHREDDED LOW-FAT MOZZARELLA	OR UNTIL FLAKY TO FORK.
2 T	PARMESAN CHEESE	

BBQ SALMON

easy

SERVES 12   FAT = 8 GM EA

12	6 OZ STEAKS (CHUM OR PINK)	COMBINE & CHILL THESE FOR 3
8 CL	GARLIC, MINCED	HOURS.
1	ONION, MINCED	REMOVE THE FISH.
1 C	BROWN SUGAR	BOIL MARINADE FOR BASTING.
1/2 C	SAKE (JAPANESE WINE)	
1/2 C	FRESH ORANGE JUICE	
1/4 C	SOY SAUCE	
2 T	BUTTER BUDS	
2 T	WORCESTERSHIRE SAUCE	GRILL OR BROIL THE FISH UNTIL
1 T	CAVENDER'S GREEK SEASONING	FLAKY TO FORK.
1 T	LOUISIANA HOT SAUCE	BASTE WELL.

SALMON w BASIL SAUCE

SERVES 4   FAT = 8 GM EA
                (Including Sauce)

4	6 OZ STEAKS (CHUM OR PINK)	SPRINKLE BOTH SIDES OF FISH
1/4 C	FRESH LEMON JUICE	& SPRAY.
1/4 C	CRACKED GREEN & RED PEPPERCORN	PRESS ONTO BOTH SIDES & FRY
2 T	CAPERS, MINCED	IN A VERY HOT, SPRAYED PAN.

Remove from pan, spry & bake at 350, (10 min. per inch of thickness).   Serve with Basil Sauce.

BASIL SAUCE

2 CUPS   FAT = TR EA

1 C	FAT-FREE CHICKEN STOCK	COMBINE & ADD THESE TO THE
1/4 C	FRESH LEMON JUICE	PAN USED ABOVE.
1/4 C	FRESH BASIL, CHOPPED	HEAT TO THICKEN.
1/4 C	DRY SHERRY OR MADEIRA WINE	
2 T	CORNSTARCH	REMOVE FROM HEAT, WHISK IN
2 T	BUTTER BUDS	EGG BEATERS. RETURN TO HEAT
		SLIGHTLY.
1/2 C	EGG BEATERS !!!DO NOT OVER COOK!!!	
	SALT & PEPPER TO TASTE.	THIN w SKIM MILK IF NEEDED.

SALMON BEARNAISE

SERVES 6   FAT = 8 GM EA
                (Including Sauce)

6	6 OZ STEAKS (CHUM OR PINK), S & P	
1/4 C	FRESH LEMON JUICE	COMBINE & BRUSH ON FISH.
2 T	BUTTER BUDS	GRILL OR BROIL UNTIL FLAKY
1 t	SUGAR	TO FORK.
		SERVE WITH BEARNAISE SAUCE.

BEARNAISE SAUCE

2 CUPS   FAT = TR EA

1 C	WHITE WINE OR SHERRY VINEGAR	COMBINE & HEAT TO THICKEN.
1/2 C	GREEN ONION, MINCED	
1/4 C	FRESH TARRAGON, CHOPPED (or to taste)	
1/4 C	BUTTER BUDS	REMOVE FROM HEAT & WHISK
1 T	CORNSTARCH	IN EGG BEATERS.
		RETURN TO HEAT BRIEFLY,
1/2 C	EGG BEATERS !!!DO NOT OVER COOK!!!	
	SALT & PEPPER TO TASTE.	THIN w SKIM MILK IF NEEDED.

SALMON IN BLUEBERRY SAUCE

SERVES 8   FAT = 8 GM EA
(Including Sauce)

8	6 OZ STEAKS (CHUM OR PINK)	SIMMER FOR 10 MINUTES.
2 QT	FAT-FREE CHICKEN STOCK	REMOVE FISH & KEEP WARM.
3 T	BUTTER BUDS	REDUCE STOCK TO 3 CUPS AND STRAIN.

BLUEBERRY SAUCE

2 CUPS   FAT = TR EA

1 C	BERRIES (BLUEBERRIES, RASPBERRIES, YOUR CHOICE)	
3 T	BUTTER BUDS	PUREE THESE, ADD TO ABOVE &
3 T	CORNSTARCH	HEAT TO THICKEN.
2 T	FRESH LEMON JUICE	
------	SKIM MILK IF NEEDED TO THIN	
1 C	BERRIES (SAME AS ABOVE)	ADD & SIMMER 2 MINUTES. SALT & PEPPER TO TASTE.

Spoon sauce onto plate & place fish on top.

SALMON w SUN-DRIED TOMATOES

SERVES 8   FAT = 8 GM EA
(Including Sauces)

8	6 OZ STEAKS (CHUM OR PINK), S & P	COMBINE & DRIZZLE THESE ON
1/4 C	FRESH LEMON JUICE, HOT	THE FISH.
1 T	BUTTER BUDS (DISSOLVED IN THE JUICE	GRILL OR BROIL UNTIL FLAKY TO
1 t	SUGAR	FORK.

SUN-DRIED TOMATO SAUCE

4 CUPS   FAT = TR EA

24	SUN-DRIED TOMATOES, BLANCHED 5 MIN. IN WATER	
1 C	FAT-FREE CHICKEN STOCK	PUREE THESE INGREDIENTS.
1/2	ONION, MINCED	S & P TO TASTE & HEAT.
1/4 C	FRESH CILANTRO, CHOPPED	
4 CL	GARLIC, MINCED	
1/2	JALAPENO PEPPER, SEEDED & MINCED	SPOON SAUCE ONTO PLATES &
2 T	BUTTER BUDS	DECORATE WITH GARLIC SAUCE.

GARLIC SAUCE

2 CUPS   FAT = TR EA

24 CL	GARLIC	SPRAY WITH PAM & BAKE AT 375 FOR 45 MINUTES.
1 C	NO-FAT SOUR CREAM	
1/2 C	FAT-FREE MIRACLE WHIP	ADD TO ABOVE & PUREE.
1 T	FRESH LEMON JUICE	
1 t	CAVENDER'S GREEK SEASONING	SPOON INTO A SQUEEZE BOTTLE.

Decorate the tomato sauce & place fish on top.

GINGER SALMON

SERVES 8   FAT = 8 GM EA

8	6 OZ STEAKS (CHUM OR PINK)
1/2 C	FRESH LEMON JUICE, HOT
1/4 C	LEMON ZEST, MINCED
1/4 C	FRESH GINGER, PEELED, MINCED
2 T	BUTTER BUDS (DISSOLVED IN THE JUICE)
2 t	CAVENDER'S GREEK SEASONING
1 t	SUGAR

COMBINE & CHILL 15 MINUTES.
REMOVE THE FISH.
BOIL THE MARINADE.

GRILL OR BROIL THE FISH UNTIL
FLAKY, BASTING WELL.

CURRIED SCALLOPS

SERVES 4   FAT = 2 GM EA

1 C	FAT-FREE CHICKEN STOCK
1 C	CLAM BROTH
3 T	FRESH LEMON JUICE
3 T	CURRY POWDER
3	LEEKS, WASHED WELL, JULIENNED

SIMMER THESE FOR 4 MINUTES.

REMOVE FROM HEAT.

2 T	BUTTER BUDS
2 T	CORNSTARCH
1/4 C	SKIM MILK

PUREE, ADD & HEAT TO THICKEN.
SERVE UNDER THE SCALLOPS.

2 LBS	SEA SCALLOPS, CLEANED, DRIED WELL
4 CL	GARLIC, MINCED

BROWN IN A PAM-SPRAYED PAN
UNTIL OPAQUE.

ORIENTAL SCALLOPS

easy

SERVES 8   FAT = 2 GM EA

2 LBS	SEA SCALLOPS, CLEANED
1 LB	MUSHROOMS, SLICED
1/2 C	SOY SAUCE
1/2 C	RICE WINE VINEGAR
1/2 C	DRY SHERRY
1/4 C	BROWN SUGAR
1 t	CRUSHED RED PEPPER FLAKES
2 EA	RED & GREEN BELL PEPPERS, JULIENNED
2	ONIONS, JULIENNED
1 T	CORNSTARCH
2 T	BUTTER BUDS

COMBINE & CHILL FOR 1 HOUR.

REMOVE THE SCALLOPS.

SIMMER THE REST 3 MINUTES.

2 C	BAMBOO SHOOTS, DRAINED
2 C	WATER CHESTNUTS, DRAINED

ADD SCALLOPS & THESE TO THE
ABOVE & STIR FRY UNTIL THE
SCALLOPS ARE OPAQUE.

SCALLOPS in VERMOUTH

quick   SERVES 6   FAT = 2 GM EA

3 LBS	SEA SCALLOPS, CLEANED, DRIED	PLACE IN A SPRAYED DISH.
6 T	DRY VERMOUTH	COMBINE & SPRINKLE OVER.
1/4 C	PERNOD LIQUEUR	
4 CL	GARLIC, MINCED	BROIL UNTIL OPAQUE.

If you're not fond of the taste of pernod, you may substitute gin.

VODKA SCALLOPS

    easy   SERVES 8   FAT = 2 GM EA

3 LBS	SEA SCALLOPS, CLEANED	COMBINE & CHILL 4 HOURS.
1 1/2 C	NO-FAT SOUR CREAM	
3/4 C	VODKA	THREAD ON SKEWERS WITH THE
1/4 C	DILL, CHOPPED (OPTIONAL)	LIME SLICES AND BROIL UNTIL
2 T	LEMON ZEST, MINCED	OPAQUE.

LEMON CAPERED SCALLOPS

quick   SERVES 6   FAT = 2 GM EA

3 LBS	SEA SCALLOPS, CLEANED, DRIED WELL	BROWN IN SPRAYED PAN.
1 t	CAVENDER'S GREEK SEASONING	REMOVE & KEEP WARM.
1/4 C	FRESH LEMON JUICE	ADD TO THE HOT PAN AND TOSS
1/4 C	CAPERS, CHOPPED	JUST ENOUGH TO WILT SPINACH.
2	GREEN ONIONS, SLICED	
2 t	RED PEPPERCORNS, CRUSHED	
2 LBS	SPINACH, WASHED, TORN	SERVE UNDER SCALLOPS.

SCALLOPS & MUSHROOMS

    quick   SERVES 6   FAT = 2 GM EA

1/2 C	WATER	SIMMER THESE FOR 3 MINUTES.
1/2 C	DRY WHITE WINE	REMOVE SCALLOPS AND KEEP
2 LBS	SEA SCALLOPS, CLEANED	WARM.
2 T	BUTTER BUDS	
1	ONION, DICED	ADD & SIMMER FOR 3 MINUTES.
1 LB	MUSHROOMS, SLICED	REMOVE FROM HEAT.
1 C	SKIM MILK	WHISK THESE WELL, ADD TO THE
2 T	CORNSTARCH	ABOVE & HEAT TO THICKEN.
1 T	WORCESTERSHIRE SAUCE	
1 T	KETCHUP	RETURN SCALLOPS TO HEAT 1
		MINUTE.

Serve over pasta or rice & garnish with sliced green onions.

SEAFOOD CURRY

easy   SERVES 10   FAT = 3 GM EA

2 C	SHRIMP, CLEANED, COOKED, HALVED	SIMMER THESE UNTIL DONE.
2 C	SEA SCALLOPS, CLEANED, COOKED, HALVED	
2 C	FLOUNDER CUBES, COOKED	
5 C	CURRY BASE (SEE BELOW)	SERVE OVER RICE OR PASTA.
5 C	WATER	

CURRY BASE

quick   10 CUPS   FAT = TR EA

2 C	ONION, DICED	SIMMER THESE FOR 5 MINUTES.
1/2 C	CELERY, MINCED	
2 CL	GARLIC, MINCED	
2 C	WATER	
4	KNORR CHICKEN BOUILLON CUBE	
2	KNORR VEGGIE BOUILLON CUBE	
2 C EA	SKIM MILK, APPLESAUCE	COMBINE & ADD THESE.
1 C	RAISINS	SIMMER FOR 30 MINUTES.
1 C	CURRY POWDER	
3/4 C	FLOUR	SALT & PEPPER TO TASTE.
3/4 C	TOMATO PASTE	
3 T	LEMON JUICE	
3 T	BUTTER BUDS	YOU CAN FREEZE AT THIS POINT
3 T	BROWN SUGAR	IN 1 CUP PORTIONS.

SEAFOOD SUPREME

SERVES 12   FAT = 3 GM EA

1 C	FAT-FREE CHICKEN STOCK	SIMMER THESE FOR 5 MINUTES.
1 C EA	ONION, GREEN PEPPER, DICED	
4 CL	GARLIC, MINCED (OR TO TASTE)	
3 T	BUTTER BUDS	
2 LBS	SHRIMP, PEELED & DEVEINED & TAILED	ADD & SIMMER UNTIL SHRIMP
1 LB	SEA SCALLOPS, CLEANED, SLICED	TURN PINK.
1/2 LB	MUSHROOMS, SLICED	REMOVE FROM HEAT.
4	GREEN ONION, SLICED	
2 T	CORNSTARCH	COMBINE WELL, WHISK IN AND
2 C	SKIM MILK	HEAT TO THICKEN.
1/2 C	DRY WHITE WINE	FILL 12 SPRAYED RAMEKINS AND
2 T	WORCESTERSHIRE SAUCE	TOP w CRUSHED 0-FAT SALTINES.
1/4 t	OLD BAY SEASONING	
1 LB	CRAB MEAT, PICKED CLEAN	BAKE AT 350 UNTIL BUBBLY.

Or you could skip the ramekins & serve over pasta.

SAFFRON SHELLFISH

SERVES 8   FAT = 1 GM EA

1 C	WILD RICE	SIMMER THESE COVERED FOR 45 MINUTES.
3 C	FAT-FREE CHICKEN STOCK, BOILING	
1	ONION, DICED	
ZEST OF 1	LEMON, MINCED	
1 T	FRESH LEMON JUICE	SALT & PEPPER TO TASTE.
1 t	SAFFRON	
		ADD THESE, COVER AND SIMMER UNTIL SHELLS OPEN.
32	MUSSELS, SCRUBBED	
32	SMALL CLAMS, SCRUBBED	PLACE ON BEDS OF RICE.
3 C	DRY WHITE WINE	STRAIN THE LIQUID.
1 C	EVAPORATED SKIM MILK	ADD THESE TO THE STRAINED
1 t	SAFFRON, CRUSHED	LIQUID & SIMMER 4 MINUTES.
1 LB	BAY SCALLOPS	POUR OVER MUSSELS & CLAMS.
1	LEMON, PEELED, PITHED, MINCED	COMBINE & SPRINKLE ON EACH
2 T	FRESH CHIVES, CHOPPED	SERVING.

Use only closed shells to cook. After cooking, discard any unopened shells.

SHRIMP ALFREDO

easy   SERVES 8   FAT = 8 GM EA

2 C	EVAPORATED SKIM MILK	SIMMER THESE FOR 5 MINUTES.
1 C	NO-FAT SOUR CREAM	
1/2 C	PIMENTO STRIPS	
1 1/4 C	PARMESAN CHEESE	ADD WHEN ALMOST READY TO
48	JUMBO SHRIMP, CLEANED & COOKED	SERVE & HEAT THROUGH.
1/2 C	WINE OR VERMOUTH—TO THIN IF NEEDED	TOSS SOME SAUCE w COOKED PASTA. SPOON REST OF SAUCE
1/4 C	FRESH PARSLEY, CHOPPED	OVER PASTA & SPRINKLE WITH
1/4 C	GREEN ONIONS (GREEN PART ONLY), MINCED	PARSLEY & ONIONS.

BUFFALO SHRIMP

easy   SERVES 6   FAT = 2 GM EA

3 LBS	SHRIMP, PEELED & DEVEINED	MARINATE IN A ZIPLOC BAG FOR 15 MINUTES.
1 T	LOUISIANA HOT SAUCE	
1/4 C	PICK-A-PEPPER SAUCE	
1/4 C	FAT-FREE CHICKEN STOCK	
1 T	BUTTER BUDS	STIR-FRY ALL UNTIL PINK.
8 CL	GARLIC, MINCED	
8	GREEN ONIONS, MINCED	SERVE OVER COOKED PASTA.

You might like to thicken the sauce with No-Fat Sour Cream.

CITRUS SHRIMP

SERVES 12   FAT = 2 GM EA

5 LBS	LARGE SHRIMP, PEELED & DEVEINED	MARINATE IN A ZIPLOC BAG FOR
1 C	FRESH ORANGE JUICE	15 MINUTES.
2	LIMES, JUICED	REMOVE SHRIMP & BAKE AT 375
6 CL	GARLIC, MINCED	UNTIL SHRIMP TURN PINK.
------	SALT, PEPPER & DRIED ITALIAN HERBS	

Serve on a bed of rice & garnish with peas & pimentos.

COCONUT SHRIMP

SERVES 8   FAT = 2 GM EA

1 C	EGG BEATERS	COMBINE FOR DIPPING SHRIMP.
3 T	COCONUT FLAVORING	
3 C	FAT-FREE SALTINES, CRUSHED FINELY	FOR DREDGING SHRIMP.
48	SHRIMP, PEELED, DEVEINED & SPLIT	DIP SHRIMP IN THE EGG MIX & DREDGE IN CRUMBS.

Spray pan with Pam Butter Spray, fry or bake until pink. You could omit the crumbs totally if you like.

SHRIMP CREOLE

SERVES 8   FAT = 2 GM EA

2 C	FAT-FREE CHICKEN STOCK	SIMMER THESE FOR 30 MINUTES.
2 C	ONIONS, DICED	
1 C	CELERY, MINCED	
10 CL	GARLIC, MINCED	
1 EA	RED & GREEN BELL PEPPER, DICED	
12 OZ	CANNED WHOLE TOMATOES, CHOPPED	
12 OZ	CANNED TOMATO SAUCE	SALT & PEPPER TO TASTE.
12 OZ	TOMATO PASTE	
1 C	CLAM BROTH (AS NEEDED)	
1 T	BUTTER BUDS	
2 t	SUGAR	
1/2 t	OLD BAY SEASONING	
3. LBS	SHRIMP, PEELED & DEVEINED & TAILED	ADD SHRIMP & SIMMER UNTIL PINK. SERVE OVER RICE.

SHRIMP CURRY

 SERVES 8 FAT = 2 GM EA

1 C	FAT-FREE CHICKEN STOCK	SIMMER THESE FOR 5 MINUTES.
1 C	GREEN BELL PEPPER, DICED	
1 C	ONION, DICED	
36	MUSHROOMS, SLICED	
3 CL	GARLIC, MINCED	
1/2 C	GOLDEN RAISINS	
2 T	CURRY POWDER (OR TO TASTE)	
1 t	WORCESTERSHIRE SAUCE	
1/2 t	DRY MUSTARD	
48	SHRIMP, PEELED & DEVEINED & TAILED	ADD & SIMMER UNTIL SHRIMP
2 C	NO-FAT SOUR CREAM	TURN PINK. S & P TO TASTE.

Serve with rice & various condiments: Bananas, dates, apples, onions, etc.

CURRIED SHRIMP & SNOW PEAS

 SERVES 8 FAT = 2 GM EA

2 C	FAT-FREE CHICKEN STOCK	SIMMER THESE FOR 6 MINUTES.
2	RED BELL PEPPERS, SLICED IN STRIPS	
2	ONIONS, SLICED & QUARTERED	
2 CL	GARLIC, MINCED	
3 T	CURRY POWDER	
1 T	COCONUT FLAVORING	
1 t	FRESH GINGER, PEELED, GRATED	
1/2 t	CRUSHED RED PEPPER FLAKES	
48	SHRIMP, PEELED & DEVEINED & TAILED	ADD & SIMMER UNTIL SHRIMP
20 OZ	SNOW PEAS	TURN PINK.
1 C	NO-FAT SOUR CREAM	SERVE OVER RICE.
------	MORE COCONUT FLAVORING IF YOU'D LIKE	

SPICY ITALIAN SHRIMP

 SERVES 8 FAT = 2 GM EA

48	SHRIMP, PEELED & DEVEINED	MARINATE IN A ZIPLOC BAG
1 EA	RED, GREEN & YELLOW PEPPER, MINCED	FOR 1 HOUR.
1 T	ITALIAN HERBS, CRUSHED	
1 T	FENNEL SEEDS, GROUND	REMOVE SHRIMP & BROIL 1 MIN.
2 t	CRUSHED RED PEPPER FLAKES	TURN, TOP WITH PEPPERS.
1/2 t	GROUND GINGER	BROIL UNTIL SHRIMP ARE PINK.

SPICY GINGER SHRIMP

(*easy*)   SERVES 4   FAT = 2 GM EA

3 OZ	EGG BEATERS	TOSS THESE AND STIR-FRY UNTIL
24 LGE	SHRIMP, PEELED & DEVEINED & TAILED	THE SHRIMP ARE PINK.
1 t	GROUND GINGER	REMOVE FROM PAN.
1 C	FAT-FREE CHICKEN STOCK	ADD & STIR-FRY 3 MINUTES.
1 T	BUTTER BUDS	
1	CARROT, JULIENNED	
1 EA	GREEN & YELLOW PEPPER, JULIENNED	
2 t	CRUSHED RED PEPPER FLAKES	
1 T	SOY SAUCE	COMBINE THESE WELL, ADD TO
1 T	SUGAR	ABOVE & HEAT TO THICKEN.
1 T	FRESH GINGER, PEELED, GRATED	
1/2 C	KETCHUP	RETURN SHRIMP TO PAN & HEAT.
3 T	WATER	
1 T	CORNSTARCH	SALT & PEPPER TO TASTE.

You can either toss with pasta or serve over rice.

FLAMING SHRIMP

SERVES 4   FAT = 4 GM EA

1 C	COOKED TURKEY BREASTS, GROUND	COMBINE THESE AND STUFF THE
8	WATER CHESTNUTS, MINCED	SHRIMP.
6	GREEN ONIONS, MINCED	
4	MUSHROOMS, MINCED	CHILL FOR 15 MINUTES.
2 T	EGG BEATERS	
2 t	SOY SAUCE	
1/2 t	SALT	SPRAY SHRIMP & BROIL UNTIL
1/2 t	SUGAR	THEY TURN PINK.
24	SHRIMP, PEELED, DEVEINED & BUTTERFLIED	
1 C	FAT-FREE CHICKEN STOCK	SIMMER THESE, COVERED, FOR 5
2 LBS	CHINESE CABBAGE, SLICED	MINUTES.
6 T	SUGAR	
1/2 t	SALT	
1/4 t	5 SPICE POWDER	
1/2 C	WATER	COMBINE WELL, ADD TO ABOVE
1 T	CORNSTARCH	& HEAT TO THICKEN.

Arrange shrimp on cabbage mixture. Spoon 2 T hot rum over each & ignite.

SHRIMP JAMBALAYA

SERVES 4   FAT = 4 GM EA

24	SHRIMP, PEELED & DEVEINED & TAILED	MARINATE FOR 15 MINUTES.
2 T	FRESH LEMON JUICE	SET ASIDE.
1 T	WORCESTERSHIRE SAUCE	

2 C	FAT-FREE CHICKEN STOCK	SIMMER THESE FOR 5 MINUTES.
2 C	ONIONS, DICED	
1/2 C EA	RED, YELLOW & GREEN PEPPERS, DICED	
1/2 C	CELERY, MINCED	
4 CL	GARLIC, MINCED	
2 T	BUTTER BUDS	

2 C	TOMATO, DICED	ADD THESE AND SIMMER FOR 3
2 T	TOMATO PASTE	MINUTES.
1 C	99% FAT-FREE TURKEY HAM, DICED	
1 t	SUGAR (OPTIONAL)	ADD THE SHRIMP.

1/2 C	DRY WHITE WINE	COMBINE THESE WELL & ADD TO
2 T	CORNSTARCH	ABOVE TO THICKEN.
1 T	FRESH LEMON JUICE	SERVE OVER RICE AND GARNISH
		WITH PINEAPPLE & PARSLEY.

SHRIMP IN LOBSTER SAUCE

SERVES 8   FAT = 3 GM EA

3 C	FAT-FREE CHICKEN STOCK	SIMMER THESE FOR 30 MINUTES.
ALL OF	SHRIMP SHELLS FROM BELOW, CHOPPED	
1 t	SAFFRON	

12 CL	GARLIC, MINCED	STRAIN THE STOCK, ADD THESE
12	GREEN ONIONS, SLICED	& SIMMER FOR 8 MINUTES.
12 OZ	TURKEY BREASTS, GROUND	

48	SHRIMP, PEELED & DEVEINED & TAILED	ADD THESE AND SIMMER UNTIL
1/4 C	DRY SHERRY	THE SHRIMP TURN PINK.
1/4 C	SOY SAUCE	
1/4 C	BLACK BEAN SAUCE	
2 T	KETCHUP	
1 T	SUGAR	
1/2 C	LOBSTER JUICE (OR BOTTLED CLAM BROTH)	

| 1/2 C | CLAM BROTH | COMBINE WELL, WHISK IN AND |
| 2 T | CORNSTARCH | HEAT TO THICKEN. |

| 1/2 | EGG BEATERS | WHISK IN, HEAT & SERVE OVER |
| | | RICE. |

HOT & SPICY PRAWNS

 SERVES 6   FAT = 2 GM EA

24	SHRIMP, PEELED & DEVEINED	TOSS THESE & STIR-FRY UNTIL
1/2 C	EGG BEATERS	SHRIMP TURN PINK.
2 CL	GARLIC, MINCED	REMOVE THE SHRIMP AND KEEP
1/2 t	CAVENDER'S GREEK SEASONING	WARM.

2 C	FAT-FREE CHICKEN STOCK	ADD THESE AND SIMMER FOR 6
12	GREEN ONIONS, SLICED	MINUTES.
2	TOMATOES, CHOPPED	
1 T	BROWN SUGAR	
1 T	PICK-A-PEPPER SAUCE	
1/2 t	CRUSHED RED PEPPER FLAKES	RETURN THE SHRIMP.
------	LOUISIANA HOT SAUCE, TO TASTE	

3 T	CORNSTARCH	COMBINE WELL, WHISK IN AND
1 C	FAT-FREE STOCK	HEAT TO THICKEN.
		SERVE OVER RICE.

QUICK & SPICY SHRIMP

 SERVES 8   FAT = 2 GM EA

48	SHRIMP, PEELED & DEVEINED	MARINATE IN A ZIPLOC BAG FOR
2 T	FRESH GINGER, PEELED, MINCED	15 MINUTES.
2	LIMES, JUICED	
4 DROPS	LIQUID SMOKE	REMOVE SHRIMP & BAKE AT 450
1 t	CAVENDER'S GREEK SEASONING	FOR 10 MINUTES OR UNTIL THE
1/2 t	CRUSHED RED PEPPER FLAKES (OR TO TASTE)	SHRIMP TURN PINK.

QUICK SHRIMP & MUSHROOMS

easy SERVES 4   FAT = 2 GM EA

24	SHRIMP, PEELED & DEVEINED	COMBINE & CHILL THESE 30
		MINUTES.
1/4 C	SOY SAUCE	
1/4 C	DRY SHERRY	
1/2 t	FRESH GINGER, PEELED, GRATED	

1 C	FAT-FREE CHICKEN STOCK	SIMMER THESE FOR 5 MINUTES.
2	CELERY STALKS, w LEAVES, SLICED THIN	
6	GREEN ONIONS, SLICED	
2 T	BUTTER BUDS	ADD SHRIMP MIXTURE & SIMMER
1 LB	MUSHROOMS, SLICED	UNTIL SHRIMP TURN PINK.

1 C	NO-FAT SOUR CREAM	STIR IN BEFORE SERVING OVER
1 t	WORCESTERSHIRE SAUCE	RICE OR PASTA.

SHRIMP & VEGGIES

 SERVES 4 FAT = 2 GM EA

2 C	FAT-FREE CHICKEN STOCK	SIMMER THESE FOR 5 MINUTES.
1	ONION, DICED	
1	GREEN PEPPER, DICED	
1	ZUCCHINI, SLICED	
4 CL	GARLIC, MINCED	
2 C	TOMATOES, CHOPPED	
2 T	BUTTER BUDS	
1 t	BALSAMIC VINEGAR	
1 t	CRUSHED RED PEPPER FLAKES	
24	SHRIMP, PEELED & DEVEINED & TAILED	ADD & SIMMER 5 MINUTES OR
4	ARTICHOKE BOTTOMS, QUARTERED	UNTIL SHRIMP TURN PINK.
1/2 t	OLD BAY SEASONING	SALT & PEPPER TO TASTE.

Serve with brown & wild rice or toss veggies with pasta & place shrimp on top.

SHRIMP w CREAM VERMOUTH

 SERVES 8 FAT = 2 GM EA

48	SHRIMP, PEELED & DEVEINED & TAILED	TOSS & FRY SHRIMP IN A PAN
1/2 C	EGG BEATERS	SPRAYED WITH OLIVE OIL UNTIL
4 CL	GARLIC, MINCED	THEY TURN PINK.
1 C	MUSHROOMS, SLICED	HEAT THESE & ADD TO ABOVE.
1 C	DRY VERMOUTH	
1 C	FAT-FREE CHICKEN STOCK	
1 C	NO-FAT SOUR CREAM	SALT & PEPPER TO TASTE.

STUFFED SHRIMP   SERVES 6   FAT = 4 GM EA

1 LB	CRAB MEAT, PICKED CLEAN	COMBINE THESE AND STUFF THE
1 C	ONION, MINCED	SHRIMP.
1/4 C	CELERY, MINCED	
1/4 C	GREEN PEPPER, MINCED	SPRINKLE WITH LEMON JUICE &
1/4 C	EGG BEATERS	PAPRIKA & SPRAY WITH PAM.
1 T	BUTTER BUDS	
1 C	FAT-FREE BREAD CRUMBS, SOAKED IN SKIM MILK	
1/3 C	NO-FAT SOUR CREAM (+/- AS NEEDED)	
1/2 t	OLD BAY SEASONING	
1/4 t	CRUSHED RED PEPPER FLAKES	
36	LARGE SHRIMP, PEELED, DEVEINED & BUTTERFLIED	
2	LEMONS, JUICED	BAKE AT 400 FOR 15 MINUTES
------	PAPRIKA	OR UNTIL SHRIMP TURN PINK.

SHRIMP STIR-FRY   SERVES 4   FAT = 2 GM EA

2 C	FAT-FREE CHICKEN STOCK	SIMMER THESE FOR 3 MINUTES.
6 SL	FRESH GINGER	
1	CARROT, SLICED DIAGONALLY	
1	ONION, SLICED LENGTHWISE	
1	CELERY STALK, SLICED DIAGONALLY	
1	YELLOW BELL PEPPER, JULIENNED	ADD THESE AND SIMMER FOR 3
6	ASPARAGUS SPEARS, SLICED DIAGONALLY	MORE MINUTES.
1 C	MUSHROOMS, SLICED	
4 OZ CAN	SLICED WATER CHESTNUTS, DRAINED	ADD AND SIMMER UNTIL SHRIMP
24	SHRIMP, PEELED & DEVEINED & TAILED	TURN PINK.
1/2 C	SOY SAUCE	COMBINE WELL, WHISK IN AND
1/2 C	CLAM BROTH	HEAT TO THICKEN.
2 T	CORNSTARCH	REMOVE GINGER SLICES.

SCALLOP STIR-FRY   SERVES 4   FAT = 4 GM EA

Make as above substituting scallops & snow peas for the shrimp & asparagus. Substitute 1/4 C dry sherry for 1/4 C of the clam broth.

TARRAGON SHRIMP

SERVES 6   FAT = 2 GM EA

2 C	FAT-FREE CHICKEN STOCK	SIMMER THESE FOR 5 MINUTES.
2	ONIONS, MINCED	
1	RED BELL PEPPER, MINCED	
8 CL	GARLIC, MINCED	SALT & PEPPER TO TASTE.
6 SPRIGS	FRESH TARRAGON, STEMMED & CHOPPED	
2 T	BUTTER BUDS	
1/2 t	CAVENDER'S GREEK SEASONING (OR TO TASTE)	
36	SHRIMP, PEELED & DEVEINED	TOSS WELL, ADD AND SIMMER
2 T	CORNSTARCH	UNTIL SHRIMP TURN PINK.

Serve with pasta or rice, & always French Bread for soaking up the sauce.

SHRIMP & SCALLOP KABOBS

SERVES 4   FAT = 3 GM EA

1 LB	SHRIMP, PEELED & DEVEINED	MARINATE IN A ZIPLOC BAG FOR
1 LB	SEA SCALLOPS, CLEANED	15 MINUTES.
1 T	FRESH CILANTRO, CHOPPED	
3 CL	GARLIC, MINCED	THREAD ON SKEWERS & BROIL
3	ORANGES, JUICED	UNTIL SHRIMP TURN PINK.
1 T	BRANDY	BASTE TWICE.

SHRIMP CAKES

SERVES 4   FAT = 2 GM EA

20 OZ	SHRIMP, COOKED, CHOPPED	COMBINE ALL INGREDIENTS AND
1 C	RICE, COOKED	FORM 8 PATTIES.
1	ONION, MINCED	
1/4 C	EGG BEATERS	FRY IN A SPRAYED PAN UNTIL
1/2 t	SALT	GOLDEN.
1/2 t	FRESH LEMON JUICE	
1/4 t	DRY MUSTARD	
1/4 t	OLD BAY SEASONING	
1-2 T	FAT-FREE MIRACLE WHIP AS NEEDED TO HOLD SHAPE	

SNAPPER w ARTICHOKES & PEPPERS SERVES 8 FAT = 3 GM EA

3	ONIONS, SLICED	PLACE IN A SPRAYED DISH.
1	FISH, 4-6 LBS, CLEANED, DRIED	MAKE 12 SLITS, 1/2" DEEP AND
6 CL	GARLIC, SLICED	INSERT GARLIC & GINGER.
12 SL	FRESH GINGER	PLACE FISH ON ONIONS.
1 EA	RED, YELLOW, GREEN PEPPER, SLICED	TOP WITH REMAINING VEGGIES.
10	GREEN ONIONS, SLICED	
3 C	MARINATED ARTICHOKE HEARTS, DRAINED, TRIMMED WELL	
1 LB	NEW POTATOES, COOKED 10 MIN., QUARTERED	
1 T	DRIED SAGE	SALT & PEPPER WELL.
2	BAY LEAVES (REMEMBER TO REMOVE)	
		DRIZZLE WINE OVER ALL AND
1 C	DRY WHITE WINE	COVER TIGHTLY WITH FOIL.

Bake at 375 for approximately 1 hour or until fish flakes easily to a fork.

STUFFED SNAPPER SERVES 6 FAT = 3 GM EA

1 C	FAT-FREE CHICKEN STOCK	SIMMER THESE FOR 5 MINUTES.
2 C	ONIONS, DICED	
1 C	CELERY, MINCED	
8 OZ	SNAPPER, DICED	ADD & SIMMER 5 MINUTES.
8 OZ	SHRIMP, PEELED, DEVEINED, CHOPPED	
1/2 t	SUGAR	
------	SALT, PEPPER & CAYENNE TO TASTE	
6 SL	STALE FAT-FREE BREAD, CUBED	SOAK THESE & ADD TO ABOVE.
1 C	EGG BEATERS	STUFF THE FILLETS & ROLL OR
		FOLD UP.
6	6 OZ FILLETS, RINSED, DRIED, S & P	BAKE AT 400 FOR 10 MINUTES
		PER INCH OF THICKNESS.

ITALIAN SNAPPER *easy* SERVES 4 FAT = 4 GM EA

4	6 OZ FILLETS, RINSED, DRIED, S & P	PLACE IN A SPRAYED DISH.
2 T	FRESH LIME JUICE	DRIZZLE OVER & SIT 15 MINUTES.
14 OZ	CANNED TOMATOES, DRAINED & CHOPPED	COMBINE THESE & SPOON OVER
2 OZ	CANNED GREEN CHILIES, DICED	FISH. BAKE AT 400 FOR 15 MIN.
2 T	STUFFED OLIVES, MINCED	OR UNTIL FLAKY TO FORK.
2 CL	GARLIC, MINCED	
1 T EA	CAPERS, JALAPENO PEPPERS, MINCED	
1/2 t	ITALIAN SEASONINGS	SALT & PEPPER.

SNAPPER AU GRATIN

SERVES 6   FAT = 5 GM EA

1/2 C	FAT-FREE CHICKEN STOCK	SIMMER THESE FOR 5 MINUTES.
1/4 C	CELERY, DICED	
1/2 C	ONIONS, DICED	
1/4 C	FLOUR	COMBINE WELL, WHISK IN AND
2 T	BUTTER BUDS	HEAT TO THICKEN. S & P AND
2 C	SKIM MILK	CAYENNE TO TASTE.
1/2 LB	SHRIMP, PEELED & DEVEINED, SPLIT	ADD & SIMMER 5 MINUTES.
1/2 C	PARMESAN CHEESE	
1/2 C	SAUTERNE WINE (OR AS NEEDED)	
		LAY A FILLET IN EACH SPRAYED
6	6 OZ FILLETS, RINSED, DRIED S & P	GRATIN DISH.

Bake at 375 for 10 minutes, then pour sauce over each & sprinkle with Fat-Free Bread Crumbs & bake 5 minutes more.

GINGERED SNAPPER ORIENTAL

easy   SERVES 8   FAT = 3 GM EA

2	ONIONS, SLICED	LAY IN SPRAYED ROASTING PAN.
2	RED BELL PEPPERS, SLICED	
1	SNAPPER, 5 LBS, CLEANED, DRIED	LAY ON TOP OF VEGGIES.
1 C	FAT-FREE FISH OR CLAM BROTH	COMBINE & POUR OVER FISH.
1 C	SOY SAUCE	CHILL FOR 4 HOURS. LET SIT AT
1 C	DRY SHERRY	ROOM TEMPERATURE 30 MIN.
6 T	FRESH GINGER, PEELED, GRATED	
1 t	CRUSHED RED PEPPER FLAKES	
8 CL	GARLIC, MINCED	COVER & BAKE AT 375 FOR 45
		MINUTES OR UNTIL DONE.

Serve on a bed of rice or pasta.

LEMON GINGER SOLE

easy   SERVES 4   FAT = 2 GM EA

4	6 OZ FILLETS, RINSED	MARINATE ALL IN A ZIPLOC BAG
1/4 C	FAT-FREE CHICKEN STOCK	FOR 20 MINUTES.
1/4 C	FRESH LEMON JUICE	
3 T	FRESH GINGER, PEELED, GRATED	
1 T	FRESH THYME, CHOPPED	
4 CL	GARLIC, MINCED	BAKE AT 375 FOR 10 MINUTES
1/4 C	FRESH PARSLEY OR CILANTRO, MINCED	PER INCH OF THICKNESS.
1/4 t	OLD BAY SEASONING	

CURRIED SOLE

SERVES 8   FAT = 2 GM EA
(Including Sauce)

1	ONION, SLICED
8	6 OZ FILLETS, RINSED

LAY IN A LARGE, SPRAYED DISH & ADD REMAINING INGREDIENTS ON TOP.

1/2 C	FAT-FREE CHICKEN STOCK
2 T	BUTTER BUDS
1 T	CURRY POWDER (OR TO TASTE)
1 t	GROUND CUMIN
ZEST OF 4	LIMES (ALSO THE JUICE)
1 C	DRY WHITE WINE

SALT & PEPPER WELL.

SIMMER UNTIL ALMOST DONE. SPOON SAUCE OVER & BAKE AT 350 TO FINISH.

SAUCE

2 CUPS   FAT = TR EA

1 C	SKIM MILK
1/4 C	BUTTER BUDS
10	GREEN ONIONS, SLICED
1 LBS	MUSHROOMS, SLICED

SIMMER THESE FOR 5 MINUTES.

1/4 C	FLOUR
1/2 t	DRY MUSTARD
1/2 t	CURRY POWDER
1 C	POACHING LIQUID (MORE IF NECESSARY)

PUREE, WHISK INTO THE ABOVE HEAT TO THICKEN.

BROILED SOLE w PLUM SAUCE

quick   SERVES 8   FAT = 2 GM EA

1	RED ONION, MINCED
12 OZ	PLUMS, PEELED, MINCED
1 C	CANNED PEACHES
1/2 C	PORT WINE
2 T	SUGAR

SIMMER THESE UNTIL TENDER & PUREE.
(THIN WITH ORANGE JUICE IF NECESSARY)

8	6 OZ FILLETS, RINSED, DRIED, S & P

BRUSH WITH SAUCE AND BROIL UNTIL FLAKY TO FORK.

Heat remaining sauce, spoon onto plates & top with the fish.

LIME & CORIANDER SWORDFISH

quick   SERVES 8   FAT = 8 GM EA

8	6 OZ STEAKS
4	LIMES, JUICED
1	ORANGE, JUICED
1 T	HOT WATER
2 T	BUTTER BUDS (DISSOLVED IN THE WATER)
1/2 C	FRESH CORIANDER OR FLAT LEAF PARSLEY, MINCED
1 t	SUGAR

MARINATE FOR 15 MINUTES.

REMOVE FISH.

SALT & PEPPER WELL.

GRILL UNTIL FLAKY.

SHERRY LEMON SOLE

 SERVES 8   FAT = 2 GM EA

1	RED ONION, MINCED
1 C	DRY WHITE WINE
1 C	SHERRY VINEGAR
1/2 C	FAT-FREE CHICKEN STOCK
1 T	FRESH THYME, MINCED
1 T	FRESH LEMON JUICE

SIMMER THESE FOR 5 MINUTES.

1/4 C	BUTTER BUDS
3 T	CORNSTARCH
1/2 C	SKIM MILK

COMBINE WELL, WHISK IN AND HEAT TO THICKEN.

8	6 OZ FILLETS, RINSED, DRIED, S & P
2 T	FRESH LEMON JUICE

SPRAY FISH AND SPRINKLE WITH JUICE. BROIL UNTIL FLAKY.

SERVE WITH SAUCE.

SOY BROILED SWORDFISH

 SERVES 4   FAT = 8 GM EA

4	6 OZ STEAKS, RINSED, DRIED, S & P
1/4 C	NO-FAT SOUR CREAM
1 T	SOY SAUCE (OR TO TASTE)
1 T	BUTTER BUDS
1 T	GARLIC, MINCED
1 T	FRESH GINGER, PEELED, MINCED
1 T	FRESH LEMON JUICE

COMBINE AND SPREAD ON THE STEAKS.

BROIL 10 MIN. OR UNTIL FLAKY TO FORK.

SWORDFISH w APPLES

 SERVES 4   FAT = 8 GM EA

1/4 C	SKIM MILK
1/4 C	NO-FAT SOUR CREAM
1/4 C	BROWN SUGAR
2	APPLES, PEELED, SLICED THIN
1/2 t	NUTMEG, GRATED

SIMMER THESE FOR 5 MINUTES.

4	6 OZ STEAKS

ADD FISH, COVER & SIMMER FOR 10 MINUTES OR UNTIL FLAKY TO FORK.

SWORDFISH ROCKEFELLER

SERVES 6   FAT = 11 GM EA

Try substituting White Sea Bass & save 7 GM of fat per serving.

8	6 OZ SWORDFISH STEAKS, TRIMMED,	SPRAY, SEASON & BAKE AT 400
------	CAVENDER'S GREEK SEASONING	10 MINUTES OR ALMOST DONE.
1 C	ONION, MINCED	
1/2 C	CELERY, MINCED	SIMMER THESE FOR 5 MINUTES.
6 CL	GARLIC, MINCED	
1/2 C	FAT-FREE CHICKEN STOCK	
1/2 C	SKIM MILK (OR MORE)	ADD & SIMMER 30 SECONDS.
1/2 C	PARMESAN CHEESE	
3 C	SPINACH, MINCED	SPREAD ON FISH & BROIL JUST TO BROWN.

This could be served with Alfredo Sauce (p 289). Remember to count the extra fat.

BROOK TROUT ON A BED OF MUSHROOMS

SERVES 8   FAT = 4 GM EA

2 LBS	MUSHROOMS, SLICED	SPREAD IN A SPRAYED DISH.
8	6 OZ TROUT, CLEANED, S & P	LAY ON TOP OF MUSHROOMS.
2	ONIONS, SLICED	LAY ON TOP OF TROUT.
1/2 C	BUTTER BUDS	COMBINE THESE AND SPRINKLE
1/2 C	HOT WATER	OVER ALL.
3	LEMONS, JUICED	
2 t	PAPRIKA	BAKE AT 400 FOR 10 MINUTES OR
6	GREEN ONIONS, SLICED	UNTIL FLAKY TO FORK.
4 CL	GARLIC, MINCED	
2 C	FAT-FREE BREAD CRUMBS	

TROUT w HERBS

SERVES 4   FAT = 4 GM EA

1/2 C	FAT-FREE CHICKEN STOCK	SIMMER THESE FOR 5 MINUTES.
2	LEMONS, JUICED	
1	ONION, DICED	
2 T	FRESH OREGANO, MINCED	
2 T	FRESH BASIL, MINCED	
1 t	FRESH TARRAGON, MINCED	
1/2 C	WHITE WINE	
4	6 OZ BROOK TROUT, CLEANED, S & P	ADD FISH, COVER & SIMMER 10 MINUTES OR UNTIL FLAKY TO TO FORK.

STUFFED BROOK TROUT   SERVES 8   FAT = 4 GM EA

1 C	WILD RICE	SIMMER THESE FOR 45 MINUTES.
2 C	FAT-FREE CHICKEN STOCK, BOILING	
1	ONION, DICED	
4	GREEN ONIONS, SLICED	ADD THESE DURING THE LAST 5
2 CL	GARLIC, MINCED	MINUTES.
16	MUSHROOMS, CHOPPED	
1 T	FRESH GINGER, PEELED, GRATED	COOL, ADD FRUIT & STUFF FISH.
2 C	CHOPPED GRAPES, APPLES OR BLUEBERRIES	
3 BNCH	FRESH PARSLEY	LAY IN A SPRAYED DISH AND TOP
8	6 OZ TROUT, CLEANED, S & P	WITH THE STUFFED FISH.
1/4 C	FRESH LEMON JUICE	SPRINKLE WITH JUICE.

Cover with foil & bake at 350 for 30-40 minutes or until flaky to fork.

STUFFED TROUT   SERVES 4   FAT = 5 GM EA

1/2 C	FAT-FREE CHICKEN STOCK	SIMMER THESE FOR 5 MINUTES.
1 C	CELERY, MINCED	
1 CL	GARLIC, MINCED	
1	ONION, MINCED	
1/2 LB	MUSHROOMS, CHOPPED	REMOVE FROM HEAT & COOL.
6 OZ	CRAB MEAT, PICKED CLEAN (OR IMITATION)	ADD THESE & STUFF THE FISH.
1/4 C	EGG BEATERS	
1 T	FRESH PARSLEY, CHOPPED	
1/2 t	NUTMEG, GRATED	
1/2 LB	FAT-FREE FRENCH BREAD CUBES, SOAKED IN SKIM MILK AND SQUEEZED DRY	
		SPRAY THE FISH & BAKE AT 375
4	6 OZ BONELESS BROOK TROUT	FOR 10 MINUTES PER INCH OF THICKNESS.

TROUT w TOMATOES & HERBS

SERVES 4   FAT = 4 GM EA

1/2 C	FAT-FREE CHICKEN STOCK	SIMMER THESE FOR 5 MINUTES.
4 CL	GARLIC, MINCED	ADD JUST ENOUGH BREAD FOR
2	ONION, MINCED	A MOIST STUFFING.
1/2 BNCH	FRESH BASIL, CHOPPED	
1/2 BNCH	FRESH PARSLEY, CHOPPED	
------	FAT-FREE BREAD CUBES, AS NEEDED	
		STUFF FISH & TIE SHUT.
4	6 OZ BROOK TROUT, CLEANED, S & P	FRY IN A SPRAYED PAN FOR 2 MINUTES EACH SIDE.
3 C	TOMATO CONCASSE (p 396)	
1/2 BNCH	FRESH BASIL, CHOPPED	COMBINE & ADD THESE TO FISH.
1 T	FRESH OREGANO	
1 T	FRESH LEMON JUICE	
1/2 t	SUGAR	COVER & SIMMER 8 MINUTES OR
------	LOUISIANA HOT SAUCE TO TASTE	FLAKY TO FORK.

You might like to fry some turkey bacon & crumble into the sauce.

BAKED SEA TROUT

SERVES 12   FAT = 4 GM EA

1	FISH, 5 LBS, CLEANED, DRIED, S & P	
1/4 C	NO-FAT SOUR CREAM	COMBINE & SPREAD THESE ON
2 T	BUTTER BUDS	THE INSIDE & OUTSIDE OF FISH.
1/4 C	FRESH LEMON JUICE	
		COMBINE THESE, STUFF FISH.
1 C	FRESH PARSLEY, CHOPPED	SPRAY WITH PAM BUTTER SPRAY.
2	ONION, DICED	
2 T	BUTTER BUDS	BAKE AT 500 FOR 10 MIN., THEN
2 T	NO-FAT SOUR CREAM	AT 400 FOR 45 MINUTES OR 'TIL
2 T	FAT-FREE BREAD CRUMBS (OR MORE)	FLAKY TO FORK.

BROILED SEA TROUT

SERVES 4   FAT = 5 GM EA

4	6 OZ FILLETS, RINSED, DRIED, S & P	COMBINE & SPREAD THESE ON
1/4 C	NO-FAT SOUR CREAM	THE FILLETS.
6 T	ONION, CHOPPED	
3 T	FRESH PARSLEY, CHOPPED	
3 T	HOT WATER	
3 T	BUTTER BUDS (DISSOLVED IN THE HOT WATER)	
2 T	FRESH LEMON JUICE	BROIL 10 MINUTES OR UNTIL THE
1 t	FRESH TARRAGON, CHOPPED	FISH IS FLAKY TO FORK.
1 t	FRESH BASIL, CHOPPED	

GRILLED YELLOWTAIL TUNA w PEPPERS

SERVES 4   FAT = 2 GM EA

1/2 C	FAT-FREE CHICKEN STOCK
1	RED ONION, DICED
4	PICKLED RED BELL PEPPERS, DICED

SIMMER THESE FOR 5 MINUTES.

1/2 C	TOMATO CONCASSE (p 396)
1/2 C	WHITE WINE
1/2 C	CLAM BROTH
4	6 OZ STEAKS, S & P
4	RED BELL PEPPERS, SLICED

ADD THESE, SIMMER 3 MINUTES & PUREE.
SPRAY WITH PAM OLIVE OIL AND GRILL UNTIL FLAKY TO FORK.

Spoon sauce on plate & top with the tuna & peppers.

ORANGE TUNA

SERVES 6   FAT = 2 GM EA

6	6 OZ YELLOWTAIL STEAKS, S & P
1 C	FRESH ORANGE JUICE
1 C	DRY WHITE WINE
1/4 C	BUTTER BUDS
ZEST OF 2	ORANGES, MINCED
2 T	GRAND MARNIER
2	CARROTS, JULIENNED
4	LEEKS, WASHED WELL, JULIENNED

SIMMER THESE FOR 5 MINUTES.
REMOVE STEAKS & KEEP WARM.

REDUCE LIQUID BY 1/2.

ADD VEGGIES & SIMMER FOR 6 MINUTES.
RETURN TUNA TO THE PAN TO FINISH COOKING.

Serve sauce under fish.

GARLIC TUNA

SERVES 8   FAT = 2 GM EA

1 C	FAT-FREE CHICKEN STOCK
1/4 C	BUTTER BUDS
32 CL	GARLIC, SLICED
1	RED ONION, DICED
2 C	DRY WHITE WINE
8	6 OZ STEAKS, RINSED
1 EA	RED, YELLOW & GREEN PEPPER, DICED

SIMMER THESE FOR 15 MINUTES.

ADD PEPPERS & TUNA. COVER & POACH 10 MINUTES   OR UNTIL FLAKY TO FORK.

SALT & PEPPER TO TASTE.

If you'd like a creamier sauce, add a cup of No-Fat Sour Cream.

SAKE-SAKE TUNA

quick   SERVES 8   FAT = 2 GM EA

8	6 OZ STEAKS, RINSED
1/2 C	SAKE (JAPANESE WINE)
2 T	FRESH LEMON JUICE
2 CL	GARLIC, MINCED
1 t	SUGAR

MARINATE AT LEAST 15 MIN.

BROIL 5 MINUTES EACH SIDE OR UNTIL FLAKY TO FORK.

CAPERED TUNA

quick   SERVES 8   FAT = 2 GM EA

8	6 OZ STEAKS, RINSED, S & P
1/4 C	FRESH LEMON JUICE
2 C	MOCK OIL (p 395)
12	CAPERS, CRUSHED SLIGHTLY
1/4 C	BALSAMIC VINEGAR
1 C	ONION, MINCED
1/4 t	CINNAMON (OR TO TASTE)
1/4 t	GROUND CLOVES (OR TO TASTE)
------	SALT & PEPPER TO TASTE

SPRINKLE WITH LEMON, FRY IN A SPRAYED PAN, OR GRILL UNTIL DONE.   REMOVE THE FISH.

ADD THESE TO PAN & SIMMER 10 MINUTES.

PUREE, SPOON ONTO PLATES & TOP WITH THE FISH.

PEPPERCORN TUNA

quick   SERVES 4   FAT = 2 GM EA

4	RED ONIONS, SLICED
4 T	RED & GREEN PEPPERCORNS, CRUSHED
4	6 OZ STEAKS, RINSED, DRIED, SALTED
1 C	DRY WHITE WINE, HEATED
4	GREEN ONIONS, MINCED

LAYER IN LARGE FRY PAN.

PRESS FISH INTO PEPPERCORNS. SPRAY WITH PAM & LAY ON THE ONIONS.
POUR OVER, COVER AND POACH UNTIL FLAKY TO FORK.
SPRINKLE ON FOR GARNISH.

ORIENTAL FISH

quick   SERVES 4   FAT = 4 GM EA

1 C	CLAM JUICE OR FISH STOCK
1 C	SAKE
2 T EA	FRESH GINGER, GARLIC, PEELED, MINCED
1 T	SOY SAUCE
1/4 t	CRUSHED RED PEPPER FLAKES
1 LGE	BOK CHOY, BASE CUT OFF & DISCARDED
4	6 OZ LEAN FISH FILLETS, RINSED

SIMMER THESE FOR 5 MINUTES.

ADD BOK CHOY FOR 5 MINUTES, PLACE ON 4 PLATES AND KEEP WARM.
ADD FISH FOR 5 MINUTES OR UNTIL FLAKY TO FORK.
PLACE ON BOK CHOY AND KEEP WARM.

Boil liquid for 8 minutes & spoon over each fish.

Meats
&
Poultry

Almost everyone loves meat and most of us eat it every day. So do yourself a big favor:

Choose meat with the lowest fat content and   **ALWAYS** remove all skin &/or fat.

When using ground beef or turkey, chop your own in a food processor from the leanest meat possible, using on-off motions. The directions will say "process chop-chop".

You can then add minced yellow squash to ground meats to keep them juicy while cooking.

Bake, broil, grill or roast on a rack to allow fat to cook out.

De-fat pan juices & stocks before continuing with the recipes. If you don't have a de-fatting cup (the one with the spout at the bottom), add 4 ice cubes to the juices & pour into a Ziploc Freezer Bag.Press out air, zip shut & place in the freezer for 10 minutes. When ready, hold the bag over a clean pan, slit a small hole in a bottom corner to drain.   Pinch shut when the level of fat gets close to the hole.

Eat more vegetables, potatoes, pastas & grains than meat.

TURKEY	OZ		FAT GM
Breast	3.5	Skinless	1.8
Thighs	3.5	Skinless	6.0
Leg	3.5	Skinless	7.0

CHICKEN			
Breast	3.5	Skinless	3.5
Thighs	3.5	Skinless	7.0
Leg	3.5	Skinless	8.0

BEEF			
Eye of Round	3.5	Lean	6.0
Round, Top	3.5	Lean	6.0
Filet	3.5	Lean	9.0
Tenderloin	3.5	Lean	9.0
Sirloin Tip	3.5	Lean	9.0
Strip Loin	3.5	Lean	11.0
Flank	3.5	Lean	11.0
NY Strip	3.5	Lean	11.0
Rib Eye	3.5	Lean	12.0
Ground	3.5	Lean only	14.0
Chuck Roast	3.5	Lean	16.0

VEAL			
Cubed	3.5	Lean Only	3.5

VENISON			
Lean Cut	3.5	Lean, Roasted	3.5

PORK		OZ		FAT GM
	Tenderloin	3.5	Lean, Roasted	10.5
	Shoulder	3.0	Cured Lean, Roasted	6.0
	Center Loin	3.0	Lean, Broiled	9.0
	Ham, Fresh	3.0	Lean, Roasted	9.0
	Center Loin	3.0	Lean, Roasted	11.0

LAMB				
	Cubed	3.0	Lean, Broiled	6.0
	New Zealand	3.0	Lean, Broiled	7.0

TURKEY BEARNAISE

SERVES 6   FAT = 3 GM EA

2 LBS	BREASTS, SLICED IN MEDALLIONS	FRY IN A PAM-SPRAYED PAN AND REMOVE WHEN DONE.
1/4 C	FAT-FREE CHICKEN STOCK	ADD THESE AND SIMMER UNTIL ALMOST DRY.
1	RED ONION, SLICED & QUARTERED	
1 LB	MUSHROOMS, MINCED	
2 T	BUTTER BUDS	
1 T	FRESH TARRAGON, CHOPPED	
1 T	TOMATO PASTE	
1 C	FAT-FREE BEARNAISE SAUCE (p 156 or 257)	WHISK IN AND SPOON OVER THE TURKEY MEDALLIONS.
------	SALT & PEPPER TO TASTE.	

TURKEY BOURGUIGNON

SERVES 8   FAT = 2 GM EA

2 LBS	BREASTS, IN CUBES, S & P & FLOURED	BROWN IN A SPRAYED PAN AND REMOVE TO A CASSEROLE.
3 C	BURGUNDY WINE	BRING THESE TO A BOIL.
2 C	FAT-FREE BEEF STOCK	
1/2 C	COGNAC	ADD TO CASSEROLE & COVER.
3	RED ONIONS, SLICED	BAKE AT 325 FOR 1 HOUR.
6	CARROTS, SLICED THICK	
2 CL	GARLIC, MINCED	
3 T	TOMATO PASTE	
1	BAY LEAF (REMEMBER TO REMOVE)	
1/2 t	DRIED THYME	
1/2 C	FAT-FREE BEEF STOCK	SIMMER THESE FOR 5 MINUTES.
1 LB	MUSHROOMS, QUARTERED	STIR INTO CASSEROLE DURING LAST 10 MINUTES.
24	PEARL ONIONS, PEELED & PARBOILED	
3 T	BUTTER BUDS	

Serve over pasta.

TURKEY BURGERS

MAKES 12   6 OZ BURGERS   FAT = 1.5 GM EA

2 LBS	YELLOW SQUASH, PEELED, JULIENNED, MINCED	TOSS THESE WELL BEFORE YOU
2	ONIONS, DICED	ADD THE GROUND TURKEY.
2 C	FAT-FREE BREAD, MINCED	
1/2 C	EGG BEATERS	THE LESS YOU MIX THE TURKEY,
1/4 C	FRESH PARSLEY, CHOPPED (OPTIONAL)	THE BETTER THE END PRODUCT.
1 t	PAPRIKA	
1/2 t	DRIED SAGE	
1/2 t	DRIED OREGANO	
1/2 t	GARLIC POWDER	
2 t	SALT	FRY A TEST PATTY TO TEST THE
1 t	PEPPER	SEASONING.
2 LBS	BREASTS, DICED	ADJUST IF NECESSARY.
	(PROCESS CHOP-CHOP IN FOOD PROCESSOR)	

Form into patties & either grill or fry in a sprayed pan. These freeze well. You can add plain beet juice if you'd like a more 'Beef Like' color.

For a slightly different taste add   1 T Tarragon & 1/4 t Nutmeg or experiment on your own with different flavors & herbs.

TURKEY & BROCCOLI

easy   SERVES 8   FAT = 2 GM EA

2 LBS	BREASTS, SLICED IN THIN STRIPS	MARINATE THESE FOR 20 MIN.
1 T	CORNSTARCH	
1/4 C	DRY SHERRY	STIR-FRY IN A SPRAYED PAN.
1/4 C	SOY SAUCE	
1 C	FAT-FREE CHICKEN STOCK, HOT	ADD THESE, COVER & SIMMER
1 BNCH	BROCCOLI, FLORETS	UNTIL DONE.
1 SL	FRESH GINGER	
1	CARROT, JULIENNED	
1	RED ONION, SLICED THIN & QUARTERED	
1	YELLOW PEPPER, JULIENNED	REMOVE GINGER & ADD MORE
1/4 LB	MUSHROOMS, SLICED	CHICKEN STOCK IF NEEDED.
------	BEAN SPROUTS (OPTIONAL)	
1 C	COLD WATER	COMBINE WELL, WHISK IN AND
1 T	CORNSTARCH	HEAT TO THICKEN.
		SERVE OVER RICE.

TURKEY CANNELONI   SERVES 8   FAT = 4 GM EA

2 LBS	BREASTS, GROUND OR PROCESSED CHOP-CHOP	BROWN IN A SPRAYED PAN.
2	RED ONIONS, MINCED	
5 T	GARLIC, MINCED	
10 OZ	FROZEN SPINACH, SQUEEZED DRY, CHOPPED	ADD THESE INGREDIENTS.
1 C	COTTAGE CREAM, (p 392)	
3/4 C	EGG BEATERS	
6 T	PARMESAN CHEESE	SALT & PEPPER TO TASTE.
1 t	FRESH OREGANO, MINCED	
		PLACE 2 T IN EACH CREPE AND
16	FAT-FREE CREPES (p 120, 122)	ROLL UP. PLACE IN GLASS DISH
4 C	FAT-FREE SPAGHETTI SAUCE (p 288)	ON SOME SPAGHETTI SAUCE.
4 C	FAT-FREE BECHAMEL SAUCE (p 25, 248)	TOP WITH MORE SAUCE & THEN THE BECHAMEL SAUCE.

Bake at 375 for 20 minutes. You can broil before serving for a golden color.

You can substitute lasagna noodles (cooked al dente & cut in half) for the crepes. Serve with an Italian Salad (p 114) & Garlic Bread (p 114).

TURKEY CASSEROLE   _easy_   SERVES 8   FAT = 2 GM EA

2 LBS	BREAST, SLICED IN MEDALLIONS	BROWN IN A PAM-SPRAYED PAN & PLACE IN A SPRAYED DISH.
1 C	RAISINS	
2	ONIONS, SLICED	TOSS THESE & FILL CASSEROLE.
2 C	YAMS, SLICED	
4 C	APPLES, PEELED, SLICED	BAKE AT 350 FOR 1 HR. OR
1/4 C	SOY SAUCE	UNTIL YAMS ARE DONE.
2 T	WORCESTERSHIRE SAUCE	
2 T	BROWN SUGAR	
2 C	FAT-FREE CHICKEN STOCK	

ORIENTAL TURKEY CASSEROLE   _easy_   SERVES 8   FAT = 2 GM EA

2 LBS	BREASTS, IN STRIPS, S & P & FLOURED	BROWN IN A SPRAYED PAN & PUT IN A SPRAYED BAKING DISH.
2	ONIONS, SLICED & QUARTERED	
2	BELL PEPPERS, SLICED THIN	
1 LB	MUSHROOMS, SLICED	TOP WITH THE REST, COVER AND
16 OZ	CANNED TOMATOES, PROCESSED CHOP-CHOP	BAKE AT 350 FOR 40 MINUTES.
2 C	FAT-FREE BEEF STOCK	
1/2 C	SOY SAUCE	
3 T	MOLASSES	SERVE WITH RICE.

CHINESE TURKEY CURRY

 SERVES 4   FAT = 2 GM EA

1 LB	BREASTS, SLICED THIN	STIR-FRY IN A SPRAYED PAN.
1 1/2 C	FAT-FREE BEEF STOCK	ADD & SIMMER 20 MINUTES.
2 T	SOY SAUCE	
2 T	CURRY POWDER	
1 t	BROWN SUGAR	
1/2 t	GROUND GINGER	
2	ONIONS, SLICED & QUARTERED	
2	BELL PEPPERS, IN EIGHTHS	
1 C	RAISINS	
4	TOMATOES, PEELED, SEEDED, IN EIGHTHS	
		COMBINE WELL, WHISK IN AND
1 C	FAT-FREE BEEF STOCK, COLD	HEAT TO THICKEN.
2 T	CORNSTARCH	SERVE WITH RICE.

GRILLED TURKEY

 SERVES 8   FAT – 2 GM EA

2 LBS	BREASTS, SLICED IN MEDALLIONS	MARINATE THESE FOR AT LEAST
1 C	WHITE WINE	20 MINUTES.
1/2 C	ONION, MINCED	
1/2 C	FRESH LEMON JUICE	REMOVE BREASTS & BOIL THE
4 CL	GARLIC, MINCED	MARINADE.
1 T	CURRY POWDER (OPTIONAL)	
1 t	WORCESTERSHIRE SAUCE	GRILL & BASTE FREQUENTLY.
1 t	FRESH GINGER, PEELED, GRATED	

MARINATED GRILLED TURKEY

easy SERVES 4   FAT = 2 GM EA

2	BREAST HALVES	MARINATE 1 HOUR OR MORE.
1/2 C	DRY RED WINE	
1/2 C	SOY SAUCE	REMOVE BREASTS & BOIL THE
4	GREEN ONION, MINCED	MARINADE.
2 CL	GARLIC, MINCED	
1	LEMON, JUICED	GRILL, BASTING UNTIL DONE.
2 T	WORCESTERSHIRE SAUCE	SLICE.

INDONESIAN TURKEY

SERVES 8   FAT = 2 GM EA

2 LBS	BREASTS, SLICED IN MEDALLIONS	MARINATE THESE FOR 4 HOURS.
2 C	NON-FAT LEMON OR LIME YOGURT	
6 CL	GARLIC, MINCED	
3 T	CORIANDER, CRUSHED	
2 T	GROUND CUMIN	GRILL UNTIL DONE.
2 T	CURRY POWDER (OR MORE)	
2	ONIONS, DICED	
1	LIME, ZESTED & JUICED	
1 t	LOUISIANA HOT SAUCE	

CREAMY FRENCH TURKEY I

SERVES 8   FAT = 2 GM EA

2 LBS	BREAST, SLICED IN MEDALLIONS, S & P	DUST WITH FLOUR & BROWN IN A SPRAYED PAN. REMOVE AND KEEP WARM.
3	ONIONS, SLICED & QUARTERED	
2 CL	GARLIC, MINCED	
1 C	FAT-FREE BEEF STOCK	ADD THESE & SIMMER 30 MIN.
1 C	WHITE WINE	
2 T	BUTTER BUDS	
1 t	SOY SAUCE	RETURN TURKEY AND SIMMER UNTIL DONE.
1 t	WORCESTERSHIRE SAUCE	
1 C	NO-FAT SOUR CREAM	ADD & SERVE OVER PASTA.

CREAMY FRENCH TURKEY II

easy

SERVES 8   FAT = 2 GM EA

2 LBS	BREASTS, SLICED IN MEDALLIONS, S & P	MARINATE THESE 2 HOURS OR MORE.
2 C	NO-FAT SOUR CREAM	
1 T	WORCESTERSHIRE SAUCE	
1 t	CAVENDER'S GREEK SEASONING	REMOVE TURKEY, DREDGE IN CRUMBS & SPRAY WITH PAM.
1 t	CELERY SALT	
2 CL	GARLIC, MINCED	
1 C	PREMIUM FAT-FREE SALTINE CRACKER CRUMBS	BAKE AT 350 FOR 20 MINUTES OR UNTIL DONE.

If you'd like to use the marinade for a sauce, be sure to boil it first.

IMPERIAL TURKEY

SERVES 8   FAT = 2 GM EA

2 LBS	BREASTS, SLICED IN MEDALLIONS, S & P	SPRINKLE WITH BRANDY & LET
1/4 C	BRANDY	SIT 10 MINUTES, THEN BROWN
		IN A SPRAYED PAN & REMOVE.
1/2 C	BRANDY	
3 T	SOY SAUCE	ADD TO THE PAN & REDUCE BY
3 T	A.1. SAUCE	1/2.
3 T	HEINZ CHILI SAUCE	
1/2 C	FAT-FREE BEEF STOCK	RETURN THE TURKEY TO PAN &
2 T	BUTTER BUDS	SIMMER UNTIL DONE.
2 T	DIJON MUSTARD	SERVE WITH PASTA OR RICE.

LEMON TURKEY

SERVES 8   FAT = 2 GM EA

2 LBS	BREASTS, SLICED IN MEDALLIONS, S & P	MARINATE THESE FOR 1 HOUR.
1/2 C	FAT-FREE CHICKEN STOCK	
2 T	BUTTER BUDS	
2	LEMONS, JUICED	BAKE, BROIL OR GRILL.
1 T	PAPRIKA	
1 T	FRESH OREGANO, CHOPPED	IF YOU BROIL OR GRILL, BOIL
1 t	CAVENDER'S GREEK SEASONING	THE MARINADE & BASTE.

GRANDMA'S MEATLOAF

easy

SERVES 12   FAT = 3 GM EA

3 LBS	TURKEY BREASTS, GROUND OR PROCESSED CHOP-CHOP	
3	YELLOW SQUASH, JULIENNED & THEN MINCED	COMBINE ALL & FORM INTO 2
1	ONION, DICED	LOAVES.
1 C	FRESH PARSLEY, CHOPPED	
3/4 C	KETCHUP	
2 T	WORCESTERSHIRE SAUCE	
1/4 C	FRESH BASIL, CHOPPED (OR 1 T DRY)	TOP WITH KETCHUP OR 4 SLICES
3 CL	GARLIC, MINCED	OSCAR MAYER TURKEY BACON.
1 T	DIJON MUSTARD	
2 t	SALT	
1 t	PEPPER	
1/2 t	LOUISIANA HOT SAUCE	BAKE AT 375 FOR 1 HR. OR UNTIL
3/4 C	EGG BEATERS	DONE.
1 C	FAT-FREE BREAD CUBES (OR MORE IF NEEDED)	
1/2 C	NO-FAT SOUR CREAM	

TURKEY NORMANDY

SERVES 4   FAT = 2 GM EA

| 1 LB | BREASTS, SLICED, FLATTENED | FRY IN SPRAYED PAN & REMOVE |
| 1 C | APPLEJACK BRANDY | DEGLAZE WITH BRANDY. |

4	APPLES, PEELED, DICED	ADD THESE AND SIMMER FOR 10
1/2 t	ALLSPICE	MINUTES.
1/4 C	APPLESAUCE	
2 T	SUGAR	RETURN TURKEY TO PAN & HEAT
1 C	NO-FAT SOUR CREAM (OR MORE)	THROUGH.

TURKEY SAUSAGE

MAKES 24 3 OZ PATTIES   FAT = 1 GM EA

2 LBS	YELLOW SQUASH, PEELED, JULIENNED & DICED	TOSS THESE WELL BEFORE YOU
2 C	FAT-FREE BREAD, MINCED	ADD THE GROUND TURKEY.
3 OZ	EGG BEATERS (OR MORE IF NEEDED)	
1 T	DRIED SAGE (OR TO TASTE)	
1 T	CRUSHED RED PEPPER FLAKES (OR TO TASTE)	THE LESS YOU MIX THE TURKEY,
1 T	PAPRIKA	THE BETTER THE END PRODUCT
1 t	DRIED OREGANO	WILL BE.
1 t	ONION POWDER	
1 t	CAVENDER'S GREEK SEASONING	FRY A TEST PATTY TO TEST THE
------	SALT & PEPPER TO TASTE	SEASONINGS. ADJUST TO TASTE.

2 LBS	BREASTS, GROUND OR DICED OR	FORM INTO PATTIES & FRY IN A
	PROCESSED CHOP-CHOP	SPRAYED PAN OR WRAP AND
		FREEZE.

You can add beet juice if you'd like a more 'Beef-Like' color.

ITALIAN TURKEY SAUSAGE

Make as above substituting 3 T Ground Fennel for the Sage & add minced garlic to taste.

TURKEY SPAGHETTI SAUCE

 SERVES 8   FAT = 3 GM EA

2 LBS	BREASTS, IN 1/2" CUBES	BROWN THESE IN OLIVE OIL
2	ONIONS, MINCED	SPRAY.
4 CL	GARLIC, MINCED	
1 EA	RED, YELLOW & GREEN PEPPERS, DICED	
28 OZ	CANNED TOMATOES, PROCESSED CHOP-CHOP	ADD & SIMMER 20 MINUTES.
1 LB	MUSHROOMS, SLICED	ADD & SIMMER 15 MINUTES.
1 T	DRIED ITALIAN HERBS	TOSS 1 CUP WITH PASTA.
1 t	FRESH BASIL, MINCED	SPOON REMAINING SAUCE OVER.
1 t	GROUND FENNEL SEEDS (OR MORE)	
------	YOUR OTHER FAVORITE SPAGHETTI SEASONINGS	

If you add regular Parmesan, add 2 GM Fat per T. Weight Watcher's has a Fat-Free Parmesan that tastes all right. You might try using half of that & half regular Parmesan.

Adding very strong olives & Balsamic Vinegar changes this sauce drastically. Remember to add in the fat count for the olives, but when you start this low on the fat scale, you have room to splurge!

TURKEY RAGOUT

 SERVES 8   FAT = 2 GM EA

2 LBS	BREASTS, CUBED, S & P	SPRINKLE WITH THYME.
		BROWN IN A SPRAYED PAN.
2	ONIONS, DICE	
3 CL	GARLIC, MINCED	
1/2 C	MARSALA WINE, SWEET SHERRY OR PORT	ADD THESE & COVER.
1/2 C	FAT-FREE BEEF STOCK	
1 T	TOMATO PASTE	SIMMER 30 MINUTES.
2 LBS	MUSHROOMS, QUARTERED	ADD & SIMMER 20 MINUTES.
1 C	FROZEN TINY PEAS	
1/4 C	NO-FAT SOUR CREAM (OR MORE)	ADD TO FINISH.

TURKEY STEW I

SERVES 8   FAT = 2 GM EA

2 LBS	BREASTS, IN CUBES, S & P	DREDGE IN FLOUR, BROWN IN A
1/3 C	FLOUR	SPRAYED PAN & ADD REMAINING
		INGREDIENTS.
6 C	FAT-FREE BEEF STOCK.	
6	ONIONS, IN EIGHTHS	
6	CARROTS, THICK SLICES	COVER AND SIMMER UNTIL THE
6	POTATOES, IN EIGHTHS	VEGGIES ARE DONE.
3	CELERY STALKS, THICK SLICES	
6 CL	GARLIC, MINCED	SALT & PEPPER TO TASTE.
3	BAY LEAVES (REMEMBER TO REMOVE)	
2 T	BUTTER BUDS	
1 t	SUGAR	
1 t	PAPRIKA	
1 t	FRESH LEMON JUICE	ADD CHOPPED PARSLEY DURING
1 t	WORCESTERSHIRE SAUCE	LAST 30 SECONDS IF YOU'D LIKE.
1 /2 t	GROUND CLOVES (OPTIONAL)	

TURKEY STEW II

SERVES 8   FAT = 2 GM EA

28 OZ	CANNED TOMATOES, PROCESSED CHOP-CHOP	BRING THESE TO A BOIL.
2	ONIONS, IN EIGHTHS	
2	GREEN BELL PEPPERS, IN EIGHTHS	
1	CELERY STALK, SLICED DIAGONALLY	
4 CL	GARLIC, MINCED	
2 LBS	BREASTS, IN CUBES	ADD REMAINING ITEMS.
1 LB	MUSHROOMS, SLICED	SIMMER UNTIL DONE.
1 T	DRIED ITALIAN HERBS	
2 C	SMALL COOKED PASTA (ADD JUST BEFORE SERVING)	
	OR SUBSTITUTE 2 C COOKED DICED POTATOES	S & P TO TASTE.

OPTION:

1 t	COCONUT FLAVORING	COMBINE THESE & ADD FOR A
1 t	CURRY POWDER	COMPLETELY DIFFERENT TASTE.
1/2 C	CURRANTS OR RAISINS	
1/4 C	SKIM MILK	
1 T	CORNSTARCH	

LOBSTER STUFFED TURKEY BREASTS   SERVES 12   FAT = 3 GM EA

6	BREAST HALVES, HALVED LENGTHWISE, TENDON REMOVED, FLATTENED	SALT & PEPPER.
1 LB	COOKED LOBSTER OR IMITATION CRAB MEAT, MINCED	
1	ONION, MINCED	COMBINE ALL OF THESE AND
3 CL	GARLIC, MINCED	SPREAD ON THE FLATTENED
1/2 C	FAT-FREE BREAD CRUMBS (MORE IF NEEDED)	BREASTS.
4 OZ	FAT-FREE CREAM CHEESE	
1/2 C	EGG BEATERS	ROLL UP, PLACE SEAM SIDE
1 T	DIJON MUSTARD	DOWN IN A SPRAYED DISH &
1 T	WORCESTERSHIRE SAUCE	SPRAY WITH PAM.
1 T	FAT-FREE MIRACLE WHIP	
1 t	OLD BAY SEASONING	ADD 1/2" STOCK TO PAN.

Bake at 350 for 30 min. or until done. Make Chicken Gravy (p 255), add leftover stuffing, puree & heat. Spoon sauce onto plates & top with turkey.

APPLE STUFFED TURKEY BREASTS   SERVES 6   FAT = 3 GM EA

Make as above, substituting apples & raisins for the lobster. Omit mustard, Worcestershire Sauce & Old Bay.

Or, add Thyme, lemon juice, brandy & serve with Curry Sauce (p 272).

Or, add crushed pineapple, cinnamon, nutmeg, ginger, ground cloves to stuffing.

MUSHROOM STUFFED TURKEY BREASTS   SERVES 12   FAT = 3 GM EA

6	BREAST HALVES, HALVED LENGTHWISE, TENDON REMOVED, FLATTENED	SALT & PEPPER.
2 C	MUSHROOMS, CHOPPED	COMBINE THESE & SPREAD ON
1 C	FAT-FREE BREAD CRUMBS	THE FLATTENED BREASTS.
1/2 C	MADEIRA WINE	
2 T	EGG BEATERS	
2 T	ONION, MINCED	ROLL UP & DIP IN EGGS.
1 T	FRESH PARSLEY, CHOPPED	DREDGE IN CRUMBS AND SPRAY
1 T	FRESH TARRAGON, MINCED	WITH PAM BUTTER SPRAY.
1 C	EGG BEATERS	PLACE IN SPRAYED DISH, SEAM
------	FAT-FREE SALTINE CRACKER CRUMBS	SIDE DOWN & BAKE AT 350 FOR 30 MINUTES OR 'TIL DONE.

Make Chicken Gravy (p 255), add leftover stuffing, puree & heat to serve.

STUFFED TURKEY BREASTS w HONEY SESAME   SERVES 8   FAT = 3 GM EA

4	BREAST HALVES, HALVED LENGTHWISE, TENDON REMOVED, FLATTENED	SALT & PEPPER.
1/2 C	FAT-FREE CHICKEN STOCK	SIMMER THESE FOR 5 MINUTES.
1	ONION, CHOPPED	
2 CL	GARLIC, MINCED	COOL.
1/2 INCH	FRESH GINGER, PEELED, GRATED	
1 C	BEAN SPROUTS, CHOPPED	ADD THESE AND SPREAD ON THE
1 CAN	WATER CHESTNUTS, CHOPPED	BREASTS.
1/4 C	BREAD CRUMBS	ROLL UP AND PLACE SEAM SIDE
2 T	SOY SAUCE	DOWN IN A SPRAYED DISH.
2 T	DRY SHERRY	
1 C	FAT-FREE CHICKEN STOCK	POUR AROUND ROLLS & BAKE AT
2 T	SOY SAUCE	350 FOR 30 MINUTES.
1 C	HONEY	BASTE EVERY 10 MINUTES WITH
3 T	SOY SAUCE	HONEY MIXTURE.
2 T	SESAME SEEDS	SPRINKLE ON LAST 5 MINUTES.

TURKEY WELLINGTONS w MADEIRA SAUCE   SERVES 8   FAT = 3 GM EA

4	BREAST HALVES, HALVED LENGTHWISE, TENDON REMOVED, FLATTENED	SALT & PEPPER.
1/4 C	FAT-FREE CHICKEN STOCK	SIMMER THESE UNTIL ALMOST
1 LB	MUSHROOMS, MINCED	DRY.
1	ONION, MINCED	
2 T	DIJON MUSTARD	SPREAD ON BREASTS & ROLL UP.
2 T	DRY SHERRY	PLACE ANY EXTRA ON TOPS.
1 T	BUTTER BUDS	
		SPRAY EACH & FOLD IN HALF.
8	SHEETS OF PHYLLO DOUGH	(CREATING 8 WRAPS)

Wrap each turkey roll in phyllo & place seam side down on a sprayed pan. Spray tops with Pam & bake at 400 for 30 minutes or until done. Serve with Madeira Sauce.

MADEIRA SAUCE   2 CUPS   FAT = TR EA

1 C	FAT-FREE BEEF STOCK	
1 C	MADEIRA WINE	SIMMER FOR 20 MINUTES.
2 T	BUTTER BUDS	SPOON OVER THE WELLINGTONS.
1	LEMON, JUICED	
1 T	BOVRIL (AVAILABLE IN MOST STORES) OR DEMI GLAZE	
1 T	CORNSTARCH	

TURKEY MEATBALLS (RED)   40 PIECES   FAT = .5 GM EA

Please do not use packaged ground turkey!!

2 LBS	BREASTS, GROUND OR PROCESSED CHOP-CHOP	
10	LOW-FAT GRAHAM CRACKERS	COMBINE THESE & FORM INTO
1/2 C	SKIM MILK OR AS NEEDED	40 SMALL BALLS.
1/2 C	ONION, MINCED	
1/2 C	YELLOW ZUCCHINI, MINCED	PLACE IN A SPRAYED DISH.
------	SALT & PEPPER	
1 C	TOMATO SAUCE	COMBINE, POUR OVER & BAKE
1 C	BROWN SUGAR	AT 325 FOR 1 HOUR.
1/4 C	VINEGAR	SERVE NOW OR FREEZE.
1 C	HEINZ KETCHUP	COMBINE & BRUSH ON THE HOT
1/4 C	BALSAMIC VINEGAR	OR THAWED BALLS.
		HEAT THROUGH.

TURKEY MEATBALLS (WHITE)   40 PIECES   FAT = .5 GM EA

2 LBS	BREASTS, GROUND OR PROCESSED CHOP-CHOP	
2	ONIONS, MINCED	COMBINE THESE & FORM INTO
1 C	SKIM MILK	40 SMALL BALLS.
1 C	FAT-FREE BREAD CRUMBS	
1/2 C	EGG BEATERS	PLACE IN A SPRAYED DISH.
1/2 C	YELLOW ZUCCHINI, MINCED	
3 CL	GARLIC, MINCED	
1/2 t	DRIED SAGE	
1/2 t	DRIED THYME	
1/2 t	SALT	
1/4 t	PEPPER	
		ADD STOCK & BAKE AT 325 FOR
1 C	STRONG FAT-FREE CHICKEN STOCK	1 HOUR.
1 C	STRONG FAT-FREE CHICKEN STOCK	PUREE THESE & POUR OVER.
1 1/2 C	NO-FAT SOUR CREAM	BAKE 10 MORE MINUTES.
1 PKG	LIPTON ONION SOUP MIX (OPTIONAL)	
------	WHITE WINE TO TASTE	

TURKEY JAMBALAYA

 SERVES 10   FAT = 2 GM EA

2 LBS	BREASTS, DICED	FRY THESE IN A SPRAYED PAN
3 C	ONIONS, DICED	FOR 10 MINUTES.
2 C	GREEN PEPPER, DICED	
1 C	CELERY, DICED	
6 CL	GARLIC, MINCED (OR TO TASTE)	
1/4 C	TOMATO PASTE	ADD & SIMMER FOR 10 MINUTES.
------	SALT & PEPPER & CAYENNE TO TASTE	
------	SUGAR	
2 C	FAT-FREE STOCK (OR AS NEEDED)	ADD & SIMMER 40 MINUTES.
1/2 C	GREEN ONION TOPS, SLICED	ADD & SIMMER 5 MINUTES.
1/4 C	FRESH PARSLEY, CHOPPED	SERVE OVER RICE.
1 T	FILE' GUMBO	

PICADILLO

easy   SERVES 4   FAT = 4 GM EA

1 LB	TURKEY BREASTS, PROCESSED CHOP-CHOP	FRY THESE IN OLIVE OIL SPRAY
1	ONION, DICED	UNTIL BROWNED.
1 EA	RED, YELLOW & GREEN PEPPER, DICED	
3 CL	GARLIC, MINCED	
1 C	TOMATOES, PEELED & CHOPPED	ADD THESE & SIMMER FOR 20
1/4 C	DRY SHERRY	MINUTES.
1 T	WORCESTERSHIRE SAUCE	
1/2 t	LOUISIANA HOT SAUCE	
2	POTATOES, COOKED, DICED	
1/4 C	RAISINS	
1/4 C	GREEN OLIVES, SLICED	
1/2 C	EGG BEATERS, COOKED, CHOPPED	SPRINKLE REMAINING ITEMS
1/4 C	EARLY PEAS	OVER BEFORE SERVING.
1/4 C	PIMENTO, DICED	

REMEMBER...WHEN WE SAY BREAST HALVES, WE MEAN BONED, SKINLESS & ALL FAT REMOVED

In most of these recipes, you can substitute turkey. If you are trying to lose weight, it is well worth it!

HONEY ALMOND CHICKEN

 SERVES 8   FAT = 4 GM EA

8	BREAST HALVES, S & P	TOSS THESE TOGETHER, SHAKE
1 C	FLOUR	OFF ALL EXCESS & BROWN IN A
3 T	PAPRIKA	PAM-SPRAYED PAN.
1 C	MADEIRA WINE	ADD MADEIRA & FLAME.
6 T	SOY SAUCE	COMBINE THESE & ADD.
3/4 C	HONEY	COVER & SIMMER 25 MINUTES.
1 T	ALMOND FLAVORING	BROIL TO BROWN IF NEEDED.

OPTIONS: CELERY, ONIONS, BELL PEPPERS, WATER CHESTNUTS, BAMBOO SHOOTS
                     MUSHROOMS, GARLIC, FRESH GINGER

Place 3 slivers of almonds on each & serve over rice.

ALMOND CHICKEN in SOUR CREAM

 SERVES 8   FAT = 4 GM EA

8	BREAST HALVES	COMBINE THESE AND SPRINKLE
1 T	PAPRIKA	OVER BREASTS.
1 T	CELERY SALT	
2 t	SALT	
1 t	CURRY POWDER	SPRAY WITH PAM BUTTER.
1 t	DRIED OREGANO	COVER WITH FOIL & BAKE AT 350
1 t	PEPPER	FOR 20 MINUTES.
1 t	BUTTER BUDS	
2 C	NO-FAT SOUR CREAM	COMBINE AND POUR OVER THE
1 C	FAT-FREE CHICKEN STOCK, HOT	BREASTS.
1 T	ALMOND FLAVORING	
1/2 C	FAT-FREE BREAD CRUMBS	SPRINKLE ON, BAKE 10 MINUTES
		MORE, UNCOVERED.

APRICOT CURRANT CHICKEN

 SERVES 8   FAT = 4 GM EA

8	BREAST HALVES, S & P
1 t	GROUND GINGER
1 1/2 C	ORANGE MARMALADE
1 C	DRIED APRICOTS, SOAKED, DICED
1 C	CURRANTS
1/2 C	APPLE JUICE
1/2 C	FRESH ORANGE JUICE
1/4 C	BROWN SUGAR
2 T	CORNSTARCH
1 T	WORCESTERSHIRE SAUCE
1/2 t	NUTMEG, GRATED

COMBINE & SPREAD THESE ON BREASTS.

COVER & BAKE AT 350 FOR 30 MINUTES OR UNTIL TENDER.

BAKED CHICKEN

 SERVES 4   FAT = 6 GM EA

4	BREAST HALVES, S & P
10 OZ	LOW-FAT CREAM OF MUSHROOM SOUP
1 C	NO-FAT SOUR CREAM
1/2 C	DRY SHERRY
1/2 C	FAT-FREE CHICKEN STOCK
1/2 LB	MUSHROOMS, SLICED
12 CIRCLES	CUT FROM FAT-FREE PITA BREAD
------	PAPRIKA
------	FRESH PARSLEY, CHOPPED

PLACE IN A SPRAYED DISH.

HEAT THESE & POUR OVER THE CHICKEN.
BAKE AT 350 FOR 25 MINUTES.

PLACE CIRCLES ON TOP & SPRAY WITH PAM. SPRINKLE THESE ON. BAKE FOR 10 MINUTES OR UNTIL DONE.

CRUSTY BAKED CHICKEN

SERVES 4   FAT = 4 GM EA

4	BREAST HALVES, S & P, FLOURED
1/2 C	1% BUTTERMILK
1 T	GROUND ROSEMARY
1 T	BUTTER BUDS
------	FAT-FREE BREAD CRUMBS

SHAKE OFF EXCESS FLOUR.

MIX THESE & DIP THE CHICKEN.

SPRINKLE ON BAKE AT 350 FOR 30 MINUTES OR UNTIL DONE.

SPICY BAKED CHICKEN

SERVES 8   FAT = 4 GM EA

8	BREAST HALVES, S & P	MARINATE THESE FOR 2 HOURS.
2	ONIONS, SLICED	
1 C	APPLE JUICE	
1 C	WHITE WINE	SALT & PEPPER.
ZEST OF 2	LEMONS, MINCED	
2	LEMONS, JUICED	
1 t	GROUND GINGER	COVER & BAKE AT 350 FOR 30
1 t	CINNAMON	MINUTES OR UNTIL DONE.
1 t	SUGAR	
2 C	WHITE OR BUTTER SAUCE (p 248, 250, 270)	SPOON OVER CHICKEN.

CHICKEN IN BASIL CREAM

SERVES 8   FAT = 4 GM EA

8	BREAST HALVES, S & P, FLOURED	SHAKE OFF ALL EXCESS. BROWN IN A SPRAYED PAN.
1 C	DRY WHITE WINE	DEGLAZE PAN WITH WINE.
1 C	FAT-FREE CHICKEN STOCK	ADD THESE & SIMMER FOR 20
2	ONIONS, DICED	MINUTES OR UNTIL DONE.
1/2 C	FRESH BASIL, CHOPPED	
1/4 C	FRESH PARSLEY, CHOPPED	
1 t	DRIED THYME	REMEMBER, REMOVE THE BAY
2	BAY LEAVES	LEAVES.
1 C	NO-FAT SOUR CREAM	WHISK IN. SERVE WITH PASTA
------	CAVENDER'S GREEK SEASONING TO TASTE	OR POTATOES.

BASQUE CHICKEN

SERVES 8   FAT = 6 GM EA

8	BREAST HALVES, SALT & CAYENNE	BROWN IN A PAM-SPRAYED PAN.
2	ONIONS, SLICED	ADD THESE, COVER & SIMMER
2 EA	RED & GREEN BELL PEPPERS, SLICED	20 MINUTES OR UNTIL DONE.
6 CL	GARLIC, MINCED	
4 SL	CANADIAN BACON, TRIMMED & DICED	
8	TOMATOES, PEELED, SEEDED, CHOPPED	
8 EA	BLACK & GREEN OLIVES, SLICED	FOR GARNISH.

BBQ LEMON MUSTARD CHICKEN

 SERVES 8   FAT = 4 GM EA

8	BREAST HALVES	MARINATE THESE OVERNIGHT.
ZEST OF 4	LEMONS	REMOVE BREASTS & BOIL THE
4	LEMONS, JUICED	MARINADE.
6 CL	GARLIC, MINCED	
1 1/2 C	DRY WHITE WINE	BAKE OR GRILL UNTIL DONE.
1/2 C	GRAINY MUSTARD	
1 T	FRESH TARRAGON, CHOPPED	
2 C	OF ABOVE MARINADE	COMBINE, HEAT TO THICKEN &
2 T	CORNSTARCH	BRUSH ON CHICKEN DURING THE
1/4 C	HONEY	LAST 10 MINUTES.
2 T	FRESH LEMON JUICE	

AND OTHER BBQ SAUCES   ALL THESE BBQ SAUCES HAVE JUST A TRACE OF FAT PER OZ.

BASIC BBQ SAUCE

1 C	KETCHUP	COMBINE WELL.
1	ONION, MINCED	
2 T	VINEGAR, LEMON JUICE OR ORANGE JUICE	
1 T	WORCESTERSHIRE SAUCE	
1 CL	GARLIC, MINCED	
OPTIONS:	HONEY	YOU MIGHT LIKE TO ADD 1 OR 2
	DIJON MUSTARD	OF THESE TO THE BASIC SAUCE.
	SOY SAUCE	
	A.1. SAUCE	
	CAYENNE OR CHILI POWDER	

BBQ SAUCE (MEAT OR POULTRY)

2 C	KETCHUP	COMBINE WELL.
1/4 C	VINEGAR, LEMON JUICE OR ORANGE JUICE	
2 T	WORCESTERSHIRE SAUCE	
1 T	OLD BAY SEASONING	
3/4 C	SUGAR	
2 T	DIJON MUSTARD	

AND MORE BBQ SAUCES   ALL THESE BBQ SAUCES HAVE JUST A TRACE OF FAT PER OZ.

CHARLIE D'S BBQ SAUCE

3 C	TOMATO SAUCE	COMBINE WELL.
1/4 C	ORANGE JUICE, LEMON JUICE OR VINEGAR	
1/2 C	ONION, MINCED	
1/2 C	BELL PEPPER, MINCED	
1 T	WORCESTERSHIRE SAUCE	
1 T	DIJON MUSTARD	
2 T	MOLASSES	
2 T	LOUISIANA HOT SAUCE	
2 CL	GARLIC, MINCED (OPTIONAL)	

BBQ SAUCE FOR RIBS

1 1/2 C	KETCHUP	SIMMER THESE 20 MINUTES.
1/4 C	RED WINE VINEGAR	
1/4 C	BROWN SUGAR	
2 T	DIJON MUSTARD	
2 T	WORCESTERSHIRE SAUCE	
2	ONIONS, MINCED	
4 CL	GARLIC, MINCED	

QUICK SWEET APPLE BBQ SAUCE

1 C	BBQ SAUCE, ANY BRAND	COMBINE WELL.
1/2 C	FROZEN APPLE JUICE CONCENTRATE (OR PINEAPPLE)	
1 T	BROWN SUGAR	SALT & PEPPER TO TASTE.

BASIL/WINE BBQ SAUCE

1 C	DRY WHITE WINE	COMBINE WELL & HEAT.
1/2 C	FAT-FREE CHICKEN STOCK	
1 C	FRESH BASIL, CHOPPED	
1/2	ONION, MINCED	
3 T	BUTTER BUDS	SALT & PEPPER TO TASTE.

AND MORE BBQ SAUCES   ALL THESE BBQ SAUCES HAVE JUST A TRACE OF FAT PER OZ.

CHILI BBQ SAUCE

2 C	HEINZ CHILI SAUCE	COMBINE WELL.
1/2 C	ONION, MINCED	
2 CL	GARLIC, MINCED	
1/4 C	FRESH LEMON JUICE	
2 T	WORCESTERSHIRE SAUCE	
2 T	BROWN SUGAR	
2 t	CHILI POWDER (OR MORE)	SALT & PEPPER TO TASTE.

CRANBERRY BBQ SAUCE

2 C	JELLIED CRANBERRY SAUCE	COMBINE & HEAT.
1 C	KETCHUP	
1/2 C	BROWN SUGAR	
1/2 C	ONION, DICED	

CURRY BBQ SAUCE

1 C	ORANGE MARMALADE	COMBINE WELL.
1/4 C	FRESH LEMON JUICE	
1/2 t	CURRY POWDER	SALT & PEPPER TO TASTE.

FRENCH BBQ

1 C	FAT-FREE FRENCH DRESSING	COMBINE WELL.
2 T	WORCESTERSHIRE SAUCE	
2 T	FRESH LEMON JUICE	SALT & PEPPER TO TASTE.

HONEY MUSTARD BBQ SAUCE

1 C	APPLE JUICE	COMBINE WELL.
6 T	DIJON MUSTARD	
1/4 C	HONEY	SALT & PEPPER TO TASTE.

AND MORE BBQ SAUCES   ALL THESE BBQ SAUCES HAVE JUST A TRACE OF FAT PER OZ.

ITALIAN BBQ SAUCE

1 C	FAT-FREE ITALIAN DRESSING	COMBINE WELL.
1 T	PARMESAN CHEESE	
1 T	DRIED OREGANO	SALT & PEPPER TO TASTE.

LEMON PEPPER BBQ SAUCE

1 C	FRESH LEMON JUICE	COMBINE & SIMMER 5 MIN.
2 T	BROWN SUGAR	
2 T	LEMON ZEST	
2 T	COARSE GROUND PEPPER	SALT TO TASTE.

MAPLE BBQ SAUCE

1 C	HEINZ CHILI SAUCE	COMBINE WELL.
1/2 C	REAL MAPLE SYRUP	
1/4 C	WHITE WINE	

ONE PART BBQ SAUCE

quick

1 PART EACH:	WORCESTERSHIRE SAUCE	COMBINE WELL.
	HEINZ 57 SAUCE	
	SOY SAUCE	
	A.1. SAUCE (OPTIONAL)	

PINEAPPLE GARLIC BBQ SAUCE

quick

1 C	FROZEN PINEAPPLE JUICE CONCENTRATE	COMBINE & SIMMER 5 MIN.
1/2 C	DRY SHERRY	
6 CL	GARLIC, MINCED	
2 T	BROWN SUGAR	
1 T	SOY SAUCE	

AND MORE BBQ SAUCES   ALL THESE BBQ SAUCES HAVE JUST A TRACE OF FAT PER OZ.

JERK BBQ

2 C	DARK BEER	COMBINE ALL INGREDIENTS.
1/2 C	THYME	
1/2 C	HONEY	
1/4 C	PAPRIKA	
1 T EA	CHILI POWDER, CINNAMON, NUTMEG	
1 T	GROUND BLACK PEPPER	
2 t	CAYENNE PEPPER	
2 t	SALT	

SESAME BBQ

1/2 C	WORCESTERSHIRE SAUCE	COMBINE ALL INGREDIENTS.
1/2 C	WATER	
3 T	SUGAR	
3 T	CHILI POWDER	
1 T	GARLIC POWDER	
1/2 t	PAPRIKA	

SWEET & SOUR BBQ SAUCE

2 T	CORNSTARCH	COMBINE WELL.
1 1/2 C	SUGAR	
2/3 C	VINEGAR	HEAT JUST TO THICKEN.
1/2 C	KETCHUP	
1 CL	GARLIC, MINCED	
1 SL	FRESH GINGER, PEELED, MINCED	SALT & PEPPER TO TASTE.

TERIYAKI BBQ SAUCE

1/2 C	SOY SAUCE	COMBINE & HEAT.
2 T	SUGAR	
1/2 C	DRY WHITE WINE	
1 t	FRESH GINGER, PEELED, GRATED	
1 CL	GARLIC, MINCED	

BLACKBERRY BBQ SAUCE

1/2 C	VINEGAR	YOU CAN SUBSTITUTE YOUR
1/2 C	BLACKBERRIES	FAVORITE BERRIES.
3/4 C	STRONG FAT-FREE CHICKEN STOCK	
1/4 C	TOMATO PASTE	PUREE ALL.
2 CL	GARLIC, MINCED	
1 T	DRIED THYME	
1/2 t	OLD BAY SEASONING	

EASTERN SHORE CHICKEN

 easy   SERVES 8   FAT = 5 GM EA

8	BREAST HALVES, S & P	FRY IN A PAM-SPRAYED PAN.
2 C	RICE	ADD REMAINING ITEMS, COVER
4 SL	CANADIAN BACON, TRIMMED WELL & DICED	& SIMMER 1 HOUR.
28 OZ	CANNED STEWED TOMATOES	
17 OZ	CANNED CORN	
3	ONIONS, DICED	
1 T	OLD BAY SEASONING	
1 T	PAPRIKA	
2	KNORR CHICKEN BOUILLON CUBES	
2 C	WATER (MORE IF NECESSARY)	

BROCCOLI CHICKEN BAKE

easy   SERVES 6   FAT = 5 GM EA

1 PKG	FAT-FREE PITA BREAD, CUT IN CIRCLES	PLACE THE LEFTOVER EDGES IN A SPRAYED 13" x 9" DISH.
6	BREAST HALVES, QUARTERED	
2	ONIONS, DICED	ARRANGE THESE ON PITA EDGES
3 C	BROCCOLI FLORETS	& TOP WITH PITA CIRCLES.
3 T	PARMESAN CHEESE	
8 OZ JAR	PICKLED RED BELL PEPPERS, SLICED	
1 1/2 C	EGG BEATERS	PUREE THESE & POUR OVER THE
3 C	SKIM MILK	ABOVE.
2	KNORR CHICKEN BOUILLON CUBES	
1/2 t	CAVENDER'S GREEK SEASONING	SPRINKLE PAPRIKA OVER.
1/4 t	DRY MUSTARD	COVER & CHILL 8 HOURS.

Remove from refrigerator for 1 hour and bake at 350 for 45 minutes.

CHAMPAGNE CHICKEN BREASTS

easy   SERVES 8   FAT = 4 GM EA

8	BREAST HALVES, S & P	FRY IN PAM-SPRAYED PAN.
1 C	COGNAC	REMOVE BREASTS AND DEGLAZE PAN WITH COGNAC.
6 T	FLOUR	PUREE THESE & ADD TO ABOVE
4 t	FRESH TARRAGON	WITH THE CHICKEN & SIMMER 25
6 C	CHAMPAGNE	MINUTES.
1 C	NO-FAT SOUR CREAM	WHISK THESE & ADD.
1 C	CHAMPAGNE	SIMMER UNTIL DONE.

CHICKEN CACCIATORE

SERVES 8   FAT = 4 GM EA

8	BREAST HALVES, S & P	MARINATE THESE FOR 4 HOURS.
6 OZ	TOMATO PASTE	
1/4 C	RICE WINE VINEGAR	REMOVE THE CHICKEN.
1/4 C	FAT-FREE CHICKEN STOCK	
1/3 C	RED WINE	
2 T	FRESH LEMON JUICE	
1 t	CAJUN SPICE	
1/2 t	CAYENNE PEPPER	BROIL, GRILL, BAKE OR SLICE &
1/4 t	CRUSHED RED PEPPER FLAKES	STIR-FRY.
2 CL	GARLIC, MINCED	ADD THESE TO MARINADE AND
1/2 t	FRESH OREGANO	SIMMER 20 MINUTES.
1/2 t	DRIED MARJORAM	
1/2 t	FRESH THYME	SERVE WITH CHICKEN & PASTA
16 OZ	CANNED TOMATOES, MINCED	OR RICE.
1/2 C	DRY WHITE WINE	
2	ONIONS, DICED	
1	BELL PEPPER, DICED	
1/2 LB	MUSHROOMS, QUARTERED	

COGNAC CHICKEN CASSEROLE

SERVES 12   FAT = 4 GM EA

4 LBS	CHICKEN BREAST, CUBED	BROWN THESE IN SPRAYED PAN.
2 LGE	ONIONS, MINCED	PLACE IN SPRAYED CASSEROLE.
3 CL	GARLIC, MINCED	
------	SALT & CAYENNE TO TASTE	
2 LBS	MUSHROOMS, SLICED	ADD THESE TO PAN & SIMMER 3
2 C	KNORR BEEF STOCK	MINUTES.
1/4 t	GROUND NUTMEG	
3	BAY LEAVES	POUR OVER CHICKEN, COVER &
2	RED BELL PEPPERS, SLICED	BAKE AT 325 FOR 30 MINUTES.
1 LB	CANNED WATER CHESTNUTS, DRAINED, JULIENNED	
1 C	NO-FAT SOUR CREAM	COMBINE & ADD.
1 T	SUGAR	BAKE UNCOVERED 15 MINUTES.
1/2 C	COGNAC	(REMOVE BAY LEAVES)

CARIBBEAN CHERRY CHICKEN & RUM

easy   SERVES 8   FAT = 4 GM EA

8	BREAST HALVES, S & P & PAPRIKA	DUST WITH FLOUR, SHAKE OFF
2 T	FLOUR	ALL EXCESS, BROWN IN A PAM-SPRAYED PAN & REMOVE.
4 C	PITTED CHERRIES, HALVED (FRESH OR FROZEN)	
2 t	SUGAR	ADD THESE & BRING TO A BOIL.
1/2 t	ALLSPICE	
1/2 t	DRY MUSTARD	RETURN BREASTS TO THE PAN.
1/2 t	CINNAMON	COVER AND EITHER SIMMER OR
2 C	FAT-FREE CHICKEN STOCK	BAKE AT 325 FOR 20 MINUTES.
2 C	CRUSHED PINEAPPLE & JUICE	
1/4 C	DARK RUM	UNCOVER AND BAKE AT 375 FOR
1/4 C	BROWN SUGAR	10 MINUTES.

CHINESE SPICY CHICKEN

easy   SERVES 8   FAT = 4 GM EA

8	BREAST HALVES, IN STRIPS	COMBINE & CHILL 20 MINUTES.
6 T	SOY SAUCE	
1 T	CORNSTARCH	
1/4 C	EGG BEATERS	FRY IN SPRAYED PAN & REMOVE CHICKEN.
3 T	CRUSHED RED PEPPER FLAKES	
6 CL	GARLIC, MINCED	ADD THESE, STIR-FRY 4 MINUTES.
1	ONION, DICED	
1 EA	RED, YELLOW & GREEN BELL PEPPER, SLICED	
3 T	FRESH GINGER, PEELED, MINCED	
1 C	FAT-FREE CHICKEN STOCK	
1/2 C	SOY SAUCE	COMBINE WELL, WHISK IN, HEAT
3 T	WHITE WINE VINEGAR	TO THICKEN.
1/2 C	WHITE WINE	
1 T	CORNSTARCH	SERVE OVER RICE.
3 T	BROWN SUGAR	

CHICKEN COQ AU RIESLING

easy   SERVES 8   FAT = 4 GM EA

8	BREAST HALVES, S & P	BROWN IN A PAM-SPRAYED PAN,
2 C	MUSHROOM CAPS	REMOVE TO A SPRAYED DISH &
2 C	ASPARAGUS TIPS	TOP WITH VEGGIES.
		DEGLAZE PAN WITH WINE & ADD
2 C	RIESLING WINE	REMAINING INGREDIENTS.
2	ONIONS, MINCED	POUR OVER THE VEGGIES.
1/2 C	NO-FAT SOUR CREAM	BAKE AT 350 FOR 30 MINUTES.
		SERVE OVER PASTA.

CHICKEN COQ AU VIN   SERVES 8   FAT = 5 GM EA

8	BREAST HALVES, S & P, FLOURED	SHAKE OFF EXCESS & BROWN IN A SPRAYED PAN.
4 SL	OSCAR MAYER TURKEY BACON, FRIED, DICED	
32	SMALL ONIONS	PLACE BREASTS IN A SPRAYED
16	NEW POTATOES, QUARTERED	DISH & LAYER THESE ON TOP.
2	CARROTS, SHREDDED	
24	MUSHROOMS	SALT & PEPPER.
8 CL	GARLIC, MINCED	
1/4 C	FRESH PARSLEY, CHOPPED	
1/4 C	CELERY LEAVES, CHOPPED	DEGLAZE PAN WITH BRANDY &
2 t	DRIED THYME	POUR OVER. ADD THE REST &
2	BAY LEAVES	COVER.
		BAKE AT 350 FOR 25 MINUTES.
1/2 C	BRANDY	
3 C	BURGUNDY WINE	CHILL FOR 8 HOURS AND BAKE
3 C	FAT-FREE CHICKEN STOCK	AGAIN FOR 25 MINUTES.
4 C EA	DRY RED WINE, CHICKEN STOCK	(REMOVE BAY LEAVES)

CUBAN CHICKEN   _easy_   SERVES 8   FAT = 4 GM EA

1 1/2 C	RICE	LET THESE SIT FOR 1 HOUR.
1 t	SAFFRON	DRAIN.
3 C	HOT WATER	
8	BREAST HALVES, QUARTERED, S & P	TOSS AND PLACE IN A SPRAYED
1	LIME, JUICED	CASSEROLE.
2	ONION, DICED	ADD THESE & THE RICE.
1 EA	GREEN & RED BELL PEPPER, DICED	COVER & BAKE AT 350 FOR 40
5 CL	GARLIC, MINCED	MINUTES.
2 C	CANNED CRUSHED TOMATOES	
4 OZ JAR	PICKLED RED BELL PEPPERS, CHOPPED	
1 t	GROUND CUMIN	
1/2 C	DRY WHITE WINE	
5 C	FAT FREE CHICKEN STOCK	REMOVE BAY LEAF.
1 C	FROZEN SWEET PEAS, DRAINED	
1	BAY LEAF	

Fresh cilantro is a nice addition if you can find it.

CHINESE CHICKEN & VEGGIES

SERVES 4   FAT = 4 GM EA

4	BREAST HALVES, S & P, SLICED	BROWN IN A SPRAYED PAN.
1 C	FAT-FREE CHICKEN STOCK	ADD THESE & SIMMER 5 MIN.
1 C	ONIONS, SLICED LENGTHWISE	
1 C	CARROTS, SLICED DIAGONALLY	
2 C	SNOW PEAS	ADD THESE, SAVING THE BEAN
2 C	MUSHROOMS, SLICED	SPROUTS UNTIL LAST.
1 C	BEAN SPROUTS	
1/4 C	DRY SHERRY	COMBINE, ADD & HEAT JUST TO
1 T	CORNSTARCH	THICKEN.
2 T	SOY SAUCE	SERVE WITH PASTA OR RICE.

CHOCOLATE CHICKEN

SERVES 16   FAT = 6 GM EA

16	BREAST HALVES, S & P	BROWN IN A PAM-SPRAYED PAN
		& PLACE IN A SPRAYED DISH.
8 CL	GARLIC, CRUSHED	
6	TOMATOES, PEELED & CUBED	
6	JALAPENO PEPPERS, MINCED	PUREE THESE & POUR OVER THE
4	ONIONS, CHOPPED	CHICKEN.
1 C	RAISINS	
1/4 C	CHILI POWDER	BAKE AT 350 FOR 30 MINUTES.
2 t	CINNAMON	
2 t	SALT	
2 t	ANISE SEEDS, CRUSHED	
1 t	GROUND CLOVES	SERVE WITH RICE AND WARM
1 t	GROUND CORIANDER	FLOUR TORTILLAS.
1/2 t	PEPPER	
2	CORN TORTILLAS, TORN IN PIECES	
6 C	FAT-FREE CHICKEN STOCK	
1/4 C	COCOA POWDER	

CURRIED CHICKEN

SERVES 4   FAT = 4 GM EA

4	BREAST HALVES, SLICED, S & P	FRY IN A PAM-SPRAYED PAN.
1 C	ONION, DICED	ADD THESE & SIMMER 5 MIN.
2-4 CL	GARLIC, MINCED	
1 C	CELERY, MINCED (OPTIONAL)	
1	APPLE, DICED	
3 T	RAISINS	
2 T	CURRY POWDER (OR TO TASTE)	
2 t	SUGAR	SALT & PEPPER TO TASTE.
1/4 t	FRESH GINGER, PEELED, GRATED	
1 C	FAT-FREE CHICKEN STOCK	
1 C	SKIM MILK	WHISK THESE IN & SERVE WITH
1 C	NO-FAT SOUR CREAM	PASTA OR RICE.

OPTION:
3 T	KETCHUP	TRY ADDING THESE SOMETIME.
1 T	COCONUT FLAVORING	
1 t	PAPRIKA	
1 t	DRY MUSTARD	
----	CAYENNE PEPPER	

CURRY BASE

8 CUPS BASE   FAT = 1 GM EA

8 SL	OSCAR MAYER TURKEY BACON, FRIED, DICED	
1 C	ONION, DICED	ADD THESE TO BACON PAN AND
1/2 C	CELERY, MINCED	FRY FOR 5 MINUTES.
2 CL	GARLIC, MINCED	
3/4 C	FLOUR	COMBINE & ADD THESE.
1 1/2 C	APPLESAUCE	
3/4 C	CURRY POWDER	
9 T	TOMATO PASTE	SALT & PEPPER.
3 T	FRESH LEMON JUICE	
3 T	SUGAR	SIMMER COVERED 45 MINUTES.
6	KNORR CHICKEN BOUILLON CUBES	
4 C	WATER	FINISH NOW OR FREEZE.

TO FINISH: Heat equal parts of each: Above sauce, water, cooked turkey breast cubes.
Serve with cooked rice & Indian condiments such as apples, bananas, dates etc.

MANGO CHUTNEY CHICKEN

 easy   SERVES 8   FAT = 4 GM EA

8	BREAST HALVES, S & P	PLACE IN A SPRAYED DISH.
3 T	BUTTER BUDS	ADD THESE.
3 T	CURRY POWDER	BAKE AT 350 FOR 30 MINUTES.
1/2 C	DRY WHITE WINE	
2 C	MANGO CHUTNEY, w SYRUP	REMOVE CHICKEN & DE-FAT THE
2 t	COCONUT FLAVORING	PAN JUICES (p 396).
1/2 C	NO-FAT SOUR CREAM	WHISK IN, RETURN CHICKEN AND
3 T	CHOPPED CHIVES FOR GARNISH	SERVE OVER RICE.

MID-EAST STIR-FRY

 easy   SERVES 8   FAT = 4 GM EA

8	BREAST HALVES, S & P	TOSS THESE, FRY IN A SPRAYED
1 t	DRIED THYME	PAN.
1/2 t	CRUSHED RED PEPPER FLAKES	REMOVE WHEN DONE.
1/2 t	GROUND CUMIN	
1/2 C	FAT-FREE CHICKEN STOCK	ADD THESE TO THE PAN & STIR
2	CELERY STALKS, SLICED DIAGONALLY	FRY FOR 5 MINUTES.
2	ONIONS, DICED	
2 EA	RED & GREEN BELL PEPPERS, SLICED	
2 T	CURRY POWDER (OR TO TASTE)	
16 OZ	CANNED CRUSHED TOMATOES	ADD TO ABOVE, SIMMER 5 MIN.
1 C	RAISINS	RETURN CHICKEN & HEAT.
1/2 C	MORE STOCK, AS NECESSARY	SERVE OVER RICE.

CHICKEN w CHUNKY CUCUMBER SAUCE

 quick   SERVES 8   FAT = 4 GM EA

2	CUKES, SHREDDED, SQUEEZED DRY	COMBINE & CHILL THESE.
1 C	FAT-FREE YOGURT	
1/2 C	FRESH CHIVES, MINCED	SALT & PEPPER.
1/2 C	NO-FAT SOUR CREAM	ADD CAYENNE TO TASTE.
8	BREAST HALVES, FLATTENED	TOSS THESE & SHAKE OFF ALL
1/2 C	CORNMEAL	EXCESS.
1 T	OLD BAY SEASONING (OR TO TASTE)	
1 T	DRY MUSTARD	FRY IN A PAM-SPRAYED PAN FOR
1 t	MACE OR NUTMEG	3 MINUTES EACH SIDE.
1/2 t	CAYENNE PEPPER	SERVE WITH SAUCE.

EASY CHICKEN DIJON

 easy   FAT = 4 GM EA BREAST

Just coat trimmed & dried breasts with Honey Dijon Dressing (p 98) and set aside 20 minutes (more if you have time). Grill, broil or dry fry, basting with more dressing. Heat extra dressing & serve with sliced chicken.

Or, slice the top off a small round loaf of Sourdough Bread, scoop out & fill with salad greens tossed with dressing & croutons & lay sliced chicken on top.

CARAWAY MUSTARD CHICKEN

 quick   SERVES 8   FAT = 4 GM EA

8	BREASTS, S & P	COMBINE , SPREAD ON BREASTS.
4 CL	GARLIC, MINCED	
1/2 C	MUSTARD (YOUR CHOICE)	BAKE AT 350 FOR 30 MINUTES
2 T	GROUND CARAWAY SEEDS	OR UNTIL DONE
1 T	HONEY (OPTIONAL)	

DEWEY CHICKEN

easy   SERVES 6   FAT = 7 GM EA

6	BREAST HALVES, S & P	DREDGE CHICKEN IN CHEESE
1/4 C	FLOUR	MIXTURE & BROWN IN A PAM-
3/4 C	PARMESAN CHEESE	SPRAYED PAN. PUT IN SPRAYED DISH.
1 C	DRY VERMOUTH (OR AS NEEDED)	POUR AROUND CHICKEN AND
1 C	FAT-FREE CHICKEN STOCK	COVER WITH FOIL. BAKE AT 350 FOR 25 MINUTES.
1 C	NO-FAT SOUR CREAM (OR MORE)	

Remove chicken & keep warm. De-fat the juices & whisk in the Fat-Free Sour Cream & any extra Cheese mix in which you dredged the chicken.

Toss a little sauce with cooked Penne Pasta, serve the rest over & around pasta & chicken.

EASY CHICKEN DIABLO

 easy   SERVES 8   FAT = 4 GM EA

1/2 C	FAT-FREE CHICKEN STOCK, HEATED	COMBINE & POUR THESE OVER
1/4 C	BUTTER BUDS	BREASTS.
1 C	HONEY	
1 C	TOMATO CONCASSE (p 396)	
1/2 C	ONION, DICED	
1/2 C	DIJON MUSTARD	COVER & BAKE AT 350 FOR 20
2 T	CURRY POWDER	MINUTES. UNCOVER & BAKE 10
8	BREAST HALVES, S & P	MORE MINUTES.

CHICKEN IN DATE NUT SAUCE

SERVES 8   FAT = 4 GM EA

8	BREAST HALVES, S & P	MARINATE THESE 4 HOURS.
1/4 C	WHITE VINEGAR	REMOVE CHICKEN.
1/2 C	RASPBERRIES, PUREED	
1/2 C	RASPBERRY JAM	ADD THESE & SIMMER 20 MIN.
2	APPLES, DICED	
1/2 C	ONION, MINCED	
6 CL	GARLIC, SLICED	COMBINE ALL IN SPRAYED DISH
20	DRIED DATES, DICED, SOAKED 45 MIN.	DISH & BAKE AT 350 FOR 25 MIN.
1 C	HOT PORT FOR SOAKING DATES	
1 C	FAT-FREE CHICKEN STOCK	
1 T	WALNUT FLAVORING	SERVE WITH WILD RICE.

CHICKEN w OLD BAY SAUCE

quick

SERVES 8   FAT = 4 GM EA

1 C	WARM BEER	WHISK THESE WELL AND FOLD
1 C	FLOUR	INTO THE EGG WHITE.
1 T	OLD BAY SEASONING	
1	EGG WHITE, BEATEN STIFF	DIP THE CHICKEN STRIPS & FRY
		IN A PAM-SPRAYED PAN.
8	BREAST HALVES, SLICED IN STRIPS	

OLD BAY SAUCE

3 CUPS   FAT = TR EA

2 C	NO-FAT SOUR CREAM	WHISK ALL INGREDIENTS.
1/2 C	KETCHUP	HEAT.
2 T	BUTTER BUDS	
2 t	WORCESTERSHIRE SAUCE	SERVE HOT OR COLD.
2 t	OLD BAY SEASONING (OR TO TASTE)	
1/2 C	WHITE WINE (OPTIONAL)	

OLD BAY FRIED CHICKEN

SERVES 4   FAT = 5 GM EA

4	BREAST HALVES, FLATTENED, S & P	TOSS THESE TOGETHER & SHAKE
1 C	FLOUR	OFF ALL EXCESS.
2 T	OLD BAY SEASONING	
1 C	NON-FAT VANILLA YOGURT	DREDGE IN YOGURT MIXTURE,
2 T	BUTTER BUDS	THEN IN THE CRUSHED FAT-FREE
		SALTINES.

Fry in a Pam-sprayed pan for 3 minutes each side, depending on thickness.
You might like to serve Old Bay Sauce on the side.

OVEN BAKED CHICKEN

SERVES 8   FAT = 5 GM EA

8	BREAST HALVES, S & P
2 C	FLOUR
1 PKG	GOOD SEASONS ITALIAN DRESSING MIX
1 T	PAPRIKA

TOSS THESE & LET SIT 25 MIN.
TOSS AGAIN.
PLACE ON A SPRAYED SHEET PAN
& BAKE AT 350 FOR 30 MINUTES
OR UNTIL DONE.

OVEN FRIED CHICKEN

SERVES 8   FAT = 5 GM EA

8	BREAST HALVES, S & P
2 C	NON-FAT VANILLA YOGURT
1/4 C	BUTTER BUDS
2 C	SOFT BREAD CRUMBS (p 391)

DIP BREASTS IN YOGURT MIX.

DREDGE IN CRUMBS & PLACE ON
A SPRAYED SHEET PAN. BAKE AT
375 FOR 20 MINUTES. TURN &
BAKE 10-15 MINUTES MORE.

OPTION: Add 2 packages of Good Seasons Italian Dressing Mix to the yogurt.

OVEN FRIED CHICKEN MIX

FAT = 0 GM PER T

2 C	FLOUR
3 T	PAPRIKA
2 T	PEPPER
2 T	GARLIC POWDER
2 T	DRIED MARJORAM
2 T	SALT
1 T	ONION POWDER

COMBINE ALL & STORE AT ROOM
TEMPERATURE.

TO USE: SPRAY BREASTS WITH
PAM, TOSS IN ZIPLOC BAG WITH
ENOUGH MIX TO COAT. LET SIT
30 MINUTES. SPRAY AGAIN AND
BAKE AT 375 FOR 25 MINUTES.

GERMAN BAKED CHICKEN

SERVES 8   FAT = 4 GM EA

8	BREAST HALVES, S & P
32 OZ	SAUERKRAUT, DRAINED
12 OZ	FAT-FREE SWISS OR MOZZARELLA
2 1/2 C	FAT-FREE THOUSAND ISLAND DRESSING

LAYER IN SPRAYED DISH. COVER
BAKE AT 325 FOR 45 MINUTES
OR UNTIL DONE.

You can serve with boiled potatoes or you could slice half-cooked potatoes & place in the dish with the chicken while cooking. Serve with steamed cabbage.

GARLIC CHICKEN   SERVES 8   FAT = 4 GM EA

8	BREAST HALVES, S & P, SPRAY w BERTOLLI OLIVE OIL	
60 CL	GARLIC, SLICED	COMBINE & POUR AROUND THE CHICKEN (IN SPRAYED DISH).
1 C	FAT-FREE CHICKEN STOCK	
1/2 C	DRY WHITE WINE	
1/4 C	DRY VERMOUTH	COVER & BAKE AT 350 FOR 20 MINUTES.
1/4 C	FRESH PARSLEY, CHOPPED	
1 T	FRESH BASIL, CHOPPED	
1 T	FRESH OREGANO, CHOPPED	UNCOVER & BAKE 10 MORE. (YOU MIGHT LIKE TO BROIL TO BROWN)
1 T	BUTTER BUDS	
1	LEMON, JUICED	
------	CAVENDER'S GREEK SEASONING TO TASTE	

GARLIC CHICKEN & GRAPES   *easy*   SERVES 12   FAT = 4 GM EA

1/2 C	SOY SAUCE	MARINATE THESE 30 MINUTES.
1/2 C	HONEY	
1/2 C	DIJON MUSTARD	PLACE IN A SPRAYED DISH.
1/2 C	WHITE WINE VINEGAR	
1 T	BUTTER BUDS	COVER & BAKE AT 350 FOR 20 MINUTES. UNCOVER & BAKE FOR 10 MORE MINUTES.
8 CL	GARLIC, MINCED	
1/4 t	CAYENNE PEPPER	
12	BREAST HALVES, S & P	
6 C	RED SEEDLESS GRAPES, HALVED	ADD FOR THE LAST 2 MINUTES OF BAKING.
2 C	GOLDEN RAISINS (SOAKED, DRAINED)	

GARLIC CHICKEN STIR-FRY   *quick*   SERVES 8   FAT = 4 GM EA

8	BREAST HALVES, SLICED IN STRIPS, S & P	FRY THESE IN SPRAYED PAN FOR 5 MINUTES.
1 INCH	FRESH GINGER, PEELED, GRATED	
4 CL	GARLIC, MINCED	
2 C	MUSHROOMS, SLICED	
1/2 C	WATER CHESTNUTS, SLICED	
8	GREEN ONIONS, SLICED	
2 1/2 C	FAT-FREE CHICKEN STOCK	WHISK THESE TOGETHER & ADD TO PAN.
1/4 C	DRY SHERRY	
1/4 C	RED WINE VINEGAR	
1/4 C	HOISIN SAUCE	HEAT TO THICKEN.
1/4 C	SOY SAUCE	
1/4 t	CRUSHED RED PEPPER FLAKES	
3 T	CORNSTARCH	SERVE OVER RICE.

GINGER CHICKEN

SERVES 8   FAT = 4 GM EA

8	BREAST HALVES, S & P, SLICED IN STRIPS	MARINATE THESE FOR 1 HOUR.
1/2 C	SOY SAUCE	
1 C	DRY SHERRY	STIR-FRY 8 MINUTES.
1/4 C	FRESH GINGER, PEELED, GRATED	
12	GREEN ONIONS, SLICED	
6 CL	GARLIC, MINCED	
1/4 C	HOISIN SAUCE	
4 EA	RED, GREEN & YELLOW BELL PEPPERS, SLICED	
		COMBINE WELL, ADD & HEAT TO THICKEN.
1 1/2 C	FAT-FREE CHICKEN STOCK	
2 T	CORNSTARCH	SERVE OVER RICE.

GINGER CHICKEN & SNOW PEAS

SERVES 8   FAT = 4 GM EA

8	BREAST HALVES, SLICED, S & P	COMBINE & CHILL FOR 30 MIN.
1/2 C	EGG BEATERS	
2 T	SOY SAUCE	
2 T	DRY SHERRY	STIR-FRY 8 MINUTES.
8 CL	GARLIC, MINCED	
12 SL	FRESH GINGER	
1 T	CRUSHED RED PEPPER FLAKES	
1 PKG	FROZEN SNOW PEAS	ADD THESE INGREDIENTS.
1 CAN	SLICED WATER CHESTNUTS	
1/2 C	PICKLED RED BELL PEPPERS, SLICED	
2 T	SOY SAUCE	COMBINE, ADD AND HEAT TO THICKEN.
2 T	DRY SHERRY	
1 T	BUTTER BUDS	(REMOVE GINGER SLICES)
2 t	CORNSTARCH	SERVE OVER RICE.

CHINESE GINGER CHICKEN

SERVES 8   FAT = 4 GM EA

8	BREAST HALVES	MARINATE THESE 8 HOURS.
1 C	SOY SAUCE	
1/2 C	DRY SHERRY	
1/4 C	BROWN SUGAR	BAKE AT 350 FOR 25 MINUTES
2 INCH	FRESH GINGER, PEELED, GRATED	OR UNTIL DONE.
6 CL	GARLIC, MINCED	
12	GREEN ONIONS, SLICED	

GRILLED CHICKEN VARIATIONS

FAT = 4 GM PER BREAST

Always use skinless, boneless breasts that have been very well trimmed of fat.

MARINADE 1

easy   1 1/2 CUPS   FAT = TR

1/2 C	FAT-FREE CHICKEN STOCK	PUREE & PLACE IN ZIPLOC BAG
1/2 C	RED WINE VINEGAR	WITH CHICKEN FOR 4 HOURS.
1/4 C	FRESH LEMON JUICE	
3 T	MUSTARD (YOUR CHOICE)	DRAIN. BOIL THE MARINADE.
4 t	GROUND ROSEMARY	
1 t	GROUND GINGER	BASTE WHILE GRILLING.
6 CL	GARLIC, MINCED	
2	ONION, CHOPPED	
------	SALT & PEPPER	

MARINADE 2

Same as above but omit mustard & ginger & add the following:

1 t	FRESH BASIL
1 t	FRESH OREGANO
1 t	FRESH THYME

HERB MARINADE

easy   1 CUP   FAT = TR

1/2 C	FAT-FREE CHICKEN STOCK	PUREE & PLACE IN ZIPLOC BAG
1/2 C	SOY SAUCE	WITH MEAT FOR 2 HOURS.
6 CL	GARLIC, MINCED	
3	BAY LEAF, CRUMBLED	
2 T	DRIED THYME	DRAIN. BOIL THE MARINADE.
1 T	DRIED SAGE	
1 T	GROUND GINGER	BASTE WHILE GRILLING.
1 T	DRIED MARJORAM	
	SALT & PEPPER	

LEMON MUSTARD

quick   2 CUPS   FAT = TR

1 C	FRESH LEMON JUICE	COMBINE WELL.
1/2 C	DIJON MUSTARD	
1/2 C	FRESH BASIL, CHOPPED (OR SUBSTITUTE YOUR FAVORITE HERB)	
------	SALT & PEPPER	

HAWAIIAN CHICKEN

 easy   SERVES 8   FAT = 4 GM EA

8	BREAST HALVES, S & P	COMBINE & BAKE AT 350 FOR 15
1/4 C	SOY SAUCE	MINUTES.
1 t	DRY MUSTARD	
2 INCH	FRESH GINGER, PEELED, GRATED	
2 EA	RED, YELLOW & GREEN PEPPERS, SLICED	ADD THESE & BAKE 10 MORE.
2	ONIONS, SLICED LENGTHWISE	
28 OZ	PINEAPPLE CHUNKS w JUICE	
20 OZ	MANDARIN ORANGES w JUICE	
		COMBINE WELL, BOIL & ADD TO
3 T	CORNSTARCH	DISH. STIR IN WELL.
1/2 C	BROWN SUGAR	BAKE FOR 5 MORE MINUTES.
2 T	CIDER VINEGAR	

EAST INDIAN CHICKEN w GREEN SAUCE

easy   SERVES 8   FAT = 4 GM EA

8	BREAST HALVES, S & P	MARINATE IN A ZIPLOC BAG FOR
2	ONIONS, DICED	4 TO 12 HOURS.
8 CL	GARLIC, MINCED	
2 INCH	FRESH GINGER, PEELED, GRATED	
4 t	GROUND CUMIN	GRILL OR BROIL CHICKEN UNTIL
1 t	CRUSHED RED PEPPER FLAKES	DONE.
1/2 C	FRESH LEMON JUICE	
1/2 C	FAT-FREE CHICKEN STOCK	

GREEN SAUCE

2 CUPS   FAT = TR EA

1 C	FAT-FREE CHICKEN STOCK	PUREE THESE.
1 LB	SPINACH, COOKED	
1 C	ONIONS, CHOPPED, COOKED	SIMMER 20 MINUTES.
1 T	FRESH GINGER, PEELED, MINCED, COOKED	
1/2 t	GROUND CORIANDER	
1/2 t	CURRY POWDER	
1/4 t	GROUND CUMIN	
1/4 t	TURMERIC	REMOVE FROM HEAT & WHISK IN
------	SALT & PEPPER	SOUR CREAM & APPLE.
1/2 C	NO-FAT SOUR CREAM	PUT CHICKEN ON A BED OF RICE.
1	APPLE, MINCED	POUR OVER THE SAUCE.

EASY ITALIAN BAKED CHICKEN

easy   SERVES 8   FAT = 7 GM EA

8	BREAST HALVES, S & P	PLACE IN A SPRAYED DISH & TOP
28 OZ	CANNED TOMATOES, CHOPPED	WITH THESE.
3 C	MUSHROOMS, SLICED	
2 C	MARINATED ARTICHOKE HEARTS, DRAINED, TRIMMED WELL	
2 C	FAT-FREE ITALIAN DRESSING	
1 C	DRY WHITE WINE	
24	RIPE, PITTED OLIVES, SLICED	
2 ENV	ONION SOUP MIX	COMBINE, SPRINKLE OVER AND
1/4 C	PARMESAN CHEESE	BAKE AT 350 FOR 45 MINUTES.

SLICE & SERVE OVER PASTA.

ITALIAN CHICKEN

easy   SERVES 8   FAT = 5 GM EA

8	BREASTS, S & P	BROWN IN A SPRAYED PAN AND REMOVE CHICKEN.
1/2 C	FAT-FREE CHICKEN STOCK	
1	RED ONION, CHOPPED	ADD THESE AND SIMMER FOR 10
1	GREEN PEPPER, SLICED THIN	MINUTES.
4 CL	GARLIC, MINCED	
1 t	GROUND ROSEMARY	RETURN THE CHICKEN, COVER &
1/8 t	CRUSHED RED PEPPER FLAKES	SIMMER 20 MINUTES.
2 C	CANNED TOMATOES, CHOPPED	
		SALT & PEPPER TO TASTE.
1/4 C	PARMESAN (ADD DURING LAST MINUTE)	SERVE WITH PASTA.

CHICKEN KABOBS

easy   SERVES 8   FAT = 3 GM EA

8	BREASTS, IN 1" CUBES	MARINATE THESE IN ZIPLOC BAG
12 OZ	BEER	FOR 2 HOURS.
2 CL	GARLIC, MINCED	
1/2 C	SOY SAUCE	THREAD ALL ON SKEWERS.
1/2 C	ORANGE MARMALADE	
1/4 C	BROWN SUGAR	BOIL MARINADE & BASTE WHILE
1 EA	RED & YELLOW BELL PEPPER, CUT IN EIGHTHS	GRILLING.
2	ONIONS, QUARTERED & STEAMED 6 MINUTES	
1	YELLOW SQUASH, IN CHUNKS	SERVE OVER RICE.

Add 2 shrimp for each person if you'd like to add a little something special.

LEMON CHICKEN

SERVES 8   FAT = 4 GM EA

2 3/4 C	FAT-FREE CHICKEN STOCK	SIMMER THESE FOR 15 MINUTES.
1 C	BROWN SUGAR	
2 C	FRESH LEMON JUICE	
1	LEMON, SLICED THIN, DICED	
2	ONIONS, SLICED THIN	TOSS CHICKEN IN THE EGG MIX.
1	RED BELL PEPPER, SLICED THIN	DRAIN WELL, DREDGE IN FLOUR & SHAKE OFF ALL EXCESS.
8	BREAST HALVES, SLICED IN STRIPS	
1/2 C	EGG BEATERS	BROWN IN SPRAYED PAN & ADD
1/2 C	FLOUR	TO THE SAUCE. COVER FOR 5 MINUTES.
1 C	WATER	COMBINE WELL, WHISK IN AND
1 t	DIJON MUSTARD (OPTIONAL)	HEAT TO THICKEN.
3 T	CORNSTARCH	SERVE WITH RICE OR PASTA.

LEMON CHICKEN w VEGGIES

SERVES 6   FAT = 4 GM EA

6	BREAST HALVES, SLICED IN STRIPS	FRY IN A PAM-SPRAYED PAN.
1 C	FAT-FREE CHICKEN STOCK	ADD THESE & SIMMER 5 MIN.
1 C	CARROTS, JULIENNED	
1 C EA	GREEN, YELLOW SQUASH, SLICED	
12	GREEN ONIONS, SLICED DIAGONALLY	
1	RED BELL PEPPER, SLICED	
1/2 LB	MUSHROOMS, SLICED	
1 T	SUGAR	
1 T	LEMON ZEST, MINCED	
2 T	CORNSTARCH	COMBINE WELL, WHISK IN AND
3/4 C	CHICKEN STOCK OR SKIM MILK	HEAT TO THICKEN.
2 T	FRESH PARSLEY, CHOPPED	
1/4 C	FRESH LEMON JUICE	SERVE OVER PASTA.

EASY LEMON-DILL CHICKEN

quick   SERVES 8   FAT = 4 GM EA

8	BREAST HALVES, FLATTENED, SALT & LEMON PEPPER	
1/4 C	EGG BEATERS	TOSS THESE & DRAIN.
2 C	FAT-FREE BREAD CRUMBS	COMBINE THESE AND DREDGE
2 T	LEMON PEPPER	CHICKEN, SHAKING OFF EXCESS.
4 T	LEMON ZEST, MINCED	
2 t	DRIED DILL	FRY IN A PAM-SPRAYED PAN. DRIZZLE WITH LEMON JUICE.

CHICKEN PICCATA SUPREME

quick SERVES 8 FAT = 5 GM EA

8	BREAST HALVES, FLATTENED, S & P	TOSS THESE, SHAKE OFF EXCESS
------	FLOUR	& FRY IN A SPRAYED PAN.
		REMOVE FROM PAN.
1 C	DRY WHITE WINE (OR AS NEEDED)	
1 C	FAT-FREE CHICKEN STOCK	ADD THESE & SIMMER 5 MIN.
4 CL	GARLIC, MINCED	
2 C	MARINATED ARTICHOKE HEARTS, DRAINED, TRIMMED & DICED	
1/4 C	FRESH LEMON JUICE	POUR OVER CHICKEN.
2 OZ JAR	CAPERS, DRAINED, MINCED	GARNISH WITH THIN SLICES OF
	(RINSE IF YOU WANT A MILDER TASTE)	LEMON.

CHICKEN w LENTILS ON VEGGIE NOODLES

SERVES 8 FAT = 4 GM EA

8	BREAST HALVES, S & P	SEASON BREASTS AND GRILL OR
------	CAVENDER'S GREEK SEASONING	DRY FRY.
4 C	YELLOW OR ORANGE LENTILS	SIMMER THESE UNTIL DONE.
4 C	FAT-FREE CHICKEN STOCK	
1 C	RED ONIONS, SLICED	ADD MORE STOCK AS NEEDED.
1 C	CARROTS, SHREDDED	SERVE WITH SLICED BREASTS &
		BLANCHED VEGGIE NOODLES.
1 C	GREEN ONIONS, SLICED (ADD DURING LAST 3 MIN)	

VEGGIE NOODLES

4	SEEDLESS CUCUMBERS, CARROTS, SQUASH OR ZUCCHINI PARED WITH VEGGIE PEELER TO MAKE NOODLES & BLANCHED 2 MINUTES. SERVE UNDER CHICKEN & LENTILS.

CREAMY CHICKEN MARSALA

 quick SERVES 8 FAT = 4 GM EA

8	BREAST HALVES, FLATTENED, S & P	TOSS THESE, SHAKE OFF EXCESS
------	FLOUR	& BROWN IN A SPRAYED PAN.
		REMOVE FROM PAN.
1 C	MARSALA WINE	DEGLAZE PAN WITH WINE.
1 C	MUSHROOMS, SLICED (OPTIONAL)	ADD & SIMMER FOR 3 MINUTE.
1/2 C	NO-FAT SOUR CREAM	ADD & SIMMER FOR 1 MINUTE.
1 T	SUGAR (OPTIONAL)	ADD & RETURN CHICKEN.
		HEAT THROUGH.

CHICKEN w MUSHROOM SABAYON

SERVES 8   FAT = 4 GM EA

8	BREAST HALVES, S & P	MARINATE THESE 30 MINUTES.
6 CL	GARLIC, MINCED	
10 CL	GARLIC, WHOLE	PLACE IN SPRAYED DISH & BAKE
6 T	FRESH LEMON JUICE	AT 350 FOR 30 MINUTES.
6 T	FAT-FREE CHICKEN STOCK	PUREE DE-FATTED JUICES.
2 LBS	SHIITAKE MUSHROOMS, MINCED, STEMS DISCARDED	
1 C	EGG BEATERS	ADD AND SIMMER IN A DOUBLE
2 C	FAT-FREE CHICKEN STOCK	BOILER JUST UNTIL THICKENED.
1/2 C	SWEET WHITE WINE	

!!!DO NOT OVERCOOK!!!

1 C	NO-FAT SOUR CREAM	
1 T	FRESH LEMON JUICE	ADD THESE AND POUR OVER THE
1 T	BUTTER BUDS	CHICKEN.
1 t	GROUND ROSEMARY	
2 T	FRESH PARSLEY, CHOPPED	

EASY MANHATTAN CHICKEN

easy

SERVES 8   FAT = 4 GM EA

8	BREAST HALVES, S & P	TOSS THESE & BAKE AT 350 FOR
1 T	DRIED THYME	15 MINUTES.
------	LOUISIANA HOT SAUCE	
------	WORCESTERSHIRE SAUCE	
2 C	TOMATO CONCASSE (p 396)	
16	RED POTATOES, QUARTERED & PAR-BOILED 10 MIN.	
1/2 C	FLOUR	PUREE THESE INGREDIENTS.
3 C	FAT-FREE CHICKEN STOCK	
1/2 C	SWEET VERMOUTH	POUR OVER AND BAKE 15 MORE
1/2 C	BOURBON	OR UNTIL DONE.
3 T	KITCHEN BOUQUET	

MEXICAN CHICKEN

SERVES 4   FAT = 4 GM EA

4	BREASTS IN CHUNKS, S & P & GARLIC POWDER	
1	ONION, DICED	FRY THESE IN A SPRAYED PAN.
1 EA	RED, YELLOW & GREEN BELL PEPPERS, DICED	
1 C	FAT-FREE CHICKEN STOCK	ADD THESE & SIMMER 5 MIN.
1 C	CANNED TOMATOES, CHOPPED	
4 OZ CAN	DICED GREEN CHILIES	
4 OZ CAN	WHOLE GREEN CHILIES, SLICED	
1/2 C	SALSA	
1/2	JALAPENO PEPPER, MINCED	SERVE WITH THE HOMEMADE
1/2 t	GROUND CUMIN	TORTILLA CHIPS ON p 20.
1/2 C	FAT-FREE CHEDDAR, SHREDDED	GARNISH WITH THESE.
------	NO-FAT SOUR CREAM	
12	BLACK OLIVES, SLICED	

MOROCCAN CHICKEN w LEMON & CARROTS

SERVES 8   FAT = 4 GM EA

8	BREAST HALVES, S & P	BROWN IN A SPRAYED PAN.
2	ONIONS, DICED	REMOVE CHICKEN & ADD THESE.
4	CARROTS, SLICED	
2 C	FAT-FREE CHICKEN STOCK	SIMMER 10 MINUTES.
1 C	MANGO CHUTNEY (p 266 OR USE COMMERCIAL)	
4 t	PAPRIKA	
2 t	FRESH GINGER, PEELED, GRATED	
1/2 t	TURMERIC	RETURN CHICKEN & ADD THESE.
1/4 t	CINNAMON	
2	LEMONS, SLICED	SIMMER FOR 30 MINUTES.
2 C	MANDARIN ORANGES, CHOPPED	ADD DURING LAST 2 MINUTES.
1/2 C	GOLDEN RAISINS	
6 C	COUSCOUS, COOKED	SERVE UNDER CHICKEN.

EASY MUSTARD CHICKEN

easy   SERVES 8   FAT = 4 GM EA

8	BREAST HALVES, S & P, FLOURED	SHAKE OFF EXCESS & BROWN IN A SPRAYED PAN.
2 C	FAT-FREE CHICKEN STOCK	
2	RED ONIONS, MINCED	ADD THESE & SIMMER 30 MIN.
2 CL	GARLIC, MINCED	
1 T	DRIED ITALIAN HERBS	REMOVE CHICKEN, KEEP WARM.
1/2 C	DRY VERMOUTH	
1/4 C	DIJON MUSTARD	WHISK THESE IN.
2 t	DRY MUSTARD	
1 t	DRIED TARRAGON	
1 C	NO-FAT SOUR CREAM	RETURN CHICKEN TO HEAT.

If you'd like a sweeter version of this, just add 2 T Honey.

CHICKEN NEWBURG

SERVES 6   FAT = 4 GM EA

6 T	BUTTER BUDS	PUREE THESE & SIMMER 10 MIN.
1/3 C	FLOUR	
1/8 t	FRESH THYME, MINCED	
1 C	FAT-FREE CHICKEN STOCK	
1 C	SKIM MILK	
2 T	DRY SHERRY (OR TO TASTE)	ADD THESE & SIMMER 10 MIN.
2 C	MUSHROOMS, SLICED	
1 C	ASPARAGUS, SLICED	SALT & PEPPER TO TASTE.
1/2 C	RED ONIONS, MINCED	
1/2 C	PIMENTO, SLICED	ADD THESE JUST TO HEAT.
3 C	CHICKEN OR TURKEY BREASTS, COOKED, CUBED	
1/2 C	FRESH PARSLEY, CHOPPED	SERVE OVER PASTA.

For thicker sauce, add No-Fat Sour Cream & Parmesan. (Add 2 GM Fat for each T Parmesan added)

CHICKEN OSCAR

SERVES 8   FAT = 4 GM EA

8	BREASTS HALVES, FLATTENED, S & P	SPRINKLE WITH LEMON JUICE, DREDGE IN FLOUR, SHAKE OFF EXCESS & FRY IN SPRAYED PAN.
1/4 C	FRESH LEMON JUICE	
1/2 C	WINE OR FAT-FREE CHICKEN STOCK	DEGLAZE PAN WITH WINE AND POUR OVER CHICKEN.
16	ASPARAGUS SPEARS, COOKED	
8	LARGE SHRIMP, COOKED, SPLIT	TOP EACH WITH 2 ASPARAGUS SPEARS, A SHRIMP & SAUCE.
2 C	MOCK HOLLANDAISE SAUCE (p 257)	

ORANGE CHICKEN   *easy*   SERVES 8   FAT = 4 GM EA

8	BREAST HALVES, S & P & PAPRIKA	BROWN IN A SPRAYED PAN AND REMOVE TO SPRAYED DISH.
1/4 C	GRAND MARNIER	DEGLAZE PAN WITH LIQUEUR.
1 C	ORANGE JUICE	ADD THESE AND POUR OVER.
1 C	CHICKEN STOCK	
3	RED ONIONS, SLICED LENGTHWISE	BAKE AT 350 FOR 25 MINUTES.
1/4 C	ORANGE ZEST, GRATED	REMOVE THE CHICKEN.
1/2 C	JUICE FROM MANDARINS(+ WATER IF NEEDED)	COMBINE WELL, WHISK IN AND
2 T	CORNSTARCH	HEAT TO THICKEN. ADD THE MANDARINS & CHICKEN.
2 CANS	MANDARIN ORANGES	

OPTION: 1/2 C   HONEY
              2 INCHES   GINGER, PEELED, GRATED
              1/2 t   NUTMEG

CREAMY CHICKEN & PASTA   SERVES 8   FAT = 7 GM EA

2 BCH	BROCCOLI FLORETS, COOKED	PROCESS THESE CHOP-CHOP.
2	CARROTS, SHREDDED	(DO NOT PUREE).
2 C	NO-FAT SOUR CREAM	
1/2 C	DRY SHERRY	
------	NUTMEG	SALT & PEPPER TO TASTE.
1/4 C	FRESH LEMON JUICE	
2 C	COOKED NOODLES	TOSS WITH ABOVE AND FILL 8
6	BREAST HALVES, COOKED, CHUNKED	LARGE, SPRAYED RAMEKINS.
8	MUSHROOMS, SLICED	
1/4 C	FLOUR	PUREE THESE.
3 T	BUTTER BUDS	HEAT TO THICKEN.
2 T	DRY MUSTARD	
1 1/2 C	SKIM MILK	
1/2 C	PARMESAN CHEESE	SALT & PEPPER TO TASTE.
------	TABASCO	
1 C	NO-FAT SOUR CREAM	SPOON OVER EACH.
3 T	PARMESAN CHEESE	SPRINKLE OVER EACH & BAKE BAKE AT 350 FOR 20 MINUTES.

Or, slice the top off small round loaves of bread, scoop out the dough & fill. Sprinkle with the cheese & bake.

RUSSIAN CHICKEN

SERVES 8   FAT = 4 GM EA

8	BREASTS, S & P	BROWN IN A SPRAYED PAN.
1 C	FAT-FREE CHICKEN STOCK	PUREE THESE & ADD.
1/4 C	FLOUR	
1/4 C	RED WINE VINEGAR	COVER & SIMMER 20 MINUTES.
2 T	SUGAR	
1/4 C	BEETS, CHOPPED (COOKED OR CANNED)	
1	BAY LEAF, CRUMBLED	
1 C	NO-FAT SOUR CREAM	ADD & SIMMER 3 MINUTES.
------	FAT-FREE CHICKEN STOCK AS NEEDED	SALT & PEPPER TO TASTE.
------	VODKA IS OPTIONAL (BUT NOT TO A RUSSIAN!)	

SPICY HERBED CHICKEN

SERVES 6   FAT = 4 GM EA

6	BREAST HALVES, S & P	TOSS THESE, SHAKE OFF EXCESS
1/2 C	FLOUR	& BROWN IN A SPRAYED PAN.
1 T	FRESH PARSLEY, MINCED	
2 t	GARLIC POWDER	PLACE IN A SPRAYED DISH.
1 t	ONION POWDER	
1/2 t	DRIED SAGE	
1/2 t	GROUND ROSEMARY	
2 C	FAT-FREE CHICKEN STOCK	COMBINE & POUR AROUND THE
2 T	BALSAMIC VINEGAR	CHICKEN, COVER & BAKE AT 350
1/2 C	NO-FAT SOUR CREAM (OPTIONAL)	FOR 25 MINUTES.

CHICKEN IN MINUTES

quick

SERVES 8   FAT = 4 GM EA

8	BREAST HALVES, FLATTEN, S & P	MARINATE THESE UNTIL READY
1/2 C	BROWN SUGAR	TO GRILL.
1/4 C	SOY SAUCE	
2 T	BALSAMIC VINEGAR	IF YOU DON'T HAVE THE TIME TO
2 CL	GARLIC, MINCED	MARINATE, JUST BAKE ALL AT
1	KNORR CHICKEN BOUILLON CUBE, CRUMBLED	350 FOR 15-20 MINUTES OR UNTIL
------	KETCHUP (OPTIONAL)	DONE.

PEACH BRANDIED CHICKEN

 easy SERVES 8   FAT = 4 GM EA

8	BREAST HALVES, S & P	MARINATE THESE FOR 2 HOURS.
1/2 C	PEACH BRANDY	
1/2 C	SWEET WHITE WINE	
1/2 C	FAT-FREE CHICKEN STOCK	ADD THESE & BAKE AT 350 FOR
2 C	PEACHES, SLICED (FRESH OR CANNED)	25 MINUTES. BROIL 5 MINUTES.

CHICKEN & PEPPERS STIR-FRY

SERVES 8   FAT = 3 GM EA

6	BREAST HALVES, IN STRIPS, S & P	MARINATE THESE FOR 2 HOURS
1/2 C	RICE WINE VINEGAR	
1/2 C	FAT-FREE CHICKEN STOCK	REMOVE CHICKEN & FRY IN A
1/2 C	RED WINE	SPRAYED PAN.
2 T	CRUSHED RED PEPPER FLAKES	
		(SAVE THE MARINADE)
1/2 C	FAT-FREE CHICKEN STOCK	
6 C	RED, YELLOW & GREEN BELL PEPPERS, SLICED	
1/2 C	CARROTS, SHREDDED	ADD THESE AND SIMMER UNTIL
2 C	ONIONS, SLICED LENGTHWISE	DONE.
1/2 C	CUCUMBERS, JULIENNED	
1 T	FRESH GINGER, PEELED, GRATED	
1 t	GARLIC, MINCED (OPTIONAL)	
------	CRUSHED RED PEPPER FLAKES TO YOUR TASTE	
6 T	SOY SAUCE	COMBINE WELL, WHISK IN AND
1 1/2 C	OF THE MARINADE	HEAT TO THICKEN.
2 T	CORNSTARCH	SERVE OVER RICE.

CREAMY PEPPER CHICKEN

SERVES 8   FAT = 4 GM EA

6	BREASTS HALVES, IN STRIPS, S & P	FRY IN A SPRAYED PAN.
1 EA	RED, YELLOW & GREEN PEPPER, STRIPS	ADD THESE AND SIMMER UNTIL
2	ONIONS, SLICED LENGTHWISE	DONE.
2 CL	GARLIC, MINCED	
3 T	CRACKED RED & GREEN PEPPERCORNS	
1 C	FAT-FREE CHICKEN STOCK	
1 C	FAT-FREE CREAM CHEESE	WHISK THESE IN TO HEAT.
2 T	BUTTER BUDS	
1 T	FRESH BASIL, CHOPPED &/OR TARRAGON	SERVE OVER PASTA.
------	SKIM MILK AS NEEDED	

CHICKEN IN PLUM SAUCE

SERVES 8   FAT = 4 GM EA

8	BREAST HALVES, S & P, PAPRIKA, FLOUR	TOSS THESE & BROWN IN A PAM-SPRAYED PAN. PLACE IN A SPRAYED DISH.
1 C	DRY WHITE WINE OR DRY SHERRY	
16	BLUE PLUMS, PITTED, SLICED	PUREE THESE & POUR OVER.
2 CL	GARLIC, MINCED	
2 SL	FRESH GINGER, PEELED, MINCED	
1/4 C	ORANGE ZEST, MINCED	COVER & BAKE AT 350 FOR 25 MINUTES OR UNTIL DONE.
8	GREEN ONIONS, MINCED	
1/4 C	BROWN SUGAR	
1/4 C	RICE WINE VINEGAR	
1/4 C	SOY SAUCE	
1 t	CINNAMON	
1 C	FAT-FREE CHICKEN STOCK OR COLD WATER	
2 T	CORNSTARCH	

CHICKEN IN RASPBERRY SAUCE

easy

SERVES 8   FAT = 4 GM EA

8	BREAST HALVES, S & P	BROWN IN A PAM-SPRAYED PAN.
1 C	RICE WINE VINEGAR	ADD THESE INGREDIENTS.
1 C	RASPBERRY SEEDLESS JAM	
2 C	DRY WHITE WINE	COVER & SIMMER 25 MINUTES OR UNTIL DONE.
1	ORANGE, ZESTED & MINCED	
5 C	RASPBERRIES, PUREED, STRAINED	

CHICKEN & RICE CASSEROLE

easy

SERVES 8   FAT = 4 GM EA

3	ONIONS, LARGE DICE	BOIL THESE FOR 2 MINUTES.
6 CL	GARLIC, MINCED	
2	CELERY STALKS, MINCED	ADD THE RICE & CHICKEN AND POUR INTO A SPRAYED DISH.
4	CARROTS, SLICED THIN	
4 C	WATER	BAKE AT 350 FOR 45 MINUTES.
2	KNORR CHICKEN BOUILLON CUBE	
1	KNORR VEGGIE BOUILLON CUBE	
2 t	SAFFRON THREADS	
2 C	LONG GRAIN RICE	
8	BREAST HALVES, IN CHUNKS, S & P	

OLD FASHIONED CHICKEN CASSEROLE

SERVES 6   FAT = 4 GM EA

3 C	NOODLES, COOKED	LAYER THESE IN A SPRAYED DISH
2 C	CARROTS, DICED, COOKED (OR CANNED)	AND COVER.
1 C	TINY PEAS (FROZEN OR CANNED)	BAKE AT 375 FOR 20 MINUTES.
2 C	ONIONS, DICED, COOKED	
6	BREAST HALVES, COOKED, IN CHUNKS (OR TURKEY)	
------	SALT & PEPPER TO TASTE	
2 T	CORNSTARCH (WHISKED INTO STOCK BELOW)	
4 C	RICH FAT-FREE CHICKEN STOCK (AS NEEDED TO COVER)	
		CUT IN STRIPS & LAY ON TOP IN
2-3	FAT-FREE FLOUR TORTILLAS	LATTICE PATTERN. PRESS DOWN. BAKE AGAIN UNTIL BUBBLY.

Or, slice the tops off small round loaves of bread and scoop out the dough. Spray with Pam, fill & top with "Loaf Lid" & bake.

SESAME BUTTERMILK CHICKEN

easy   SERVES 8   FAT = 5 GM EA

8	BREAST HALVES, SOAKED OVERNIGHT IN BUTTERMILK, DRAINED	
3 T	BUTTER BUDS	COMBINE & SPRINKLE OVER EA
2 T	FRESH LEMON JUICE	BREAST.
2 CL	GARLIC, MINCED	
		COMBINE & DREDGE EACH.
1 1/2 C	FAT-FREE BREAD CRUMBS	BAKE AT 375 FOR 15 MINUTES.
1/4 C	SESAME SEEDS	SPRAY WITH PAM AND BAKE 15 MORE MINUTES.

CHICKEN & SNOW PEAS

quick   SERVES 8   FAT = 4 GM EA

6	BREAST HALVES, IN STRIPS, S & P	FRY IN A PAM-SPRAYED PAN.
1 C	FAT-FREE CHICKEN STOCK	ADD THESE AND SIMMER UNTIL
1	RED ONION, SLICED & QUARTERED	VEGGIES ARE TENDER CRISP.
1 LB	SNOW PEAS	
2 C	MUSHROOMS, SLICED	
1 C	WATER CHESTNUTS, SLICED	
1 JAR	BABY CORN	
1 t	SUGAR	
		COMBINE WELL, WHISK IN AND
1/2 C	FAT-FREE CHICKEN STOCK	HEAT TO THICKEN.
1 T	CORNSTARCH	SERVE OVER RICE.
1 T	DRY SHERRY	
1 T	SOY SAUCE OR MINCED GINGER OR MINCED GARLIC—YOUR CHOICE	

CHUTNEY STUFFED CHICKEN

SERVES 8   FAT = 4 GM EA

1/2 C	FAT-FREE CHICKEN STOCK	SIMMER THESE FOR 10 MINUTES.
2	ONIONS, DICED	
2	CELERY STALKS, MINCED	
2	RED APPLES, DICED	COOL.
2 SL	FAT-FREE BREAD, DICED	ADD THESE TO ABOVE.
2 t	CURRY POWDER (OR TO TASTE)	STUFF BREASTS, ROLL UP AND
1/2 C	CHUTNEY, CHOPPED	SECURE WITH A PICK.
1/2 C	GOLDEN RAISINS	
8	BREAST HALVES, FLATTENED, S & P	BROWN THE STUFFED ROLLS IN SPRAYED PAN.
3	APPLES, SLICED	
1	LEMON, JUICED	ADD & SIMMER FOR 30 MINUTES.
1 C	FAT-FREE CHICKEN STOCK	
2 T	CORNSTARCH	COMBINE WELL, WHISK IN AND
1/2 C	APPLE JUICE	HEAT TO THICKEN.

CURRIED CHICKEN ROLLS

SERVES 4   FAT = 4 GM EA

1 C	RICE	COOK RICE AS DIRECTED.
2 C	BOILING WATER	(WITH THESE INGREDIENTS)
2	ONIONS, MINCED	
2	KNORR CHICKEN BOUILLON CUBES	COOL SLIGHTLY.
1 C	RAISINS	ADD THESE, STUFF THE BREASTS
3 T	FRESH PARSLEY, CHOPPED	& ROLL UP.
1 T	CURRY POWDER (OR TO TASTE)	SECURE WITH A PICK.
2 t	POULTRY SEASONING	
1 T	BROWN SUGAR	BROWN IN A SPRAYED PAN.
1/2 t	GARLIC POWDER	
8	BREAST HALVES, FLATTENED, S & P	
2 C	WHITE WINE	ADD THESE, COVER AND SIMMER
2	KNORR CHICKEN BOUILLON CUBES	30 MINUTES.

FRUIT STUFFED CHICKEN I

SERVES 8   FAT = 4 GM EA

1 C	DATES, CHOPPED	COMBINE THESE AND PLACE ON EACH BREAST.
2	APPLES, CHOPPED	
1/2 C	GRAPES, HALVED	
1	ONION, DICED	ROLL UP & SECURE WITH A PICK.
1/3 C	FRESH LEMON JUICE	
1 T	CINNAMON	PLACE IN A SPRAYED DISH, SEAM
1 t	ALLSPICE	SIDE DOWN.
1/2 t	GROUND CUMIN	
8	BREAST HALVES, FLATTENED, S & P	
2 C	DRY WHITE WINE, HOT	PUREE THESE & BRUSH ON EACH.
1/4 C	SOY SAUCE	
1/2 C	HONEY	
1 C	APRICOTS, CHOPPED, SOAKED 30 MIN	BAKE AT 350 FOR 30 MINUTES OR UNTIL DONE.

FRUIT STUFFED CHICKEN II

SERVES 8   FAT = 4 GM EA

8	BREASTS, FLATTENED, S & P	
1	RED ONION, MINCED	TOSS THESE & PLACE ON EACH.
1 C	DRIED MIXED FRUIT, DICED	
1/2 C	MADEIRA WINE FOR SOAKING ABOVE FRUIT 30 MIN.	
2 CL	GARLIC, MINCED	
1 T	FRESH PARSLEY, CHOPPED	ROLL UP & SECURE WITH A PICK.
1/4 t	MACE OR ALLSPICE	
1/8 t	DRY MUSTARD	
1/8 t	GROUND CLOVES	
1/2 C	BROWN SUGAR	WHISK THESE & BRUSH ON EACH.
1 T	DRY MUSTARD	
1/2 C	DRY SHERRY OR AS NEEDED	PLACE IN A SPRAYED DISH.
1 C	WHITE WINE	POUR AROUND, BAKE AT 350 FOR 30 MINUTES OR UNTIL DONE.

ITALIAN STUFFED CHICKEN

SERVES 8   FAT = 6 GM EA

8	BREAST HALVES, FLATTENED, S & P

1 C	FRESH BASIL LEAVES, CHOPPED	COMBINE & SPREAD ON EACH.
8	PLUM TOMATOES, SLICED THIN	ROLL UP & SECURE WITH A PICK.
1/4 C	EGG BEATERS	
1 C	FAT-FREE BREAD CRUMBS	BROWN IN A SPRAYED PAN AND
1/2 C	PARMESAN CHEESE	PLACE IN SPRAYED DISH.

1 C	DRY WHITE WINE	ADD & BAKE AT 350 FOR 45 MIN.
		REMOVE CHICKEN.
1 C	NO-FAT SOUR CREAM	DE-FAT THE DRIPPINGS & WHISK
3 T	FRESH BASIL, CHOPPED	IN THESE INGREDIENTS.

CHICKEN KIEV

SERVES 8   FAT = 4 GM EA

1/2 C	NO-FAT SOUR CREAM	COMBINE THESE, SPREAD ON EA
1/4 C	BUTTER BUDS (OR TO TASTE)	BREAST, ROLL UP & SECURE EA
2 T	DIJON MUSTARD	WITH A PICK.
1/4 C	FRESH CHIVES, MINCED	
2 T	FRESH PARSLEY	YOU CAN WRAP & FREEZE NOW
4 CL	GARLIC, MINCED	OR CONTINUE...
------	FAT-FREE BREAD CRUMBS AS NEEDED	
	TO MAKE FIRM MIXTURE	DIP EACH IN EGG MIX, DREDGE
		IN CRUMBS & BROWN IN A PAM-
8	BREAST HALVES, FLATTENED, S & P	SPRAYED PAN.
3/4 C	EGG BEATERS	PLACE IN A SPRAYED DISH.
2 C	FAT-FREE BREAD CRUMBS	BAKE AT 350 FOR 30 MINUTES.

TRADITIONALLY STUFFED CHICKEN BREASTS

SERVES 4   FAT = 4 GM EA

1	CARROT, SHREDDED	COMBINE & SIMMER 15 MINUTES.
1	CELERY STALK, MINCED	
1	ONION, DICED	COOL.
1	APPLE, DICED	ADD BREAD CUBES & SPREAD ON
1 C	MUSHROOMS, DICED (OPTIONAL)	BREASTS. ROLL UP & SECURE w
1 C	FAT-FREE CHICKEN STOCK	PICKS.
------	FAT-FREE BREAD CUBES AS NEEDED	POUR STOCK AROUND & BAKE AT
4	BREAST HALVES, FLATTENED, S & P	350 FOR 30 MINUTES OR UNTIL
2 C	FAT-FREE CHICKEN STOCK	DONE.

Puree leftover stuffing with de-fatted drippings, heat & spoon over breasts.
Serve with Fat-Free Mashed Potatoes, Gravy & Peas (p 282, 255, 314).

SPINACH STUFFED BREASTS

SERVES 4   FAT = 4 GM EA

4	BREAST HALVES, FLATTENED, S & P	COMBINE & CHILL FOR 2 HOURS.
1/2 C	RICE WINE VINEGAR	
1/2 C	SOY SAUCE	
1 t	FRESH GINGER, PEELED, GRATED	DRAIN.
1 t	FRESH THYME, MINCED	
1 PKG	FROZEN SPINACH, SQUEEZED DRY	PROCESS THESE CHOP-CHOP.
1/2 C	ONION, MINCED	
1/2 C	NO-FAT SOUR CREAM	SPREAD ON BREASTS.
------	NUTMEG	
1 T	BUTTER BUDS	
1 C	MUSHROOMS, MINCED	COMBINE & SPREAD THESE ON
1 T	BUTTER BUDS	THE SPINACH MIX.
2	EGG WHITES, BEATEN STIFF, NOT DRY	
		ARRANGE 3 TIPS ON EACH AND
12	ASPARAGUS TIPS	ROLL UP IN MICROWAVE SARAN WRAP.

Poach to internal temperature of 160. Remove wrap, Slice & serve with Wild Rice & Fat-Free Chicken Gravy (p 298, 255).

Or...chill, slice & serve on bed of greens with a Light Vinaigrette (p 106, 107).

WILD RICE STUFFED BREASTS

easy   SERVES 8   FAT = 4 GM EA

1 C	WILD RICE	SIMMER THESE FOR 30 MINUTES.
2	ONIONS, MINCED	COOL.
2 C	FAT-FREE CHICKEN STOCK	
		ADD THESE, STUFF BREASTS AND
1 C	MUSHROOMS, SLICED	ROLL UP. SECURE WITH PICKS &
1/4 C	FAT-FREE MIRACLE WHIP	SPRAY WITH PAM.
1/4 C	FRESH CHIVES, CHOPPED	BAKE AT 350 FOR 30 MINUTES
		OR UNTIL DONE.
8	BREAST HALVES, FLATTENED, S & P	

SOUTHWESTERN CHICKEN

easy   SERVES 8   FAT = 6 GM EA

8	BREAST HALVES, S & P	LAY IN A SPRAYED DISH.
2	ONIONS, CHOPPED	ADD THESE & LET SIT 30 MIN.
3 CL	GARLIC, MINCED	
28 OZ CAN	TOMATOES, CHOPPED	
11 OZ CAN	CORN	
6 OZ	TOMATO PASTE	BAKE AT 350 FOR 30 MINUTES
6 OZ	GREEN CHILIES, CHOPPED	OR UNTIL DONE.
2 t	CHILI POWDER	
1/2 t	CORIANDER	
1/2 t	CAVENDER'S GREEK SEASONING	
1/2 t	GROUND CUMIN	
16 SL	BLACK OLIVES, SLICED	SPREAD OLIVES OVER.
4 OZ	FAT-FREE CHEDDAR, SHREDDED	SPRINKLE CHEESE, SPRAY AND
------	PAM OLIVE OIL SPRAY	BROIL TO MELT CHEESE.

SWEET & SOUR CHICKEN

  quick   SERVES 8   FAT = 5 GM EA

7	BREAST HALVES, IN STRIPS	FRY THESE IN A SPRAYED PAN 5
1 EA	RED, GREEN & YELLOW BELL PEPPER IN STRIPS	MINUTES.
1	ONION, SLICED LENGTHWISE	
5 SL	FRESH GINGER	
2 CL	GARLIC, MINCED	
1 C	FAT-FREE CHICKEN STOCK	COMBINE & ADD TO ABOVE.
3 T	BROWN SUGAR	SIMMER UNTIL DONE.
3 T	CORNSTARCH	
2 T	WORCESTERSHIRE SAUCE	
2 C	PINEAPPLE JUICE	
1/2 C	RICE WINE VINEGAR	REMOVE GINGER SLICES.
1/2 C	SOY SAUCE	
1/2 C	KETCHUP	SERVE OVER RICE.
2 T	SESAME SEEDS, TOASTED	SPRINKLE OVER.

THAI CHICKEN & VEGGIES

SERVES 8   FAT = 7 GM EA

6	BREAST HALVES, IN STRIPS, S & P	
2 C	FAT-FREE CHICKEN STOCK	SIMMER THESE FOR 5 MINUTES.
4 CL	GARLIC, MINCED	
1	ONION, SLICED, QUARTERED	
1	CARROT, JULIENNED	
1	RED BELL PEPPER, JULIENNED	
1 C	BROCCOLI FLORETS (OPTIONAL)	
1	CELERY STALK, SLICED DIAGONALLY	
5 SL	FRESH GINGER	
1/4 C	HEALTH VALLEY PEANUT BUTTER	COMBINE & ADD THESE.
1 T	MOLASSES	SIMMER UNTIL DONE.
1 T	SOY SAUCE	
1 T	FRESH LEMON JUICE	
1 T	COCONUT FLAVORING (OR TO TASTE)	SALT & PEPPER TO TASTE.
6 DROPS	LOUISIANA HOT SAUCE	REMOVE GINGER SLICES.
1/2 C	WATER CHESTNUTS, SLICED	SERVE OVER RICE.

CHICKEN in CREAMY VINEGAR

easy   SERVES 8   FAT = 4 GM EA

8	BREAST HALVES, S & P, FLOURED	FRY IN A PAM-SPRAYED PAN. PLACE IN A SPRAYED DISH.
1/2 C	RED WINE VINEGAR	
1/2 C	BRANDY	DEGLAZE PAN & POUR OVER THE CHICKEN.
2 C	WHITE WINE	
2	ONIONS, DICED	ADD THESE & BAKE AT 350 FOR
2 LBS	MUSHROOMS, QUARTERED	30 MINUTES.
3 C	FAT-FREE CHICKEN STOCK	DE-FAT THE DRIPPINGS.
1/4 C	FLOUR	PUREE THESE AND ADD TO THE
1 C	SKIM MILK	DRIPPINGS.
1	KNORR CHICKEN BOUILLON CUBE	HEAT TO THICKEN.
------	SALT & PEPPER TO TASTE	

CHICKEN in WINE SAUCE

 SERVES 4   FAT = 5 GM EA

4	BREAST HALVES, IN STRIPS	FRY IN A SPRAYED PAN, REMOVE
------	SALT & PEPPER & GARLIC POWDER	& KEEP WARM.
1 C	SKIM MILK	PUREE THESE, ADD AND HEAT TO
1	KNORR CHICKEN BOUILLON CUBE	THICKEN.
2 T	PARMESAN CHEESE	
1/2 t	DRIED BASIL	
2 t	CORNSTARCH	RETURN CHICKEN & HEAT.
1/2 C	DRY WHITE WINE OR CHICKEN STOCK	

For a change, you might like to finish off this dish with No-Fat Sour Cream.

GRILLED YOGURT CHICKEN

 SERVES 8   FAT = 4 GM EA

8	BREAST HALVES, S & P	MARINATE THESE FOR 8 HOURS.
1 C	FAT-FREE LEMON YOGURT	
6 CL	GARLIC, MINCED	
4 SL	FRESH GINGER	
4	GREEN ONIONS, SLICED	REMOVE CHICKEN AND GRILL OR
2 T	DRY SHERRY	BROIL UNTIL DONE.
1 T	FRESH LEMON JUICE	
1 T	LEMON ZEST, MINCED	ADD 1 T CORNSTARCH TO COLD
1 t	CRUSHED RED PEPPER FLAKES	MARINADE & BOIL TO THICKEN.
1/2 t	GROUND ROSEMARY	
1/2 t	PAPRIKA	
1/2 t	GROUND CUMIN	REMOVE GINGER SLICES.
1/2 t	TURMERIC	
2	SEEDLESS CUCUMBER, JULIENNED	ADD JUST BEFORE SERVING.

EASY DEVILED CHICKEN

 SERVES 8   FAT = 4 GM EA

8	BREAST HALVES, S & P	MARINATE THESE FOR 6 HOURS.
1/2 C	HONEY	REMOVE THE CHICKEN.
1/2 C	SOY SAUCE	
3 T	BALSAMIC VINEGAR	BOIL THE MARINADE, ADDING
3 T	ORANGE JUICE CONCENTRATE	THE MUSTARD & DRESSING.
2 T	ORANGE ZEST	
		BRUSH ON THE CHICKEN & BAKE
1/2 C	DIJON MUSTARD	AT 350 FOR 30 MINUTES.
1/2 C	FAT-FREE RANCH DRESSING	

PORT & HONEY CHICKEN

easy   SERVES 8   FAT = 4 GM EA

8	BREAST HALVES, S & P	BROWN IN A SPRAYED PAN AND REMOVE TO A SPRAYED DISH. DEGLAZE PAN & POUR OVER THE CHICKEN.
1/2 C	PORT WINE	
1/2 C	FAT-FREE CHICKEN STOCK	
1/2 C	ONION, MINCED	ADD THESE & BAKE AT 350 FOR 25 MINUTES.
1 C	PORT WINE	
1/2 C	RED WINE	
2 T	BALSAMIC VINEGAR	REMOVE CHICKEN, REDUCE THE STOCK BY 1/2 & DE-FAT.
5 C	FAT-FREE CHICKEN STOCK	
1/2 C	PORT WINE	COMBINE WELL, WHISK IN AND HEAT TO THICKEN.
1 T	CORNSTARCH	
1 T	HONEY	SERVE WITH PASTA.

JUNIPER CHICKEN

SERVES 8   FAT = 4 GM EA

8	BREAST HALVES, S & P	MARINATE THESE FOR 8 HOURS. DRAIN & FRY IN A SPRAYED PAN. REMOVE & KEEP WARM.
1 C	CRUSHED JUNIPER BERRIES	
1 C	DRY VERMOUTH	
2 C	WATER	ADD THESE & REDUCE BY 1//2.
1	KNORR BEEF BOUILLON CUBE	
1	KNORR CHICKEN BOUILLON CUBE	
1 T	BALSAMIC VINEGAR	WHISK IN THE SOUR CREAM.
1 C	NO-FAT SOUR CREAM	PLACE THE CHICKEN ON BEDS OF SPINACH & SPOON ON SAUCE.
2 LBS	SPINACH LEAVES, BLANCHED	

CHICKEN IN HOISIN SAUCE

easy   SERVES 8   FAT = 4 GM EA

8	BREAST HALVES, S & P	MARINATE THESE FOR 4 HOURS.
1 BCH	GREEN ONIONS, MINCED	
1/2 C	HOISIN SAUCE	
1/2 C	SOY SAUCE	COVER & BAKE AT 350 FOR 30 MINUTES.
1	LEMON, JUICED	
1 T	WALNUT FLAVORING	
1/2 t	GARLIC, MINCED	
1/2 t	FRESH GINGER, PEELED, GRATED	
1/4 t	NUTMEG	SERVE OVER RICE.
1/4 t	CINNAMON	
------	GROUND CLOVES	

SIMPLY APPLES & CHICKEN

(quick)   SERVES 8   FAT = 4 GM EA

8	BREAST HALVES, S & P	FRY IN A PAM-SPRAYED PAN.
1	ONION, DICED	ADD THESE & SIMMER COVERED
2	APPLES, SLICED	FOR 20 MINUTES.
1 C	DRY WHITE WINE	
1/2 C	APPLE LIQUOR	
1/2 C	COLD FAT-FREE CHICKEN STOCK	COMBINE WELL, WHISK IN AND HEAT TO THICKEN.
2 T	CORNSTARCH	SERVE WITH BOILED POTATOES & APPLE WINGS.

APPLE WINGS

16 WINGS

4   RED APPLES, QUARTERED, SLICED AS PICTURED
        DIP IN ORANGE JUICE & MICROWAVE FOR 1 MINUTE.

Make 2 small diagonal cuts in the center of each apple quarter creating a small wedge. Make 2 more cuts following the lines of the original cuts creating a slightly larger wedge (around the smaller wedge). Do this again, creating a larger wedge if you have enough apple left, thus creating 4 wedges, 3 of which have a smaller wedge within. Separate these wedges, dip in orange juice & put back together, but slide each wedge slightly to one side to create the wing effect.

EVEN EASIER APPLES & CHICKEN

SERVES 8   FAT = 4 GM EA

8	BREAST HALVES, S & P	PLACE IN A SPRAYED PAN.
1/2 C	DIJON MUSTARD	SPREAD OVER BREASTS.
1 C	BROWN SUGAR	SPRINKLE OVER ALL.
------	GARLIC POWDER	
------	CINNAMON	
2 C	CHUNKY APPLESAUCE	SIMMER THESE AND SPOON ON
1	APPLE, DICED	BREASTS.

Bake at 350 for 30 minutes or until done.

Remember...... All beef, veal & pork in these recipes are trimmed **EXTREMELY** well, even to the point of trimming large marbling inside the meat. An ounce = 28 grams, so if you can remove even 1/2 ounce of fat, you're saving almost 14 grams of fat right there. It may take extra time, but, believe me, it's really worth it! If, while trimming, you end up losing the shape of the meat, just cut in cubes & make kabobs.

ALMOND BEEF

 quick   SERVES 8   FAT = 7 GM EA

2 LBS	TOP ROUND OR TENDERLOIN, IN STRIPS	FRY IN A PAM-SPRAYED PAN.
3	CARROTS, JULIENNED	ADD THESE AND STIR-FRY UNTIL
2	ONIONS, SLICED LENGTHWISE	ALMOST DONE.
3	CELERY STALKS, SLICED THIN DIAGONALLY	
1 T	CURRY POWDER	
2 C	FAT-FREE CHICKEN STOCK	COMBINE & ADD TO THICKEN.
1 T	ALMOND FLAVORING	
2 T	BUTTER BUDS	
1 t	WORCESTERSHIRE SAUCE	
1/4 t	LOUISIANA HOT SAUCE (OPTIONAL)	SERVE WITH RICE OR PASTA.
2 T	CORNSTARCH	

BBQ STEAK

easy   SERVES 8   FAT = 10 GM EA

1 C	A. 1. SAUCE	MARINATE THESE FOR 2 HOURS.
ZEST OF 1	LEMON, MINCED	
1/4 C	FRESH LEMON JUICE	DRAIN ONIONS & STEAKS.
4	ONIONS, SLICED THICK	BOIL THE MARINADE.
4 CL	GARLIC, MINCED	
1 t	OLD BAY SEASONING	GRILL OR BROIL THE ONIONS &
1 t	CAVENDER'S GREEK SEASONING	THE STEAKS, BASTING WITH THE
8	4 OZ TENDERLOIN STEAKS	MARINADE.

BURGERS in CREAM SAUCE

easy   SERVES 12   FAT = 7 GM EA

2 LBS	TOP ROUND STEAK	PROCESS CHOP-CHOP.
2 LBS	YELLOW ZUCCHINI, JULIENNED & THEN MINCED	ADD THESE & FORM INTO 6 OZ
4 SL	FAT-FREE BREAD, DICED	BURGERS.
2	ONION, DICED	
2 CL	GARLIC, MINCED	
2 T	BUTTER BUDS	SALT & PEPPER.
1 t	DRIED SAGE	FRY IN SPRAYED PAN.
1 C	NO-FAT SOUR CREAM	COMBINE & SIMMER THESE.
2 T	BUTTER BUDS	SERVE WITH BURGERS.
2 CL	GARLIC, MINCED	
2 t	FRESH LEMON JUICE	ADD FAT FREE STOCK TO THIN
1 t	SUGAR (OPTIONAL)	SAUCE AS NEEDED.

BURGERS w WINE SAUCE

SERVES 12   FAT = 7 GM EA

Make burgers as above adding these ingredients:

1/4 C	HEINZ CHILI SAUCE	SHAPE & FRY PATTIES.
2 T	WORCESTERSHIRE SAUCE	REMOVE BURGERS.
1/2 C	RED WINE	WHISK THESE INTO PAN AND
1/4 C	TOMATO PASTE	RETURN THE BURGERS FOR 3
1 C	NO-FAT SOUR CREAM	MINUTES.

BEEF CURRY

quick   SERVES 8   FAT = 9 GM EA

2 LBS	TENDERLOIN, IN STRIPS	FRY IN A SPRAYED PAN.
3	ONIONS, DICED	
3	YELLOW PEPPERS, DICED	
6 C	BOILING WATER	ADD THESE & SIMMER 5 MIN.
2	KNORR BEEF BOUILLON CUBE	
1	KNORR VEGGIE BOUILLON CUBE	
3 T	CURRY POWDER	COMBINE THE CORNSTARCH AND
1 C	GOLDEN RAISINS	WATER, ADD & BOIL.
1/2 C	CHUTNEY	
		SERVE w RICE, CHOPPED APPLES,
5 T	CORNSTARCH	BANANAS, RAISINS, ONIONS AND
1/2 C	COLD WATER	CHUTNEY.

STUFFED CABBAGE

20 ROLLS   FAT = 2 GM EA

20	CABBAGE LEAVES, BLANCHED 5 MIN.	
1 LB	TURKEY BREAST, PROCESSED CHOP-CHOP & BROWNED, DRAINED	
1 LB	TOP ROUND, PROCESSED CHOP-CHOP & BROWNED, DRAINED	
2 C	BROWN RICE, COOKED	
2	ONIONS, DICED	COMBINE THESE, STUFF LEAVES
1/4 C	EGG BEATERS	& ROLL UP.
1/2 C	FAT-FREE BEEF STOCK	
2	ONIONS, MINCED	
2 CL	GARLIC, MINCED	
2 T	BUTTER BUDS	
1 t EA	SALT & PEPPER	
1 t	CAVENDER'S GREEK SEASONING	
4	CARROTS, SLICED THICK	SCATTER ON THE BOTTOM OF A
4	CELERY STALKS, SLICED THICK	SPRAYED DISH.
2	ONIONS, SLICED THICK	
1 C	RAISINS	TOP WITH CABBAGE ROLLS.
1 C	BROWN SUGAR	COMBINE & POUR OVER.
1/2 C	FRESH LEMON JUICE	
32 OZ	CANNED TOMATOES, CRUSHED	COVER, BAKE AT 350 FOR 1 HOUR.
10 OZ	TOMATO SAUCE	DE-FAT THE PAN JUICES.
2 C	NO-FAT SOUR CREAM (OR MORE)	MIX WITH JUICES FOR SAUCE.

STEAK w CORIANDER SAUCE

quick   SERVES 6   FAT = 12 GM EA

1 1/2 LBS	FLANK STEAK	MARINATE THESE 20 MINUTES.
4 CL.	GARLIC, MINCED	
1 C	CORIANDER, CHOPPED	
1/2 C	DRY RED WINE	REMOVE STEAK & GRILL.
1/4 C	FAT-FREE BEEF STOCK	
		ADD ONIONS TO MARINADE AND
1	RED ONION, MINCED	BOIL TO REDUCE FOR SAUCE.

Add No-Fat Sour Cream if you want a creamier sauce.

STEAK DIANE I

quick　　SERVES 6　　　　FAT = 10 GM EA

6	4 OZ TENDERLOINS	FRY 3 MINUTES EACH SIDE.
1/2 C	BRANDY	REMOVE & DEGLAZE THE PAN.
2 C	ONIONS, DICED	ADD THESE TO PAN .
2 C	MUSHROOMS, SLICED	SIMMER FOR 2 MINUTES.
6 T	DIJON MUSTARD	
2 T	WORCESTERSHIRE SAUCE	
2 T	SUGAR (OPTIONAL)	
2 C	SKIM MILK	COMBINE WELL, WHISK IN AND
3 T	BUTTER BUDS	HEAT TO THICKEN.
2 T	CORNSTARCH	RETURN BEEF UNTIL DONE THE
		WAY YOU LIKE IT.

(You can substitute No-Fat Sour Cream for the cornstarch slurry)

STEAK DIANE II

quick　　SERVES 8　　　　FAT = 10 GM EA

8	4 OZ FILLETS	RUB SEASONING ON STEAKS, FRY
3 T	DRY MUSTARD	IN A SPRAYED PAN & REMOVE.
------	FRESHLY GROUND PEPPER	
1 C	RED ONIONS, MINCED	ADD THESE & STIR-FRY 5 MIN.
1 LB	MUSHROOMS, SLICED	
1/2 C	WORCESTERSHIRE SAUCE	
1/2 C	BOVRIL (AVAILABLE IN MOST STORES)	
2 C	FAT-FREE BEEF STOCK	RETURN STEAKS TO PAN AND
1/2 C	BRANDY	SIMMER UNTIL DONE.
------	FRESH PARSLEY, CHOPPED	ADD DURING THE LAST MINUTE.

MELISSA'S FAVORITE BEEF DIJON

easy　　SERVES 12　　　　FAT = 10 GM EA

3 LBS	TENDERLOIN, S & P	
1/2 C	DIJON MUSTARD	RUB ON THE ROAST.
1/4 C	BROWN SUGAR	PAT INTO THE MUSTARD.
2 C	DRY SHERRY	POUR THESE AROUND BEEF AND
1/2 C	SOY SAUCE	BAKE AT 375 FOR 25 MINUTES OR
		TO DESIRED DONENESS.
		DE-FAT JUICES & WHISK IN THE
1 C	NO-FAT SOUR CREAM (OR MORE)	SOUR CREAM.

STEAK EUGENE

easy SERVES 8 FAT = 10 GM EA

8	4 OZ TENDERLOINS	MARINATE THESE 2 HOURS.
4 CL	GARLIC, MINCED	
1/2 C	WORCESTERSHIRE SAUCE	DRAIN. FRY IN A SPRAYED PAN &
2 T	FRENCH'S MUSTARD	REMOVE.
1 C	ONIONS, DICED	ADD & SIMMER FOR 5 MINUTES.
1 C	MARINATED ARTICHOKE BOTTOMS, DRAINED, SLICED	
2 C	MUSHROOMS, SLICED	
2 C	CANNED PLUM TOMATOES, DICED	
3 T	GARLIC, MINCED	
1/4 C	FRESH CHIVES, CHOPPED	RETURN STEAK, ADD THESE AND
1/2 C	BRANDY (& STEAK JUICES)	SIMMER UNTIL DONE.
1 C	NO-FAT SOUR CREAM (OPTIONAL)	

GERMAN BEEF

easy SERVES 8 FAT = 7 GM EA

2 LBS	TOP ROUND, S & P	MARINATE THESE 4 HOURS.
1 T	CAVENDER'S GREEK SEASONING	
1 T	FRESH GINGER, PEELED, GRATED	
4 CL	GARLIC, MINCED	BROWN STEAK IN A SPRAYED
1 C	WATER	PAN & PUT IN A SPRAYED DISH.
1 C	RED WINE VINEGAR	
1/2 C	VERMOUTH	STRAIN MARINADE & POUR OVER
1/2 C	BROWN SUGAR	THE STEAK.
2	ONIONS, DICED	
10	WHOLE CLOVES	BAKE AT 325 TO AN INTERNAL
3	BAY LEAVES	TEMP OF 120 FOR RARE
1 T	PICKLING SPICE	130 FOR MEDIUM
1/2 t	DRY MUSTARD	150 FOR WELL DONE
		DE-FAT THE PAN JUICES AND ADD
10	LOW-FAT GINGERSNAPS, CRUSHED FINE	COOKIES TO THICKEN.

GRILLED FLANK

easy SERVES 8 FAT = 12 GM EA

2 LBS	FLANK STEAK	MARINATE THESE FOR 4 HOURS.
4 CL	GARLIC, MINCED	
1 T	ONION POWDER	
1 T	CELERY SALT	
1 t	CAVENDER'S GREEK SEASONING	GRILL 4 MINUTES EACH SIDE OR
1 C	RICE WINE VINEGAR	TO DESIRED DONENESS.
1/4 C	WORCESTERSHIRE SAUCE	SLICE MEAT ON DIAGONAL.

BEEF GORGONZOLA

 SERVES 8   FAT = 14 GM EA

8	SMALL THICK 4 OZ FILLETS	GRILL EACH UNTIL ALMOST AT DESIRED DONENESS.
1/4 C	GORGONZOLA, CRUMBLED	
1/4 C	PARMESAN CHEESE	MIX THESE & PAT ON TOPS OF
1/4 C	FAT-FREE BREAD CRUMBS	EACH STEAK.
1/4 C	NO-FAT SOUR CREAM (OR MORE)	
2 T	BUTTER BUDS	BROIL UNTIL BUBBLY.
2 T	FRESH PARSLEY, CHOPPED	

BEEF MADEIRA

 SERVES 8   FAT = 10 GM EA

8	4 OZ FILLETS, S & P	FRY IN A SPRAYED PAN.
1/2 C	MADEIRA WINE	REMOVE & DEGLAZE.
3 OZ	BOVRIL (AVAILABLE IN MOST STORES)	ADD THESE & SIMMER 3 MIN.
1 C	WATER OR AS NEEDED	
2 T	BUTTER BUDS	RETURN STEAKS AND FINISH TO
2 C	MUSHROOMS. SLICED	DESIRED DONENESS.

EASY STEAKS MED STYLE

 SERVES 8   FAT = 11 GM EA

8	4 OZ FILLETS, S & P	FRY UNTIL ALMOST DONE.
1/4 C	FRESH BASIL, MINCED	COMBINE THESE & SPREAD ON
1/4 C	FRESH PARSLEY, MINCED	TOP OF EACH STEAK & BROIL.
1/4 C	CAPERS, MINCED	
1/4 C	PIMENTO, MINCED	
1/4 C	NO-FAT SOUR CREAM	
1/4 C	PARMESAN CHEESE	

STEAK & MUSHROOM PASTA

 SERVES 8   FAT = 10 GM EA

2 LBS	TENDERLOIN, IN STRIPS, S & P	BROWN IN A SPRAYED PAN.
3 CL	GARLIC, MINCED	ADD THESE & SIMMER 20 MIN.
1	RED ONION, MINCED	
1 T	FRESH OREGANO, MINCED	
1 t	FRESH THYME, MINCED	
2 C	FAT-FREE BEEF STOCK	ADD FAT-FREE SOUR CREAM TO
1/2 C	RED WINE	FINISH THE SAUCE.
2 C	MUSHROOMS, SLICED	SERVE OVER PASTA.

ORIENTAL KABOBS

easy   SERVES 8   FAT = 10 GM EA

2 LBS	TENDERLOIN CUBES, S & P	MARINATE THESE 2 HOURS.
1/3 C	PINEAPPLE JUICE (FROM BELOW)	
2 T	GARLIC, MINCED	
1 T	SOY SAUCE	
1 T	SUGAR	
1/4 t	5 SPICE POWDER (AVAILABLE IN MOST STORES)	
1 CAN	PINEAPPLE CHUNKS, RESERVE JUICE	THREAD ALL ON SKEWERS AND
3	ONIONS, QUARTERED, BLANCHED	GRILL 3-4 MINUTES EACH SIDE.
1 EA	RED, YELLOW & GREEN PEPPERS, IN CHUNKS, BLANCHED	

ORIENTAL FISH SAUCE

2 CUPS   FAT = TR EA

1 1/2 C	FAT-FREE BEEF STOCK	COMBINE THESE TO SERVE WITH
3/4 C	FISH SAUCE	KABOBS.
6 CL	GARLIC, MINCED	
1 t	FRESH LEMON JUICE (OR TO TASTE)	
------	LOUISIANA HOT SAUCE TO TASTE	

BEEF in OYSTER SAUCE

SERVES 8   FAT = 10 GM EA

2 LBS	TENDERLOIN, IN STRIPS, S & P	MARINATE THESE 2 HOURS.
1/2 C	OYSTER SAUCE	
1/2 C	FAT-FREE BEEF STOCK	REMOVE THE BEEF & BOIL THE
1/4 C	RED WINE	MARINADE.
1/4 C	SOY SAUCE	
1 T	WORCESTERSHIRE SAUCE	
1 T	CORNSTARCH	
1 t	SUGAR	
12	GREEN ONIONS, SLICED	FRY THESE IN A SPRAYED PAN
6 CL	GARLIC, MINCED	FOR 3 MINUTES.
3	CARROTS, SLICED PAPER THIN	
1 LB	SNOW PEAS	ADD BEEF FOR 3 MINUTES.
3 C	MUSHROOMS, SLICED	
10 OZ	WATER CHESTNUTS, SLICED, DRAINED	ADD MARINADE AND SIMMER
10 OZ	BAMBOO SHOOTS	FOR 4 MINUTES.
1 JAR	BABY CORN	
1 C	SPINACH CHIFFONADE (p 396)	SERVE OVER RICE.

EASY PEPPER STEAK

SERVES 8   FAT = 7 GM EA

2 LBS	TOP ROUND, POUNDED, SCORED, S & P	MARINATE THESE FOR 15 MIN.
1/2 C	RED WINE VINEGAR	
1 C	FAT-FREE BEEF STOCK	
2 T	CRACKED PEPPER	PRESS PEPPER INTO STEAK AND
2 T	FRESH THYME, MINCED	SPRAY WITH PAM OLIVE OIL.
2 T EA	RED, YELLOW & GREEN PEPPERCORNS, CRUSHED	SEASON AND GRILL OR BROIL TO
------	CAVENDER'S GREEK SEASONING	DESIRED DONENESS.

BEEF PEPPERONATA

SERVES 8   FAT = 12 GM EA

2 LBS	TENDERLOINS, IN STRIPS, S & P	MARINATE THESE FOR 30 MIN.
1/4 C	RED WINE VINEGAR	
1/4 C	FAT-FREE BEEF STOCK	
2 T	FRESH LEMON JUICE	
1 EA	RED, YELLOW & GREEN PEPPER, SLICED	FRY THESE IN A SPRAYED PAN.
2	ONIONS, HALVED & SLICED	
2 CL	GARLIC, MINCED	
------	CAJUN BLACKENED MEAT SEASONING	COAT BEEF, ADD TO PAN AND STIR-FRY 3 MINUTES.
1/4 C	CAPERS, MINCED, w JUICE	ADD & SIMMER TO FINISH.
16	OLIVES, SLICED	
2 T	RED WINE VINEGAR	
------	FRESH PARSLEY, CHOPPED	

BEEF w RED PEPPER BUTTER

SERVES 8   FAT = 10 GM EA

1/4 C	NO-FAT SOUR CREAM	
1/4 C	FAT-FREE PROMISE ULTRA MARGARINE	
1/4 C	BUTTER BUDS	
4 OZ JAR	PICKLED RED BELL PEPPERS, MINCED & PATTED DRY	
1/4 C	NON-FAT MILK POWDER	WHISK THESE TOGETHER AND
2 T	FRESH PARSLEY, CHOPPED	ROLL UP IN PLASTIC WRAP LIKE A 2" LOG. CHILL.
8	4 OZ FILLETS, S & P	

Broil steaks until almost done, place a thin pat or two of Pepper Butter on each fillet & broil to finish.

HERBED ROAST BEEF

easy   SERVES 10   FAT = 12 GM EA

3 LBS	TENDERLOIN	RUB SALT ON THE LOIN & CHILL
------	HERBED SALT (p 22)	2 HOURS.

BAKE AT 375 TO AN INTERNAL
TEMP. OF: 120 FOR RARE
             130 FOR MEDIUM
             150 FOR WELL DONE

Serve with Pepper Sauce.

PEPPER SAUCE

2 CUPS   FAT = TR EA

1	RED ONION, MINCED	FRY IN A SPRAYED PAN.
2 CL	GARLIC, MINCED	
1/2 C	BRANDY	ADD THESE & HEAT THROUGH.
1/4 C	BUTTER BUDS	
2 T	DIJON MUSTARD	
2 T EA	BLACK, GREEN & RED PEPPERCORNS, CRUSHED	
1 C	NO-FAT SOUR CREAM (OR MORE)	SALT TO TASTE.

BEEF STROGANOFF

quick   SERVES 8   FAT = 10 GM EA

2 LBS	TENDERLOIN, IN STRIPS, S & P	SHAKE WITH FLOUR & FRY IN A SPRAYED PAN.
3 CL	GARLIC, MINCED	
3	ONIONS, DICED	ADD THESE & SIMMER 10 MIN.
1 C	MUSHROOMS, SLICED	
2 t	PAPRIKA	
3/4 C	RED WINE	ADD THESE & SIMMER 15 MIN.
1/4 C	BRANDY	
1 T	KITCHEN BOUQUET	
2 C	BEEF GRAVY (p 255)	
1 C	NO-FAT SOUR CREAM (OR MORE)	ADD DURING LAST 5 MINUTES.
1/4 C	FRESH PARSLEY, CHOPPED	

You might like to add a can of peeled plum tomatoes, chopped.

STEAKS PROVENCAL

 SERVES 8   FAT = 10 GM EA

8	4 OZ FILLETS	MARINATE THESE FOR 2 HOURS.
1/4 C EA	DIJON MUSTARD, SOY SAUCE	
1/4 C	WORCESTERSHIRE SAUCE	GRILL STEAKS UNTIL DONE.
3 C EA	ONIONS, MUSHROOMS, TOMATOES, DICED	BOIL MARINADE & ADD THESE.
6 CL	GARLIC, MINCED	
2 C	MARINATED ARTICHOKE HEARTS, DRAINED, TRIMMED WELL	
1/4 C	BRANDY	RETURN STEAKS TO SAUCE JUST TO HEAT THROUGH.

BOURBON ROAST VENISON

 SERVES 8   FAT = 6 GM EA

3 LBS	VENISON LOIN, SPRAYED WITH PAM	COMBINE THESE IN ZIPLOC BAG
1/2 C	BOURBON	FOR 4 HOURS & DRAIN.
3 SPRIGS EA	FRESH THYME, SAGE, MARJORAM, MINCED	
4 CL	GARLIC, MINCED	SEAR (p 398), IN A VERY HOT
1	ONION, MINCED	SPRAYED PAN.
1 t	GROUND BLACK PEPPER	BAKE AT 350 FOR 35 MINUTES OR UNTIL DONE, BASTING.

HEARTY VENISON STEAKS

 SERVES 6   FAT = 5 GM EA

1/2 C	FAT-FREE CHICKEN STOCK	SIMMER THESE FOR 5 MINUTES.
2 LBS	ASSORTED FRESH MUSHROOMS, STEMS REMOVED	
2 T	FRESH THYME, MINCED	
		FRY IN A VERY HOT, SPRAYED
6	5 OZ STEAKS, S & P	PAN, 3 MINUTES EACH SIDE.
1 1/2 C	FAT-FREE BEEF STOCK	ADD THESE AND SHROOMS TO
1 C	DRY RED WINE	FINISH COOKING.

CRANBERRY VENISON

easy   SERVES 4   FAT = 6 GM EA

1 1/2 LBS	BONELESS LOIN, SPRAYED WITH PAM	COMBINE THESE IN ZIPLOC BAG
1 C	DRY RED WINE	FOR 8 HOURS & DRAIN. SPRAY
1 C	ONIONS, MINCED	AGAIN, SEAR (p 398) ALL OVER IN
10	JUNIPER BERRIES	A VERY HOT SPRAYED PAN.
1 t	GROUND BLACK PEPPER	PUT IN A ROASTING PAN & ADD REMAINING ITEMS & MARINADE.
2 C	CRANBERRIES	BAKE AT 400 FOR 24 MINUTES.
1/2 C	ORANGE JUICE	REMOVE & KEEP WARM.
1 T	ORANGE ZEST, MINCED	REDUCE JUICES BY HALF.
1 t	FRESH GINGER, PEELED, GRATED	
1 C	FAT-FREE BEEF STOCK	ADD & REDUCE AGAIN.

Sauces & Marinades

Barbecue Sauces can be found in the Meat Section.

BECHAMEL SAUCE (or WHITE SAUCE)

 4 CUPS   FAT = TR EA

6 T	BUTTER BUDS	PUREE & POUR INTO A DOUBLE
1/2 C	FLOUR	BOILER.
4 C	SKIM MILK	
2 C	NON-FAT MILK POWDER	
1 t	BUTTER FLAVORING (OR TO TASTE)	HEAT TO THICKEN.
1/4 t	SALT	SEASON TO TASTE.
1/4 t	WHITE PEPPER	

Try simmering minced red onion in Fat-Free Chicken Stock or wine & adding a dash of nutmeg.

MEDIUM WHITE SAUCE

 1 CUP   FAT = TR EA

1 C	SKIM MILK	WHISK THESE INGREDIENTS.
1 T	CORNSTARCH	
1 T	BUTTER BUDS	SIMMER TO THICKEN, WHISKING
1/2 t	SALT	CONSTANTLY. IF LUMPS FORM,
1/4 t	WHITE PEPPER	PUREE BEFORE SERVING. THIN
		w MORE SKIM MILK IF NEEDED.

WHITE SAUCE

 1 1/2 C UPS   FAT = TR EA

1 1/2 C	SKIM MILK, SCALDING	PUREE THESE INGREDIENTS.
3 T	UNCOOKED CREAM OF RICE	
1 1/2 T	BUTTER BUDS	SIMMER TO THICKEN, WHISKING
1/2 t	SALT	CONSTANTLY.
		THIN w SKIM MILK IF NEEDED.

WHITE SAUCE MIX

4 CUPS   FAT = TR EA

2 C	NON-FAT MILK POWDER	BLENDERIZE ALL.
1 1/2 C	CORNSTARCH	
6 T	CHICKEN BOUILLON GRANULES	STORE IN AIR-TIGHT CONTAINER.
1/4 C	BUTTER BUDS	
4 t	ONION POWDER	
1 t	DRIED THYME	TO USE: 1/4 C MIX, 1 C SKIM
1 t	DRIED BASIL	MILK, HEATING AND WHISKING.
1/2 t	SALT	
1/4 t	WHITE PEPPER	THIN w SKIM MILK IF NEEDED.

MORNAY SAUCE

Make Bechamel or White Sauce (see recipe opposite page) and add Parmesan Cheese—Remember to add 2 GM FAT for each Tablespoon of Parmesan added.

BASIL SAUCE

3 CUPS   FAT = TR EA

2 C	FAT-FREE STOCK (FISH, CHICK, BEEF—DEPENDING ON HOW SAUCE IS USED)	
1	RED ONION, MINCED	
2 CL	GARLIC, MINCED	SIMMER FOR 10 MINUTES.
2 T	BUTTER BUDS	ADD & REDUCE BY 1/2.
1/4 C	VERMOUTH	
1	BAY LEAF	
1 C	NO-FAT SOUR CREAM (OR MORE)	ADD THESE TO FINISH.
1/2 C	FRESH BASIL, MINCED	SALT & PEPPER TO TASTE.
		REMOVE BAY LEAF.

BASIC BROWN SAUCE

2 1/2 CUPS   FAT = 1 GM EA

2 C	WATER	SIMMER FOR 10 MINUTES.
4	KNORR BEEF BOUILLON CUBES	
1 T	BOVRIL (AVAILABLE IN MOST STORES)	
2 T	BUTTER BUDS	
		COMBINE WELL, WHISK IN AND
2 T	CORNSTARCH	HEAT TO THICKEN.
1/2 C	COLD WATER	SALT & PEPPER TO TASTE.

RICHER BROWN SAUCE

3 CUPS   FAT = 1 GM EA

Add these ingredients while making the Basic Brown Sauce: (recipe above)

2 T	TOMATO PASTE, BROWNED w ABOVE BOVRIL	
1	BAY LEAF	
1/4 t	GROUND THYME	
1/2 C	SHERRY, PORT OR MADEIRA	REMOVE BAY LEAF.

MOCK BUTTER SAUCE   3 CUPS   FAT = 1 GM EA

2 T	CORNSTARCH	COMBINE THESE IN THE TOP OF
1/2 C	BUTTER BUDS	DOUBLE BOILER & HEAT UNTIL
1/2 C	FAT-FREE CHICKEN STOCK	SLIGHTLY THICK.
1 C	SKIM MILK	
1 t	BUTTER FLAVORING	WHISK IN THE SOUR CREAM AND
		REMOVE FROM HEAT.
1/2 C	NO-FAT SOUR CREAM	
1 C	EGG BEATERS	WHISK IN EGG BEATERS & HEAT
		UNTIL THICK AGAIN.
------	MORE BUTTER BUDS IF NECESSARY	!!!DO NOT OVER COOK!!!

This should be the consistency of a squeeze margarine.

CHEESE SAUCE

To make a Cheese Sauce, add Parmesan Cheese to the Butter Sauce recipe...Remember, each Tablespoon you add has 2 Grams of Fat.

BURGUNDY BUTTER   *quick*   1 1/2 CUPS   FAT = TR EA

1/4 C	BURGUNDY WINE (OR TO TASTE)	WHISK THESE TOGETHER.
1/4 C	FAT-FREE SOUR CREAM	
1/4 C	PROMISE ULTRA FAT-FREE MARGARINE	
1/2 C	BUTTER BUDS	
1 C	NON-FAT MILK POWDER	
2 CL	GARLIC, MINCED	SALT & PEPPER TO TASTE.
1	RED ONION, MINCED	
1 T	FRESH PARSLEY, CHOPPED	GREAT ON TURKEY BURGERS OR
		STUFF MUSHROOMS & BROIL.

MEDITERRANEAN BUTTER   *quick*   2 CUPS   FAT = 1 GM EA

1/2 C	FAT-FREE CREAM CHEESE	WHISK ALL INGREDIENTS.
1/4 C	FAT-FREE SOUR CREAM	
1/4 C	PROMISE ULTRA FAT-FREE MARGARINE	
1/4 C	BUTTER BUDS	
1	RED ONION, MINCED	
3 OZ JAR	CAPERS, DRAINED, MINCED (RINSE FOR MILDER TASTE)	
4 T	PICKLED RED BELL PEPPERS, MINCED & PATTED DRY	
1 T	CARAWAY SEED, CRUSHED	
1 t	DIJON MUSTARD	SALT & PEPPER TO TASTE.

OLD BAY BUTTER

 2 CUPS   FAT = 1 GM EA

1 C	FAT-FREE CREAM CHEESE	WHISK THESE TOGETHER.
1/2 C	NO-FAT SOUR CREAM	
1/2 C	PROMISE ULTRA FAT-FREE MARGARINE	
1/2 C	BUTTER BUDS	
2 T	FRESH LEMON JUICE	SALT & PEPPER TO TASTE.
2 T	PICKLED RED BELL PEPPERS, MINCED (OPTIONAL)	
2 T	OLD BAY SEASONING	
1/2	RED ONION, MINCED	SPREAD ON PITAS WHEN YOU
1 CL	GARLIC, MINCED (OPTIONAL)	MAKE SEAFOOD SALAD PITAS.

(p 85)

ROQUEFORT BUTTER

 24 OZ   FAT = 1 GM EA

1 C	FAT-FREE CREAM CHEESE	WHISK ALL INGREDIENTS.
1/2 C	NO-FAT SOUR CREAM	
1/2 C	PROMIS ULTRA FAT-FREE MARGARINE	
1/2 C	BUTTER BUDS	
1/2 C	NON-FAT MILK POWDER	SALT & PEPPER TO TASTE.
2 OZ	ROQUEFORT OR BLEU CHEESE, CRUMBLED	
2 T	FAT-FREE PARMESAN CHEESE	ROLL UP IN PLASTIC WRAP LIKE
1 T	FRESH LEMON JUICE	LIKE A 2" LOG & CHILL.
1 T	BRANDY	
1 t	WORCESTERSHIRE SAUCE	SLICE IN THIN PATS.

CURRIED CHUTNEY SAUCE

 2 1/2 CUPS   FAT – TR EA

1 C	FAT-FREE CHICKEN STOCK	SIMMER UNTIL HOT.
1/2 C	MANGO CHUTNEY, CHOPPED	
2 T	CURRY POWDER	REMOVE FROM HEAT.
1 T	FRESH LEMON JUICE	
1 C	NO-FAT SOUR CREAM	WHISK IN.

CURRIED MANGO SAUCE

 3 CUPS   FAT = TR EA

3	MANGOES, PEELED, DICED	PUREE & HEAT.
1 1/2 C	FAT-FREE CHICKEN STOCK	
2 T	CURRY POWDER	
2 T	FRESH LEMON JUICE	
2 T	FRESH MINT (OPTIONAL)	

COCKTAIL SAUCE

 2 CUPS   FAT = TR EA

1 C	HEINZ KETCHUP	WHISK ALL & CHILL.
1/2 C	TOMATO PUREE	
1/2 C	HEINZ CHILI SAUCE	
1 T	FRESH LEMON JUICE (OR TO TASTE)	
2 T	HORSERADISH (OR TO TASTE)	
1 t	WORCESTERSHIRE SAUCE (OR TO TASTE)	
------	LOUISIANA HOT SAUCE	

BOURBON COCKTAIL SAUCE

 2 CUPS   FAT = TR EA

1 C	KETCHUP OR TOMATO PUREE	WHISK ALL & CHILL.
1 C	FAT-FREE MIRACLE WHIP	
1 T	HORSERADISH (OR TO TASTE)	
1 T	BOURBON (OR TO TASTE)	

CREAMY COCKTAIL SAUCE

 1 CUP   FAT = TR EA

1/2 C	HEINZ CHILI SAUCE OR KETCHUP	WHISK ALL & CHILL.
1/2 C	NO-FAT SOUR CREAM	
2 t	HORSERADISH (OR TO TASTE)	
1 t	FRESH LEMON JUICE (OR TO TASTE)	
	SUGAR TO TASTE	
	FRESH DILL, CHOPPED (OPTIONAL)	

DELMARVA COCKTAIL SAUCE

2 CUPS   FAT = TR EA

1 C	HEINZ CHILI SAUCE	WHISK ALL & CHILL.
1/2 C	FAT-FREE MIRACLE WHIP	
4 CL	GARLIC, MINCED	
2 T	FRESH LEMON JUICE (OR TO TASTE)	
1	ONION, MINCED	
1 t	HORSERADISH (OR TO TASTE)	
1 t	PAPRIKA	
1 t	MUSTARD	
1 t	WORCESTERSHIRE SAUCE	
1/2 t	CAVENDER'S GREEK SEASONING	
------	LOUISIANA HOT SAUCE TO TASTE	

PLUM COCKTAIL SAUCE

quick   3 CUPS   FAT = TR EA

2 C	HEINZ CHILI SAUCE	WHISK ALL TOGETHER.
2 T	DIJON MUSTARD	
2 T	FRESH LEMON JUICE (OR TO TASTE)	
1	LIME, JUICED	
2 t	HORSERADISH	
2 PKG	EQUAL	
1/4 C	DRY SHERRY	
1/4 C	ONIONS, MINCED	
1/4 C	PLUM JAM, SEEDLESS	
1 t	WORCESTERSHIRE SAUCE	
------	LOUISIANA HOT SAUCE TO TASTE	

ZIPPY COCKTAIL SAUCE

quick   2 1/2 CUPS   FAT = TR EA

2 C	HEINZ KETCHUP	WHISK ALL TOGETHER.
2 T	HORSERADISH	
2 T	PICANTE SAUCE	
2 T	FRESH LEMON JUICE	
1 T	WORCESTERSHIRE SAUCE	
1 t	ONION POWDER	
1/2 t	CAVENDER'S GREEK SEASONING	

CHILI SAUCE

easy   6 CUPS   FAT = TR EA

10	TOMATOES, PEELED, DICED	SIMMER THESE FOR 1 HOUR.
3	ONIONS, DICED	
2	RED BELL PEPPERS, DICED	
1	CELERY STALK, MINCED	
2 C	BROWN SUGAR (OR TO TASTE)	
1 C	WHITE VINEGAR	
1/4 C	PICKLING SPICE (WRAPPED IN CHEESECLOTH)	
1 T	PICKLING SALT	REMOVE SPICE BAG.
1/8 t	CAYENNE OR LOUISIANA HOT SAUCE TO TASTE	

FRUIT CHILI SAUCE

easy   6 CUPS   FAT = TR EA

8	TOMATOES, PEELED, DICED	SIMMER THESE FOR 1 HOUR.
3	PEACHES, PEELED, DICED	
3	PEARS, PEELED, DICED	
3	ONIONS, DICED	SALT & PEPPER TO TASTE.
2 C	BROWN SUGAR	
1 t	LOUISIANA HOT SAUCE (OR TO TASTE)	
1 T	PICKLING SPICE IN CHEESECLOTH	REMOVE SPICE BAG.

SWEET & TANGY DIPPING SAUCE

 quick   2 CUPS   FAT = TR EA

1 C	FRESH ORANGE JUICE	SIMMER FOR 10 MINUTES.
1/2 C	BROWN SUGAR	
1/3 C	CIDER VINEGAR	
1/4 C	TOMATO PASTE	
1/4 C	SOY SAUCE	
2 T	CORNSTARCH	
1 T	WORCESTERSHIRE SAUCE	
1/2 t	LOUISIANA HOT SAUCE	

CREOLE SAUCE

quick   6 CUPS   FAT = TR EA

2	ONIONS, DICED	SIMMER UNTIL ALMOST DRY.
4 CL	GARLIC, MINCED (OR MORE)	
1 EA	RED, YELLOW & GREEN BELL PEPPER, DICED	
1	CELERY STALK, MINCED	
1/2 C	FAT-FREE CHICKEN STOCK	
2 C	TOMATOES, PEELED, DICED	ADD THESE & SIMMER 10 MIN.
1 C	WINE (YOUR CHOICE—RED OR WHITE)	
1 T	FRESH LEMON JUICE	
1 T	HONEY	
1 T	CREOLE MUSTARD (OR BROWN)	SUGAR IF NEEDED .

OPTIONS: 1 C NO-FAT SOUR CREAM (OR MORE) &/OR 2 C CRAB OR SHRIMP.

RED CURRANT SAUCE

quick   3 CUPS   FAT = TR EA

Great for Beef, Pork or Game.

1	ORANGE, ZESTED, MINCED	BOIL FOR 5 MINUTES & DRAIN.
1 C	WATER	(SAVE THE LIQUID)
1/2 C	DRIED CURRANTS	
1 C	RED CURRANT JAM	ADD TO CURRANTS & PUREE 1 C
1 C	PORT WINE	OF THIS. ADD RESERVED LIQUID
1 T	FRESH ORANGE JUICE	AS NEEDED.

GLAZE FOR GRILLING FRUITS OR VEGGIES

 quick   1 CUP   FAT = TR EA

6 T	FRESH LEMON JUICE	COMBINE AND BRUSH ON ITEMS
6 T	HONEY	TO BE GRILLED.
3 T	BRANDY	

Serve Hot Pepper Jelly or Fruit Chili Sauce on the side.

BASIC CHICKEN GRAVY 2 CUPS FAT = 1 GM EA

1 3/4 C	WATER OR SKIM MILK	BOIL THESE & REMOVE FROM
1	KNORR CHICKEN BOUILLON CUBE	HEAT.
1	KNORR VEGGIE BOUILLON CUBE	
1/4 C	COLD WATER	COMBINE WELL, WHISK IN AND
2 T	CORNSTARCH	HEAT TO THICKEN.

DARK CHICKEN GRAVY 2 CUPS FAT = 1 GM EA

Add these ingredients to above gravy:

1 T	BOVRIL (OR MORE, AVAILABLE IN MOST STORES)	
------	CAVENDER'S GREEK SEASONING TO TASTE	

BEEF GRAVY 2 CUPS FAT = 1 GM EA

1 3/4 C	WATER	BOIL THESE & REMOVE FROM
1	KNORR BEEF BOUILLON CUBE	HEAT.
1	KNORR VEGGIE BOUILLON CUBE	
1/4 C	COLD WATER	COMBINE WELL, WHISK IN AND
2 T	CORNSTARCH	HEAT TO THICKEN.

DILL SAUCE 2 CUPS FAT = TR EA

2 C	NO-FAT SOUR CREAM	COMBINE ALL INGREDIENTS.
1/4 C	BUTTER BUDS	
1 T	FRESH LEMON JUICE	SERVE HOT OR COLD.
1 T	CAPERS, MINCED	
1 T	FRESH DILL (OR MORE)	
1 t	DIJON MUSTARD	ADD SKIM MILK IF NEEDED.
1/2 t	CAVENDER'S GREEK SEASONING	
------	LOUISIANA HOT SAUCE (OPTIONAL)	SERVE ON OR UNDER FISH.

DUCK SAUCE 2 CUPS FAT = TR EA

2 C	ORANGE MARMALADE	SIMMER 10 MINUTES.
2 T	SOY SAUCE	
2 T	DRY SHERRY	
1 T	FRESH GINGER, PEELED, MINCED	
2	GREEN ONIONS, MINCED	
ZEST OF 1	ORANGE (ALSO THE JUICE)	
ZEST OF 1	LEMON (ALSO THE JUICE)	

FRUIT SAUCE FOR MEAT

quick   1 1/2 CUPS   FAT = TR EA

1/2 C	APPLE JELLY
1/2 C	PINEAPPLE JAM
1/2 C	ORANGE MARMALADE
3 t	HORSERADISH
2 T	DRY MUSTARD

WHISK THESE INGREDIENTS.

GARLIC SAUCE

quick   1 CUP   FAT = TR EA

1/2 C	FAT-FREE MIRACLE WHIP
1/2 C	NO-FAT SOUR CREAM
4 CL	GARLIC, CRUSHED (MORE FOR GARLIC LOVERS)
ZEST OF 1/2	LEMON, MINCED
1/2	LEMON, JUICED
1/2 t	CAVENDER'S GREEK SEASONING
------	SKIM MILK AS NEEDED

PUREE ALL INGREDIENTS.

SALT & PEPPER TO TASTE.

GINGER PUREE

easy   2 CUPS   FAT = TR EA

1 C	FRESH GINGER, PEELED, GRATED
1 C	RICE WINE VINEGAR
1 C	DRY WHITE WINE
1/4 C	SUGAR (OR TO TASTE)

SIMMER THESE FOR 1 HOUR.

PUREE & STRAIN.

HORSERADISH SAUCE

 easy   2 CUPS   FAT = TR EA

1 C	SKIM MILK
4 SL	FAT-FREE WHITE BREAD CUBES, CRUSTS REMOVED
1/4 C	GRATED HORSERADISH (OR MORE)
2 T	CIDER VINEGAR
1 T	DRY MUSTARD
2 T	POWDERED SUGAR (OR TO TASTE)

PUREE ALL INGREDIENTS.

CHILL.

MOCK HOLLANDAISE

20 OZ   FAT = TR EA

2 T	CORNSTARCH	COMBINE IN THE TOP OF DOUBLE
1/4 C	BUTTER BUDS	BOILER & HEAT TO THICKEN.
1/2 C	FAT-FREE CHICKEN STOCK	
1/2 C	SKIM MILK	
3/4 C	NO-FAT SOUR CREAM	REMOVE FROM HEAT, ADD AND
3/4 C	EGG BEATERS	WHISK IN. RETURN TO HEAT.
3 T	FRESH LEMON JUICE	ADD TO TASTE.

You can store this in a Ziploc Freezer Bag & put in very hot water (not boiling) to re-heat.

BEARNAISE SAUCE

1 CUP   FAT = TR EA

1 C	MOCK HOLLANDAISE SAUCE (HOT)	COMBINE ALL INGREDIENTS.
2 t	TARRAGON VINEGAR	
1 t	ONION, MINCED	
1/2 t	FRESH TARRAGON, MINCED	
1/2 t	FRESH PARSLEY, MINCED	

LEEK SAUCE

easy   2 CUPS   FAT = TR EA

8	LEEKS, GREEN PART, CHOPPED	SIMMER UNTIL WELL DONE AND
1 C	FAT-FREE STOCK (FISH OR CHICKEN)	PUREE.
1/2 C	NO-FAT SOUR CREAM (OR MORE)	WHISK IN AS MUCH AS NEEDED FOR CONSISTENCY.

LEMON SAUCE (or ORANGE)

quick   3 CUPS   FAT = TR EA

1 C	FRESH LEMON OR ORANGE JUICE	COMBINE AND SIMMER THESE
1 C	WATER	TO THICKEN.
1 C	SUGAR	
1/4 C	BUTTER BUDS	
2 T	LEMON OR ORANGE ZEST	
2 T	CORNSTARCH	

EASY MEAT SAUCE

quick   2 CUPS   FAT = TR EA

| 2 C | RED WINE | COMBINE & REDUCE BY 1/2. |
| 3 T | BOVRIL, OR VEGIMATE, OR MARMITE (OR AS NEEDED) | |

CAJUN MAYO

quick   1 CUP   FAT = TR EA

1 C	FAT-FREE MIRACLE WHIP		2 t	SPICY MUSTARD
1 CL	GARLIC, MINCED		2 t	HORSERADISH
2 T	KETCHUP		1/2 t	DRIED TARRAGON
1 T	CAPERS, MINCED		1/2 t	DRIED OREGANO
1 T	PARSLEY, MINCED		1/4 t	WORCESTERSHIRE
1/8 t	LOUISIANA HOT SAUCE (OR TO TASTE)			

WHISK ALL INGREDIENTS.

CURRY MAYO

quick   1 CUP   FAT = TR EA

1/2 C	FAT-FREE MIRACLE WHIP (OR MAYO)		2 t	DIJON MUSTARD
1/2 C	NON-FAT YOGURT		1 t	FRESH LEMON JUICE
2 t	CURRY POWDER (OR TO TASTE)		1 t	PICKLE RELISH
1 CL	GARLIC, MINCED		1/4 t	GROUND GINGER
3	GREEN ONION, MINCED			

WHISK ALL INGREDIENTS.

TEX MEX MAYO SAUCE

quick   1 1/2 CUPS   FAT = TR EA

| 1 C | FAT-FREE MIRACLE WHIP | COMBINE WELL. |
| 1/2 C | SALSA (OR TO TASTE), HOMEMADE OR COMMERCIAL | |

SALSA

2	TOMATOES, PEELED, CHOPPED		1	ONION, MINCED
3 CANS	DICED GREEN CHILIES		2 CL	GARLIC, MINCED
2 T	FRESH CILANTRO, MINCED		1 T	FRESH LIME JUICE
------	JALAPENO PEPPER, MINCED TO YOUR TASTE			

I sometimes substitute No-Fat Sour Cream for the Miracle Whip.

MISO SAUCE

quick   25 T   FAT = .5 GM EA T

1 C	MISO PASTE	WHISK THESE INGREDIENTS.
6 T	BROWN SUGAR	
1/4 C	FRESH GINGER, PEELED, GRATED	
2 T	SAKE OR SHERRY	
2 T	GREEN ONIONS, MINCED	

This goes well with grilled chicken, fish or beef.

MINT SAUCE   (THESE MAKE GREAT GIFTS!)   3 CUPS   FAT = TR EA

2 C	FRESH MINT, STEMMED, CHOPPED	COMBINE FOR 10 MINUTES.
4 SPRIGS	FRESH ROSEMARY, STEMMED, CHOPPED	PUREE & STRAIN THROUGH WET
1 C	BOILING WATER	CHEESECLOTH.
1 C	FROZEN ORANGE JUICE CONCENTRATE	ADD & BOIL HARD FOR 1 MIN.
3 C	SUGAR	REMOVE FROM HEAT, SKIM AND
1 OR 2	DROPS GREEN FOOD COLOR	STIR FOR 3 MINUTES.
1/2 C	LIQUID PECTIN	

Pour into sterile jars & seal or serve in hollowed out zucchini cups.

EASY MINT SAUCE   *easy*   3 CUPS   FAT = TR EA

1 C	APPLE OR CURRANT JELLY	SIMMER THESE 5 MINUTES.
1 C	RASPBERRY VINEGAR	
1/2 C	WATER	
1/4 C	POWDERED SUGAR	
1 C	FRESH MINT, MINCED	REMOVE FROM HEAT & ADD THE MINT.

Serve in hollowed out zucchini cups or radicchio leaves.

MUSHROOM SAUCE   *quick*   4 CUPS   FAT = TR EA

1	RED ONION, DICED	FRY IN A SPRAYED PAN 3 MIN.
2 CL	GARLIC, MINCED	
24	MUSHROOMS, SLICED	
2 C	FAT-FREE BEEF STOCK	ADD & SIMMER UNTIL DONE.
1/2 C	WINE (RED OR WHITE DEPENDING ON USE)	
2 T	BUTTER BUDS	
1 C	NO-FAT SOUR CREAM	ADD AND S & P TO TASTE.

PARSLEY SAUCE   *quick*   2 1/2 CUPS   FAT = TR EA

1/2 LB	FRESH PARSLEY, CHOPPED	SIMMER UNTIL THE ONIONS ARE
1/4 C	ONIONS, DICED	VERY TENDER.
1 C	FAT-FREE BEEF STOCK	
		ADD THESE & PUREE.
1/2 C	FAT-FREE CREAM CHEESE	
1/2	LEMON, JUICED	ADD MORE STOCK OR CREAM
1/3 C	COLD FAT-FREE BEEF STOCK	CHEESE IF NEEDED. S & P.

MUSTARD SAUCE

1 CUP   FAT = TR EA

1 T	DIJON MUSTARD (OR TO TASTE)	
1/2 T	STONE GROUND MUSTARD	
1 C	NO-FAT SOUR CREAM	
1/2 t	CAVENDER'S GREEK SEASONING	
1/2 t	WORCESTERSHIRE SAUCE	

WHISK ALL INGREDIENTS.

ADD DRY SHERRY IF NEEDED FOR THINNING.

HONEY MUSTARD SAUCE

1 CUP   FAT = TR EA

1 C	HONEY
2 T	DIJON MUSTARD
1/4 C	STONE GROUND MUSTARD (TRY OTHER FLAVORS TOO)
2 T	ONIONS, MINCED
	WHITE WINE OR SHERRY FOR TASTE & THINNING

WHISK ALL INGREDIENTS.

SALT & PEPPER TO TASTE.

OPTIONS: BEER, NO-FAT SOUR CREAM OR   FAT-FREE CREAM CHEESE

ORANGE MUSTARD SAUCE

1 CUP   FAT = TR EA

1/2 C	ORANGE MARMALADE
1/4 C	STONE GROUND MUSTARD (OR TO TASTE)
6 T	ONIONS, MINCED & BLANCHED 3 MINUTES.
1/4 C	RED WINE
1 t	PAPRIKA

WHISK ALL INGREDIENTS.

SWEET & SOUR MUSTARD SAUCE

2 CUPS   FAT = TR EA

1/2 C	BROWN SUGAR
2 T	FLOUR
1/2 C	MUSTARD (YOUR CHOICE)
1/2 C	VINEGAR
1/2	KNORR BEEF BOUILLON CUBE
1/2 C	SKIM MILK
1/2 C	EGG BEATERS

COMBINE IN A DOUBLE BOILER TO THICKEN.

REMOVE FROM HEAT.

WHISK IN.

RED PEPPER COULIS

 4 CUPS FAT = TR EA

4	RED BELL PEPPERS, MINCED	SIMMER ALL UNTIL WELL DONE
1	RED ONION, MINCED	& PUREE.
2 CL	GARLIC, SLICED	
3 C	FAT-FREE STOCK (FISH OR CHICKEN)	
1/2 t	CAVENDER'S GREEK SEASONING	SALT & PEPPER TO TASTE.
------	SUGAR IF NEEDED	
------	DRIED THYME TO TASTE	THIS IS GOOD HOT OR COLD.

OPTIONS: TARRAGON, RED WINE OR BALSAMIC VINEGAR
CAPERS, RINSED & MINCED

YELLOW PEPPER COULIS

 4 CUPS FAT = TR EA

Make the same as Red Pepper Coulis but substitute Yellow Bell Peppers.

These sauces are great for decorating plates. You can make a Green Pepper Sauce too.

PEPPERCORN SAUCE I

2 CUPS FAT = TR EA

Great for broiled fish, poultry or beef.

1/2 C	GREEN ONIONS, MINCED	SIMMER THESE FOR 5 MINUTES.
1/2 C	FAT-FREE CHICKEN STOCK	
1	KNORR CHICKEN BOUILLON CUBE	
2 T	GREEN PEPPERCORNS, CRUSH WELL	
3 T	BRANDY	WHISK THESE TOGETHER & ADD.
1 T	DIJON MUSTARD (OR TO TASTE)	
1 C	NO-FAT SOUR CREAM	

PEPPERCORN SAUCE II

4 CUPS FAT = 1 GM EA

6 T	GREEN PEPPERCORNS, CRUSHED	SIMMER THESE UNTIL ALMOST
1 C	RED ONIONS, MINCED	DRY.
1/2 C	WHITE WINE	
1/4 C	BRANDY	
4 C	EASY MEAT SAUCE (p 257)	ADD & SIMMER 3 MINUTES.
------	SALT & PEPPER TO TASTE	

CHUNKY PROVENCAL SAUCE

 easy   4 CUPS   FAT = TR EA

6	TOMATOES, PEELED, DICED	SIMMER THESE FOR 20 MINUTES.
2	ONIONS, DICED	
4 CL	GARLIC, MINCED	
2 T	TOMATO PASTE	

1 LB	MUSHROOMS, SLICED	ADD & SIMMER FOR 10 MORE.
10 EA	PITTED BLACK & GREEN OLIVES, SLICED	
1 t	DRIED ITALIAN HERBS	SALT & PEPPER TO TASTE.
1 t	FRESH BASIL, MINCED	

SAUCE REMOULADE

 quick   1 1/2 CUPS   FAT = TR EA

1 C	FAT-FREE MIRACLE WHIP	WHISK ALL INGREDIENTS.
1/2 C	NO-FAT SOUR CREAM	
4	GREEN ONIONS, MINCED	
2 T	PICKLE RELISH	
2 T	CAPERS, MINCED	
2 T	FRESH PARSLEY, CHOPPED	
2 T	KETCHUP	
2 t	MUSTARD, YOUR CHOICE	

SATE' SAUCE

 quick   1 1/2 CUPS   FAT = TR EA

1 C	SOY SAUCE	SIMMER THESE INGREDIENTS.
1 T	BUTTER BUDS	
1/2 C	WATER	
2 T	FRESH LEMON JUICE	
1 T	LEMON ZEST, MINCED	
1 t	LOUISIANA HOT SAUCE	

OPTIONS:	HEALTH VALLEY PEANUT BUTTER (REMEMBER TO ADD TO FAT COUNT)
	COCONUT FLAVORING

THAI SWEET & SOUR GARLIC SAUCE

quick   2 CUPS   FAT = TR EA

1 C	VINEGAR	PUREE ALL INGREDIENTS.
1/2 C	BROWN SUGAR	
1/2 C	WATER	
6 T	FISH SAUCE	
4 CL	GARLIC, GRATED	
1	RED CHILI PEPPER, SEEDED, MINCED	

TARTAR SAUCE

quick   1 1/2 CUPS   FAT = TR EA

1/2 C	NO-FAT SOUR CREAM	WHISK ALL INGREDIENTS.
1/2 C	FAT-FREE MIRACLE WHIP	
1/4 C	PICKLE RELISH	
2 T	BUTTER BUDS	
1 T	FRESH PARSLEY, CHOPPED	
1 T	CAPERS, CRUSHED	SALT & PEPPER TO TASTE.
1 T	RED ONION, MINCED	
1 t	REGULAR MUSTARD, OR DIJON	
1 t	FRESH LEMON JUICE	
1 t	SUGAR	
1/2 t	CAVENDER'S GREEK SEASONING	
------	SKIM MILK AS NEEDED	

OPTIONS: GARLIC, PIMENTO, MORE LEMON JUICE, BASIL

TOMATO CAPER SAUCE

quick   8 CUPS   FAT = TR EA

7 C	TOMATO CONCASSE (p 396)	SIMMER THESE FOR 5 MINUTES.
1	ONION, MINCED	
1/2 C	CAPERS, MINCED	
1/2 C	FRESH BASIL, CILANTRO OR ITALIAN PARSLEY, CHOPPED	
1/2 C	DRY WHITE WINE	SALT & PEPPER TO TASTE.

TOMATO COULIS

quick   5 CUPS   FAT = TR EA

4 C	TOMATO CONCASSE (p 396)	PUREE ALL INGREDIENTS.
1/3 C	RED ONIONS, DICED	
2 CL	GARLIC, CRUSHED	
2 T	TOMATO PASTE	SALT & PEPPER TO TASTE.
1 t	FRESH THYME (OR TO TASTE)	
1 t	FRESH ROSEMARY (OR TO TASTE)	
1/2 C	FAT-FREE CHICKEN STOCK	THIS IS GOOD HOT OR COLD.
1/2 t	CAVENDER'S GREEK SEASONING	

OPTIONS: FRESH BASIL, BALSAMIC VINEGAR OR GREEK OLIVE JUICE, BROWN SUGAR,
CANADIAN BACON, TRIMMED & JULIENNED, GRATED CARROT, THYME

TZAZIKI

5 CUPS   FAT = TR EA

2	CUCUMBERS, PEELED, GRATED
2 C	YOGURT CHEESE (p 393)
8 CL	GARLIC, MINCED
1/2 t	FRESH DILL (OPTIONAL)

PUREE THESE INGREDIENTS.

SALT & PEPPER TO TASTE.

A Greek Sauce for dipping or to go with veggies when serving hot spicy food, usually East Indian or Greek.

VEGGIE VEAL SAUCE

6 CUPS   FAT = TR EA

5	CARROTS, SHREDDED
1	ONION, SHREDDED
1 CL	GARLIC, CRUSHED
1	GREEN PEPPER, DICED
1	ZUCCHINI, DICED (OPTIONAL)
4 C	FAT-FREE BEEF STOCK
	SALT & PEPPER TO TASTE

SIMMER UNTIL VERY TENDER.
PUREE WELL.

ADJUST CONSISTENCY w STOCK
SHERRY, SKIM MILK OR FAT-FREE
SOUR CREAM.

VEGGIE FISH SAUCE

6 CUPS   FAT = TR EA

1	ONION, SHREDDED
1	CUCUMBER, SLICED THIN
1	YELLOW SQUASH, SHREDDED
1 CL	GARLIC, CRUSHED
ZEST OF 1	LEMON, MINCED
1/2 t	LEMON PEPPER
4 C	FAT-FREE FISH STOCK OR CLAM BROTH
1/2 t	CAVENDER'S GREEK SEASONING

SIMMER UNTIL VERY TENDER.
PUREE WELL.

ADJUST CONSISTENCY w STOCK
SKIM MILK OR FAT-FREE SOUR
CREAM.
SALT & PEPPER TO TASTE.

VEGGIE CHICKEN SAUCE

6 CUPS   FAT = TR EA

1	ONION, DICED
12	ASPARAGUS SPEARS, SLICED THIN
1	ZUCCHINI, DICED
1 BNCH	FRESH PARSLEY
1	POTATO, PEELED & DICED
3-4 C	FAT-FREE CHICKEN STOCK
------	SALT & PEPPER TO TASTE

SIMMER UNTIL VERY TENDER.
PUREE WELL.

ADJUST CONSISTENCY w STOCK
VERMOUTH OR SKIM MILK.

VIETNAM SAUCE

 2 CUPS   FAT = TR EA

1 C	WATER	BOIL THESE AND REMOVE FROM HEAT.
1/2	KNORR FISH BOUILLON CUBE	
1 C	FISH SAUCE*	ADD THESE & PUREE.
1/3 C	FRESH LIME JUICE (OR LEMON IF OUT OF LIME)	
1/4 C	SUGAR	
4 CL	GARLIC, MINCED	CHILL.
4	RED OR GREEN CHILIES, SEEDED & MINCED	
1 t	BOVRIL (AVAILABLE IN MOST STORES)	

* You can find this in Oriental Markets.

WATERCRESS COULIS

 2 CUPS   FAT – TR EA

1 LB	WATERCRESS, TRIMMED, BLANCHED, SHOCKED	PUREE THESE.
1	LEMON, JUICED	
2 C	FAT-FREE CHICKEN STOCK (MORE IF NECESSARY)	
1/2 C	FAT-FREE CREAM CHEESE	
		SALT & PEPPER TO TASTE.

CARROT CHUTNEY

 8 CUPS   FAT = TR EA

1 LB	CARROTS, DICED	SIMMER 20 MINUTES OR MORE.
2	ONIONS, DICED	
1 C EA	RED, YELLOW & GREEN PEPPERS, DICED	
1 C	RAISINS	
1 C	SUGAR	
1 C	VINEGAR	
1 t	DRY MUSTARD	
1/2 t	SALT	

HOT CHILI CHUTNEY

 2 CUPS   FAT = TR EA

3	TOMATOES, PEELED, CHOPPED	PUREE THESE.
6 CL	GARLIC, MINCED	SERVE COLD OR SIMMER FOR 10 MINUTES & SERVE HOT.
1 C EA	RED & GREEN BELL PEPPER, DICED	
1/2 C	FRESH CORIANDER (CILANTRO), CHOPPED	
2 T	FRESH RED CHILIES, MINCED (OR TO TASTE)	

MANGO CHUTNEY

4 CUPS   FAT = TR EA

6	MANGOES, PEELED, DICED	SIMMER THESE 30 MINUTES.
1 C	RAISINS OR CURRANTS	
1 C	ONIONS, MINCED	
1	LEMON, JUICE & PEEL, MINCED	
1 C	BROWN SUGAR	
1 C	VINEGAR (YOUR CHOICE)	
3 CL	GARLIC, MINCED	SALT & PEPPER TO TASTE.
2 T	FRESH GINGER, PEELED, MINCED	
1 t	CRUSHED RED PEPPER FLAKES	
1/2 t	ALLSPICE (OR TO TASTE)	

PEACH CHUTNEY

6 CUPS   FAT = TR EA

16	PEACHES, PEELED & CHOPPED	SIMMER THESE 30 MINUTES.
1 C	RAISINS	
1	RED ONION, MINCED	
1/4 C	FRESH GINGER, PEELED, GRATED	
2 CL	GARLIC, MINCED	
4 C	BROWN SUGAR	
2 C	VINEGAR	SALT & PEPPER TO TASTE.
2 t	DRY MUSTARD	
2 t	ALLSPICE	

APPLE BERRY RELISH

3 CUPS   FAT = TR EA

4	TART APPLES, DICED	
2	RED ONIONS, DICED	SIMMER THESE 20 MINUTES.
1 C	JUICE FROM 24 OZ SIEVED RASPBERRIES	
5 T	RASPBERRY VINEGAR	
3 T	SUGAR	PUREE 1/3 OF THIS.
1/2 t	FRESH GINGER, PEELED, GRATED	
1/4 t	ALLSPICE	SEASON w SALT & VINEGAR TO TASTE.

EASY BEET RELISH

1 1/2 CUPS   FAT = TR EA

1 C	BEETS, COOKED, DICED	COMBINE ALL & CHILL.
3 T	HORSERADISH	
2 T	FRESH LEMON JUICE	
1 T	SAUERKRAUT, MINCED	YOU COULD EVEN USE CANNED BEETS.
1 T	POWDERED SUGAR	
1/2 t	SALT	

APPLE CUCUMBER RELISH   6 CUPS   FAT = TR EA

3	CUCUMBERS, PEELED, DICED	SIMMER THESE 20 MINUTES.
2	ONIONS, DICED	
2	TART APPLES, DICED	
1	RED BELL PEPPER, DICED	
1	CELERY STALKS, MINCED	
2 C	WHITE WINE VINEGAR	
2 C	SUGAR	
1 T	DRY MUSTARD (OR TO TASTE)	REMOVE FROM HEAT & ADD THE
1 T	TURMERIC	FLOUR MIXTURE.
2 T	PICKLING SALT	
1/2 C	FLOUR	COMBINE, ADD SOME HOT JUICE
3 T	COLD WATER	& RETURN TO HEAT.

Simmer 5 minutes, pour into sterile jars & seal.

CORN RELISH   8 CUPS   FAT = TR EA

2 C	TOMATO CONCASSE (p 396)	TOSS THESE AND LET SIT FOR 1
2 C	CORN	HOUR.
1 C	ONIONS, DICED	
1 C	CUCUMBERS, PEELED, DICED	
1 EA	RED & GREEN BELL PEPPER, DICED	
2 T	COARSE SALT	
1 1/2 C	VINEGAR	BOIL THESE & ADD TO ABOVE.
1 1/2 C	SUGAR	
2 T	DRY MUSTARD	SIMMER 20 MINUTES.
2 T	FLOUR	
1/2 t	TURMERIC	
1/4 C	VINEGAR (OR TO TASTE)	ADD AT END, IF NEEDED, TO TASTE.

CRANBERRY RELISH   *easy*   2 CUPS   FAT = TR EA

2 C	CRANBERRIES	SIMMER THESE 20 MINUTES.
1/2 C	WATER	
1	RED ONION, MINCED	
2 C	MANDARIN ORANGES, CHOPPED	ADD & SIMMER 30 MINUTES.
1	TART APPLE, GRATED	
1/2 C	SUGAR	

CURRY RELISH   4 CUPS   FAT = TR EA

2	ONIONS, DICED	SIMMER 1 HOUR.
2	CARROTS, DICED	
2	CELERY STALKS, DICED	
2	TART APPLES, DICED	
1/4 C	CURRY POWDER	
1/4 C	FLOUR	
3 C	FAT-FREE CHICKEN STOCK	
1/2 C	APPLE JELLY	
2 T	FRESH LEMON JUICE	SALT & PEPPER TO TASTE.
2 T	LEMON ZEST, MINCED	
2 T	HONEY	REMOVE GINGER SLICES AND
2 T	TOMATO PASTE	STORE IN STERILE JARS.
1 T	COCONUT FLAVORING	
6	CARDAMOM SEEDS, CRUSH WELL	
5 CL	GARLIC, MINCED	
1/2 t	CINNAMON	
1 INCH	FRESH GINGER, SLICED	

PEAR CURRANT RELISH   *easy*   2 CUPS   FAT = TR EA

4	PEARS, PEELED, DICED	COMBINE ALL & LET SIT 4
1	TART APPLE, GRATED	HOURS.
1	RED ONION, MINCED	
1 C	RED CURRANTS	SIMMER 20 MINUTES. PUREE 1/3
1/2 C	VINEGAR	RETURN ALL TO HEAT.
1/2 C	SUGAR	
1/2 t	DRIED THYME	SALT & PEPPER & VINEGAR TO
1/2 t	ALLSPICE	TASTE.

THREE PEPPER RELISH   *easy*   2 CUPS   FAT = TR EA

4	CARROTS, GRATED	SIMMER THESE 30 MINUTES.
2	ONIONS, SLICED THIN	
1 EA	RED, YELLOW & GREEN BELL PEPPER, SLICED THIN	
1/2 C	GOLDEN RAISINS (OPTIONAL)	
3 CL	GARLIC, MINCED	COOL.
1/2 C	SUGAR	SALT & PEPPER & VINEGAR TO
1/4 C	VINEGAR	TO TASTE.

SAUCES FOR FISH

MUSHROOM SAUCE

 2 CUPS   FAT = 4 GM EA

2 C	MUSHROOMS, SLICED	SIMMER THESE 5 MINUTES.
1 C	RED ONIONS, DICED	
1/2 C	FAT-FREE CHICKEN STOCK	

1 C	NON-FAT YOGURT	COMBINE AND ADD TO ABOVE
4 T	PARMESAN CHEESE	TO HEAT THROUGH.
1 t	CORNSTARCH	

Add white wine or skim milk if too thick.

MUSTARD SAUCE

 1 CUP   FAT = TR EA

1/4 C	DIJON MUSTARD	SIMMER THESE 10 MINUTES.
1/4 C	RICE WINE VINEGAR	
1/2 C	FISH STOCK	

TOMATO HERB SAUCE

 2 CUPS   FAT = TR EA

2 C	TOMATO CONCASSE (p 396)	
2 T	FISH STOCK	PUREE & HEAT.
1 T	DIJON MUSTARD	
1 T	FRESH PARSLEY, STEMS REMOVED	
1 T	FRESH TARRAGON, STEMS REMOVED	
1 T	FRESH CILANTRO, STEMS REMOVED	
1 T	FRESH BASIL, STEMS REMOVED	
1 CL	GARLIC, MINCED	

LEMON WINE SAUCE

 1 CUP   FAT = TR EA

1/2 C	FRESH LEMON JUICE	
1/2 C	WHITE WINE VINEGAR	HEAT & REDUCE BY 1/2.
1 C	FISH STOCK	

If you like, you could thicken this with a mixture of cornstarch & cold stock. Use thin strips of green onion & red pepper for garnish.

SAUCES FOR MUSHROOMS:

BUTTER CREAM SAUCE

quick   1 CUP   FAT = TR EA

1/2 C	NO-FAT SOUR CREAM
1/4 C	SKIM MILK
1/4 C	BUTTER BUDS (OR TO TASTE)
1 T	FRESH LEMON JUICE
1	ONION, MINCED
2 T	FRESH PARSLEY, CHOPPED

SIMMER AND PUREE THESE.

ADD MUSHROOMS AND SIMMER
5 MINUTES.

WINE SAUCE

easy   1 CUP   FAT = TR EA

1 C	BURGUNDY WINE
2 CL	GARLIC, MINCED
1	RED ONION, MINCED
1/2 t	CAVENDER'S GREEK SEASONING

SIMMER WITH MUSHROOMS FOR
10 MINUTES.

SPICY SAUCE

easy   1 CUP   FAT = TR EA

1/2 C	WORCESTERSHIRE SAUCE
1/2 C	WATER
2 T	BUTTER BUDS
1 T	SOY SAUCE
2 T	A.1. SAUCE OR PICK-A-PEPPER (YOUR CHOICE)
	(TRY IT EACH WAY, THEY'RE BOTH GREAT)
------	CAVENDER'S GREEK SEASONING TO TASTE

SIMMER ALL WITH MUSHROOMS
FOR 10 MINUTES.

ORIENTAL SAUCE

easy   1 1/2 CUPS   FAT = TR EA

1/4 C	HOISIN SAUCE
1/4 C	TOMATO SAUCE
1/4 C	SOY SAUCE
1/4 C	CHUTNEY
1/4 C	RICE WINE VINEGAR
1/4 C	HONEY

SIMMER AND PUREE THESE.

ADD MUSHROOMS AND SIMMER
5 MINUTES.

SAUCES FOR SALMON:

BLACK BEAN SAUCE

 2 CUPS   FAT = TR EA

1 C	FAT-FREE CHICKEN STOCK	PUREE & HEAT UNTIL SLIGHTLY
1/4 C	RICE WINE OR SAKE	THICKENED.
1/2 C	FERMENTED BLACK BEANS, RINSED & DRAINED	
2 T	SOY SAUCE	
2 T	GARLIC, MINCED	
1 T	SUGAR	
1 T	CORNSTARCH, HEAPING	

YOGURT CUCUMBER SAUCE

 3 CUPS   FAT = TR EA

2 C	NON-FAT YOGURT	WHISK ALL INGREDIENTS.
1 C	CUCUMBER, PEELED, SEEDED & MINCED	
1/4 C	SHALLOTS, MINCED	
1/2 t	CAVENDER'S GREEK SEASONING (OR TO TASTE)	

YOGURT DILL SAUCE

 2 CUPS   FAT = TR EA

2 C	NON-FAT PLAIN YOGURT	
2 T	FRESH DILL, MINCED	WHISK ALL & SERVE UNDER THE
1 T	STRONG MUSTARD	SALMON.

MUSTARD SAUCE

 2 CUPS   FAT = TR EA

1 3/4 C	NO-FAT SOUR CREAM	WHISK ALL INGREDIENTS.
1 T	DIJON MUSTARD (OR TO TASTE)	
4 T	SKIM MILK (OR AS NEEDED)	SALT & PEPPER TO TASTE.
------	CAYENNE PEPPER	
------	FRESH DILL (OPTIONAL)	SERVE UNDER SALMON.

ARTICHOKE MAYONNAISE

quick   2 CUPS   FAT = TR EA

1 C	FAT-FREE MIRACLE WHIP	PUREE THESE.
1 C	MARINATED ARTICHOKE HEARTS, DRAINED, TRIMMED WELL	
1/4 t	CAVENDER'S GREEK SEASONING	SALT & PEPPER TO TASTE.

SAUCES FOR SEAFOOD:

STONE CRAB VINAIGRETTE

easy   3 CUPS   FAT = TR EA

1 C	MOCK OIL (p 395)	PUREE ALL INGREDIENTS.
1/2 C	RED WINE VINEGAR (OR TO TASTE)	
1/2 C	CAPERS, CHOPPED (OPTIONAL)	
1/2 C	ONIONS, DICED	
1/2 C	EGG BEATERS, SCRAMBLED, DICED	SALT & PEPPER TO TASTE.
1/4 C	PARSLEY	
1/4 C	CHOPPED PIMENTO	
1 t	SUGAR (OR TO TASTE)	
1/2 t	CAYENNE PEPPER (OR TO TASTE)	

CURRY CREAM SAUCE

quick   1 CUP   FAT = TR EA

1/2 C	DRY WHITE WINE	SIMMER THESE 10 MINUTES.
1/4 C	FAT-FREE CHICKEN STOCK	
3	SHALLOTS, MINCED	
2 CL	GARLIC, MINCED	
1 T	FRESH LEMON JUICE	
3/4 t	CURRY POWDER (OR TO TASTE)	
------	SAFFRON THREADS	
1/2 C	NO-FAT SOUR CREAM	WHISK IN & HEAT THROUGH.

CARROT TOP SAUCE

quick   3 CUPS   FAT = TR EA

1 LB	CARROT TOPS	BLANCH 2 MINUTES IN STOCK & DRAIN.
1 C	FAT-FREE CHICKEN STOCK, BOILING	ADD SOUR CREAM & PROCESS CHOP-CHOP.
1 1/2 C	NO-FAT SOUR CREAM	
1/2 t	CAVENDER'S GREEK SEASONING	HEAT & SERVE UNDER FISH.

LEMON CARROT SAUCE

easy   2 CUPS   FAT = TR EA

6	CARROTS, GRATED	SIMMER UNTIL WELL DONE.
1 C	WATER (OR TO COVER)	
1	KNORR CHICKEN BOUILLON CUBE	
1/2	RED ONION, MINCED	PUREE WELL.
ZEST OF 2	LEMONS, MINCED	ADD THESE, HEAT & SERVE
2	LEMONS, JUICED	UNDER FISH.
1/4 t	CAVENDER'S GREEK SEASONING	

APPLE HERB MARINADE

 1 1/2 CUPS   FAT = TR EA

This is good for lamb, pork, beef or poultry.

1 C	BALSAMIC VINEGAR
6 T	APPLE JUICE CONCENTRATE
1/4 C	HOT WATER
1 T	DIJON MUSTARD
2 CL	GARLIC, MINCED
1 t	GROUND ROSEMARY
1 t	FRESH BASIL, CHOPPED

WHISK ALL TOGETHER.

HONEY MUSTARD HERB

 1 CUP   FAT = TR EA

This is great for beef & poultry.

1/2 C	HONEY
1/2 C	DIJON MUSTARD
1/4 C	FRESH BASIL, CHOPPED
1/4 C	FRESH DILL, CHOPPED

MAKE A PASTE & RUB ON THE MEAT 20 MIN. BEFORE COOKING.

SHERRY VINAIGRETTE MARINADE

 1 CUP   FAT = TR EA

This is a good basic marinade for all meats.

1 C	RED WINE
1/2 C	BALSAMIC VINEGAR
1/2 C	DRY SHERRY
1/2 C	FAT-FREE STOCK
1	ONION, MINCED
1 t	DRIED SAGE

COMBINE THESE WELL.

HEAT TO REDUCE.

SHERRY APPLE SOY MARINADE

quick 2 CUPS   FAT = TR EA

3/4 C	DRY SHERRY
1/2 C	APPLE JUICE CONCENTRATE
1/2 C	SOY SAUCE
1/4 C	TOMATO PASTE
2 T	DIJON MUSTARD
2 T	FRESH GINGER, PEELED, GRATED
1 T	GARLIC, MINCED

SIMMER FOR 10 MINUTES .

PUREE WELL.

ADD LOUISIANA HOT SAUCE AND SALT & PEPPER TO YOUR TASTE.

CITRUS MARINADE

 2 CUPS FAT = TR EA

This is good for fish & poultry.

2 T	ORANGE ZEST	BOIL THESE & REMOVE FROM HEAT.
1 C	FRESH ORANGE JUICE	
1/2 C	FRESH GRAPEFRUIT JUICE	ADD THESE & MIX WELL.
2 T	LIME ZEST	
1/4 C	HONEY	
2 T	RED WINE VINEGAR	
1 T	WORCESTERSHIRE SAUCE	
1 t	DIJON MUSTARD	

GINGER CILANTRO MARINADE

 3 CUPS FAT = TR EA

This is great for fish, poultry & vegetables before & during grilling.

2 C	FRESH GRAPEFRUIT JUICE	
1/2 C	WHITE WINE	COMBINE THESE WELL.
1/4 C	FRESH ORANGE JUICE	
1/4 C	FRESH LIME JUICE	
8 CL	GARLIC, MINCED	
1 t	CRUSHED RED PEPPER FLAKES	
1/2 C	CILANTRO, CHOPPED	
2 INCH	FRESH GINGER, PEELED, GRATED	

MARINADE FOR CHEVRE (GOAT CHEESE)

 8 OZ FAT = 3 GM EA

1/2 C	WHITE WINE	PUREE THESE INGREDIENTS.
4 CL	GARLIC, MINCED	
6	GREEN ONIONS, MINCED	
20	RED & GREEN PEPPERCORNS, CRUSHED	
2 t	DRIED BASIL	
2 t	DRIED THYME	
2 t	DRIED OREGANO	
8 OZ	LOW-FAT GOAT CHEESE, SLICED THICKLY	ADD & MARINATE 12 HOURS AT ROOM TEMPERATURE.

Drain & serve cheese with Fat-Free Crackers or French Bread.

RASPBERRY MARINADE

 easy

2 CUPS   FAT = TR EA

This one is good for pork or poultry.

2 C	RASPBERRIES (OR BLUE OR STRAWBERRIES)	COMBINE & LET SIT IN A DARK PLACE FOR 2 WEEKS.
2 C	WHITE WINE VINEGAR	

DISCARD THE BERRIES.

HONEY & ORANGE MARINADE

 quick

3 CUPS   FAT = 2 GM EA

This is great for fish & poultry for grilling, broiling or stir-frying.

2 C	FRESH ORANGE JUICE	COMBINE ALL INGREDIENTS.
1/2 C	WINE VINEGAR	
1/2 C	SOY SAUCE	
3 T	HONEY	
1/2 t	TOASTED SESAME OIL	

LEMON SOY MARINADE

 quick

1 1/2 CUPS   FAT = TR EA

This is great for fish & poultry for grilling or broiling.

1/2 C	FRESH LEMON JUICE	COMBINE ALL INGREDIENTS.
1/2 C	WATER	
1/2 C	SOY SAUCE	
1 t	GARLIC POWDER	
1/2 t	LOUISIANA HOT SAUCE	

MANDARIN MARINADE

quick

3 CUPS   FAT = TR EA

This is especially good for shrimp, chicken & other stir-fry dishes.

1 C	RICE WINE VINEGAR	PUREE ALL INGREDIENTS.
1 3/4 C	FROZEN PINEAPPLE JUICE CONCENTRATE	
1/4 C	SOY SAUCE	
1 T	FRESH GINGER, PEELED, MINCED	
3 CL	GARLIC, MINCED	
1/2 T	TOASTED SESAME OIL	
1/2 t	CRUSHED RED PEPPER FLAKES	

ORANGE MARINADE

 2 CUPS   FAT = 2 GM EA

This is great for fish & poultry.

1 C	FRESH ORANGE JUICE	COMBINE ALL INGREDIENTS.
1 C	FRESH GRAPEFRUIT JUICE	
8 CL	GARLIC, MINCED	
2 INCH	FRESH GINGER, PEELED, GRATED	
1/4 C	SOY SAUCE	
1/2 t	TOASTED SESAME OIL	

PICANTE MARINADE

 3 CUPS   FAT = TR EA

This is good for beef or poultry.

2 C	TOMATO SAUCE	HEAT ALL INGREDIENTS.
1/2 C	ONION, MINCED	
2 T	JALAPENO PEPPER, MINCED	
2 T	SUGAR	
2 T	BALSAMIC VINEGAR	
5 CL	GARLIC, CRUSHED	

PINEAPPLE MARINADE

 2 CUPS   FAT = TR EA

This is good for beef, poultry or fish.

3/4 C	SOY SAUCE	COMBINE ALL INGREDIENTS.
3/4 C	PINEAPPLE JUICE
1/2 C	RED OR WHITE WINE (DEPENDING ON BEEF OR POULTRY, FISH)

PINEAPPLE SOY MARINADE

2 CUPS   FAT = TR EA

This is good for beef, poultry or fish.

1 C	PINEAPPLE JUICE	COMBINE ALL INGREDIENTS.
1/4 C	SOY SAUCE	
2 T	FRESH GINGER, PEELED, MINCED	
3 CL	GARLIC, MINCED	
3/4 C	FAT-FREE ITALIAN DRESSING	

SHERRY SOY MARINADE

2 1/4 CUPS   FAT = TR EA

This is great for anything stir-fried.

1 C	SOY SAUCE	PUREE ALL INGREDIENTS.
1 C	DRY SHERRY	
4 CL	GARLIC, MINCED	
2 T	FRESH GINGER, PEELED, MINCED	ADD LOUISIANA HOT SAUCE TO
1/4 C	HONEY	TASTE.

RAISIN SOUR CREAM MARINADE

2 1/2 CUPS   FAT = TR EA

This is great for ham, pork & lamb.

1/2 C	RAISINS, SOAKED, DRAINED	PUREE ALL & CHILL.
2 C	NO-FAT SOUR CREAM	
2 T	HORSERADISH	
1 T	FRESH LEMON JUICE	

SHERRY KABOB MARINADE & SAUCE

1 CUP   FAT = TR EA

This is for grilling all meats & poultry.   After grilling, boil the marinade to serve on the side.

6 T	SOY SAUCE	COMBINE ALL INGREDIENTS.
1 T	CURRY POWDER	
1 T	PAPRIKA	
2 T	SWEET SHERRY OR KIRSCHWASSER	SALT & PEPPER TO TASTE.
1/4 C	KETCHUP	
1/4 C	FRESH ORANGE JUICE	

SHERRY MARINADE

2 CUPS   FAT = 3 GM EA

The is a good basic for all meats.

1/2 C	WORCESTERSHIRE SAUCE	COMBINE ALL INGREDIENTS.
1/2 C	DRY SHERRY	
1/2 C	WATER	
1/4 C	FRESH LEMON JUICE	
1/4 C	SOY SAUCE	
2 t	TOASTED SESAME OR WALNUT OIL	
1 T	DRY MUSTARD	
3 CL	GARLIC, MINCED	
1 T	FRESH PARSLEY, CHOPPED	

TERIYAKI MARINADE I

quick 2 CUPS FAT = TR EA

1 C	SOY SAUCE
1 C	DRY SHERRY OR BOURBON
1/4 C	BROWN SUGAR
3 CL	GARLIC, MINCED
1 INCH	FRESH GINGER, PEELED, MINCED

PUREE ALL INGREDIENTS.

TERIYAKI MARINADE II

quick 3 CUPS FAT = TR EA

1 1/2 C	SOY SAUCE
1 C	WATER
1/2 C	SAKE (JAPANESE WINE)
6 T	GARLIC, MINCED
4 T	GROUND GINGER
2 T	SUGAR

PUREE ALL INGREDIENTS.

TROPICAL MARINADE

quick 4 CUPS FAT = TR EA

2 1/2 C	SOY SAUCE
1 C	FRESH ORANGE JUICE
2/3 C	BROWN SUGAR
1/2 C	RUM
2 T	FRESH GINGER, PEELED, GRATED
4 CL	GARLIC, CRUSHED

PUREE ALL INGREDIENTS.

ROSEMARY MARINADE

quick 1 1/2 CUPS FAT = TR EA

1 C	MOCK OIL (p 395)
1/4 C	FRESH ROSEMARY, MINCED
1/4 C	FRESH LEMON JUICE
8 CL	GARLIC, MINCED
1 t EA	SALT & PEPPER

PUREE ALL INGREDIENTS.

CURRY MARINADE

quick 1 1/2 CUPS FAT = TR EA

1 C	MOCK OIL (p 395)
1/4 C	WHITE WINE VINEGAR
1/4 C	ORANGE JUICE
4 CL	GARLIC, CRUSHED
2 t	CURRY POWDER
1 t	CRUSHED RED PEPPER FLAKES (OR TO TASTE)

PUREE ALL INGREDIENTS.

SALT TO TASTE.

Potatoes, Grains & Pastas

Unless I specifically want plain white rice, I always cook it in fat-free stock with diced onions. Sometimes I add garlic, herbs, Butter Buds, chopped fruit etc.

NOTE: Add bay leaf &/or garlic to the water when cooking pasta.

GARLIC POTATOES

 SERVES 6   FAT = TR EA

24	NEW RED POTATOES, QUARTERED	BOIL 10 MIN., DRAIN & PAT DRY.
10 CL	GARLIC, MINCED	TOSS WITH THE POTATOES.
1/4 C	BUTTER BUDS (DISSOLVED IN THE WATER)	LAY ON A SPRAYED PAN & BAKE
1/4 C	HOT WATER	AT 375 FOR 10 MINUTES OR 'TIL
------	SALT & PEPPER AS DESIRED	DONE.

PARSLIED POTATOES

 SERVES 6   FAT = TR EA

The Quick & Easy Way:

Prepare as Garlic Potatoes, substituting 1/2 C Chopped Parsley for the Garlic.

The Fancier Way, Almost As Quick:

12	BAKING POTATOES, PEELED	USING MELON BALLER, SCOOP OUT LITTLE BALLS AND BOIL
------	HOT WATER TO COVER WELL	UNTIL ALMOST DONE. DRAIN & PAT DRY.
4 T	BUTTER BUDS (DISSOLVED IN THE WATER)	COMBINE, TOSS WITH POTATOES
4 T	HOT WATER	& FRY IN A SPRAYED PAN.
1/2 C	FRESH PARSLEY, CHOPPED	
------	SALT & PEPPER AS DESIRED	

BASIL POTATOES

 SERVES 6   FAT = TR EA

Prepare as Garlic Potatoes substituting BASIL for the Garlic.

RANCH POTATOES

 SERVES 6   FAT = TR EA

Prepare as Garlic Potatoes substituting for the Garlic:

1/2 PKG	HIDDEN VALLEY RANCH DRESSING OR DIP MIX	ADD THESE TO THE BUTTER BUD
1/2 C	NO-FAT SOUR CREAM	MIXTURE & BAKE AT 375 FOR 10 MINUTES OR UNTIL DONE.

This method works well with other pre-packaged dressing & dip mixes on potatoes as well as on vegetables. Try the old favorite mix, Lipton's Onion Soup (blenderize before tossing with the potatoes).

HOME FRIES

 SERVES 8 — FAT = 1 GM EA

| 8-10 | POTATOES, SCRUBBED, CUT LENGTHWISE IN EIGHTHS, SOAKED IN COLD WATER |
| ------ | SALT OR CAVENDER'S GREEK SEASONING |

Pat dry & spray with Pam Butter Spray. Sprinkle with seasonings and bake at 350 for 30 minutes or until done.   Spray again & broil if necessary to brown.

Try different seasonings (p 21).

DOWN HOME FRIES

 SERVES 8 — FAT = 1 GM EA

| 8-10 | POTATOES, PEELED, BOILED 'TIL ALMOST DONE | COOL & CUBE THE POTATOES. |
| ------ | SALT & PEPPER | FRY IN A HOT, WELL SPRAYED PAN, STIRRING ONLY WHEN IT'S NECESSARY. |

ROSTI POTATOES   (HASH-BROWNS)

 SERVES 6 — FAT = 1 GM EA

8	POTATOES, PEELED, SHREDDED	TOSS & MICROWAVE 5 MINUTES.
2	ONIONS, SHREDDED	FORM INTO PATTIES & FRY IN A
2 T	BUTTER BUDS (DISSOLVED IN THE WATER)	VERY HOT SPRAYED PAN,
2 T	HOT WATER	TURN ONLY ONCE WHEN THEY
------	SALT & PEPPER AS DESIRED	ARE GOLDEN.

For more formal service, use a biscuit cutter & cut each in uniform circles.

MASHED POTATOES

 easy SERVES 6 FAT = TR EA

10	POTATOES, PEELED, DICED	BOIL FOR 15 MINUTES, RINSE,
------	WATER TO COVER WELL	& DRAIN.
------	HOT WATER TO COVER WELL AGAIN	BOIL AGAIN, UNTIL POTATOES ARE VERY TENDER. DRAIN &
1/4 C	HOT SKIM MILK (OR MORE)	MASH VERY WELL.
6 T	EGG BEATERS	ADD THESE & WHIP FLUFFY.
2 T	BUTTER BUDS (OR MORE)	SALT & PEPPER TO TASTE.

Serve with Chicken or Beef Gravy (p 255) or with Mock Butter Sauce (p 250) & 2 strips of Oscar Mayer Turkey Bacon, fried & minced.

EMERALD POTATOES

SERVES 6 FAT = TR EA

Make Mashed Potatoes, adding 1 C Zucchini Peels (blanched), cut in tiny diamond shapes, or add 1 C Sliced Green Onion Tops.

GARLIC MASHED POTATOES

SERVES 6 FAT = TR EA

Make Mashed Potatoes, adding 6 CL Garlic, minced (or Garlic Powder), or make Horseradish Potatoes instead, using Creamy Horseradish Sauce.

CHEESY POTATOES

SERVES 6 FAT = 2 GM EA

Make Mashed Potatoes, adding 6 T Parmesan Cheese, or add 1 1/2 OZ Bleu Cheese or Roquefort Cheese, crumbled.

RUBY POTATOES

SERVES 6 FAT = TR EA

Make Mashed Potatoes, adding 1 C Pickled Red Bell Peppers, diced, or add 1 C Pimentos, diced, or add 1 C Red Bell Peppers, diced & blanched.

POTATO & ONION SOUFFLE

easy   SERVES 6   FAT = TR EA

3 C	MASHED POTATOES, (p 283)	COMBINE WELL & FOLD IN THE
1	RED ONION, MINCED	BEATEN EGG WHITES.
1/4 C	GREEN ONION TOPS, MINCED	
1 T	FRESH PARSLEY	SPOON IN 6 SPRAYED RAMEKINS.
1/4 C	EGG BEATERS	
4	EGG WHITES, BEATEN STIFF, NOT DRY	BAKE AT 350 FOR 30 MINUTES.

TWICE BAKED POTATOES I

SERVES 6   FAT = 2 GM EA

Scrub 3 BAKING POTATOES, puncture 3 times & bake at 425 for 1 hour. Slice lengthwise in half, scoop out centers of each (not too close to shells).

Make 1 recipe Mashed Potatoes (p 282), your choice; Plain, Emerald, Ruby or Garlic & add these ingredients while whipping:

1/4 C	PARMESAN CHEESE	SALT & PEPPER TO TASTE.
1/4 C	NO-FAT SOUR CREAM	
2 T	BUTTER BUDS	SPOON OR PIPE INTO EA SHELL.
------	SCOOPED OUT CENTERS FROM SHELLS	
6 t	PARMESAN CHEESE, SPRINKLED ON TOP	SPRAY w PAM BUTTER & BAKE AT 350 FOR 20 MINUTES.

TWICE BAKED POTATOES II

SERVES 6   FAT = 4 GM EA

Make 1 recipe Cheesy Potatoes (p 282) & add the following while whipping:

10 OZ PKG	CHOPPED SPINACH, DRAINED WELL	
1/2 C	NO-FAT SOUR CREAM	FINISH AS ABOVE.

PUFFY TWICE BAKED POTATOES

SERVES 6   FAT = 2 GM EA

Make 1 recipe Mashed Potatoes (p 282) & add the following while whipping:

10	GREEN ONIONS, MINCED	
1 T	FRESH PARSLEY, CHOPPED	
1/2 t	CAVENDER'S SEASONING (OR TO TASTE)	
6	EGG WHITES, BEATEN STIFF, NOT DRY	FOLD IN, & SPRINKLE CHEESE ON
2 T	PARMESAN CHEESE	THE TOPS.

Spoon or pipe into potato shells. Bake at 350 for 20 minutes.

CRAB STUFFED POTATOES   SERVES 6   FAT = TR EA

Make 1 recipe of Mashed Potatoes (p 282) & add the following while whipping:

1 LB	CRAB MEAT, SHRIMP OR LOBSTER	
1 t	OLD BAY SEASONING	FOLD IN THE WHITES & SPOON
1 C	COTTAGE CREAM (p 392)	INTO THE POTATO SHELLS.
1/2 C	PIMENTOS, CHOPPED	
1/2 C	GREEN ONION TOPS, MINCED	BAKE AT 350 FOR 20 MINUTES.
3	EGG WHITES, BEATEN TO STIFF, NOT DRY	

STUFFED POTATOES   SERVES 6   FAT = TR EA

Scrub 6 BAKING POTATOES, Puncture 3 times & bake at 425 for 1 hour. Slice off each end & scoop out a small cylindrical hole lengthwise through the center. Pack this hole with the Mushroom Mix below & keep warm.

2 LBS	MUSHROOMS, MINCED	SIMMER UNTIL ALMOST DRY.
2	RED ONIONS, MINCED	
3 CL	GARLIC, MINCED	
1 t	CAVENDER'S GREEK SEASONING	ADD ENOUGH POTATO CENTERS
1/2 C	FAT-FREE CHICKEN OR BEEF STOCK	TO HOLD MIXTURE TOGETHER.

Slice potatoes in 1/2" slices to show the design.

POTATO CAKES   SERVES 6   FAT DEPENDS ON
                                                           BASE RECIPE USED

1 RECIPE	MASHED POTATOES (p 282), YOUR CHOICE	
1 C	RED ONIONS, MINCED	FORM 12 FIRM PATTIES & FRY IN
1/2 C	INSTANT POTATO FLAKES (OR MORE)	A SPRAYED PAN.

quick

POTATO LATKES   SERVES 6   FAT = TR EA

6	POTATOES, PEELED, COOKED, SHREDDED	TOSS THESE TOGETHER.
2 T	FLOUR	
1 t	BAKING POWDER	
1	RED ONION, MINCED	FORM PATTIES & FRY IN A HOT
1/2 C	EGG BEATERS	SPRAYED PAN.

Serve with No-Fat Sour Cream and applesauce.

SCALLOPED POTATOES

 easy   SERVES 6   FAT = TR EA

8-10	POTATOES, PEELED, SLICED THIN	LAYER THESE IN A SPRAYED DISH
4	ONIONS, SLICED THIN & IN RINGS	& SEASON EACH LAYER.
------	FLOUR, SALT & PEPPER	

3-4 C	HOT SKIM MILK	POUR OVER, COVER WITH FOIL &
1/2 C	BUTTER BUDS (DISSOLVED IN ABOVE MILK)	BAKE AT 375 FOR 1 HOUR. LET
		SIT 15 MINUTES, UNCOVERED.

POTATOES AU GRATIN

SERVES 6   FAT = 2 GM EA

Make the same as above, adding 4 T Parmesan while layering. Sprinkle 2 T Parmesan on top after adding the skim milk.

POTATO PEPPER CASSOULETS

 easy   SERVES 6   FAT = TR EA

16	GREEN CHERRY PEPPERS, SLICED IN CIRCLES	ALTERNATE THESE IN LAYERS IN
4	RED BELL PEPPERS, SLICED IN CIRCLES	SPRAYED DISHES.
8	POTATOES, PEELED, SLICED THIN	
1	RED ONION, SLICED THIN & IN RINGS	
2 T	FRESH MARJORAM LEAVES, CHOPPED	
------	SALT & PEPPER	
		POUR OVER, COVER & BAKE AT
3 C	FAT-FREE CHICKEN OR BEEF STOCK (OR MORE)	425 FOR 45 MIN. OR UNIL DONE.

Try adding 6 OZ 99% Fat-Free Ham or Turkey Ham, diced, while layering either of the 3 recipes above, This would add 1 GM Fat for each serving.

POTATO PANCAKES

 easy   SERVES 10   FAT = TR EA

8-10	POTATOES, PEELED, GRATED, DRAINED	COMBINE ALL & FRY LIKE SMALL
------	SALT & PEPPER	PANCAKES IN A SPRAYED PAN.
1 C	EGG BEATERS	
3/4 C	SKIM MILK	
1/2 t	BAKING POWDER	

OPTIONS: ONION, GARLIC, HERBS OR PARMESAN, (ADD 2 GM PER TABLESPOON)

POTATOES AU JUS SERVES 6 FAT = 1 GM EA

8-10	NEW POTATOES, PEELED, QUARTERED	PLACE IN A SPRAYED DISH.

2 C	WATER, BOILING	COMBINE, POUR OVER & BAKE
1	KNORR VEGGIE BOUILLON CUBE	AT 400 FOR 45 MINUTES.
1	KNORR BEEF BOUILLON CUBE	
2 T	BOVRIL (AVAILABLE IN MOST STORES)	

POTATOES VERMOUTH SERVES 6 FAT = TR EA

8	LONG, LIGHT-SKINNED POTATOES	BOIL UNTIL JUST DONE & SLICE 1/2" THICK.

1/2 C	DRY VERMOUTH	PUREE THESE & TOSS WITH THE
1/2 C	MOCK OIL (p 395)	POTATOES.
2 T	DIJON MUSTARD	
1 T	WHITE WINE VINEGAR	SALT & PEPPER TO TASTE.
1 T	FRESH LEMON JUICE	

1/4 C	CAPERS, MINCED	ADD JUST BEFORE SERVING.

DIAMOND POTATOES SERVES 8 FAT = TR EA

This procedure is hard to explain, but easy to do, so don't be afraid to try.

4	BAKING POTATOES, SCRUBBED, HALVED LENGTHWISE	DIAMOND CUT*
1/2 C	BUTTER BUDS (DISSOLVED IN THE HOT WATER)	SPREAD POTATOES SLIGHTLY &
1/2 C	HOT WATER	BRUSH WITH BUTTER MIXTURE.
------	SALT & PEPPER	

Bake at 375 for 35-45 minutes or until done, depending on size. You could add your favorite seasoning to the Butter Bud mixture.

* DIAMOND CUT: Cut potatoes almost to the skin every 1/2" lengthwise. Make another set of similar cuts but at a 35 degree angle to the first cuts. Soak in ice cold water for 15 minutes. Drain upside down.

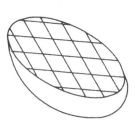

For an easy & delicious BAKED SWEET POTATO: Scrub, puncture & wrap in foil, bake at 400 for 1 hour or until done. Squeeze with oven mitts & split open. Drizzle liquid Butter Buds over & sprinkle with a little cinnamon.

SWEET POTATO PUFFS

SERVES 8   FAT = TR EA

4 C	SWEET POTATOES, COOKED, PEELED	PUREE THESE WELL.
3 T	BROWN SUGAR	
1/2 t	GROUND GINGER	
1/2 t	CINNAMON	POUR INTO 8 PAM-SPRAYED AND
1/2 t	MACE	SUGARED RAMEKINS.
1 C	EGG BEATERS	
1/2 C	FRESH ORANGE JUICE	BAKE AT 350 FOR 30 MINUTES.
1 t	ORANGE ZEST	
2 T	MEYER'S RUM	
1 T	SALT & PEPPER	

PUFFY SWEET POTATO

SERVES 6   FAT = TR EA

4 C	SWEET POTATOES, SHREDDED	SPRAY BAKING DISH & SPRINKLE
1/4 C	APPLESAUCE	WELL WITH FAT-FREE BREAD
2 T	BROWN SUGAR	CRUMBS.
3 T	BUTTER BUDS	PRESS AGAINST THE SIDES AND
1/2 t	GROUND GINGER	BOTTOM.
1/2 t	CINNAMON	
1/4 t	GROUND CLOVES	COMBINE ALL & POUR INTO THE
1 C	EGG BEATERS	PREPARED DISH.
1/3 C	FROZEN ORANGE JUICE CONCENTRATE	
1/4 C	MEYER'S RUM	BAKE AT 375 IN A WATER BATH
1 T	ORANGE ZEST, MINCED	FOR 1 HOUR.
1 t	SALT & PEPPER	

Serve with Non-Fat Vanilla Yogurt & cinnamon or a Fruit Compote.

HERBED SWEET POTATOES

quick   SERVES 6   FAT = TR EA

3	SWEET POTATOES, PEELED & DICED	BOIL 10 MINUTES & DRAIN.
------	WATER TO COVER	
1/2 C	FAT-FREE CHICKEN STOCK	ADD THESE & SIMMER UNTIL
1/4 C	BUTTER BUDS	DONE.
1/2 C	RED ONION, MINCED	
1 t	FRESH THYME, CHOPPED	
1 t	FRESH BASIL, CHOPPED	
1 t	FRESH ROSEMARY, GROUND	SALT & PEPPER TO TASTE.

MOCK ANCHOVY PASTA

SERVES 8   FAT = 4 GM EA

6 CL	GARLIC, MINCED	SIMMER THESE 5 MINUTES.
1	RED ONION, MINCED	
1/2 C	FAT-FREE CHICKEN STOCK	
8 OZ	TUNA IN WATER, UNDRAINED, SHREDDED	ADD & SIMMER 5 MINUTES.
4 OZ	CAPERS, MINCED	
1/4 C	FRESH PARSLEY, MINCED	
1/4 C	PARMESAN CHEESE	TOSS WITH COOKED PASTA.
16	CALAMATA OLIVES, SLICED	
1 PKG	BUTTER BUDS	

Adding TOMATO SAUCE or No-Fat Sour Cream would change this dish drastically.

SPAGHETTI SAUCE

5 CUPS   FAT = 2 GM EA

1 LB	TURKEY BREASTS, PROCESSED CHOP-CHOP	FRY THESE IN A SPRAYED PAN
2	ONIONS, DICED	PAN UNTIL TURKEY IS DONE.
4 CL	GARLIC. MINCED (OR MORE)	
1 EA	RED & GREEN BELL PEPPER, MINCED	
2	CARROTS, SHREDDED	
20 OZ	CANNED TOMATOES, CHOPPED	ADD & SIMMER 1 HOUR.
1/2 C	RED WINE (OR TO TASTE)	
2 t	DRIED ITALIAN HERBS	
2 t	GROUND FENNEL	SERVE OVER COOKED PASTA.
2	KNORR BEEF BOUILLON CUBES	

SUN-DRIED TOMATO SAUCE

4 CUPS   FAT = 2 GM EA

2	RED ONIONS, MINCED	FRY THESE IN A SPRAYED PAN
4 CL	GARLIC, MINCED	FOR 3 MINUTES.
1	RED BELL PEPPER, MINCED	
26	SUN-DRIED TOMATOES, BLANCHED, MINCED	ADD & SIMMER 30 MINUTES.
3 C	TOMATOES, PEELED, CHOPPED	
2	KNORR BEEF BOUILLON CUBES	
1 t	DRIED ITALIAN HERBS (OR TO TASTE)	SALT & PEPPER TO TASTE.
1 t	SAFFRON THREADS	
ZEST OF 1	LEMON, MINCED	
1 C	NO-FAT SOUR CREAM	WHISK IN BEFORE SERVING ON
1/4 C	PARMESAN CHEESE	COOKED PASTA.

PASTA ALFREDO

quick SERVES 8 FAT = 6 GM EA

2 C	NO-FAT SOUR CREAM	SIMMER THESE 10 MINUTES.
1 C	SKIM MILK	
2 C	MUSHROOMS, SLICED	
1/4 C	WINE OR VERMOUTH (OR TO TASTE)	
1 C	PARMESAN CHEESE	ADD THESE & TOSS 1/2 WITH
1/4 C	FRESH PARSLEY, CHOPPED	COOKED PASTA.
1/4 C	PIMENTO, CHOPPED	
------	FRESH LEMON JUICE (OPTIONAL)	TOP WITH REMAINDER.

OPTION: ADD COOKED SHRIMP TO THE REMAINDER & SPOON OVER. (ADDS NO FAT)

BLEU CHEESE PASTA

quick SERVES 8 FAT = 5 GM EA

2 C	NO-FAT SOUR CREAM	SIMMER THESE 10 MINUTES.
1/2 C	TOMATO PASTE	
2 OZ	BLEU CHEESE OR ROQUEFORT	
1/4 C	PARMESAN CHEESE	ADD THESE AND TOSS WITH
1/4 C	FAT-FREE PARMESAN CHEESE	COOKED PASTA.
1/4 C	BRANDY	
1/2 C	FRESH BASIL, CHOPPED	

PASTA CARBONARA

SERVES 8 FAT = 5 GM EA

2 C	NO-FAT SOUR CREAM	SIMMER IN A DOUBLE BOILER
1/4 C	BUTTER BUDS	UNTIL HOT.
1/4 C	WHITE WINE	
8 SL	OSCAR MAYER TURKEY BACON, FRIED DICED	ADD THESE JUST BEFORE YOU
4 SL	CANADIAN BACON, TRIMMED, DICED	SERVE OVER THE PASTA.
1/4 C	FRESH PARSLEY, CHOPPED	
1 C	EGG BEATERS	TOSS WITH PASTA WHILE IT IS
3/4 C	PARMESAN CHEESE	STILL VERY HOT.
3/4 C	FAT-FREE PARMESAN CHEESE	
1 1/2 LBS	PASTA, COOKED, DRAINED, BUT STILL VERY HOT	

PASTA VERDE & CREAM SAUCE

quick SERVES 8   FAT = 2 GM EA

1	RED ONION, MINCED	SIMMER THESE 10 MINUTES.
4 CL	GARLIC, MINCED	
2 C	FAT-FREE CHICKEN STOCK	

2 C	NO-FAT SOUR CREAM	WHISK IN THESE.
1/2 C	BUTTER BUDS	
1/2 C	WHITE WINE	

1 C	FRESH PARSLEY, CHOPPED	WHEN READY TO SERVE, ADD THESE & TOSS WITH COOKED SPINACH PASTA.
1/4 C	PARMESAN CHEESE	
1/4 C	FAT-FREE PARMESAN CHEESE	

| 1/4 C | PARSLEY, CHOPPED | COMBINE & SPRINKLE OVER EA. |
| 1/4 C | PARMESAN CHEESE | |

PASTINA & CHIVES

quick SERVES 4   FAT = 1 GM EA

1 C	FAT-FREE CHICKEN STOCK	SIMMER THESE 5 MINUTES.
1/4 C	BUTTER BUDS	
1 C	RED ONIONS, MINCED	
2 CL	GARLIC, MINCED (OR MORE)	

| 1 C | NO-FAT SOUR CREAM | WHISK IN &TOSS WITH COOKED PASTA. |
| 1 C | FRESH CHIVES, CHOPPED | SALT & PEPPER TO TASTE. |

| 2 C | PASTINA (TINY PASTA BEADS), COOKED | |

PASTA & RED CLAM SAUCE

easy SERVES 8   FAT = 1 GM EA

8 CL	GARLIC, MINCED	SIMMER THESE 30 MINUTES.
2	RED ONIONS, MINCED	
1	GREEN BELL PEPPER, MINCED	
4 C	TOMATO SAUCE	ADD RINSED, CANNED CLAMS &
1/2 C	FRESH BASIL, CHOPPED	SIMMER 2 MINUTES.
2 T	FRESH PARSLEY, CHOPPED	SERVE OVER COOKED PASTA.
------	JUICE OF 20 OZ CAN OF BABY CLAMS (STRAINED)	

If you sprinkle 1 T Parmesan over each, remember to add 2 GM FAT a serving.

ITALIAN PASTA & MUSHROOMS

SERVES 4 FAT = 4 GM EA

12 OZ	TURKEY BREASTS, PROCESSED CHOP-CHOP	FRY THESE IN A SPRAYED PAN
1	ONION, MINCED	UNTIL TURKEY IS DONE.
1	YELLOW SQUASH, MINCED	
4 CL	GARLIC, MINCED	
2 t	GROUND FENNEL (OR TO TASTE)	
1 1/2 C	FAT-FREE CHICKEN STOCK	ADD THESE INGREDIENTS.
1 LB	MUSHROOMS, DICED	
1 T	LEMON ZEST, MINCED	SALT & PEPPER TO TASTE.
1 C	NO-FAT SOUR CREAM	
1/4 C	WHITE WINE	
1/4 C	BUTTER BUDS	SERVE OVER COOKED SPIRAL
1 T	FRESH PARSLEY, CHOPPED	PASTA.
2 T	PARMESAN CHEESE	SPRINKLE OVER.

PASTA PARMESAN

quick SERVES 4 FAT = 4 GM EA

2 CL	GARLIC, MINCED	SIMMER THESE 10 MINUTES.
1	RED ONION, MINCED	
2 C	FAT-FREE CHICKEN STOCK (OR AS NEEDED)	
1/2 C	PARMESAN CHEESE	ADD THESE AND TOSS WITH
1 C	FAT-FREE PARMESAN CHEESE	COOKED PASTA.
1 C	NO-FAT SOUR CREAM	
1/4 C	FRESH PARSLEY, CHOPPED	

PESTO PASTA

SERVES 8 FAT = 2 GM EA

3 C	FRESH BASIL	PUREE THESE INGREDIENTS.
20 CL	GARLIC, DICED	
1 C	FRESH PARSLEY	SALT & PEPPER TO TASTE.
1	ONION, DICED	
1/2 C	PARMESAN CHEESE	
1/2 C	FAT-FREE PARMESAN CHEESE	SERVE OVER COOKED PASTA.
1/4 C	BUTTER BUDS (DISSOLVED IN THE STOCK)	
1 C	FAT-FREE CHICKEN STOCK, BOILING	THIS IS EVEN GREAT THE NEXT
1 t	CAVENDER'S GREEK SEASONING	DAY.
1 C	MOCK OIL (p 395 MADE w CHICKEN STOCK)	

This also makes a great base sauce for pizza.

SALMON PASTA

quick   SERVES 8   FAT = 2 GM EA

8	GREEN ONIONS, SLICED	SIMMER THESE 5 MINUTES.
3 CL	GARLIC, MINCED	
1/4 t	OLD BAY SEASONING	
1 C	FAT-FREE CHICKEN STOCK	
3 C	FAT-FREE CREAM CHEESE	WHISK IN THESE.
1/4 C	BUTTER BUDS	
1/2 C	GIN OR VODKA	SIMMER 3 MINUTES.
1/2 C	FROZEN TINY PEAS	
4	TOMATOES, PEELED, DICED	
3/4 LB	SMOKED SALMON, JULIENNED	
1 C	FRESH SPINACH, CHIFFONADE (p 396)	TOSS WITH COOKED PASTA AND SPOON THE SAUCE OVER.
1/4 C	PARMESAN CHEESE (OPTIONAL—ADDS 8 GM FAT)	

STUFFED PASTA

SERVES 8   FAT = 4 GM EA

2 C	NON-FAT COTTAGE CHEESE	COMBINE THESE IN THE FOOD PROCESSOR.
1 C	PARMESAN CHEESE	
1/2 C	FAT-FREE PARMESAN CHEESE	
2 PKG	FROZEN SPINACH, CHOPPED & SQUEEZED DRY	
10	GREEN ONIONS, DICED	SALT & PEPPER TO TASTE.
1/2 C	EGG BEATERS	
4 CL	GARLIC, DICED	
1/4 C	FRESH BASIL	STUFF THE SHELLS, COVER WITH
1/4 t	NUTMEG, GRATED	SPAGHETTI SAUCE AND BAKE AT 350 FOR 30 MINUTES.
24	JUMBO PASTA SHELLS,(ALLOWING FOR BREAKAGE), COOKED AL DENTE	

Or you could form into finger shapes, dip in Egg Beaters, dredge in flour, chill 20 minutes, & boil for 3 minutes before baking with spaghetti sauce.

BARLEY CASSEROLE

quick   SERVES 4   FAT = TR EA

1 C	PEARL BARLEY	COMBINE IN SPRAYED DISH.
2	ONIONS, DICED	COVER & BAKE AT 350 FOR 20
1/2 LB	MUSHROOMS, SLICED THICK	MINUTES OR UNTIL DONE.
2 C	FAT-FREE CHICKEN STOCK, BOILING	
------	SALT & PEPPER AS DESIRED	

BULGUR w MUSHROOMS

quick SERVES 4 FAT = TR EA

1 C	BULGUR (CRACKED WHEAT)	SIMMER THESE FOR 20 MINUTES
1	ONION, MINCED	OR UNTIL DONE.
2 C	FAT-FREE CHICKEN STOCK, BOILING	
16	MUSHROOMS, SLICED	
1 T	FRESH THYME, CHOPPED	

BULGUR PILAF

quick SERVES 4 FAT = TR EA

2 C	FAT-FREE CHICKEN STOCK, BOILING	SIMMER THESE FOR 20 MINUTES.
1 C	BULGUR (CRACKED WHEAT)	
1	RED ONION, MINCED	
1 EA	RED, YELLOW & GREEN BELL PEPPER, MINCED	
1/4 C	FRESH PARSLEY, CHOPPED	DRAIN AND ADD PARSLEY AND
1/4 C	CANNED WATER CHESTNUTS, DICED	CHESTNUTS.

CURRIED COUSCOUS

quick SERVES 4 FAT = TR EA

1	ONION, MINCED	COMBINE THESE AND POUR ON
1 C	FAT-FREE CHICKEN STOCK, BOILING	COUSCOUS.
1 t	SOY SAUCE	COVER & LET SIT 5 MINUTES.
1 T	CURRY POWDER	
1/2 t	SUGAR	FLUFF WITH A FORK.
1 C	COUSCOUS	SALT & PEPPER TO TASTE.

ALLSPICE RICE

easy SERVES 8 FAT = TR EA

2 C	BROWN RICE	COMBINE, COVER & SIMMER 20
1	ONION, DICED	MINUTES OR UNTIL DONE.
1/4 t	ALLSPICE	
4 C	BOILING FAT-FREE CHICKEN STOCK	
1	BOUQUET GARNI OF CLOVE, CARDAMOM, CINNAMON STICK (WRAP IN CHEESECLOTH)	
1/2 C	RAISINS OR CURRANTS	REMOVE BOUQUET & ADD.

ALMOND RICE

SERVES 8   FAT = TR EA

4 C	FAT-FREE CHICKEN STOCK	COVER & SIMMER THESE FOR 20
2 C	BROWN RICE	MINUTES OR UNTIL DONE.
2 t	ALMOND FLAVORING	
12	DRIED APRICOTS, MINCED	
ZEST OF 1	ORANGE, MINCED	
4 SL	FRESH GINGER, PEELED, MINCED	
1/2 t	SAFFRON THREADS	
1/4 C	GOLDEN RAISINS	ADD THESE DURING THE LAST 5
1 T	CAPERS, RINSED & MINCED	MINUTES OF COOKING.
1/2 t	GROUND CUMIN	

BLACK BEANS & RICE

SERVES 8   FAT = TR EA

2 C	RICE	
1	KNORR VEGGIE BOUILLON CUBE	COVER & SIMMER 20 MINUTES.
1	KNORR HAM BOUILLON CUBE	
2	RED ONIONS, DICED	
1	ORANGE, JUICE & PULP OF	
4 C	WATER, BOILING	
2 C	BLACK BEANS, SOAKED OVERNIGHT	DRAIN, COVER WITH NEW WATER
6	ONIONS, DICED	& ADD THESE.
9	TOMATOES, PEELED & DICED	
4 CL	GARLIC, MINCED (OR MORE)	
3	CARROTS, DICED	SIMMER 1 HOUR OR MORE.
2	KNORR HAM BOUILLON CUBES	SALT & PEPPER TO TASTE.
2	KNORR BEEF BOUILLON CUBES	PUREE 1/3 OF THIS.
1 t	CUMIN (OR MORE)	
1 t	LOUISIANA HOT SAUCE (OR TO TASTE)	SERVE OVER THE RICE.
------	SHERRY (OPTIONAL)	

CURRIED RICE

easy

SERVES 4   FAT = TR EA

2 C	FAT-FREE CHICKEN STOCK, BOILING	COVER & SIMMER 20 MINUTES.
1 C	RICE	
1	ONION, DICED	
2 t	CURRY POWDER (OR TO TASTE)	ADD CAYENNE, IF YOU LIKE.

OPTION FOR LAST 5 MINUTES OF COOKING:
     ADD

1/2 C	WHITE WINE
4 OZ	99% FAT-FREE HAM OR TURKEY HAM
2	APPLES, DICED, TOSSED IN ORANGE JUICE, DRAINED

GREEN RICE

quick SERVES 8 FAT = TR EA

2 C	FAT-FREE CHICKEN STOCK	
1 C	RICE	
1 BNCH	GREEN ONIONS, MINCED	

COVER & SIMMER 20 MINUTES.

1/4 C	FRESH PARSLEY, MINCED
1 C	RAW SPINACH, CHOPPED

ADD DURING LAST 3 MINUTES & TOSS.

FRIED RICE

easy SERVES 8 FAT = 1 GM EA

6	GREEN ONIONS, SLICED
2 CL	GARLIC, MINCED
2	CARROTS, COOKED, MINCED
4 SL	CANADIAN BACON, TRIMMED, DICED

FRY IN A HOT SPRAYED PAN.

SALT & PEPPER TO TASTE.

1 C	SHRIMP, COOKED, DICED
4 C	COOKED RICE, COOLED
1 C	EGG BEATERS, FRIED, DICED

ADD SHRIMP AND RICE. WHEN HOT, STIR IN EGG BEATERS.

MUSHROOM RICE

quick SERVES 8 FAT = TR EA

2 C	RICE (OR BARLEY)
2	ONIONS, DICED
1/2 LB	MUSHROOMS, SLICED
1/2 t	CAVENDER'S SEASONING
4 C	BOILING WATER
2	KNORR BEEF BOUILLON CUBES

SIMMER THESE COVERED FOR 20 MINUTES OR UNTIL DONE.

SAVORY RICE PILAF

quick SERVES 8 FAT = TR EA

2 C	RICE, SPRAYED w PAM & TOSSED
2	ONIONS, DICED

FRY THESE IN A SPRAYED PAN 3 MINUTES.

1/2 LB	MUSHROOMS, SLICED
2 CL	GARLIC, MINCED
2 C	WATER, BOILING
1/2	KNORR VEGGIE BOUILLON CUBE
1	KNORR BEEF BOUILLON CUBE (OR CHICKEN)
1 C	PICKLED RED PEPPERS (OPTIONAL)
2 T	FRESH PARSLEY, CHOPPED (OPTIONAL)

ADD THESE AND POUR INTO A SPRAYED DISH.

BAKE AT 350 FOR 20 MINUTES OR UNTIL DONE.

ADD WATER AS NEEDED.

SAFFRON RICE

 easy   SERVES 8   FAT = 1 GM EA

2 C	LONG GRAIN RICE	COVER & SIMMER THESE FOR 20
2	ONIONS, DICED	MINUTES OR UNTILDONE.
1/4 C	DRY WHITE WINE	
1 EA	RED & GREEN BELL PEPPER, DICED	
3 CL	GARLIC, MINCED	
1/4 t	SAFFRON THREADS	ADD PARSLEY.
1/4 t	TURMERIC	
4 C	FAT-FREE CHICKEN STOCK, BOILING	FLUFF WITH FORK.
2 T	PARSLEY, CHOPPED	
1 T	PARMESAN CHEESE (OPTIONAL—ADD 2 GMS FAT)	

Turn this easy dish into PAELLA by adding the following during last 5 minutes:

1/2 t	GROUND CUMIN
------	CAYENNE PEPPER
	COOKED TURKEY CHUNKS, SHRIMP, LOBSTER, CANADIAN BACON, TOMATOES, PEELED & CHOPPED, FROZEN TINY PEAS, CLAMS & MUSSELS

SESAME (or POPPY) RICE

 quick   SERVES 8   FAT = 5 GM EA

2 C	RICE	COVER & SIMMER THESE FOR 20
2	ONIONS, DICED	MINUTES OR UNTIL DONE.
3 CL	GARLIC, MINCED.	
1/2 C	TOASTED SESAME SEEDS (OR POPPY SEEDS)	
4 C	BOILING FAT-FREE CHICKEN STOCK	
2 T	FRESH PARSLEY, CHOPPED	TOSS & SERVE.

RICE w SALMON & GREEN ONIONS

 easy   SERVES 8   FAT = 2 GM EA

2 CL	GARLIC, MINCED	FRY THESE IN A HOT SPRAYED
1 BNCH	GREEN ONION, SLICED	PAN FOR 3 MINUTES.
1 C	NO-FAT SOUR CREAM	ADD THESE & HEAT THROUGH.
1 T	DIJON MUSTARD (OR TO TASTE)	
4 T EA	BUTTER BUDS, HOT WATER (COMBINED)	
1/2 LB	SMOKED SALMON, DICED	
4 C	HOT COOKED RICE	TOSS WITH ABOVE.
1 C	FROZEN TINY PEAS, BLANCHED 2 MIN.	SALT & PEPPER TO TASTE.
1/4 C	PARMESAN CHEESE (OPTIONAL—ADDS 8 GMS FAT)	

SPINACH RICE

easy   SERVES 8   FAT = TR EA

2 C	LONG GRAIN RICE	COVER & SIMMER THESE FOR 20
1	ONION, DICED	MINUTES OR UNTILDONE.
4 C	WATER, BOILING	
1	KNORR CHICKEN BOUILLON CUBE	
1	KNORR VEGGIE BOUILLON CUBE	
1/2 C	FRESH PARSLEY, CHOPPED	ADD DURING LAST 5 MINUTES
2 C	FRESH SPINACH, CHOPPED	OF COOKING.
1 T	PARMESAN (OPTIONAL—ADDS 2 GMS FAT)	SPRINKLE OVER.

SWEET-SCENTED RICE

easy   SERVES 8   FAT = TR EA

2 C	LONG GRAIN RICE, SPRAYED w PAM, TOSSED	FRY THESE IN A SPRAYED PAN
1	ONION, CHOPPED	FOR 5 MINUTES.
2	CARROTS, SHREDDED	
4	WHOLE CLOVES	WRAP SPICES IN CHEESECLOTH.
4	CARDAMOM SEEDS, CRUSHED	
10	PEPPERCORNS, CRUSHED	
1	CINNAMON STICK (2" LONG)	ADD TO RICE, POUR IN SPRAYED
4 C	WATER, BOILING	DISH, COVER & BAKE AT 325 FOR
1	KNORR CHICKEN BOUILLON CUBE	20 MINUTES.
1	KNORR VEGGIE BOUILLON CUBE	REMOVE SPICE BAG.
1/2 C	RAISINS	ADD JUST BEFORE SERVING.

RICE w SMOKED TROUT

easy   SERVES 8   FAT = 1 GM EA

2 CL	GARLIC, MINCED	FRY THESE IN A SPRAYED PAN 5
8	GREEN ONION BOTTOMS, SLICED	MINUTES.
2 C	NO-FAT SOUR CREAM	WHISK IN THESE ITEMS.
2 T	DIJON MUSTARD (OR TO TASTE)	
8 OZ	SMOKED TROUT, DICED	
4 C	COOKED RICE, HOT	TOSS THESE WITH SAUCE.
1/2 C	FROZEN TINY PEAS (OPTIONAL)	
8	GREEN ONION TOPS, SLICED	

You can substitute Turkey & Broccoli. This would lower the fat content.

WHEAT-BERRY RICE

 easy   SERVES 8   FAT = TR EA

1 C	WHOLE-WHEAT BERRIES	SPRAY, TOSS AND FRY IN A HOT
1 C	BASMATI RICE	SPRAYED PAN FOR 5 MINUTES.
12	GREEN ONIONS, SLICED	
1 EA	RED, YELLOW & GREEN BELL PEPPER, DICED	
4 C	WATER, BOILING	ADD, COVER & SIMMER FOR 20
2	KNORR CHICKEN BOUILLON CUBES	MINUTES OR UNTIL DONE.
ZEST OF 1	LEMON, MINCED	TOSS WITH ABOVE & SERVE.
1	LEMON, JUICED	
2 T	FRESH PARSLEY, MINCED	

WILD RICE & MUSHROOMS

 easy   SERVES 8   FAT = TR EA

1/2 C	WILD RICE	SIMMER THESE FOR 25 MINUTES.
4 C	WATER, BOILING	
1 1/2 C	RICE	
1	KNORR VEGGIE BOUILLON CUBE	ADD, COVER & SIMMER FOR 20
1	KNORR CHICKEN OR BEEF CUBE	MINUTES OR UNTIL DONE.
1	ONION, DICED	
2 CL	GARLIC, MINCED	
1/2 LB	MUSHROOMS, SLICED	ADD THESE DURING THE LAST 5
2 T	FRESH PARSLEY, CHOPPED	MINUTES OF COOKING.
1 T	FRESH LEMON JUICE (OPTIONAL)	
------	SALT & PEPPER AS DESIRED	

WILD RICE w VEGETABLES

easy   SERVES 8   FAT = TR EA

1/2 C	WILD RICE	COVER & SIMMER FOR 25 MIN.
4 C	BOILING WATER	
1 1/2 C	RICE	ADD, COVER & SIMMER FOR 20
2	ONION, DICED	MINUTES OR UNTIL DONE.
1	KNORR VEGGIE BOUILLON CUBE	
1	KNORR CHICKEN BOUILLON CUBE	
2 PKG	FROZEN SNOW PEAS	ADD THESE DURING THE LAST 5
2 C	MUSHROOMS, SLICED	MINUTES OF COOKING.
2 CANS	WATER CHESTNUTS, SLICED	

WILD ORZO

easy SERVES 8 FAT = TR EA

1 C	WILD RICE	SIMMER 45 MINUTES AND SET
2	RED ONION, DICED	ASIDE.
1	GREEN BELL PEPPER, DICED	
2 C	WATER	DRAIN & KEEP WARM.
2	KNORR CHICKEN BOUILLON CUBE	SAVE STOCK.
1 C	ORZO	BOIL THESE 6 MINUTES, DRAIN
------	STOCK ABOVE & WATER TO COVER WELL	& ADD RICE MIXTURE
1	RED BELL PEPPER, DICED	
1	KNORR CHICKEN BOUILLON CUBE	SALT & PEPPER TO TASTE.

ORZO, PEPPERS & SUN-DRIED TOMATOES

SERVES 8 FAT – 3 GM EA

2 C	ORZO, COOKED IN BOILING, SALTED WATER 6 MINUTES & DRAINED WELL	
2 EA	RED, YELLOW, GREEN BELL PEPPERS, ROASTED, PEELED, SEEDED & DICED	
1	RED ONION, DICED	BOIL THESE FOR 5 MINUTES.
6 CL	GARLIC, MINCED	
1 1/2 C	FAT-FREE CHICKEN STOCK	
1 t	GROUND BLACK PEPPER	
1 C	SUN-DRIED TOMATOES, JULIENNED	ADD THESE, THE ORZO, PEPPERS
1 C	FRESH BASIL, CHOPPED	AND STIR UNTIL THE LIQUID IS ABSORBED.
8 T	PARMESAN CHEESE	REMOVE FROM HEAT. STIR IN CHEESE & SERVE IMMEDIATELY.

ORZO & TOMATOES

easy SERVES 6 FAT = 1 GM EA

1 1/2 C	ORZO, COOKED IN BOILING, SALTED WATER FOR 8-10 MIN, DRAINED	
1/4 C	FAT-FREE BEEF STOCK	SIMMER THESE FOR 5 MINUTES.
1	RED ONION, DICED	
4 CL	GARLIC	
1 t	GROUND BLACK PEPPER	
1 LB	TOMATOES, DICED	ADD THESE FOR 2 MINUTES AND
1/4 C	FRESH BASIL, MINCED (OR PARSLEY)	THEN STIR IN THE ORZO.
3 T	PARMESAN	SERVE & SPRINKLE EACH WITH CHEESE.

QUINOA TIMBALES

 SERVES 6   FAT = TR EA

2 C	FAT-FREE CHICKEN STOCK, BOILING
1 C	QUINOA, RINSED, DRAINED
1	RED ONION, DICED
1/3 C	CURRANTS OR RAISINS
1/3 C	TOMATOES, PEELED, SEEDED, CHOPPED
1 t	GROUND CUMIN
1/4 t	CINNAMON
1/4 t	TURMERIC
------	SAFFRON

COVER & SIMMER 15 MINUTES.

SPRAY 6 TIMBALE MOLDS, PACK
WITHE QUINOA MIX., INVERT EA
ONTO PLATES & REMOVE MOLDS
WHEN READY TO SERVE.

SPRINKLE WITH PARSLEY.

BULGUR TIMBALES

 SERVES 6   FAT = TR EA

2 C	FAT-FREE CHICKEN STOCK, BOILING
1 C	BULGAR (CRACKED WHEAT)
2 C	GREEN ONIONS, SLICED THINLY
ZEST OF 1	LEMON, MINCED

COVER & SIMMER 10 MINUTES.

LET SIT 5 MINUTES, FLUFF AND
SEASON WITH SALT & PEPPER.

Spray 6 timbale molds, pack each with the Bulgur mix.Invert each onto a plate. Remove mold when ready to serve. Garnish w strips of lemon peel.

BARLEY CASSEROLE

easy SERVES 8   FAT = TR EA

3 1/2 C	FAT-FREE CHICKEN STOCK
1 C	BARLEY, RINSED
1/2 C	DRY WHITE WINE
2	CARROTS, SLICED DIAGONALLY
1	RED ONION, DICED
1 C	MUSHROOMS, SLICED
1 t	GROUND ROSEMARY
1 t	FRESH BASIL, MINCED
1/2 t	THYME
1 t	CRUSHED RED PEPPER FLAKES

COMBINE ALL IN A SPRAYED 3 QT
BAKING DISH.

COVER AND BAKE AT 350 FOR 2
HOURS.

Vegetables

Most vegetables have only trace amounts of fat, so unless you add fat in the cooking, you can eat all you want. But remember to only put fat-free toppings or sauces on them.

ARTICHOKE POTATO SAUTE

SERVES 4   FAT = 2 GM EA

2 C	MARINATED ARTICHOKE HEARTS, DRAINED, TRIMMED WELL, DICED	
8	NEW RED POTATOES, BOILED, QUARTERED	
1	RED ONION, MINCED	FRY THESE IN A SPRAYED PAN.
2 T	FRESH MARJORAM, MINCED	SALT & PEPPER TO TASTE.
2 T	PARMESAN CHEESE	SPRINKLE OVER TO SERVE.

STUFFED ARTICHOKES

SERVES 4   FAT = 3 GM EA

1/2	SPAGHETTI SQUASH, HALVED, CUT SIDE DOWN IN 1" WATER. BAKE AT 350 FOR 45 MINUTES & SCRAPE OUT SPAGHETTI.	
4	ARTICHOKES, TRIMMED, BOILED 45 MIN.	PRY APART, REMOVE CENTER & THE CHOKE & DISCARD.
2 JARS	MARINATED ARTICHOKE HEARTS, DRAINED, TRIMMED WELL, DICED.	
2	ONIONS, DICED	
4 CL	GARLIC, MINCED	FRY THESE IN A SPRAYED PAN.
1 C	MUSHROOMS, DICED	
1 t	DRIED ITALIAN HERBS	
1/2 t	CAVENDER'S GREEK SEASONING	TOSS WITH THE SPAGHETTI.
1/4 C	PARMESAN CHEESE	ADD & STUFF THE ARTICHOKES.
1 C	SPAGHETTI SAUCE (p 288)	BAKE AT 375 FOR 15 MINUTES.

ASPARAGUS w HERBED HOLLANDAISE

SERVES 8   FAT = TR EA

2 LBS	ASPARAGUS, TRIMMED	BLANCH 5 MINUTES.
1 C	MOCK HOLLANDAISE (p 257)	ADD HERBS TO SAUCE & SPOON
2 T	FRESH PARSLEY, MINCED	OVER ASPARAGUS.
1 T	FRESH THYME OR ROSEMARY OR TARRAGON, MINCED—PICK YOUR FAVORITE.	

ASPARAGUS w ORANGE SAUCE

SERVES 6   FAT = TR EA

1 1/2 LBS	ASPARAGUS, TRIMMED	BLANCH 5 MINUTES.
1/2 C	FROZEN ORANGE JUICE CONCENTRATE	SIMMER THESE & SPOON OVER
1/2 C	NO-FAT SOUR CREAM	ASPARAGUS.
1 T	BUTTER BUDS	
2 T	ORANGE ZEST	SPRINKLE OVER TO SERVE.

CHINESE ASPARAGUS

 SERVES 8   FAT = 1 GM EA

2 LBS	ASPARAGUS PIECES	BLANCH 5 MINUTES & SHOCK.
2 T	SOY SAUCE	ADD THESE & CHILL.
1 T	SUGAR	
1 T	RICE WINE VINEGAR	TO SERVE, SPRINKLE WITH 1 T
8 DROPS	LOUISIANA HOT SAUCE (OR TO TASTE)	SESAME SEEDS.

ASPARAGUS & ONIONS

 SERVES 4   FAT = TR EA

1 LB	ASPARAGUS PIECES	SIMMER THESE 5 MINUTES.
2	RED ONIONS, DICED	DRAIN.
2 C	FAT-FREE CHICKEN STOCK, BOILING.	
2 T	NO-FAT SOUR CREAM	TOSS THESE WITH ABOVE.
2 T	RICE WINE VINEGAR	
1 T	DIJON MUSTARD	SALT & PEPPER TO TASTE.

GREEN BEANS & MUSHROOMS

 SERVES 8   FAT = TR EA

2 LBS	GREEN BEANS, SNAPPED	SIMMER THESE UNTIL ALMOST
2 CL	GARLIC, MINCED	DONE.
1	RED ONION, DICED	
2 C	WATER	
2	KNORR BEEF BOUILLON CUBES	
2 T	BUTTER BUDS	
2 C	MUSHROOMS, SLICED	ADD & SIMMER 2 MINUTES.
1/4 C	COLD WATER	COMBINE WELL, WHISK IN AND
2 T	CORNSTARCH	HEAT TO THICKEN.
1 T	PARSLEY, CHOPPED	SPRINKLE OVER TO SERVE.

MINI STRING BEANS, CARROTS & RADICCHIO

SERVES 6   FAT = TR EA

1 LB	GREEN BEANS, SNAPPED, BLANCHED 5 MIN.	SIMMER THESE 2 MINUTES.
1/2 LB	CARROTS, JULIENNED, BLANCHED 5 MIN.	
1	RED ONION, DICED	
2 T	BUTTER BUDS	PEPPER TO TASTE.
1 C	FAT-FREE BEEF STOCK, BOILING	
1/2 t	GROUND ROSEMARY	
2 HD	RADICCHIO, SHREDDED	ADD RADICCHIO JUST FOR 30 SECONDS & SERVE.

ORIENTAL GREEN BEANS

 quick SERVES 4 FAT = 2 GM EA

1	RED ONION, DICED	FRY IN A HOT SPRAYED PAN FOR
3 CL	GARLIC, MINCED	2 MINUTES.
3 SL	FRESH GINGER (REMEMBER TO REMOVE)	
1 C	FAT-FREE CHICKEN STOCK	COMBINE WELL, WHISK IN AND
2 T	SOY SAUCE	HEAT TO THICKEN.
1 t	SUGAR	
1/4 t	CRUSHED RED PEPPER FLAKES	
1 T	CORNSTARCH	ADD BEANS & TOSS.
1 LB	GREEN BEANS, SNAPPED, BLANCHED 5 MIN.	
1 T	TOASTED SESAME SEEDS	SPRINKLE OVER TO SERVE.

HOT FOUR BEAN

quick SERVES 8 FAT = TR EA

1/2 C	SUGAR	SIMMER THESE TO THICKEN.
1 T	CORNSTARCH	
2/3 C	RED WINE VINEGAR	
1 CAN	GREEN BEANS, DRAINED	ADD THESE & HEAT THROUGH.
1 CAN	WAX BEANS, DRAINED	
1 CAN	KIDNEY BEANS, DRAINED WELL	
1 CAN	CHICK PEAS, DRAINED	
1 SM JAR	PICKLED RED BELL PEPPERS, DRAINED, DICED	
1 LGE	RED ONION, SLICED, QUARTERED	
2 T	DRIED ITALIAN HERBS	SALT & PEPPER TO TASTE.

BROCCOLI & SAUCES

SERVES 4 FAT DEPENDS ON SAUCE

1 HD	BROCCOLI, FLORETS	STEAM 5 MINUTES OR TO THE
1 C	FAT-FREE STOCK, UNDER VEGGIE STEAMER	DONENESS YOU LIKE.

Any of these sauces are great on steamed veggies:

MOCK HOLLANDAISE (p 257)   LEMON SAUCE (p 146, 257)
MOCK BUTTER SAUCE (p 250)   ORANGE SAUCE (p 148, 257, 302)
CHEESE SAUCE (p 250, 395)   OR EXPERIMENT WITH NEW ONES

Or simmer these ingredients & toss with the cooked florets:

1/4 C	FRESH LEMON JUICE
1/4 C	OYSTER SAUCE
1/4 C	FAT-FREE MIRACLE WHIP
1 t	DRY MUSTARD

GARLIC BROCCOLI

 SERVES 4   FAT = TR EA

1/4 C	HOT WATER	
1/4 C	BUTTER BUDS	
1	RED ONION, MINCED	
3 CL	GARLIC, MINCED	
------	SALT & PEPPER	

SIMMER THESE 5 MINUTES &
POUR OVER BROCCOLI.

1 HD   BROCCOLI, IN FLORETS, STEAMED TO DESIRED DONENESS

If you'd like this creamy, just whisk in some No-Fat Sour Cream before pouring.

BROCCOLI w SESAME

SERVES 4   FAT = 1 GM EA

1 HD	BROCCOLI, IN FLORETS	
2 CL	GARLIC, MINCED	
1 C	FAT-FREE CHICKEN STOCK, UNDER VEGGIE STEAMER	

STEAM THESE 5 MINUTES.

1/4 C	WHITE WINE	
1/4 C	SOY SAUCE	
1/2 C	WATER CHESTNUTS, SLICED	
1/8 t	GROUND GINGER (OPTIONAL)	

COMBINE AND TOSS WITH THE
BROCCOLI & SESAME SEEDS.

SALT & PEPPER TO TASTE.

2 t   TOASTED SESAME SEEDS

SESAME VEGGIE STIR-FRY

SERVES 8   FAT = 1 GM EA

1 C	FAT-FREE CHICKEN STOCK	
1/4 C	SOY SAUCE	
1/4 t	GROUND GINGER	
2 T	BUTTER BUDS	
2	ONIONS, CHOPPED	
2	CARROTS, SHREDDED	
1 C	CAULIFLOWER FLORETS	
1 C	BROCCOLI FLORETS	
1 C	GREEN ZUCCHINI, DICED	
1 C	YELLOW ZUCCHINI, DICED	
1	RED BELL PEPPER, JULIENNED	

STIR-FRY & ADD THESE IN THE
ORDER THEY ARE LISTED.

ADD MORE STOCK AS NEEDED.

1/2 C	FAT-FREE CHICKEN STOCK, COLD	
1 T	CORNSTARCH	
1/4 C	TOASTED SESAME SEEDS	

COMBINE WELL, WHISK IN AND
HEAT TO THICKEN.
SPRINKLE OVER TO SERVE.

CHAMPAGNE CARROTS

SERVES 8   FAT = TR EA

2 LBS	CARROTS, SLICED	SIMMER UNTIL JUST TENDER.
1/2 C	WATER	
1 C	CHAMPAGNE (BUBBLY OR FLAT)	
1	KNORR BEEF BOUILLON CUBE	
1 T EA	FRESH LEMON JUICE, SUGAR	

CURRIED CARROTS

SERVES 4   FAT = TR EA

8	CARROTS, SLICED, BOILED 6 MIN IN FAT-FREE CHICKEN STOCK & DRAINED.	
4 T	STOCK FROM COOKING CARROTS	
1 T	BUTTER BUDS	SIMMER THESE UNTIL TENDER.
1 t	CURRY POWDER (OR TO TASTE)	
------	FRESH LEMON JUICE, SALT & PEPPER TO TASTE	

CARROTS & FENNEL

SERVES 6   FAT = TR EA

10	CARROTS, JULIENNED	SIMMER THESE 10 MINUTES OR UNTIL DONE.
2 BULBS	FENNEL, JULIENNED	
1 C EA	WATER, WHITE WINE	
1	KNORR CHICKEN BOUILLON CUBE	SALT & PEPPER TO TASTE.
1 t	BOVRIL (AVAILABLE IN MOST STORES)	

GINGER CARROTS

SERVES 6   FAT = TR EA

10	CARROTS, SLICED OR JULIENNED	BLANCH 8 MINUTES & DRAIN.
1/4 C EA	HOT WATER, BROWN SUGAR	ADD & SIMMER UNTIL DONE.
1/4 C	BUTTER BUDS	
1/2 t	GROUND GINGER (OR TO TASTE)	
1/4 t	NUTMEG	

MOROCCAN CARROTS

quick

SERVES 4   FAT = TR EA

8	CARROTS, SLICED, BOILED 6 MIN IN FAT-FREE CHICKEN STOCK & DRAINED.	
4 T	STOCK FROM COOKING CARROTS	
2 T	BUTTER BUDS	SIMMER UNTIL TENDER.
2 CL	GARLIC, MINCED	
1 t	SUGAR	SALT & PEPPER TO TASTE.
1/2 t	GROUND CUMIN	
1/4 t	CINNAMON	SERVE HOT OR ROOM TEMP.
------	CAYENNE & FRESH LEMON JUICE TO TASTE	

ORANGE SPICED CARROTS

 SERVES 8   FAT = TR EA

4 C	CARROTS, SLICED, BOILED 6 MIN IN FAT-FREE CHICKEN STOCK & DRAINED.	
1 C	FRESH ORANGE JUICE	
1/4 C	BROWN SUGAR	SIMMER ALL UNTIL THICKENED.
1 T	CORNSTARCH	
1/4 t	GROUND GINGER	
1/8 t	NUTMEG	

MADEIRA CARROTS

 SERVES 8   FAT = TR EA

2 LBS	CARROTS, JULIENNED	BOIL THESE UNTIL TENDER.
1/2 C EA	MADEIRA WINE, WATER	
1 t EA	FRESH PARSLEY, TARRAGON, CHOPPED	ADD JUST BEFORE SERVING. SALT & PEPPER TO TASTE.

CARROT PUREE

 SERVES 8   FAT = TR EA

1 1/2 LBS	CARROTS, SHREDDED	SIMMER 30 MINUTES, DRAIN & PUREE, USING SOME STOCK TO
1 t	SUGAR	GET THE DESIRED CONSISTENCY.
2 C	FAT-FREE CHICKEN STOCK	(LIKE MASHED POTATOES)
2 T	BUTTER BUDS	ADD THESE & SALT & PEPPER TO
1/4 t	NUTMEG	TASTE.
------	DRIED THYME TO TASTE	

TEX MEX CARROTS

 SERVES 8   FAT = TR EA

4 C	CARROTS, COOKED IN FAT-FREE CHICKEN STOCK & DRAINED	
1/4 C	TEQUILA	
1/3 C EA	RED, YELLOW & GREEN BELL PEPPER, DICED	SIMMER FOR 3 MINUTES.
1 T	JALAPENO PEPPER, MINCED	
1/4 t EA	GROUND CUMIN, SALT	

TROPICAL CARROTS

 SERVES 8   FAT = TR EA

2 C EA	COOKED, SLICED CARROTS & COOKED CUBED SWEET POTATOES	
20 OZ CAN	PINEAPPLE CHUNKS, DRAINED	
1 C	JUICE FROM PINEAPPLE (ADD WATER IF NECESSARY)	
3 T EA	RAISINS, BROWN SUGAR	SIMMER THESE 3 MINUTES.
1 T EA	SOY SAUCE, CORNSTARCH	COMBINE WELL & ADD TO THE
1 t	BALSAMIC VINEGAR	ABOVE. BOIL TO THICKEN.

WHISKEY CARROTS

 SERVES 8   FAT = TR EA

4 C	CARROTS, SLICED, COOKED IN FAT-FREE CHICKEN STOCK & DRAINED
6 T	STOCK FROM ABOVE
3 T EA	BUTTER BUDS, BROWN SUGAR, HONEY
3 T EA	WHISKEY OR BRANDY, FRESH PARSLEY

SIMMER TO DISSOLVE SUGAR.

RED CABBAGE & APPLES

 SERVES 6   FAT = TR EA

1 HD	RED CABBAGE, SLICED
3 EA	GRANNY SMITH APPLES, ONIONS, SLICED
2 CL	GARLIC, MINCED
1 C	FAT-FREE CHICKEN STOCK

SIMMER THESE 10 MINUTES.

OPT: ADD 1/4 C BALSAMIC
    VINEGAR IN LAST 2 MIN.

CABBAGE w MUSHROOMS

 SERVES 6   FAT = TR EA

1 HD	CABBAGE, SLICED
2	ONIONS, SLICED
4 CL	GARLIC, MINCED
1 C	FAT-FREE CHICKEN STOCK
1 LB	MUSHROOMS, SLICED
1/2 t	CAVENDER'S GREEK SEASONING
1 C	NO-FAT SOUR CREAM

SIMMER THESE TOSSING WELL.

SALT & PEPPER TO TASTE.

WHEN DONE, REMOVE WITH A
SLOTTED SPOON.

WHISK INTO DRIPPINGS.

CABBAGE & RICE

 SERVES 6   FAT = TR EA

1 C	RICE
1	ONION, DICED
2 C	FAT-FREE CHICKEN STOCK, BOILING
2	BAY LEAVES

COVER & SIMMER FOR 20
MINUTES OR UNTIL DONE.

REMOVE BAY LEAVES.

1 HD	CABBAGE, CHOPPED
2	ONIONS, CHOPPED
1/2 C	FAT-FREE CHICKEN STOCK
2 SPRIGS	ITALIAN PARSLEY, CHOPPED

COVER & SIMMER THESE 10 MIN.

TOSS WITH RICE AND SALT &
PEPPER TO TASTE.

CARAWAY CABBAGE

 SERVES 6   FAT = TR EA

1 HD	CABBAGE, SHREDDED
2 EA	APPLES, ONIONS, SLICED
1 C	FAT-FREE CHICKEN STOCK
1/4 C	RED WINE VINEGAR
2 T	BROWN SUGAR
1 T	CARAWAY SEED, GROUND

SIMMER THESE TOSSING WELL.

SALT & PEPPER TO TASTE.

GOOD HOT OR COLD.

SWEET & SOUR CABBAGE

 SERVES 8 — FAT = TR EA

2 T	DRY SHERRY	SIMMER THESE 5 MINUTES AND
2 T	RICE WINE VINEGAR	COOL.
2 T	BROWN SUGAR	
2 T	SOY SAUCE	
4 CL	GARLIC, MINCED	
1 t	FRESH GINGER, PEELED, GRATED	
1 t	HOISIN SAUCE	
1 t	CRUSHED RED PEPPER FLAKES	
2 LBS	BOK CHOY, SLICED, SALTED & DRAINED	COMBINE & TOSS THESE WITH
1	RED BELL PEPPER, DICED	ABOVE DRESSING.
1	CELERY STALK, SLICED DIAGONALLY	
16	FRESH CORIANDER LEAVES, MINCED	

CAULIFLOWER w CURRY

 SERVES 4 — FAT = TR EA

1 C	NO-FAT SOUR CREAM	HEAT THESE INGREDIENTS.
1/4 C	BUTTER BUDS	
1 T	CURRY POWDER (OR TO TASTE)	
2 t	WORCESTERSHIRE SAUCE (OR TO TASTE)	
4 C	CAULIFLOWER FLORETS, COOKED	COMBINE & TOSS WITH ABOVE.
1 t	FRESH LEMON JUICE	

CAULIFLOWER PUREE

 SERVES 4 — FAT = TR EA

1	CAULIFLOWER, VERY WELL COOKED	PUREE THESE WELL.
1 C	NO-FAT SOUR CREAM	
1/4 C	PARMESAN CHEESE	POUR INTO A SPRAYED DISH &
1/2 t	ALLSPICE	BAKE AT 350 FOR 15 MINUTES.

You can use asparagus, broccoli, carrots, turnips or almost any vegetable.

TEX MEX CORN

 SERVES 4 — FAT = 2 GM EA

2 C	CORN	SIMMER THESE INGREDIENTS.
1 EA	RED & GREEN BELL PEPPER, DICED, STEAMED	
1/4 C	NO-FAT SOUR CREAM	
1/4 C	PARMESAN CHEESE	ADD JUST BEFORE SERVING.
------	SKIM MILK IF NEEDED	

CORN & GARBANZO BEANS

quick SERVES 4 FAT = TR EA

1 C	CORN (WITH JUICE)	
1 C	CANNED GARBANZO BEANS, DRAINED	
1	RED ONION, DICED	
1	RED BELL PEPPER, DICED	
2 CL	GARLIC, MINCED	
1 T	FRESH BASIL, CHOPPED (OPTIONAL)	

SIMMER THESE 5 MINUTES.

SALT & PEPPER TO TASTE.

CORN SOUFFLE

easy SERVES 6 FAT = TR EA

2 C	CORN	
1/4 C	FAT-FREE CHICKEN STOCK	
4	GREEN ONIONS, MINCED	

SIMMER THESE 5 MINUTES.

1/3 C	FLOUR	
3/4 C	SKIM MILK	
2 T	BUTTER BUDS	

PUREE THESE, ADD TO ABOVE &
SIMMER 5 MINUTES.
COOL.

1/2 C	EGG BEATERS	
------	SALT & PEPPER AS DESIRED	

WHISK INTO ABOVE MIX.

4	EGG WHITES, BEATEN STIFF, NOT DRY	

FOLD IN WHITES, POUR INTO A
SPRAYED SOUFFLE DISH & BAKE
AT 350 FOR 25 MINUTES.

DILLY CUCUMBERS

easy SERVES 6 FAT = TR EA

2	SEEDLESS CUCUMBERS, SLICED	

SALT & LET SIT 20 MINUTES.
RINSE & DRAIN.
COMBINE ALL INGREDIENTS AND
CHILL 2 HOURS.

1/4 C	NO-FAT SOUR CREAM	
1/4 C	FAT-FREE MIRACLE WHIP	
2 T	DRY SHERRY	
2 T	FRESH CHIVES, CHOPPED	
1 t	FRESH DILL, CHOPPED	
1/2 t	CAVENDER'S GREEK SEASONING	

ADD DROPS OF LOUISIANA HOT
SAUCE IF DESIRED.

ROSEMARY CUCUMBERS

easy SERVES 6 FAT = TR EA

2	SEEDLESS CUKES, SLICED	

SALT & LET SIT 20 MINUTES.
RINSE & DRAIN.

1/2 C	FAT-FREE MIRACLE WHIP	
1/2 C	BALSAMIC VINEGAR	
2 T	DIJON MUSTARD	
1 t	GROUND ROSEMARY	
------	SUGAR, IF NEEDED	

COMBINE ALL INGREDIENTS AND
CHILL 2 HOURS.

CUCUMBERS in VINEGAR   *easy*   SERVES 6   FAT = TR EA

2	SEEDLESS CUCUMBERS, GROOVED & SLICED	COMBINE ALL ITEMS EXCEPT
2	RED ONIONS, SLICED & QUARTERED	TOMATOES.
1/2 C	SUGAR	
2 C	CIDER VINEGAR	CHILL 2 HOURS.
1 C	WATER (OR AS NEEDED TO DILUTE TO YOUR TASTE)	
1 t	DRIED ITALIAN HERBS (OPTIONAL)	
2 C	CHERRY TOMATOES, HALVED	ADD THE TOMATOES 10 MINUTES BEFORE SERVING.

SAUTEED EGGPLANT, ONIONS, & PEPPERS   *quick*   SERVES 6   FAT = 1 GM EA

2	ONIONS, SLICED & QUARTERED	SPRAY ALL VEGGIES & TOSS.
4 CL	GARLIC, MINCED	SALT & PEPPER & FRY IN A PAM-
4	ITALIAN PEPPERS, SEEDED, JULIENNED	SPRAYED PAN.
2	MINI EGGPLANTS, PEELED & SLICED LIKE FRENCH FRIES	

MINI EGGPLANTS & SQUASH   SERVES 6   FAT = 3 GM EA

12	MINI EGGPLANTS, BLANCHED 8 MIN.	SPRAY ALL w OLIVE OIL SPRAY.
24	ASSORTED MINI SQUASH, BLANCHED 6 MIN.	SALT & PEPPER.
2	RED ONIONS, MINCED	FRY IN A SPRAYED PAN.
4 CL	GARLIC, MINCED (OPTIONAL)	
1 1/2 C	NON-FAT COTTAGE CHEESE	COMBINE THESE & SPOON ONTO
6 T	PARMESAN CHEESE	6 COLD PLATES.
1 t	CAVENDER'S GREEK SEASONING	TOP WITH VEGGIES.
2 T	HIDDEN VALLEY RANCH POWDER FOR DIP OR DRESSING	

BRAISED ENDIVE   *quick*   SERVES 4   FAT = TR EA

8	ENDIVE, HALVED LENGTHWISE	SIMMER FOR 3 MINUTES AND
1 C	FAT-FREE CHICKEN STOCK	DRAIN.
1/4 C	BUTTER BUDS	
2 CL	GARLIC, MINCED	

SAUTEED FENNEL   *easy*   SERVES 4   FAT = TR EA

1 C	FAT-FREE CHICKEN STOCK	SIMMER ALL UNTIL TENDER.
2 BULBS	FENNEL, JULIENNED	
2 CL	GARLIC, MINCED	SALT & PEPPER TO TASTE.
2 T	BUTTER BUDS	
12	SUN-DRIED TOMATOES, BLANCHED 5 MIN., JULIENNED	

MIXED VEGETABLES

quick   SERVES 6   FAT = TR EA

2	CARROTS, SLICED	SIMMER FOR 5 MINUTES.
2	WHITE TURNIPS, QUARTERED, SLICED	
1 C	FAT-FREE CHICKEN STOCK	
2 T	BUTTER BUDS	
1	ONION, SLICED, QUARTERED	ADD & SIMMER UNTIL ALMOST
1 EA	RED & YELLOW BELL PEPPER, SLICED	DONE.
1/2 t	FRESH THYME	
ZEST OF 1	LEMON, MINCED	SALT & PEPPER TO TASTE.
1/2 LB	SNOW PEAS	ADD DURING LAST 2 MINUTES.

ROSEMARY VEGETABLES

easy   SERVES 6   FAT = TR EA

1/2	BUTTERNUT SQUASH, PEELED, CUBED	SIMMER THESE UNTIL DONE.
3	TURNIPS, PEELED, CUBED	
2 C	WATER, BOILING	
2	KNORR CHICKEN BOUILLON CUBE	DRAIN PARTIALLY.
2 T	BUTTER BUDS	TOSS WITH ABOVE.
1/2 t	GROUND ROSEMARY (OR TO TASTE)	SALT & PEPPER TO TASTE.

VEGGIE STIR-FRY

SERVES 8   FAT = TR EA

4 SL	FRESH GINGER	SIMMER UNTIL ALMOST DONE.
1	ONION, SLICED, QUARTERED	
4 CL	GARLIC, MINCED	
1 C	CARROTS, JULIENNED	
1 C	CELERY, SLICED THIN DIAGONALLY	
1 C	BROCCOLI FLORETS	
2 C	FAT-FREE CHICKEN STOCK	
1 T	FRESH LEMON JUICE	
1 C	ZUCCHINI OR SQUASH, JULIENNED	ADD & SIMMER FOR 2 MINUTES.
8 OZ	SNOW PEAS	
2 T	OYSTER SAUCE	
1 T	LEMON ZEST, MINCED	REMOVE GINGER SLICES.
1/4 C	DRY SHERRY	
2 T	SOY SAUCE	
1/2 t	CAVENDER'S SEASONING	
1/4 C	COLD WATER	COMBINE WELL, WHISK IN AND
2 T	CORNSTARCH	HEAT TO THICKEN.
		SERVE OVER RICE.

MUSHROOM TOMATO KABOBS

  quick   SERVES 8   FAT = TR EA

2 LBS	MUSHROOMS	THREAD ON SKEWERS, SPRAY w
1 LB	CHERRY TOMATOES	BERTOLLI OLIVE OIL SPRAY.
1 T	CAVENDER'S SEASONING	TOSS THESE & SPRINKLE ON THE
6 CL	GARLIC, MINCED (OR GARLIC POWDER)	KABOBS.
1 T	DRIED ITALIAN HERBS	SALT & PEPPER & GRILL.

Try fresh basil & oregano. You can add crushed red pepper flakes if you like.

MUSHROOM CUPS

  quick   SERVES 6   FAT = TR EA

1/2 C	HOT SKIM MILK	COMBINE & SET ASIDE 10 MIN.
2 T	BUTTER BUDS	
1 C	FAT-FREE BREAD CRUMBS	
2	ONIONS, MINCED	FRY THESE IN A PAM-SPRAYED
4 CL	GARLIC, MINCED	PAN FOR 3 MINUTES.
		SALT & PEPPER.
1 LB	MUSHROOMS, DICED	ADD & SIMMER 4 MINUTES.
1/2 C	EGG BEATERS	COMBINE ALL INGREDIENTS.

Fill sprayed muffin tins 3/4 full & bake at 350 for 20 minutes or until firm.

MUSHROOM SPIRAL

SERVES 8   FAT = TR EA

2 LBS	MUSHROOMS, CHOPPED	COMBINE ALL EXCEPT THE EGG
6	GREEN ONION TOPS, MINCED	WHITES.
1	YELLOW BELL PEPPER, MINCED, BLANCHED 3 MIN.	
1/2 C	EGG BEATERS	
2 T	FRESH LEMON JUICE	FOLD IN WHITES & POUR ONTO A
1/2 t	CAVENDER'S SEASONING	SPRAYED SHEET PAN LINED WITH
		PARCHMENT PAPER.
6	EGG WHITES, BEATEN STIFF, NOT DRY	SPREAD TO EDGES.

Bake at 350 for 20 minutes. Cool, roll up, slice & serve with Honey Mustard Sauce (p 260).

STUFFED ONIONS

easy   SERVES 4   FAT = 1 GM EA

4	ONIONS, HOLLOWED OUT, BLANCHED 10 MIN.	
------	INSIDES OF ABOVE, CHOPPED	COMBINE THESE & STUFF THE ONIONS.
1/4 C	CHOPPED PIMENTOS	
2 C	BROWN & WILD RICE, COOKED IN CHICKEN STOCK	
1/4 C	FRESH PARSLEY, MINCED	SALT & PEPPER LIGHTLY.
1/4 C	FAT-FREE BREAD CRUMBS (OR MORE AS NEEDED)	
1/4 C	SKIM MILK (OR AS NEEDED)	
2 T	BUTTER BUDS	
2 T	FAT-FREE BREAD CRUMBS	COMBINE & SPRINKLE THESE ON THE TOPS.
2 T	PARMESAN CHEESE	BAKE AT 375 FOR 20 MINUTES.

SNOW PEAS & ESCAROLE

quick   SERVES 8   FAT = TR EA

2 C	SNOW PEAS	SIMMER THESE FOR 3 MINUTES.
1	RED BELL PEPPER, IN STRIPS	
1 C	FAT-FREE CHICKEN STOCK	
2 T	BUTTER BUDS	
1 t	SUGAR	
2 HDS	ESCAROLE, SLICED	ADD JUST BEFORE SERVING.
------	ORANGE OR LEMON ZEST (OPTIONAL)	SALT & PEPPER TO TASTE.

CANADIAN PEAS

quick   SERVES 4   FAT = 1 GM EA

2 C	TINY JUNE PEAS	SIMMER THESE 2-3 MINUTES.
4 SL	CANADIAN BACON, TRIMMED, DICED	
1	RED ONION, MINCED	
1/2 C	FAT-FREE CHICKEN STOCK	
1/4 C	NON-FAT MILK POWDER	
1/2 t	DRIED SAGE	

GRILLED PEPPERS

easy   SERVES 8   FAT = TR EA

2 EA	RED, YELLOW & GREEN BELL PEPPERS, QUARTERED	
6	RED ONIONS, BLANCHED 10 MIN., QUARTERED	
4 CL	GARLIC, MINCED	COMBINE ALL INGREDIENTS IN A ZIPLOC BAG FOR 10 MINUTES.
1/2 C	SHERRY WINE VINEGAR	DRAIN.
2 T	FRESH BASIL, CHOPPED	
2 T	FRESH PARSLEY, CHOPPED	GRILL OR STIR-FRY.
1/2 t	CAVENDER'S GREEK SEASONING	SALT & PEPPER TO TASTE.

PEPPERS & SNOW PEAS

 quick   SERVES 8   FAT = TR EA

2 LBS	SNOW PEAS	SIMMER THESE FOR 5 MINUTES.
2 EA	RED & YELLOW BELL PEPPER, IN STRIPS	
4 CL	GARLIC, MINCED (OPTIONAL)	
1/2 C	FAT-FREE CHICKEN STOCK	SALT & PEPPER TO TASTE.
1 T	FRESH BASIL, CHOPPED	

STUFFED YELLOW PEPPERS

easy   SERVES 4   FAT = TR EA

4	YELLOW PEPPERS, TOPS SLICED OFF, CORED	BLANCH 2 MINUTES & DRAIN.
1 C	RICE	COVER & SIMMER THESE FOR 20
1	ONION, DICED	MINUTES.
3 CL	GARLIC, MINCED	
2 C	FAT-FREE CHICKEN STOCK	
1 t	GROUND CORIANDER	COMBINE & TOSS WITH RICE.
1 T	FRESH CILANTRO, CHOPPED	SALT & PEPPER TO TASTE.
1 T	FRESH BASIL, CHOPPED	
1 T	FRESH ITALIAN PARSLEY, CHOPPED	STUFF THE PEPPERS & SPRAY THE
1 C	TINY COOKED SHRIMP	TOPS.
5 T	CURRANTS, SOAKED IN 1/4 C ORANGE JUICE	BAKE AT 350 FOR 20 MINUTES.
1/4 C	SUN-DRIED TOMATOES, BLANCHED 5 MIN. & CHOPPED	

RATATOUILLE

HOT OR COLD   SERVES 10   FAT = TR EA

1 LGE	EGGPLANT, CUBED, SALTED, DRAINED	COMBINE ALL INGREDIENTS AND
2	ONIONS, DICED	EITHER CHILL...
2	GREEN BELL PEPPERS, DICED	
2 EA	GREEN & YELLOW SQUASH, CUBED	OR COMBINE ALL ITEMS EXCEPT
1 LB	MUSHROOMS, QUARTERED	VINEGAR & SIMMER FOR 1 HOUR.
6	TOMATOES, PEELED & CHOPPED	
5 CL	GARLIC, MINCED	ADD VINEGAR TO TASTE.
1/2 C	WATER	
6 OZ	TOMATO PASTE	
2 t	FRESH BASIL	SALT & PEPPER TO TASTE.
2	BAY LEAVES	
1 t	GROUND CUMIN	REMOVE BAY LEAVES.
1/4 C	FRESH PARSLEY, CHOPPED	
1/4 C	RED WINE	SERVE HOT OR COLD.
1/4 C	BALSAMIC VINEGAR (OR TO TASTE)	

OPTIONAL ADDITIONS: MARINATED ARTICHOKE HEARTS, DRAINED & TRIMMED; CAPERS; ROASTED RED PEPPERS; CALAMATA OLIVES, PITTED; CRUSHED RED PEPPER FLAKES; PARMESAN FOR GARNISH.

RUTABAGA RAMEKINS

easy   SERVES 8   FAT = 1 GM EA

4 C	RUTABAGAS, DICED	SIMMER 1 HOUR OR 'TIL TENDER.
	WATER TO COVER	DRAIN & COOL.
1 C	EGG BEATERS	ADD TO ABOVE & POUR INTO 8
4	GREEN ONION TOPS, SLICED	SPRAYED RAMEKINS.
1 C	FAT-FREE CHEDDAR CHEESE, SHREDDED	
1/4 C	BREAD CRUMBS	COMBINE & SPRINKLE OVER.
2 T	PARMESAN CHEESE	BAKE AT 350 FOR 25 MINUTES.

SPINACH CASSEROLE

easy   SERVES 4   FAT = 2 GM EA

3 LBS	SPINACH, STEAMED, SQUEEZED DRY	COMBINE & POUR IN A SPRAYED
1 C	COTTAGE CREAM (p 392)	CASSEROLE.
1/2 C	NO-FAT SOUR CREAM	
1	RED ONION, MINCED	
1 C	EGG BEATERS	
2 T	BUTTER BUDS	BAKE AT 350 FOR 30 MINUTES.
2 T	FLOUR	STIR WELL AND SPRINKLE WITH
1/4 t	ALLSPICE	PARMESAN. BAKE AGAIN FOR 15
		MINUTES.
2 T	PARMESAN CHEESE	

ACORN SQUASH CUPS

easy   SERVES 4   FAT = TR EA

2	SQUASH, HALVED, SEEDS REMOVED	BAKE FACE DOWN IN WATER AT
		375 FOR 45 MINUTES.
2 C	CHUNKY APPLESAUCE	
2	APPLES, DICED	SIMMER THESE, FILL THE BAKED
2 t	SUGAR OR EQUAL (OR TO TASTE)	SQUASH & SPRINKLE WITH MORE
1 T	BUTTER BUDS	CINNAMON.
2 t	CINNAMON (OR TO TASTE)	BAKE 10 MINUTES MORE.

ACORN SQUASH RINGS

easy   SERVES 4   FAT = TR EA

2	SQUASH, SLICED IN 1" SLICES	USE A COOKIE CUTTER TO CUT
		OUT SEEDS. SPRAY WITH PAM.
1 C	BROWN SUGAR	
1/4 C	BUTTER BUDS	COMBINE & SPRINKLE OVER EA.
1/2 t	ALLSPICE	

Place on a sprayed sheet pan, surrounded with water & bake at 350 for 30 minutes.

PUREED BUTTERNUT SQUASH

easy   SERVES 4   FAT = TR EA

| 1 | SQUASH, PEELED, CUBED | SIMMER UNTIL VERY TENDER & |
| | WATER TO COVER | DRAIN. |

3 T	BUTTER BUDS	ADD THE REST & PUREE.
1/4 C	EVAPORATED SKIM MILK	
1/4 C	NON-FAT MILK POWDER (OR MORE FOR CONSISTENCY)	
1/4 t	GROUND GINGER	
------	NUTMEG (OPTIONAL)	SALT & PEPPER TO TASTE.

SQUASH SOUFFLE

SERVES 4   FAT = TR EA

1 LB	SQUASH, COOKED & PUREED	COMBINE ALL & PUREE AGAIN.
1/4 C	EVAPORATED SKIM MILK	
1/4 C	NON-FAT MILK POWDER	
1/2 C	EGG BEATERS	
1/4 t	LEMON PEPPER & SALT	FOLD IN THE STIFF WHITES AND
		FILL 8 SPRAYED RAMEKINS.
2	EGG WHITES, BEATEN STIFF, NOT DRY	BAKE AT 350 FOR 25 MINUTES.

TROPICAL SQUASH SALAD

quick   SERVES 4   FAT = TR EA

| 1 | BUTTERNUT SQUASH, PEELED, CUBED | SIMMER UNTIL JUST TENDER & |
| | WATER TO COVER | COOL. |

1 C	CANNED PINEAPPLE TIDBITS, DRAINED	WHISK THESE IN AND HEAT TO
1 C	JUICE OF ABOVE & ORANGE JUICE	THICKEN.
1/4 C	MEYER'S RUM	
2 T	CORNSTARCH	SALT & PEPPER TO TASTE.

| 1 t | COCONUT FLAVORING (OR AS NEEDED) | ADD THESE & TOSS ALL. |
| 1 C | MANDARIN ORANGES | |

TOMATOES w ARTICHOKES

easy   SERVES 8   FAT = TR EA

1 C	RED ONIONS, CHOPPED	FRY IN A SPRAYED PAN 3 MIN.
2 T	FRESH BASIL, CHOPPED	
1 T	BROWN SUGAR	

28 OZ	CANNED TOMATOES, DRAINED & QUARTERED	ADD & SIMMER 15 MINUTES.
2 C	MARINATED ARTICHOKE HEARTS, DRAINED,	
	TRIMMED WELL & QUARTERED	

BROILED TOMATOES

 SERVES 4   FAT = 2 GM EA

| 4 | TOMATOES, HALVED & SPRINKLED w CAVENDER'S GREEK SEASONING. |

1/4 C	NO-FAT SOUR CREAM	COMBINE THESE & SPREAD ON
1/4 C	COTTAGE CREAM (p 392)	TOMATO HALVES.
1/4 C	PARMESAN CHEESE	
1 t	CAVENDER'S GREEK SEASONING	
1	LEMON, JUICED	BAKE AT 375 FOR 10 MINUTES.
1 T	FRESH PARSLEY, CHOPPED	THEN BROIL UNTIL BUBBLY.
3	GREEN ONIONS, MINCED	

GRILLED CHEESE TOMATOES

 SERVES 6   FAT = 2 GM EA

| 12 | THICK SLICES OF TOMATOES | PLACE ON SPRAYED SHEET PAN. |

1	GREEN PEPPER, MINCED	COMBINE & SPRINKLE THESE ON
4	GREEN ONIONS, MINCED	TOMATOES.
1/2 C	FAT-FREE BREAD CRUMBS	
6 T	PARMESAN CHEESE	BAKE AT 375 FOR 20 MINUTES.
3 T	BUTTER BUDS	
2 T	DRIED ITALIAN HERBS	BROIL IF NEEDED TO BROWN.
1 T	BROWN SUGAR	
------	SALT & CAYENNE PEPPER	

TOMATOES ROCKEFELLER

 SERVES 6   FAT = 3 GM EA

| 12 | THICK SLICES OF TOMATOES |

20 OZ	FROZEN SPINACH, COOKED, DRAINED, CHOPPED	
1 C	GREEN ONIONS, CHOPPED	COMBINE & SPREAD OVER
1 C	FAT-FREE BREAD CRUMBS	TOMATO SLICES
1/2 C	PARMESAN CHEESE	
3/4	EGG BEATERS	
1/4 C	BUTTER BUDS	BAKE AT 375 UNTIL BUBBLY.
2 T	GARLIC, MINCED	
1/2 t	GROUND ROSEMARY	
1/2 t	FRESH THYME, MINCED	
------	EVAPORATED SKIM MILK AS NEEDED	

TOMATO FLORENTINE CUPS

SERVES 8   FAT = TR EA

8	TOMATO CUPS, SCOOPED OUT, SALTED & DRAINED	
20 OZ	FROZEN SPINACH, COOKED, DRAINED, CHOPPED	
8 SL	OSCAR MAYER TURKEY BACON, FRIED CRUMBLED	
1 C	FAT-FREE BREAD CUBES	COMBINE THESE & STUFF THE
1/4 C	NO-FAT SOUR CREAM	TOMATO CUPS.
1/4 C	EGG BEATERS	
2 T	BUTTER BUDS	BAKE AT 350 FOR 20 MINUTES.
------	SALT, PEPPER & NUTMEG TO TASTE	

STUFFED CHERRY TOMATOES

 quick

SERVES 4   FAT = 1 GM EA

16	CHERRY TOMATOES, HALVED	
4	GREEN ONIONS, MINCED	COMBINE & PIPE THESE ONTO
6 T	NO-FAT SOUR CREAM	TOMATO HALVES.
2 T	PARMESAN CHEESE	
2 T	HORSERADISH	
2 T	FRESH PARSLEY, CHOPPED	SALT & PEPPER TO TASTE.
1	LEMON, JUICED	

FRENCH TURNIPS

easy

SERVES 4   FAT = 2 GM EA

2 C	YELLOW TURNIPS, COOKED, MASHED WELL	COMBINE & POUR THESE INTO
1/2 C	EGG BEATERS	A SPRAYED DISH.
2 T	BUTTER BUDS	
1/2 C	FAT-FREE CHEDDAR CHEESE, SHREDDED	
1/4 C	PARMESAN CHEESE	SPRINKLE w CRUMBS & SPRAY
------	SALT & PEPPER	WITH PAM.
		BAKE AT 375 FOR 20 MINUTES.
2 T	FAT-FREE BREAD CRUMBS	

CHINESE VEGETABLES

SERVES 8   FAT = TR EA

1 C	FAT-FREE BEEF STOCK	SIMMER THESE FOR 4 MINUTES.
1 C	BROCCOLI FLORETS	
1 C	CARROTS, SLICED DIAGONALLY	
1 C	CAULIFLOWER FLORETS	
1 C	GREEN BEANS, SLICED DIAGONALLY	ADD & SIMMER 2 MINUTES.
1	RED ONIONS, SLICED LENGTHWISE	
1 EA	RED & YELLOW BELL PEPPER, SLICED	
1/2 LB	MUSHROOMS	
2 t	DARK SESAME OIL	
1/2 C	FAT-FREE BEEF STOCK OR DRY SHERRY, COLD	COMBINE THESE WELL, WHISK IN
1/4 C	OYSTER SAUCE	& HEAT TO THICKEN.
1/4 C	SOY SAUCE	
2 T	CORNSTARCH	
	BABY CORN COBS (OPTIONAL)	ADD & SERVE OVER RICE.

VEGETABLE FRITTATA

SERVES 4   FAT = 2 GM EA

1	ONION, DICED	FRY THESE IN A SPRAYED, OVEN-
1 C	ZUCCHINI, DICED	PROOF PAN FOR 4 MINUTES.
1 C	BELL PEPPERS, DICED	
12	MUSHROOMS, SLICED	ADD & SIMMER 3 MINUTES.
1 C	POTATOES, COOKED, JULIENNED	
1 T	FRESH BASIL, CHOPPED	COMBINE & POUR OVER ABOVE.
1/4 t	CAYENNE PEPPER	BAKE AT 350 FOR 20 MINUTES.
2 C	EGG BEATERS	
1/4 C	BUTTER BUDS	PLACE A PLATE OVER THE PAN &
12	BLACK OLIVES, SLICED	FLIP BOTH OVER. SLIDE OFF THE
		PLATE BACK INTO THE PAN.
1/2 C	TOMATO OR SPAGHETTI SAUCE	POUR ON THE SAUCE & BAKE 10
2 T	PARMESAN CHEESE, SPRINKLED OVER	MORE MINUTES OR UNTIL FIRM.

ZUCCHINI CAKES

SERVES 6   FAT = TR EA

4 C	ZUCCHINI, GRATED	TOSS ALL INGREDIENTS.
1 C	EGG BEATERS	
2 C	FAT-FREE BREAD CRUMBS	FORM INTO PATTIES & FRY IN A
1 C	RED ONION, MINCED	SPRAYED PAN.
1/4 C	NO-FAT SOUR CREAM	
1/2 t EA	OLD BAY SEASONING, CAVENDER'S GREEK SEASONING	

JULIENNED ZUCCHINI & SUMMER SQUASH

quick SERVES 4 FAT = TR EA

2 SM	ZUCCHINI, JULIENNED	SIMMER THESE FOR 2 MINUTES.
2 SM	YELLOW SQUASH, JULIENNED	
1	RED ONION, SLICED LENGTHWISE	
1 C	FAT-FREE CHICKEN STOCK	SALT & PEPPER TO TASTE.
1 T	BUTTER BUDS	
1 t	GROUND ROSEMARY	

SHERRY ZUCCHINI

quick SERVES 6 FAT = TR EA

1 C	WATER	SIMMER THESE UNTIL ALMOST
1	KNORR CHICKEN BOUILLON CUBE	TENDER.
4	ZUCCHINI, SLICED	
4 CL	GARLIC, MINCED	
1/2 t	CELERY SALT	
		ADD DURING LAST 2 MINUTES
1/4 C	DRY SHERRY	OF COOKING.

ZUCCHINI, TOMATOES & BASIL

easy SERVES 6 FAT = TR EA

3	ZUCCHINI, CUBED, BOILED 2 MIN., DRAINED	COMBINE ALL INGREDIENTS.
2 C	CHERRY TOMATOES, QUARTERED	
1	RED ONION, DICED	EITHER SIMMER 3 MINUTES &
2 T	GARLIC, MINCED	SERVE....
2 T	BUTTER BUDS	
2 T	FRESH BASIL, CHOPPED	OR CHILL OVERNIGHT & SERVE
1 T	FRESH LEMON JUICE	COLD.
1/2 t	LEMON PEPPER	
1 t	LEMON ZEST, MINCED	
	SALT & PEPPER TO TASTE	

ZUCCHINI in WHITE SAUCE

SERVES 4 FAT = TR EA

2	ZUCCHINI, SLICED OR JULIENNED	SIMMER UNTIL ALMOST DONE.
1 C	RED ONION, MINCED	
1/2 C	FAT-FREE CHICKEN STOCK	
1 C	THICK WHITE SAUCE (p 248)	ADD THESE TO FINISH.
1/4 C	WHITE WINE	
2 T	FRESH PARSLEY, CHOPPED	

GLAZED VEGGIES

 SERVES 6   FAT = TR EA

1/2 C	FAT-FREE CHICKEN STOCK	BOIL THESE & REDUCE BY HALF.
2 t	FRESH LEMON JUICE	STRAIN.
1/2 t	FRESH GINGER, PEELED, GRATED	
1/4 t	LEMON ZEST, MINCED	SALT & PEPPER TO TASTE
1-2 LBS	VEGGIES, COOKED (ASPARAGUS, BROCCOLI, CARROTS OR ANY FAVORITE)	

When ready to serve, place hot veggies on plate & brush with glaze.

HONEY GLAZED ONIONS

 SERVES 4   FAT = TR EA

| 4 | VIDALIA ONIONS, PEELED,SPRAYED w PAM BUTTER, WRAPPED IN FOIL. |
| | Bake at 350 for 30 minutes. Unwrap & place in sprayed baking dish. |

3 T	WHISKEY OR BRANDY	COMBINE AND BASTE EVERY 15
3 T EA	HONEY, MUSTARD	MINUTES. BAKE AT 350 FOR 45
2 t EA	FRESH LEMON JUICE, BUTTER BUDS	MINUTES OR UNTIL DONE.
------	SALT & PEPPER	

PICKLED BELL PEPPERS

 1 QT   FAT = TR

2 C	RED WINE VINEGAR	BOIL THESE & POUR OVER THE
1 C EA	BROWN SUGAR, WATER	PEPPERS.
1/4 C	PEPPERCORNS	
1 t	CAVENDER'S GREEK SEASONING	CHILL AT LEAST 12 HOURS.
8	RED BELL PEPPERS, QUARTERED & SEEDED	

WEST COAST VEGGIES

SERVES 6   FAT = 2 GM EA

1 C	ASPARAGUS, STEAMED	TOSS HOT VEGGIES WITH ONE
1 C	CARROTS, SLICED THIN, COOKED	OF THE SAUCES BELOW.
2	RED ONIONS, DICED, STEAMED	
1/4 LB	MUSHROOMS, SLICED, COOKED	SERVE HOT OR COLD.
1 C	CAULIFLOWER FLORETS, STEAMED	

	SAUCE I	**OR**		**SAUCE II**
1/4 C	SOY SAUCE		1/4 C	NO-FAT SOUR CREAM
1/4 C	RICE WINE VINEGAR		6 T	PARMESAN CHEESE
1 T	DIJON MUSTARD (OPTIONAL)		2 T	BUTTER BUDS
2 T	TOASTED SESAME SEEDS		------	SKIM MILK
	Simmer 5 minutes.			Simmer 5 minutes.

Breakfast Ideas

The LIQUADA, a Mexican term I use for "LIQUID AHHS", is Mother Nature's start to the perfect breakfast. It's so smooth, so comforting, so rich and creamy, you just know you're being bad. But you're not. Liquadas are so good and good for you, you can have one anytime, all day long if you're on a low-fat diet.

I'll list a few here, but experiment on your own. The banana is necessary in them all, as it gives the drink its thick texture (or you can substitute non-fat yogurt). Any kind of juice is good or you can replace this with skim milk. More than three fruit combinations tend to be too much. Ice is optional.

If you like yogurt, substitute non-fat vanilla yogurt for the banana or go with 1/2 banana & 1/2 yogurt.

PINEAPPLE LIQUADA

SERVES 4   FAT = TR EA

1	RIPE BANANA	BLENDERIZE.
1/2	HONEYDEW	
1 1/2 C	PINEAPPLE CHUNKS	
6	ICE CUBES	
	HONEY OR EQUAL (OPTIONAL)	

Add skim milk if you'd like it thinner.

STRAWBERRY LIQUADA

SERVES 4   FAT = TR EA

1	RIPE BANANA	BLENDERIZE.
1 C	STRAWBERRIES	
1 C	SKIM MILK	
1 t	REAL VANILLA EXTRACT	
6	ICE CUBES	
	HONEY OR EQUAL (OPTIONAL)	

Add more skim milk if you'd like it thinner.

BLUEBERRY LIQUADA

SERVES 4   FAT = TR EA

1	RIPE BANANA	BLENDERIZE.
1 C	BLUEBERRIES	
1 C	ORANGE JUICE OR SKIM MILK	
1 t	HONEY OR EQUAL	
6	ICE CUBES	

Add more juice if you'd like it thinner.

MANGO LIQUADA

SERVES 4   FAT = TR EA

1	RIPE BANANA	BLENDERIZE.
2 C	MANGO SLICES	
1 C	SKIM MILK	
1 t	HONEY OR EQUAL	
1 t	COCONUT FLAVORING	
6	ICE CUBES	

Add more skim milk if you'd like it thinner.

These make great gifts for your Fat-Free-Loving Friends!!

APPLE BUTTER

easy 4 CUPS FAT = TR EA

| 15 | MACINTOSH APPLES, SLICED |
| 1/2 C | WATER (OR MORE) |

SIMMER THESE FOR 25 MINUTES.
PUREE & SIEVE.

4 C	BROWN SUGAR
1/4 C	RED WINE VINEGAR
1/2 C	DARK CORN SYRUP
3 T	BUTTER BUDS
2 T	BRANDY (OPTIONAL)
1 T	CINNAMON

ADD REMAINING INGREDIENTS &
SIMMER 2 HOURS.
STIR OFTEN.

PUREE & COOL.

This is also good on Sweet Potatoes or Gingerbread.

BANANA BUTTER

 quick 3 CUPS FAT = TR EA

12	BANANAS, MASHED
3 C	BROWN SUGAR
1 C	FRESH ORANGE JUICE
ZEST OF 1	ORANGE, MINCED
ZEST OF 1/2	LEMON, MINCED

SIMMER ALL UNTIL THE SUGAR
DISSOLVES.

PUREE ALL & COOL.

FRUIT SPREAD

quick 1 CUP FAT = 1 GM EA

1/2 C	FRUIT OF YOUR CHOICE, FRESH, FROZEN OR CANNED, DRAINED WELL
1 C	YOGURT CHEESE (p 393)
1/2 t	REAL VANILLA EXTRACT
	HONEY TO TASTE

PUREE ALL.

FRUIT SYRUP

 easy 2 CUPS FAT = TR EA

1 C	PUREED FRUIT (YOUR FAVORITE)
1 1/4 C	WATER
1 T	ARROWROOT OR CORNSTARCH
3 T	COLD WATER

SIMMER THESE FOR 20 MINUTES.

COMBINE WELL, WHISK IN AND
HEAT TO THICKEN.

Remember, when scrambling Egg Beaters, always use a non-stick pan that has been sprayed with Pam Butter Spray & don't stir too much.

Also: Add Butter Buds to the egg mixture to give a richer taste.

EGGS BENEFIT

SERVES 4   FAT = 3 GM EA

2 C	EGG BEATERS	WHISK & SCRAMBLE TO DESIRED
2 T	BUTTER BUDS	DONENESS. S & P.
------	SALT & PEPPER TO TASTE	
		PLACE BACON ON A TOASTED
8 SL	CANADIAN BACON, TRIMMED, BROWNED	ENGLISH MUFFIN & TOP WITH
4	ENGLISH MUFFINS	EGGS.
3/4 C	MOCK HOLLANDAISE SAUCE	SPOON OVER EACH SERVING.
	(p 257)	GARNISH WITH FRESH FRUIT.

Remember to trim **ALL FAT** from the Canadian Bacon!

EGGS FLORENTINE

SERVES 4   FAT = 2 GM EA

2 C	EGG BEATERS	WHISK & SCRAMBLE THESE.
2 T	BUTTER BUDS	SALT & PEPPER TO TASTE.
2 STRIPS	OSCAR MAYER TURKEY BACON, FRIED, PATTED DRY & DICED	
------	SALT & PEPPER TO TASTE	
		DIVIDE INTO 4 SPRAYED GRATIN
2 LBS	SPINACH, STEAMED 30 SEC., DRAINED	DISHES & TOP WITH EGGS.
3/4 C	CHEESE SAUCE (p 250, 395)	COMBINE & SPOON OVER EACH.
1 t	DIJON MUSTARD	
		SPRINKLE OVER EACH & BROIL
4 t	PARMESAN CHEESE	UNTIL BUBBLY.
2 STRIPS	OSCAR MAYER TURKEY BACON, FRIED, PATTED DRY & DICED	

Serve with Fat-Free Bagels topped with Fat-Free Cream Cheese, sprinkled with Cavender's Greek Seasoning.

Try scrambling Egg Beaters with Smoked Oysters & Chives & serve on English Muffins. Be sure to rinse the oil from the oysters & pat dry first.

EGG & CRAB NEW ORLEANS   SERVES 6   FAT = 1 GM EA

1 C	MOCK BUTTER SAUCE (p 250)	COMBINE & KEEP WARM.
2 T	BRANDY	
1/8 t	NUTMEG	
1/8 t	OLD BAY SEASONING	
4 DROPS	LOUISIANA HOT SAUCE (OPTIONAL)	
3 C	EGG BEATERS	SCRAMBLE THESE & PLACE ON
2 T	BUTTER BUDS	MUFFINS.
------	SALT & PEPPER TO TASTE	
		TOP WITH CRAB, SOME SAUCE
6	ENGLISH MUFFINS, TOASTED	& SPRINKLE WITH PAPRIKA.
1 LB	BACKFIN LUMP CRAB, WARMED	
------	PAPRIKA	

EGGS w CURRY & WATER CHESTNUTS   *quick*   SERVES 6   FAT = TR EA

2 C	EGG BEATERS	COMBINE THESE & SCRAMBLE.
2 T	BUTTER BUDS	
3	GREEN ONIONS, MINCED	
2 t	CURRY (OR TO TASTE)	SERVE WITH APPLE & BANANA
1 CAN	WATER CHESTNUTS, DICED	SLICES, TOSSED WITH ORANGE
------	CAYENNE PEPPER & SALT TO TASTE	JUICE.

Try scrambling Egg Beaters with diced Sun-Dried Tomatoes & Parmesan. They're very good. (When you blanch your Sun-Dried Tomatoes, store them in water, NOT oil.)

A small amount of grated Parmesan in scrambled Egg Beaters makes a surprisingly good breakfast with very little fat.

STUFFED OMELET

SERVES 6   FAT = 1 GM EA

1 C	ONION, DICED	SIMMER THESE & DRAIN.
1 C EA	RED & GREEN BELL PEPPERS, DICED	(SAVE THE BROTH)
2 C	FAT-FREE CHICKEN STOCK	
2 T	CORNSTARCH	COMBINE THESE WELL & ADD TO
1/4 C	SKIM MILK	THE BROTH WITH 1/2 OF THE
1 t	CAVENDER'S GREEK SEASONING	VEGGIES.
1 C	NO-FAT SOUR CREAM	
2 T	PARMESAN CHEESE	HEAT TO THICKEN.
3 C	EGG BEATERS (SEE "MAKING OMELETS" p 397)	USE OTHER 1/2 OF VEGGIES TO
3 T	BUTTER BUDS	STUFF OMELETS.
------	SALT & PEPPER TO TASTE	

Top with thickened Vegetable Sauce. Serve with toasted English Muffins topped with Fruit Spread. (p 325).

SEAFOOD OMELET

SERVES 4   FAT = 2 GM EA

1 C	ONIONS, MINCED	SIMMER THESE FOR 5 MINUTES.
1/2 C	FISH STOCK OR BOTTLED CLAM JUICE	
1/2 t	OLD BAY SEASONING	
1 1/2 C	TINY COOKED SHRIMP	ADD & REMOVE FROM HEAT.
1 1/2 C	SCALLOPS, COOKED	DRAIN & SAVE ANY JUICES.
3 C	EGG BEATERS (SEE "MAKING OMELETS" p 397)	USE 2 C OF THE SEAFOOD FOR
3 T	BUTTER BUDS	THE FILLING.
------	SALT & PEPPER TO TASTE	
1 C	STOCK FROM ABOVE (ADD BOTTLED CLAM JUICE IF NECESSARY)	HEAT FOR SAUCE.
1 T	CORNSTARCH	COMBINE WELL, WHISK INTO
1/2 C	SKIM MILK	STOCK & HEAT TO THICKEN.
1/8 t	OLD BAY SEASONING (OR TO TASTE)	
1 C	SHRIMP & SCALLOPS (LEFT FROM ABOVE)	ADD TO SAUCE.

Serve sauce over omelets on a bed of Spinach Angel Hair Pasta. Garnish with orange sections & Orange Marmalade Toast Points.

OPTIONS: MUSHROOMS, CANADIAN BACON, ARTICHOKE HEARTS OR ANY OF YOUR FAVORITES.

MANDARIN FRENCH TOAST

 SERVES 4   FAT = 1 GM EA

1 C	EGG BEATERS	WHISK THESE FOR DIPPING THE BREAD.
1/4 C	FROZEN ORANGE JUICE CONCENTRATE	
1/4 t	CINNAMON	
1/4 t	REAL VANILLA EXTRACT	
3 T	GRAND MARNIER (OR TO TASTE)	
		DIP BREAD & FRY IN A SPRAYED PAN.
12	SLICES FAT-FREE BREAD	
20 OZ	MANDARIN ORANGES (SAVE 12 SECTIONS)	PUREE THESE & HEAT.
3 T	ARROWROOT OR CORNSTARCH	
1/4 C	FROZEN ORANGE JUICE CONCENTRATE	SPOON OVER AND GARNISH WITH MANDARINS.
2 T	HONEY (OR TO TASTE)	
3 T	GRAND MARNIER	

BUTTERMILK PANCAKES

 20 PANCAKES   FAT = .5 GM EA

3 C	FLOUR (OR 1/2 REGULAR & 1/2 BUCKWHEAT)	WHISK THESE & LET SIT FOR 15 MINUTES.
2 T	SUGAR	
1 t	SALT	
2 t	BAKING POWDER	SPOON ONTO A HOT, SPRAYED GRIDDLE AND FLIP ONLY WHEN BUBBLES APPEAR OVER MOST OF THE SURFACE.
2 t	BAKING SODA	
1 /2 C	EGG BEATERS, BEATEN 5 MIN.	
3 1/2 C	1% BUTTERMILK (OR AS NEEDED)	
1 T	MELTED BUTTER	

Serve with Butter Buds dissolved in hot water.

Remember, Maple Syrup (plain, not containing butter) has no fat.

PINEAPPLE PANCAKES

 20 PANCAKES   FAT = .5 GM EA

Make batter as above, spoon onto griddle sprayed with Pam Butter. Sprinkle drained, crushed pineapple on each before flipping.

20 OZ	PINEAPPLE CHUNKS(SAVE 10 FOR GARNISH)	PUREE & HEAT TO THICKEN.
2 T	CORNSTARCH	
1 T	HONEY (OR TO TASTE)	

Try substituting Apple Juice and Applesauce with Cinnamon, or Mango Juice and Mangoes, Peaches, Blueberries, Strawberries, etc.   Have fun...be creative.

GOOD MORNING STRUDEL

SERVES 6   FAT = 1 GM EA

1 C	RAISINS	TOSS THESE IN A GLASS DISH.
	BRANDY TO COVER RAISINS	MICROWAVE FOR 2 MINUTES,
8 C	APPLES, PEELED & SLICED & DICED	STIRRING ONCE.
3/4 C	BROWN SUGAR	
2 T	BUTTER BUDS	
2 t	CINNAMON	
1 t	NUTMEG	
2 t	ALMOND FLAVORING	
1 t	REAL VANILLA EXTRACT	DRAIN & COOL.
------	MACE	
8	SHEETS OF PHYLLO	

Lay out a sheet of Phyllo, spray with Pam Butter and top with another sheet. Repeat for a total of 4 sheets. Do this again for a second stack of 4.

Spread 1/2 of the mixture on the pastry (the long way). Roll up tightly, slash tops diagonally, spray with Pam Butter. Repeat with the second stack of pastry.

Place on cookie sheet covered with parchment paper. Bake the two strudels at 400 for 15-20 minutes.

ICING

quick

2 C	POWDERED SUGAR	WHISK OVER HOT WATER.
2 T	BUTTER BUDS	
2 T	SKIM MILK (OR AS NEEDED)	DRIZZLE OVER BAKED STRUDEL.

FRUIT BROCHETTES (KABOBS)

quick

FAT = TR EA

Thread your favorite fruit on skewers: STRAWBERRIES, PINEAPPLE, KIWI, BANANAS ETC.

2 T	HONEY	WHISK THESE WELL & BRUSH ON
2 t	LEMON ZEST	THE KABOBS.
1 T	FRESH ORANGE JUICE	
------	NUTMEG	BROIL UNTIL BUBBLY.

Place 1/2 of a Cantaloupe face down & insert the kabobs into the rind just far enough so they'll stand up.

Breads

If you love to bake bread...great, here are some recipes you'll enjoy!

If you don't enjoy baking bread, don't worry. There are plenty of fat-free breads on the market that taste almost homemade. These recipes will let you experiment with the breads that you can't find at your market.

BEER BREAD

easy   1 LOAF   FAT = TR EA

3 C	BREAD FLOUR	
2 T	BAKING POWDER	
1 T	BUTTER BUDS	
2 t	BAKING SODA	
5 T	SUGAR	
1 t	SALT	
1 1/4 C	COORS BEER	
1/2 C	EGG BEATERS	
1/4 C	SKIM MILK	

COMBINE DRY INGREDIENTS.

COMBINE WET INGREDIENTS & BLEND LIGHTLY WITH ABOVE.

POUR IN A SPRAYED LOAF PAN.

BAKE AT 350 FOR 1 HOUR OR UNTIL PICK COMES OUT CLEAN.

Cover with foil if the bread is browning too much, to soon.

SWEET BEER BREAD

easy   1 LOAF   FAT = TR EA

3 C	BREAD FLOUR	
1 C	SUGAR	
1	COORS BEER	
1/2 C	EGG BEATERS	
2 T	BAKING POWDER	
1 T	BUTTER BUDS	
1 t	SALT	

LIGHTLY COMBINE THESE AND POUR IN A SPRAYED LOAF PAN.

SPRAY WITH PAM BUTTER AND BAKT AT 350 FOR 1 HOUR OR UNTIL PICK COMES OUT CLEAN.

BROWN BREAD

easy   1 LOAF   FAT = TR EA

1 C	SUGAR	
1/2 C	APPLESAUCE	
1 t	REAL VANILLA EXTRACT	
1 C	EGG BEATERS	
1	BANANA, MASHED VERY WELL	
5 T	COCOA POWDER	
2 T	INSTANT DECAF COFFEE POWDER	
1 C	BREAD FLOUR	
1/4 C	OAT BRAN	
2 T	TOASTED WHEAT GERM	
1 T	BAKING SODA	
1/4 t	SALT	

WHIP THESE FOR 5 MINUTES.

ADD THESE TO ABOVE.

THEN ADD THESE.

POUR IN A SPRAYED LOAF PAN & BAKE IN PRE-HEATED, 350 OVEN FOR 45 MINUTES OR UNTIL PICK COMES CLEAN.

FRENCH BAGUETTES   2 LOAVES   FAT = TR EA

2 C	WARM WATER (115 DEGREES)	COMBINE AND SET ASIDE FOR 10
1 PKG	ACTIVE DRY YEAST	MINUTES.
1 T	SUGAR	
		MIX IN THESE AND LET REST 15
3 C	SEMOLINA FLOUR	MINUTES.
2 C	BREAD FLOUR	
1 T	SALT	KNEAD 10 MINUTES, PLACE IN A
1 T	BUTTER BUDS (OPTIONAL)	SPRAYED BOWL, SPRAY, COVER &
		LET RISE UNTIL TRIPLED IN VOL.
1 C	BREAD FLOUR (OR AS NEEDED)	(APPROXIMATELY 1 HOUR)

Punch down well, divide into 2 baguettes (long loaves). Place on a baking sheet sprinkled with cornmeal, let rise 45 minutes. Brush with Egg Beaters, slash tops & bake in a pre-heated oven at 375 for 40 minutes.

EASY SOURDOUGH BREAD   2 LOAVES   FAT = TR EA

2 PKG	DRY YEAST	COMBINE THESE AND LET SIT 10
1 C	WARM WATER (115 DEGREES)	MINUTES.
1 T	SUGAR	
2 C	BREAD FLOUR	ADD THESE INGREDIENTS.
1 C	NO-FAT SOUR CREAM	
2 T	VINEGAR	
1 T	BUTTER BUDS	ADD REMAINING FLOUR AS YOU
2 t	SALT	KNEAD FOR 5 MINUTES.
1 t	BAKING SODA	LET RISE 30 MINUTES, PUNCH
2 1/2 C	BREAD FLOUR (OR AS NEEDED)	DOWN & LET RISE 15 MINUTES.

Divide into 2 baguettes (long loaves) & place on a pan sprinkled with corn-meal. Slash tops, spray & let rise 20 minutes. Bake in pre-heated, 375 oven for 25 minutes.

WHOLE WHEAT BREAD   2 LOAVES   FAT = TR EA

1 C	WARM WATER (115 DEGREES)	COMBINE AND SETASIDE FOR 10
1 PKG	DRY YEAST	MINUTES.
1 T	BROWN SUGAR	
		ADD THESE AND KNEAD FOR 10
2 C	BREAD FLOUR	MINUTES. LET RISE FOR 30 MIN.
1/2 C	WHOLE WHEAT FLOUR (MORE IF NEEDED)	
1 t	SALT	SPRINKLE A LITTLE CORNMEAL
		ON A SHEET PAN.

Form dough into 2 baguettes (long loaves), place on cornmeal, slash the tops & spray with Pam Butter. Let rise another 30 minutes. Bake in a pre-heated oven at 400 for 10 minutes, then 325 for 15-20 minutes.

MOM'S DINNER ROLLS

 easy   24 ROLLS   FAT = TR EA

1 PKG	DRY YEAST	COMBINE THESE AND LET SIT 10
1/4 C	WARM WATER (115 DEGREES)	MINUTES.
1 T	SUGAR (OR MORE IF YOU LIKE SWEETER ROLLS)	
2 T	INSTANT POTATO FLAKES	COMBINE THESE & COOL TO 115.
3/4 C	BOILING WATER	
1/2 C	SUGAR	ADD YEAST MIX & REST OF THE
1 T	BUTTER BUDS	ITEMS AND KNEAD FOR 10 MIN.
1 t	SALT	(ADD MORE FLOUR, AS NEEDED)
1/4 C	EGG BEATERS	LET RISE 1 HOUR. KNEAD 2 MIN.
1/4 C	PROMISE FAT-FREE MARGARINE	
3 C	FLOUR (+ UP TO 1/2 CUP WHILE KNEADING)	

At this point you can cover & refrigerate for later use or divide into small 1" balls. Place 3 little balls in each cup of a sprayed muffin tin and let rise 1 hour. Bake in a 350 oven for 12-15 minutes.

By the way, this dough makes unbelievably great cinnamon buns!!!!! (p 341)

If you can't get Fat-Free Margarine, substitute 1 t Olive Oil & 1 T Butter Buds.

WHOLE GRAIN RYE BREAD

2 LOAVES   FAT = TR EA

1/2 C	WARM WATER (115 DEGREES)	COMBINE AND LET SIT FOR 10
2 PKG	DRY YEAST	MINUTES.
2 T	HONEY	
1/2 C	CORNMEAL (SEE NOTE BELOW)	COMBINE THESE & COOL TO 115.
1/3 C	PACKED BROWN SUGAR	
1 T	CAVENDER'S GREEK SEASONING	ADD THE YEAST MIX.
2 C	BOILING WATER	
1/2 C	WHOLE WHEAT FLOUR	ADD THESE AND KNEAD FOR 10
1/2 C	RYE FLOUR	MINUTES.
5 C	BREAD FLOUR (OR AS NEEDED)	
1 t	SALT	LET RISE 1 HOUR.

Punch down, shape into 2 loaves & place in sprayed loaf pans. Cover & let rise 45 minutes. Bake in pre-heated oven at 350 for 45 minutes or until they sound hollow when tapped.

You might like to add 1-2 T Caraway Seeds with the cornmeal mix.

HONEY OAT BREAD

2 LOAVES   FAT = TR EA

2 1/2 C	WATER, 115 DEGREES	WHISK THESE & LET SIT 10 MIN.
1/2 C	MOLASSES	
1/2 C	HONEY	
2 PKG	YEAST	
3 C	BREAD FLOUR	WHISK THESE TOGETHER & ADD
1 C	CRACKED (OR WHOLE) WHEAT FLOUR	TO ABOVE.
1/2 C	QUAKER OATS, QUICK COOKING	
1 t	SALT	KNEAD 10 MINUTES, ADD MORE
		FLOUR IF NEEDED.

Let rise 1 hour, punch down, place in 2 sprayed loaf pans & let rise for 1 hour. Spray tops with Pam Butter Spray, Slash down the middle & drizzle honey mixture (below) in centers. Sprinkle with extra oats.

3 T	HOT WATER (OR AS NEEDED TO DISSOLVE BUDS)	
1/4 C	BUTTER BUDS	COMBINE THESE TO DRIZZLE
1/4 C	HONEY	OVER TOPS BEFORE BAKING.

Bake in a pre-heated oven at 350 for 30 minutes or until done.

ITALIAN HERB BUNS

24 BUNS   FAT = TR EA

3 1/2 C	BREAD FLOUR	COMBINE THESE.
1/2 C	WHOLE WHEAT FLOUR	
2 T	BAKING POWDER	
2 T	BUTTER BUDS	
1 t	SALT	
3/4 C	SUGAR	COMBINE & BLEND THESE INTO
2 C	SKIM MILK (WARM)	ABOVE.
1	RED ONION, MINCED	
1/2 C	EGG BEATERS	
1 1/2 T	DRIED ITALIAN HERBS (OR YOUR FAVORITE)	ADD BEER,SPOON INTO SPRAYED MINI (OR REGULAR SIZE) MUFFIN
1/4 C	COORS BEER	PANS.

Bake in pre-heated oven at 350 for 25-30 minutes or until golden. (Longer for regular sized muffins).

SPINACH CHEESE BREAD

2 LOAVES   FAT = 8 GM EA

1/4 C	SUGAR	WHIP THESE FOR 5 MINUTES.
1/2 C	APPLESAUCE	
1 C	EGG BEATERS	
5 C	BREAD FLOUR	BLEND THESE TOGETHER.
2 1/2 t	SALT	
2 T	BAKING SODA	
2 T	BUTTER BUDS	
2 t	CAVENDER'S GREEK SEASONING	
1/4 t	OLD BAY SEASONING	
2 1/2 C	1% BUTTERMILK	BLEND THESE & ADD TO ABOVE.
1 t	WORCESTERSHIRE SAUCE	
2 C	FRESH SPINACH, MINCED	
1/4 C	FRESH PARSLEY, MINCED	
2 C	FAT-FREE CHEDDAR CHEESE, SHREDDED	FOLD IN THE WHIPPED EGG MIX.
1/2 C	PARMESAN CHEESE (*SEE NOTE)	
1 t	POULTRY SEASONING	

Pour into sprayed loaf pans & bake in pre-heated oven at 350 for 40 minutes.

*Note: You can substitute Fat-Free Parmesan for 1/2 of the required Parmesan.

If you're not trying to lose weight, try adding diced pepperoni.

WHEAT SODA BREAD

easy

2 CIRCLES   FAT = TR EA

4 1/2 C	BREAD FLOUR	WHISK THESE & ADD ENOUGH OF THE BUTTERMILK TO FORM A SLIGHTLY MOIST DOUGH.
1/2 C	WHOLE WHEAT FLOUR (OPTIONAL)	
1/4 C	TOASTED WHEAT GERM	
1 T	BAKING SODA	
1 T	BUTTER BUDS	
1 t	SALT	KNEAD 30 SECONDS AND PRESS INTO A FLOURED CAKE PAN.
2 1/4 C	1% BUTTERMILK (OR MORE)	SLASH THE TOPS.

Bake in pre-heated oven at 375 for 35 minutes, turn out & wrap in towel to cool.

PHYLLO PIZZA CRUST

1 PIZZA BASE   FAT = 7 GM

Lay out a sheet of Phyllo, spray with Pam Butter, top with another sheet, spray again & sprinkle with 1 t Parmesan. Press lightly each time before sprinkling the cheese.
Repeat this until you have a stack of 8 sheets & have used 8 t Parmesan.

Top with your favorite low-fat toppings & bake in pre-heated oven at 375 for 25 minutes or until toppings are done.

PIZZA DOUGH

1 PIZZA BASE   FAT = TR EA

1 C	WATER, 115 DEGREES	WHISK TOGETHER & LET SIT FOR 10 MINUTES.
1 T	HONEY	
1 PKG	YEAST	
2 1/2 C	BREAD FLOUR (OR MORE IF NEEDED)	ADD & KNEAD FOR 5 MINUTES.
2 T	BUTTER BUDS	LET RISE UNTIL DOUBLED.
1/2 t	SALT	

Roll out in large circle, place on pan that has been sprinkled with cornmeal. Let rise 20 minutes. Spray with Pam Olive Oil & top as you like. Bake at 375 for 25 min. or until golden on the bottom & toppings are done.

HERBED PIZZA DOUGH

1 PIZZA BASE   FAT = TR EA

1 PKG	YEAST	COMBINE AND LET SIT FOR 10 MINUTES.
1/2 C	WATER (115 DEGREES)	
1 T	SUGAR	
2 C	BREAD FLOUR (OR MORE IF NEEDED)	COMBINE, ADD TO ABOVE AND KNEAD 5 MINUTES.
1/4 C	EGG BEATERS	
2 T	OREGANO	
2 t	GROUND ROSEMARY	LET RISE 1 HOUR.
2 t	GARLIC POWDER	
1 t	SALT	KNEAD & ROLL OUT FLAT.

Place on pan that has been sprinkled with cornmeal. Let rise 20 minutes. Top with your favorite low-fat toppings & bake at 375 for 25 minutes or until golden & the toppings are bubbly.

BANANA RUM BREAD

 easy 1 LOAF FAT = TR EA

1/2 C	SUGAR	WHIP THESE FOR 5 MINUTES.
1/2 C	BROWN SUGAR	
1/4 C	APPLESAUCE	
1 t	REAL VANILLA EXTRACT	
1/4 C	EGG BEATERS	
2 C	CAKE FLOUR	SIFT THESE & ADD TO ABOVE.
1 T	BUTTER BUDS	
2 t	BAKING SODA	
2 t	BAKING POWDER	!!!DO NOT OVER MIX!!!
1/2 C	BANANA RUM	FOLD THESE IN.
1/4 t	SALT	
1 T	FAT-FREE YOGURT	POUR INTO A LINED & SPRAYED
3	BANANAS, MASHED	LOAF PAN.

Bake in pre-heated oven at 350 for 90 minutes or until knife comes out clean.

ZUCCHINI BREAD

easy 1 LOAF FAT = TR EA

1 C	APPLESAUCE	WHIP THESE FOR 5 MINUTES.
2 C	SUGAR	
1 T	REAL VANILLA EXTRACT	
1/4 C	EGG BEATERS	
1 T	FAT-FREE YOGURT	ADD THESE INGREDIENTS.
2 C	ZUCCHINI, GRATED	
3 C	CAKE FLOUR	SIFT & FOLD INTO ABOVE.
2 t	BAKING SODA	!!!DO NOT OVER MIX!!!
2 t	BAKING POWDER	
1 t	CINNAMON	ADD FLOURED RAISINS & POUR
1 t	SALT	INTO A SPRAYED & LINED LOAF
		PAN.
1 C	RAISINS, TOSSED IN ABOVE FLOUR MIXTURE	

Bake in pre-heated oven at 350 for 80 minutes or until knife comes out clean.

FRUIT BREADS

Prepare as above, Substituting Blueberries, Chopped Cherries, Mandarins, Mangoes, Pineapples, Apricots or any diced fruit for the raisins..

FRUIT & BRAN LOAF

 easy   2 LOAVES   FAT = TR EA

2 C	BRAN CEREAL	COMBINE & LET SIT 15 MINUTES.
1 C	SKIM MILK	
1 C	ORANGE JUICE	
1/2 C	CARROTS	

1 C	BROWN SUGAR	WHIP THESE FOR 5 MINUTES &
1/2 C	APPLESAUCE	& FOLD INTO ABOVE.
1 C	EGG BEATERS	

2 1/2 C	CAKE FLOUR	SIFT & FOLD INTO ABOVE.
1/2 C	WHOLE WHEAT FLOUR	!!!DO NOT OVER MIX!!!
2 T	BAKING POWDER, ROUNDED	
1 T	BAKING SODA	POUR INTO 2 SPRAYED & LINED
1 t	CINNAMON	LOAF PANS.
1 t	SALT	
1/2 t	ALLSPICE	BAKE IN A PRE-HEATED 350 OVEN FOR 30-40 MINUTES.

This recipe also makes great muffins.

MANDARIN NUT BREAD

easy   1 LOAF   FAT = TR EA

1/4 C	APPLESAUCE	BLEND & LET SIT 15 MINUTES.
3/4 C	BROWN SUGAR	

1/2 C	EGG BEATERS	ADD THESE & WHIP FLUFFY.
3/4 C	APRICOT JAM	

		SIFT & FOLD INTO ABOVE.
2 1/2 C	CAKE FLOUR	!!!DO NOT OVER MIX!!!
2 T	BAKING POWDER	
1 T	BUTTER BUDS	ADD MANDARINS & POUR INTO
1 t	BAKING SODA	A LINED & SPRAYED LOAF PAN.
1 t	CINNAMON	
1/2 t	SALT	SPRINKLE THE GRAPE-NUTS ON
1/4 t	NUTMEG	TOP.

1 C   MANDARIN ORANGE SECTIONS, CHOPPED, DRAINED.

1/4 C   GRAPE-NUTS

Bake in pre-heated oven at 350 for 55-60 minutes. After baking, brush off the excess grape-nuts.

BLUEBERRY MUFFINS

easy   32 MUFFINS   FAT = TR EA

1 C	APPLESAUCE	BLEND THESE & SET ASIDE FOR
2 1/2 C	SUGAR	15 MINUTES.
1 C	EGG BEATERS	ADD & WHIP 5 MINUTES.
4 C	CAKE FLOUR	SIFT THESE & ADD TO ABOVE.
2 T	BAKING POWDER	
1 t	BAKING SODA	!!!DO NOT OVER MIX!!!
1 T	BUTTER BUDS	
1 t	SALT	
1/4 C	SKIM MILK (OR MORE AS NEEDED)	FOLD THESE IN & FILL THE
3 C	BLUEBERRIES (DRAIN IF FROZEN)	SPRAYED MUFFIN TINS.

Sprinkle with sugar & bake in pre-heated oven at 350 for 40-45 minutes or until pick comes out clean.

Try substituting Raspberries, Blackberries etc.

ORANGE POPPY SEED MUFFINS

32 MUFFINS   FAT = 1 GM EA

Make as above substituting Diced Orange Sections (patted dry) for the BLUEBERRIES & adding 3 T
Poppy Seeds & 1 T Orange Flavored Extract.

PEACH MUFFINS

easy   16 MUFFINS   AT = TR EA

1/2 C	APPLESAUCE	BLEND THESE & SET ASIDE FOR
1 C	SUGAR	15 MINUTES.
1 t	REAL VANILLA EXTRACT	
1/2 C	EGG BEATERS	ADD AND WHIP UNTIL ALMOST FLUFFY.
2 C	CAKE FLOUR	FOLD THESE IN LIGHTLY.
1 T	BAKING POWDER	
1 t	BAKING SODA	
1 t	BUTTER BUDS	
1/2 t	SALT	!!!DO NOT OVER MIX!!!
1 C	GRAPE-NUTS	
3/4 C	1% BUTTERMILK (OR MORE AS NEEDED)	FOLD INTO ABOVE AND FILL
1 C	PEACHES, DICED SMALL	SPRAYED MUFFIN TINS.

Bake in pre-heated oven at 350 for 45 minutes or until pick comes out clean.

PINEAPPLE RAISIN MUFFINS

easy   18 MUFFINS   FAT = TR EA

1 C	BROWN SUGAR	BLEND & LET SIT 15 MINUTES.
1/2 C	APPLESAUCE	
1/2 C	EGG BEATERS	ADD & WHIP 5 MINUTES.
2 C	CAKE FLOUR	SIFT THESE AND FOLD INTO THE
1 T	BAKING POWDER	ABOVE.
1 T	BUTTER BUDS	
1 t	BAKING SODA	!!!DO NOT OVER MIX!!!
1/2 t	CINNAMON	
1/2 t	GROUND GINGER	
1 C	RAISINS	
1 C	CRUSHED PINEAPPLE, DRAINED VERY WELL	COMBINE THESE & FOLD IN.
1 C	SHREDDED CARROT	SPOON INTO SPRAYED MUFFIN
1 t	REAL VANILLA EXTRACT	TINS. BAKE IN A PRE-HEATED OVEN AT 350 FOR 35 MINUTES.

UNBELIEVABLE CINNAMON BUNS

10 BUNS   FAT = TR EA

1/2 RECIPE	MOM'S DINNER ROLLS (p 334)	ROLL OUT ON A FLOURED SPACE
2 T	PROMISE ULTRA FAT-FREE MARGARINE	IN A RECTANGLE & SPREAD THE
------	CINNAMON (DON'T SKIMP)	BUTTER ALL OVER.
------	SUGAR (DON'T SKIMP)	SPRINKLE ON LOTS OF SUGAR & CINNAMON.

Roll up tightly & cut the 'LOG' of dough into 10 pieces. Place in a sprayed cake pan. Cover & let rise 1 hour. Bake in a pre-heated 350 oven for 15 minutes.

SUGAR ICING

1 C	POWDERED SUGAR	COMBINE WELL & DRIZZLE OVER
1 T	SKIM MILK (OR AS NEEDED)	BUNS WHILE WARM.

GARLIC BREAD

quick   SERVES 6   FAT = TR EA

1 LOAF	FAT-FREE FRENCH BREAD, SLICED HORIZONTALLY	
1/4 C	PROMISE ULTRA FAT-FREE MARGARINE	COMBINE AND SPREAD ON THE
1/4 C	GARLIC, MINCED	BREAD. BAKE OR BROIL UNTIL GOLDEN.

SOURDOUGH RYE BREAD

2 LOAVES   FAT = TR

1 PKG	ACTIVE DRY YEAST	COMBINE THESE AND LET SIT 10 MINUTES.
1 T	SUGAR	
1/3 C	WARM WATER (115 DEGREES)	

1 C	WARM WATER (115 DEGREES)	COMBINE THESE & ADD TO THE YEAST MIXTURE.
1 T	SALT	
2 C	SOUR DOUGH STARTER (BELOW)	
2 T	CARAWAY SEEDS	
2 T	DARK MOLASSES	
1/2 C	RYE FLOUR	

1 1/2 C	RYE FLOUR	COMBINE & ADD AS NEEDED. KNEAD FOR 10 MIN. & PLACE IN A SPRAYED BOWL. SPRAY & COVER.
3 1/2 C	BREAD FLOUR	

Let rise until doubled, about 1 1/2 hours. Punch down, cover & let rise 30 more minutes. Spray a baking sheet & sprinkle with Cornmeal. Create 2 ovals of dough & place on pan. Cover, let rise for 45 minutes. Spray, bake in a pre-heated oven at 400 for 1 hour or until bottoms sound hollow when tapped.

SOURDOUGH STARTER

easy

3 C EA	BREAD FLOUR, WARM WATER (115 DEGREES)	BEAT THESE UNTIL SMOOTH. COVER LOOSELY & SIT AT ROOM TEMPERATURE FOR 2 DAYS.
1 T	SUGAR	
1 PKG	ACTIVE DRY YEAST	

FOOD PROCESSOR BURGER BUNS

easy   12 ROLLS   FAT = TR EA

1 PKG	ACTIVE DRY YEAST	COMBINE THESE & LET SIT 10 10 MINUTES.
1 T	SUGAR	
1 1/2 C	WARM WATER (115 DEGREES)	

3 1/2 C	BREAD FLOUR	PROCESS, ADD YEAST MIX WHILE RUNNING, FOR 1 MINUTE AFTER BALL FORMS.
1 t	SALT	
1/2 t	CAVENDER'S GREEK SEASONING	

Place in a sprayed bowl, spray again, cover & let rise for 1 hour. Punch down Divide into 12 smooth balls. Place on a sprayed sheet pan, sprinkled with Cornmeal. Flatten slightly. Cover & rise again for 45 minutes. Slash the tops of each roll 4 times (like a Tic Tac Toe). Spray with Pam, sprinkle with 1 T Sesame Seeds. Bake in a pre-heated oven at 400 for 15-20 minutes.

Desserts

BANANAS FOSTER

 quick   SERVES 4   FAT = TR EA

1/2 C	BROWN SUGAR	COMBINE & SIMMER THESE.
1/2 C	BANANA OR MEYERS DARK RUM	
1/4 C	WATER	
2 T	BUTTER BUDS	
1 t	BUTTER FLAVORING	
1/4 t	CINNAMON OR ALLSPICE (OR TO TASTE)	ADD THE BANANAS JUST TO HEAT THROUGH.
3	BANANAS, PEELED & QUARTERED	PLACE 1 SCOOP FROZEN YOGURT ON EA PLATE & SURROUND WITH THE BANANA MIXTURE.
4 SCOOPS	FAT-FREE FROZEN VANILLA YOGURT	
1/2 C	MEYERS DARK RUM, HEATED	SPOON OVER & IGNITE.

PEACHES FLAMBE

 quick   SERVES 4   FAT = TR EA

1/2 C	JUICE FROM PEACHES	SIMMER THESE INGREDIENTS.
1/2 C	ARMAGNAC	
1/2 C	BROWN SUGAR	ADD PEACHES JUST TO HEAT.
2 T	BUTTER BUDS	
1	ORANGE, ZESTED, MINCED	
8	PEACH HALVES	PLACE CUT SIDE UP ON 4 PLATES WITH JUICES. PLACE 2 SCOOPS YOGURT BESIDE EACH.
8	SMALL SCOOPS FAT-FREE FROZEN YOGURT	
1/2 C	ARMAGNAC, HEATED	SPOON INTO PEACH CENTERS & IGNITE.

If you can't find Armagnac, just use 1/2 Amaretto & 1/2 Cognac.

ORANGES IN CREAM SAUCE

quick   SERVES 6   FAT = TR EA

12	ORANGE SLICES, PEELED, SLICED, SEEDED	SPRINKLE SLICES & BROIL UNTIL BUBBLY.
------	BROWN SUGAR TO SPRINKLE ON ORANGES	
1 C	NO-FAT SOUR CREAM	COMBINE & SIMMER THESE.
1/4 C	POWDERED SUGAR	
1/4 C	CONTREAU	
1 t	REAL VANILLA EXTRACT	SAUCE 4 PLATES AND PLACE 3 BROILED ORANGE SLICES ON EA.
1/2 t	CINNAMON	
1/4 t	MACE	
2 T	ORANGE ZEST	

CHOCOLATE PEARS

 SERVES 8   FAT = TR EA

1 C	HERSHEY'S CHOCOLATE SYRUP	BOIL THESE AND REMOVE FROM
1/2 C	GRAND MARNIER	HEAT.
1/4 C	COLD WATER	COMBINE WELL, ADD & HEAT TO
2 T	ARROWROOT (DISSOLVED IN ABOVE WATER)	THICKEN. THIN w MORE LIQUEUR IF IT GETS TOO THICK.
6	RIPE PEARS, PEELED, CORED	SLICE LENGTHWISE & TOSS WITH
1/4 C	ORANGE JUICE	ORANGE JUICE & DRAIN.

Place 5 slices on each plate to look like a starfish. Spoon sauce between the slices.

RASPBERRY PEARS

 SERVES 6   FAT = TR EA

2 C	WATER	BOIL, THEN SIMMER THESE 15
2 C	SUGAR	MINUTES.
3	FIRM RIPE PEARS, PEELED, CORED	DRAIN & CHILL.
1 1/2 C	RASPBERRY JAM, SEEDLESS	HEAT THESE FOR 5 MINUTES &
1/2	KIRSCHWASSER	REMOVE FROM HEAT.
1/4 C	COLD WATER	COMBINE WELL, WHISK IN AND
2 T	CORNSTARCH	HEAT TO THICKEN. SPOON ONTO
1 t	REAL VANILLA EXTRACT	6 PLATES.

Cut pears in half lengthwise. Lay cut side down & slice lengthwise almost to stem end 6 or 8 times. Press lightly & spread like a fan. Place each on a sauced plate.

RED PEAR CROWNS

 SERVES 8   FAT = TR EA

8	PEARS, PEELED, CORED LEAVING STEMS	SIMMER THESE (PLACE A PLATE
6 C	RED WINE	ON TOP TO SUBMERGE PEARS), FOR 30 MINUTES. CHILL.
2 C	SUGAR	DRAIN, PAT DRY & SLICE FROM
1 t	LEMON ZEST	THE MIDDLES TO THE BOTTOMS
1	CINNAMON STICK	IN CURVED LINES, 6 TIMES FOR
8	WHOLE CLOVES	EACH PEAR.
2 DROPS	RED FOOD COLORING	
8 SCOOPS	FAT-FREE FROZEN YOGURT	SPREAD OPEN SLIGHTLY & STUFF
2 C	RASPBERRY SAUCE (SEE ABOVE)	WITH THE FROZEN YOGURT.

Freeze. Remove 10 minutes before standing each upright on a sauced plate.

BRANDIED STRAWBERRIES & CREAM

easy   SERVES 6   FAT = 1 GM EA

4 C	STRAWBERRIES, HALVED	COMBINE & LET SIT 30 MINUTES.
1/2 C	POWDERED SUGAR	DRAIN & SAVE THE LIQUID.
1/4 C	CONTREAU	
1/4 C	BRANDY	COMBINE DREAM WHIP, BERRIES
		& FILL 6 BRANDY SNIFTERS.
1 C	PREPARED DREAM WHIP	CHILL.
		DRIZZLE LIQUID ON EACH.

PINEAPPLE MADAGASCAR

quick   SERVES 4   FAT = TR EA

4 SLICES	PINEAPPLE, FRESH IF POSSIBLE, PAT DRY	PRESS SLICES IN PEPPERCORNS &
1/4 C	GREEN & RED PEPPERCORNS, CRUSHED	SPRINKLE WITH BROWN SUGAR.
1/4 C	BROWN SUGAR	PLACE ON A SPRAYED PAN.
1/2 C	ORANGE JUICE	COMBINE & DRIZZLE ON SLICES.
1/2 C	DARK RUM	
2 T	HONEY	BROIL UNTIL BUBBLY.
4 SCOOPS	FAT-FREE FROZEN YOGURT	TOP EACH SLICE & SERVE.

KAHLUA PINEAPPLE

quick   SERVES 4   FAT = TR EA

4 SLICES	PINEAPPLE	PLACE ON A SPRAYED PAN.
3 T	BROWN SUGAR	COMBINE & DRIZZLE ON SLICES.
1 T	BUTTER BUDS	
1/4 t	CINNAMON	
1/2 C	KAHLUA	BAKE AT 400 FOR 15 MINUTES.
4	SCOOPS, FAT-FREE FROZEN YOGURT	SERVE ON PINEAPPLE.

SPICY BAKED APPLES

easy   SERVES 4   FAT = TR EA

1 C	APPLE JUICE	SIMMER THESE FOR 5 MINUTES.
1/2 C	RAISINS	DRAIN & SAVE THE JUICES.
2 T	BRANDY	
4	APPLES, CORED	SPOON RAISINS INTO THE APPLES
1/4 C	HONEY	& DRIZZLE REMAINING OVER.
2 t	FRESH LEMON JUICE	BAKE AT 350 FOR 30 MINUTES.

BROWNIES TO DIE FOR

 9 BROWNIES   FAT = 1.5 GM EA

3/4 C	SUGAR	WHIP THESE 5 MINUTES OR
1/2 C	APPLESAUCE	MORE.
1/2 C	EGG BEATERS	
1/4 C	KARO CORN SYRUP	ADD THESE INGREDIENTS.
1 t	REAL VANILLA EXTRACT	
1 1/4 C	CAKE FLOUR	SIFT THESE & ADD.
3/4 C	HERSHEY'S COCOA POWDER	
1/2 C	SUGAR	!!!DO NOT OVER MIX!!!
1 T	BUTTER BUDS	
2 t	BAKING POWDER	FOLD IN BEATEN EGG WHITES.
1/8 t	SALT	

POUR INTO A LINED & SPRAYED

2   EGG WHITES, BEATEN STIFF, NOT DRY   9" x 9" PAN. (Glass works well here)
     (Use fewer whites if you like gooey-chewy brownies)

Bake at 350 for 35 minutes or until pick comes out almost clean. It's better to under bake these, otherwise they tend to be too tough. Cool before cutting into 9 squares.
If you double this recipe, **DO NOT** pour into 1 larger pan. You must use 2 pans. This is a thick batter & needs the heat dispersement of smaller pans.

CAKE-LIKE BROWNIES

16 BROWNIES   FAT = 1 GM EA

2 1/2 C	CAKE FLOUR	SIFT THESE INGREDIENTS.
2 C	COCOA	
2 1/2 C	SUGAR	
1 1/2 T	BAKING SODA	
1/2 t	SALT	
1 3/4 C	SKIM MILK, WARM (or 1/2 applesauce, 1/2 skim milk)	PUREE & ADD TO ABOVE.
1	BANANA, MASHED	
1 C	KARO CORN SYRUP	
1/2 C	EGG BEATERS	
8	EGG WHITES, BEATEN STIFF, NOT DRY	FOLD INTO THE BATTER.

QUICK CHOCOLATE PUDDING   SERVES 6   FAT = 1 GM EA

4 C	SKIM MILK	WHISK THESE IN THE TOP OF A
1/2 C	NON-FAT MILK POWDER	DOUBLE BOILER UNTIL THICK.
1 C	SUGAR	
1/3 C	COCOA POWDER	
1/4 C	CORNSTARCH, SLIGHTLY ROUNDED	TEMPER WITH EGGS & RETURN
2 T	BUTTER BUDS	TO HEAT SLIGHTLY.

!!!DO NOT OVER COOK!!!

1 C	EGG BEATERS	ADD VANILLA & POUR INTO 6
2 t	REAL VANILLA EXTRACT	CUPS.

Lay a piece of plastic wrap directly on the pudding & chill 4 hours.

QUICK COFFEE CUSTARDS   SERVES 6   FAT = TR EA

4 C	SKIM MILK	WHISK THESE IN THE TOP OF A
1 C	SUGAR	DOUBLE BOILER UNTIL THICK.
1/2 C	NON-FAT MILK POWDER	
1/4 C	CORNSTARCH, SLIGHTLY ROUNDED	
2 T	BUTTER BUDS	TEMPER WITH EGGS & RETURN
2 t	INSTANT COFFEE GRANULES	TO HEAT SLIGHTLY.

!!!DO NOT OVER COOK!!!

1 C	EGG BEATERS	ADD VANILLA & POUR INTO 6
2 t	REAL VANILLA EXTRACT	CUPS.

Lay a piece of plastic wrap directly on the custard & chill 4 hours.

CHOCOLATE CHEESE CUSTARD   SERVES 6   FAT = 2 GM EA

1 PKG	KNOX GELATIN (SPRINKLED ON THE MILK)	LET SIT FOR 2 MINUTES.
3/4 C	SKIM MILK	
1 C	SUGAR	PUREE THESE & HEAT.
1/2 C	COCOA	ADD GELATIN MIX & HEAT JUST
1 C	SKIM MILK	TO DISSOLVE.
1 C	COTTAGE CREAM (p 392)	
2 T	BUTTER BUDS	CHILL, WHISKING UNTIL THICK.
1 1/2 C	PREPARED DREAM WHIP (from a package)	WHISK THESE INTO ABOVE.
2 t	REAL VANILLA EXTRACT	

Pour into 6 dishes or fill a Graham Cracker Pie Crust (p 372) & chill. If using as a pie, remember to add the fat count of the crust when figuring total fat.

CHOCOLATE MOUSSE
SERVES 6   FAT = 1 GM EA

1 PKG	KNOX GELATIN (SPRINKLED OVER THE MILK)	LET SIT FOR 2 MINUTES.
1/4 C	SKIM MILK	
1/2 C	SKIM MILK	COMBINE, HEAT AND ADD THE
1 C	SUGAR	GELATIN MIX JUST TO DISSOLVE.
1/2 C	COCOA POWDER	
1/2 t	INSTANT DECAF COFFEE GRANULES	
1 T	BUTTER BUDS	
		ADD MILK AND WHISK OVER AN
1 C	SKIM MILK, ICE COLD	ICE BATH UNTIL COOL & THICK.
4	EGG WHITES, BEATEN FOAMY	COMBINE & BEAT STIFF.
1/2 t	CREAM OF TARTAR	(NOT DRY)

Fold in the whites & spoon into brandy snifters. Chill 4 hours. Top with a dollop of Dream Whip or Whipped Cream Topping (p 390).

If you do not let this cool enough, you will end up with 2 different layers of chocolate....(so, rename it 'TWO LAYER CHOCOLATE MOUSSE', it's still great!)

EASY CHOCOLATE MOUSSE
easy   SERVES 6   FAT = 2 GM EA

1/2 C	SKIM MILK	BLENDERIZE THESE.
1 C	EGG BEATERS	
1 1/2 C	SKIM MILK	HEAT THESE TO THICKEN.
1 C	NON-FAT MILK POWDER	
1/2 C	COCOA POWDER	
1/2 C	HONEY (OR 1 CUP SUGAR)	POUR INTO BLENDER WHILE IT
2 T	CORNSTARCH, SLIGHTLY ROUNDED	IS RUNNING.
1/2 t	INSTANT DECAF COFFEE GRANULES	
1/4 C	RUM OR ORANGE LIQUEUR	WHISK OVER AN ICE BATH UNTIL
		ALMOST COLD & THICKENED.
1 C	PREPARED DREAM WHIP (from a package)	FOLD INTO ABOVE & SPOON
	or FAT FREE COOL WHIP	INTO PARFAIT GLASSES.

CARAMEL CUSTARDS

 SERVES 6   FAT = 1 GM EA

4 C	SKIM MILK, WARM	WHISK THESE VERY WELL.
2 C	EGG BEATERS	
1 C	SUGAR	
1 C	NON-FAT MILK POWDER	POUR INTO 6 CUSTARD CUPS
1 t	BUTTER FLAVORING (OPTIONAL)	THAT HAVE CARAMEL GLAZE
2 t	REAL VANILLA EXTRACT	IN THE BOTTOM. (BELOW)
1/4 t	NUTMEG	
1/4 t	SALT	PRE-HEAT OVEN AT 300.

Bake in a water bath for 50 minutes or until knife inserted comes out clean. To serve, turn upside down on dessert plates. Serve as is or decorate with fresh fruit.

When doing the knife test, there should be no milky residue left on the blade. If blade is clear, but particles of custard are attached, that's done.

CARAMEL GLAZE

 1 CUP   FAT = TR EA

1 C	WATER	BOIL TO A DARK AMBER COLOR.
2 C	SUGAR	POUR A LITTLE INTO EACH CUP & COOL.

APRICOT BRULEE

SERVES 6   FAT = 1 GM EA

6	APRICOT HALVES, PATTED DRY	PLACE EACH CUT SIDE UP IN THE CENTER OF EACH CUSTARD CUP.
	CARAMEL GLAZE (SEE ABOVE)	POUR THE GLAZE AROUND EACH APRICOT & LET COOL.
4 C	SKIM MILK, WARM	
2 C	EGG BEATERS	WHISK THESE VERY WELL
1 C	SUGAR	& POUR INTO THE ABOVE CUPS.
1 C	NON-FAT MILK POWDER	
2 t	REAL VANILLA EXTRACT	BAKE IN A WATER BATH IN A
1/2 t	CINNAMON	PRE-HEATED, OVEN AT 300 FOR
1/4 C	ARMAGNAC (OR 1/2 BRANDY, 1/2 AMARETTO)	50 MIN. OR UNTIL KNIFE COMES
1/4 C	ORANGE ZEST, MINCED	OUT CLEAN.

To serve, turn upside down on dessert plates.

When doing the knife test, there should be no milky residue left on the blade. If the blade is clear, but particles of custard are attached, that's done.

SOUTHERN CREME BRULEE

SERVES 6   FAT = 1 GM EA

4 C	SKIM MILK	WHISK THESE VERY WELL AND
2 C	EGG BEATERS	POUR INTO 6 CUSTARD CUPS.
1 C	SUGAR	
1 C	NON-FAT MILK POWDER	
1 t	BUTTER FLAVORING (OPTIONAL)	BAKE IN A WATER BATH IN A
2 t	REAL VANILLA EXTRACT	PRE-HEATED OVEN AT 300 FOR
1/4 t	SALT	50 MINUTES OR UNTIL KNIFE
		INSERTED COMES CLEAN.
		CHILL 4 HOURS.
1/2 C	BROWN SUGAR	SPRINKLE OVER THE TOPS.

When cool, pack ice around cups & broil to caramelize the brown sugar.

When doing the knife test, there should be no milky residue left on the blade. If blade is clear, but particles of custard are attached, that's done.

QUICK VANILLA PUDDING

SERVES 6   FAT = 1 GM EA

4 C	SKIM MILK	WHISK THESE IN THE TOP OF A
1 C	SUGAR	DOUBLE BOILER UNTIL THICK.
1 C	NON-FAT MILK POWDER	
1/4 C	CORNSTARCH, SLIGHTLY ROUNDED	
2 T	BUTTER BUDS	
1 C	EGG BEATERS	TEMPER WITH EGG MIX AND
2 t	REAL VANILLA EXTRACT	RETURN TO HEAT SLIGHTLY.
	!!!DO NOT OVER COOK!!!	ADD VANILLA & POUR INTO 6
		CUPS.

Lay a piece of plastic wrap on the pudding & chill.

BLUEBERRY CUSTARD

SERVES 6   FAT = 1 GM EA

4 C	SKIM MILK	WHISK THESE IN THE TOP OF A
1 C	SUGAR	DOUBLE BOILER UNTIL THICK.
1 C	NON-FAT MILK POWDER	
1/4 C	CORNSTARCH	
2 T	BUTTER BUDS	TEMPER WITH EGG MIX AND
1/4 t	SALT	RETURN TO HEAT SLIGHTLY.
	!!!DO NOT OVER COOK!!!	
1 C	EGG BEATERS	ADD VANILLA & 1/2 OF BERRIES.
2 t	REAL VANILLA EXTRACT	POUR INTO CUPS & DROP IN THE
2 C	FRESH BERRIES	REST OF THE BERRIES.

Lay a piece of plastic wrap directly on the custard & chill 4 hours.

ORANGE CREME BRULEE

 easy   SERVES 6   FAT = 1 GM EA

4 C	SKIM MILK	WHISK THESE VERY WELL.
2 C	EGG BEATERS	
1 C	SUGAR	POUR INTO CUSTARD CUPS THAT
1 C	NON-FAT MILK POWDER	CARAMEL GLAZE (p 350) IN THE
1/4 C	GRAND MARNIER	BOTTOMS.
1/4 C	ORANGE ZEST	
2 t	REAL VANILLA EXTRACT	PRE-HEAT OVEN AT 300.

Bake in a water bath for 50 minutes or until *knife inserted comes out clean. Turn upside down on dessert plates & sprinkle with threads of orange zest.

LEMON CREME BRULEE

easy   SERVES 6   FAT = 1 GM EA

4 C	SKIM MILK, WARM	WHISK THESE AND POUR INTO 6
2 C	EGG BEATERS	CUSTARD CUPS THAT HAVE THE
1 C	SUGAR	CARAMEL GLAZE (p 350) IN THE
1 C	NON-FAT MILK POWDER	BOTTOMS (p 350).
1/4 C	LEMON ZEST, MINCED	
1 T	FRESH LEMON JUICE	
2 t	REAL VANILLA EXTRACT	PRE-HEAT OVEN AT 300.

Bake in a water bath for 50 minutes or until *knife inserted comes out clean. Turn upside down on dessert plates & sprinkle with lemon zest threads.

PUMPKIN CUSTARDS

easy   SERVES 6   FAT = TR EA

4 C	SKIM MILK	PUREE THESE AND POUR INTO 6
2 C	PUMPKIN PUREE	SPRAYED CUSTARD CUPS.
2 C	EGG BEATERS	
1 C	NON-FAT MILK POWDER	
1 C	SUGAR	BAKE IN A WATER BATH IN A
1 1/2 t	CINNAMON	PRE-HEATED OVEN AT 300 FOR
2 t	REAL VANILLA EXTRACT	50 MINUTES OR UNTIL A KNIFE
1/4 t	NUTMEG	COMES OUT CLEAN.
1/4 t	SALT	

*When doing the knife test, there should be no milky residue left on the blade. If the blade is clear, but particles of custard are attached, that's done.

CLASSIC TIRAMISU   SERVES 8   FAT = 2 GM EA

1 1/2 t	KNOX GELATIN (SPRINKLED OVER THE WATER)	LET SIT 2 MINUTES, THEN HEAT
1/4 C	COLD WATER	TO DISSOLVE.
2 t	INSTANT COFFEE POWDER	
3 C	NON-FAT COTTAGE CHEESE, PUREED WELL	PUREE THESE &ADD COFFEE MIX
1 1/2 C	POWDERED SUGAR	WHILE BLENDER IS RUNNING.
	(SEE CHOCOLATE OPTION-- BELOW)	CHILL 4 HOURS.
1 1/2 t	KNOX GELATIN (SPRINKLED ON THE MARSALA)	LET SIT 2 MINUTES, THEN HEAT
1 C	SUGAR	TO DISSOLVE IN THE TOP OF A
1 1/2 C	MARSALA	DOUBLE BOILER.
		TEMPER WITH EGGS & RETURN
3 C	EGG BEATERS !!!DO NOT OVER COOK!!!	TO HEAT UNTIL THICK. COOL.
1 LAYER	MOM'S GOLDEN CAKE (p 361, leave in springform)	ROUGH UP COOLED CAKE TOP
4 T	MARSALA	WITH FORK. COMBINE COCOA,
1 T	HERSHEY'S COCOA POWDER	MARSALA & BRUSH ON CAKE.
		SPREAD CHEESE ON CAKE AND
1 t	HERSHEY'S COCOA POWDER	CHILL 2 HOURS. SPREAD ON
2 T	BITTER-CHOCOLATE DRIZZLE (p 362)	THE COOLED CUSTARD.

Lay a wax paper cut out design on top (a palm tree ?), sift cocoa over. Drizzle edges with Bitter Chocolate.
Chill 12 hours & remove the cut out design.

CHOCOLATE OPTION: Add 3 T Hershey's Cocoa Powder & 1/4 C Powdered Sugar to the cheese mixture.
This is my al time favorite. It creates a Chocolate Tiramisu & adds 3 GM Fat total.

* It's easiest if the cake is baked in a springform pan & left in the pan while creating all the other layers on top.

PUMPKIN CHEESE PIE   _easy_   SERVES 8   FAT = 2 GM EA

3 C	COTTAGE CREAM (p 392)	PUREE THESE INGREDIENTS.
1 1/2 C	PUMPKIN PUREE	
1/2 C	BROWN SUGAR	FOLD IN THE WHITES.
3/4 C	EGG BEATERS	
1/3 C	REAL MAPLE SYRUP	POUR INTO A PHYLLO PIE CRUST.
3 T	FLOUR	(p 372).
1 t EA	BRANDY, CINNAMON	
1 t	REAL VANILLA EXTRACT	BAKE IN PRE-HEATED, 325 OVEN
1 t	PUMPKIN PIE SPICE OR ALLSPICE	FOR 45 MINUTES OR UNTIL KNIFE
1/4 t	SALT	COMES CLEAN.
2	EGG WHITES, BEATEN STIFF, NOT DRY	PIPE ROSETTES OF DREAM WHIP
		TO GARNISH.

FRANGELICO MERINGUES w CREME ANGLAISE   SERVES 4   FAT = TR EA

FRANGELICO CREME ANGLAISE

2 C	SKIM MILK	COMBINE AND HEAT THESE IN A
1/2 C	SUGAR	DOUBLE BOILER UNTIL THICK.
1/2 C	EGG BEATERS	
1/4 C	NON-FAT MILK POWDER	
1 1/2 T	CORNSTARCH	!!!DO NOT OVER COOK!!!
1 T	BUTTER BUDS	
		WHISK IN & COOL.
2 T	FRANGELICO (HAZELNUT LIQUEUR)	SPOON ONTO PLATES & TOP WITH
		THE COOKED MERINGUES.

MERINGUES

4	EGG WHITES, BEATEN TO MEDIUM PEAKS	COMBINE AND WHIP TO MEDIUM
1/2 C	SUGAR	PEAKS.
1 T	BUTTER BUDS	
1/4 t	CREAM OF TARTER	
1/2 t	REAL VANILLA EXTRACT	
		SIMMER MILK AND ADD LARGE
2 C	SKIM MILK IN LARGE FRY PAN	DOLLOPS OF MERINGUE.
1 C	NON-FAT MILK POWDER	COVER & SIMMER 8 MINUTES.

CARAMEL DRIZZLE   Make this just before serving.

1/2 C	SUGAR	HEAT THESE TO A DARK AMBER.
1/4 C	WATER	DRIZZLE OVER THE MERINGUES.

CHOCOLATE CLOUDS   SERVES 8   FAT = 1 GM EA

1 PKG	DREAM WHIP (1.3 OZ)	WHIP THESE UNTIL STIFF.
1/2 C	SKIM MILK	
1/2 C	NON-FAT MILK POWDER	FOLD IN WHITES AND SPOON 8
2 T	COCOA POWDER	MOUNDS ONTO A PAN, LINED w
2 T	POWDERED SUGAR	WAX PAPER.
1/2 t	REAL VANILLA EXTRACT	
		CREATE A HOLLOW IN EACH &
4	EGG WHITES, BEATEN STIFF, NOT DRY	FREEZE 4 HOURS.

To serve, fill w fruit & drizzle Chocolate Sauce over (p 379, 387, 388), or top with Dream Whip.

APRICOT CREAM CAKE

SERVES 10   FAT = 2 GM EA

1 C	GINGERSNAP CRUMBS	COMBINE AND PRESS INTO A 9"
2 T	BUTTER BUDS	SPRINGFORM, BAKE AT 375 FOR
1 T	APPLESAUCE (OR AS NEEDED)	8 MINUTES.

2 PKG	KNOX GELATIN (SPRINKLED ON THE JUICE)	LET SIT FOR 2 MINUTES, THEN
3/4 C	DARK BROWN SUGAR	HEAT TO DISSOLVE.
1 C	APRICOT JUICE FROM APRICOTS	

3 C	COTTAGE CREAM (p 392)	PUREE THESE AND ADD GELATIN
2 C	NO-FAT SOUR CREAM	MIXTURE.
3 T	FRESH LEMON JUICE	
2 T	BUTTER BUDS	
1 t	REAL VANILLA EXTRACT	ADD APRICOTS, POUR INTO THE
1 t	BUTTER FLAVORING	CRUST & CHILL FOR 6 HOURS.

1 LB CAN	APRICOT HALVES, DRAINED, MINCED

1 LB CAN	APRICOT HALVES, DRAINED, SLICED	PAT DRY & LAY ON TOP.
1/4 C	FRESH BLUEBERRIES	SPRINKLE BERRIES OVER.
1/4 C	SEEDLESS RASPBERRY JAM, HEATED	DRIZZLE JAM OVER & CHILL.

NO-BAKE CHEESECAKE

 easy

SERVES 10   FAT = 2 GM EA

1 PKG	KNOX GELATIN (SPRINKLED OVER THE MILK)	LET SIT 2 MINUTES AND THEN
1/4 C	SKIM MILK	HEAT JUST TO DISSOLVE.

2 1/2 C	COTTAGE CREAM (p 392)	PUREE WELL, ADDING GELATIN
2 1/2 C	NO-FAT SOUR CREAM	MIX LAST.
1/2 C	SUGAR	
2 t	FRESH LEMON JUICE	POUR IN A GRAHAM CRACKER
2 t	BUTTER FLAVORING	CRUST MADE IN A SPRINGFORM
1 t	REAL VANILLA EXTRACT	PAN (SEE BELOW).
		CHILL 6 HOURS.
		GARNISH WITH FRESH FRUIT.

GRAHAM CRACKER CRUST

 quick

1 CRUST   FAT = 10 GM

1 C	GRAHAM CRACKERS, CRUSHED	WHIRL IN FOOD PROCESSOR.
2 T	BUTTER BUDS	
		ADD TO GET CONSISTENCY FOR
1 T	APPLESAUCE (+ OR -)	PRESSING INTO PAN.

CREAMY RICH CHEESECAKE   SERVES 10   FAT = 2 GM EA

1	GRAHAM CRACKER CRUST (p 355)	MAKE IN A SPRINGFORM PAN.
1 PKG	KNOX GELATIN (SPRINKLED OVER THE MILK)	LET SIT 2 MINUTES AND HEAT TO
1/2 C	SKIM MILK	DISSOLVE.
3 C	COTTAGE CREAM (p 392)	PUREE THESE, ADDING GELATIN
2 C	NO-FAT SOUR CREAM	MIX SLOWLY.
1 C	EGG BEATERS	
1 C	SUGAR	POUR INTO CRUST.
2 T	FLOUR	
2 t	BUTTER FLAVORING	BAKE IN A PRE-HEATED OVEN AT
1 t	REAL VANILLA EXTRACT	300 FOR 1 HOUR.
1 t	FRESH LEMON JUICE	TURN OFF OVEN & LEAVE DOOR
		AJAR FOR 1 HOUR.
		CHILL OVERNIGHT.

TOPPING

6 T	MEYERS RUM (OR ANY LIQUEUR)	COMBINE, SPREAD ON TOP AND
6 T	BROWN SUGAR	BROIL JUST UNTIL BUBBLY.

Or try the Orange Topping below.

ORANGE TOPPING   ZERO FAT

1 C	ORANGE MARMALADE OR PEACH JAM	WARM THESE JUST TO BLEND.
1/4 C	GRAND MARNIER	COOL & SPREAD ON THE CAKE.
1 T	REAL VANILLA EXTRACT	

Or use a can of your favorite fruit pie filling.

BLUEBERRY CHEESECAKE

Make the batter for the above cheesecake & pour all but 1 C into the crust.

1 C	BATTER FROM ABOVE CHEESECAKE	PUREE THESE & SWIRL INTO THE
1/2 C	BLUEBERRIES	CAKE.
1/2 C	BLUEBERRIES	DROP BERRIES INTO THE SWIRLS
		& BAKE AS ABOVE.

You can leave plain or top with a Blueberry Pie Filling. Try experimenting with various berries & pie fillings.

CHOCOLATE MARBLE CHEESECAKE

SERVES 10   FAT = 3 GM EA

1	CHOCOLATE GRAHAM CRACKER CRUST (p 372)	MAKE IN A SPRINGFORM PAN.
1 PKG	KNOX GELATIN (SPRINKLED OVER THE MILK)	LET SIT FOR 2 MINUTES & HEAT
1/2 C	SKIM MILK	JUST TO DISSOLVE.
3 C	COTTAGE CREAM (p 392)	PUREE THESE AND ADD GELATIN
2 C	NO-FAT SOUR CREAM	MIX.
1 C	SUGAR	POUR ALL EXCEPT 1 CUP OF THE
1 C	EGG BEATERS	BATTER INTO THE CRUST.
2 T	FLOUR	
1 t	REAL VANILLA EXTRACT	WHISK CHOCOLATE MIX WITH 1
2 t	BUTTER FLAVORING	CUP OF BATTER & SWIRL IN.

CHOCOLATE MIX

1/2 C	COCOA	
1/2 C	HOT WATER	BAKE IN PRE-HEATED, 300 OVEN
1/2 C	SUGAR	FOR 1 HOUR.
2 T	BUTTER BUDS	
3 T	HONEY	TURN OFF OVEN, LEAVE DOOR
1/2 t	REAL VANILLA EXTRACT	AJAR FOR 1 HOUR.
		CHILL.

CHOCOLATE CHEESECAKE

Mix the Chocolate Mix well into all of the batter above before pouring into crust.

LEMON CHEESECAKE

SERVES 10   FAT = 2 GM EA

1	GRAHAM CRACKER CRUST (p 355).	MAKE IN A SPRINGFORM PAN.
1 PKG	KNOX GELATIN (SPRINKLED OVER MILK)	LET SIT 2 MINUTES & HEAT TO
1/2 C	SKIM MILK	DISSOLVE.
3 C	COTTAGE CREAM (p 392)	PUREE ALL, POUR INTO
2 C	NO-FAT SOUR CREAM	GRAHAM CRACKER CRUST.
1 C	EGG BEATERS	BAKE IN A PRE-HEATED OVEN AT
1 C	SUGAR	300 FOR 1 HOUR.
6 T	FRESH LEMON JUICE	
2 T	FLOUR	TURN OVEN OFF & LEAVE DOOR
1 t	BUTTER FLAVORING	AJAR FOR 1 HOUR.
1 t	REAL VANILLA EXTRACT	CHILL OVERNIGHT.

PEACH CHEESE PIE

SERVES 10   FAT = 2 GM EA

1	CINNAMON GRAHAM CRACKER CRUST (p 372)	MAKE IN A PIE PLATE.
1 PKG	KNOX GELATIN (SPRINKLED OVER THE MILK)	LET SIT 2 MINUTES & HEAT TO
2 T	SKIM MILK	DISSOLVE.
1 1/2 C	CANNED PEACHES, DRAINED	PUREE THESE, ADDING GELATIN
3 C	COTTAGE CREAM (p 392)	MIX LAST.
3/4 C	SUGAR	
2 T	BUTTER BUDS	POUR INTO CRUST AND CHILL 6 HOURS.
1 C	CANNED PEACHES, SLICED, PATTED DRY	PLACE ON TOP.

MANDARIN CHEESECAKE

SERVES 10   FAT = 2 GM EA

1	GRAHAM CRACKER CRUST (p 355)	MAKE IN A SPRINGFORM PAN.
1 PKG	KNOX GELATIN (SPRINKLED ON THE JUICE)	LET SIT 2 MINUTES, ADD BUTTER
1 C	FRESH ORANGE JUICE	BUDS & HEAT JUST TO DISSOLVE.
2 T	BUTTER BUDS	
1 1/2 C	NO-FAT SOUR CREAM	PUREE & ADD GELATIN MIX.
1 1/2 C	COTTAGE CREAM (p 392)	
1/4 C	NON-FAT MILK POWDER	
1/2 C	SUGAR	
		FOLD IN THE MANDARINS.
1 C	MANDARIN ORANGE SECTIONS (MINCED & PATTED DRY)	POUR INTO CRUST & CHILL 6 HR.
1 C	MANDARIN ORANGE SLICES, PATTED DRY	PLACE AROUND EDGE OF CAKE.

HEAVENLY CLAFOUTI SAUCE

easy   2 CUPS   FAT = TR EA

2 C	SKIM MILK	WHISK IN A DOUBLE BOILER TO
1 C	SUGAR	THICKEN.
1/2 C	NON-FAT MILK POWDER	
2 T	BUTTER BUDS	REMOVE FROM THE HEAT.
1 T	FLOUR	
		TEMPER WITH EGG BEATERS. RETURN TO HEAT.
1/2 C	EGG BEATERS	SLIGHTLY THICKEN AGAIN.

!!!DO NOT OVER COOK!!!

RUM CHARLOTTE   SERVES 8   FAT = TR EA

Spray a souffle' dish & line with Angel Food Cake (p 391 made in a 9" x 13" pan & cut like Lady Fingers).

1 PKG	KNOX GELATIN (SPRINKLED ON THE MILK)	LET SIT 2 MINUTES.
1 1/2 C	SKIM MILK	COMBINE & HEAT TO THICKEN.
1 C	NON-FAT MILK POWDER	STIR CONSTANTLY.
1 C	SUGAR	
1 T	CORNSTARCH	
		TEMPER THESE INTO ABOVE &
1 C	EGG BEATERS	RETURN TO HEAT UNTIL IT IS
2 t	BUTTER FLAVORING	SLIGHTLY THICK AGAIN.
	!!!DO NOT OVER COOK!!!	
6 T	MEYERS RUM	ADD THESE & STRAIN INTO THE
2 t	REAL VANILLA EXTRACT	PREPARED DISH. LAY A SHEET
1/2 C	SKIM MILK	OF PLASTIC WRAP ON SURFACE
		& CHILL 6 HOURS.

FRESH PEACH CLAFOUTI   SERVES 4   FAT = TR EA

2 C	PEELED PEACH SLICES	PLACE IN A SPRAYED & SUGARED CASSEROLE.
1 C	SKIM MILK	
1/2 C	NON-FAT MILK POWDER	WHISK WELL & POUR OVER THE
1/2 C	EGG BEATERS	PEACHES
1 C	FLOUR	
3/4 C	SUGAR	BAKE IN A PRE-HEATED OVEN AT
1 T	BUTTER BUDS	350 FOR 35 MINUTES OR UNTIL
1 t	REAL VANILLA EXTRACT	KNIFE COMES OUT CLEAN.
1 t	BAKING POWDER	
1/2 t	SALT	SERVE WARM WITH HEAVENLY
1/2 t	NUTMEG (OPTIONAL)	CLAFOUTI SAUCE. (p 358)

APRICOT CLAFOUTI   SERVES 4   FAT = TR EA

2 C	APRICOTS, SLICED	PLACE IN A SPRAYED & SUGARED CASSEROLE.
1 C	SKIM MILK	
1/2 C	NON-FAT MILK POWDER	WHISK WELL & POUR OVER THE
3/4 C	EGG BEATERS	APRICOTS.
1/2 C	ARMAGNAC (OR BRANDY, ETC.)	
3/4 C	SUGAR	BAKE IN A PRE-HEATED OVEN AT
1 C	FLOUR	350 FOR 35 MINUTES.
1 t	REAL VANILLA EXTRACT	SERVE WARM WITH HEAVENLY
1 t	BAKING POWDER	CLAFOUTI SAUCE. (p 358)
1/2 t	SALT	

PEACHES w CUSTARD SAUCE

 SERVES 8   FAT = TR EA

2 1/2 C	SKIM MILK	WHISK IN A DOUBLE BOILER TO THICKEN.
1/2 C	EGG BEATERS	
1/2 C	SUGAR	!!!DO NOT OVER COOK!!!
1/2 C	NON-FAT MILK POWDER	
1 T	BUTTER BUDS	
1 T	CORNSTARCH	
		ADD LIQUEUR & VANILLA.
2 T	CONTREAU OR ORANGE LIQUEUR	
1 T	REAL VANILLA EXTRACT	TOSS FRUIT IN JUICE, PAT DRY & PUT FACE DOWN ON PLATES.
4	RIPE PEACHES, PEELED, HALVED	
1/2 C	ORANGE JUICE	SPOON SAUCE ON EACH.
------	NUTMEG	SPRINKLE WITH NUTMEG.

RHUBARB FOOL

 SERVES 8   FAT = TR EA

4 C	RHUBARB, TRIMMED, CUBED	SIMMER THESE FOR 1 HOUR.
1 C	POWDERED SUGAR	DRAIN WELL.
1/3 C	APPLESAUCE	PUREE HALF, CHILL BOTH.
1 1/2 t	KNOX GELATIN (SPRINKLED OVER THE RUM)	LET SIT FOR 2 MINUTES & HEAT
1/4 C	RUM	TO DISSOLVE.
2 C	PUREED RHUBARB (ABOVE)	ADD THESE TO THE GELATIN MIX
2 C	COTTAGE CREAM (p 392)	& CHILL.
1/2 C	POWDERED SUGAR	

Fill 8 parfait glasses alternately with cream puree & rhubarb. Chill 4 hours.

STRAWBERRY FOOL

easy SERVES 8   FAT = TR EA

3 C	STRAWBERRIES, SLICED	TOSS & SET ASIDE 30 MINUTES.
1/2 C	SUGAR	DRAIN.
1 PKG	KNOX GELATIN (SPRINKLED ON THE JUICES)	LET SIT FOR 2 MINUTES & HEAT
1/4 C	GRAND MARNIER	JUST TO DISSOLVE.
1/4 C	OF THE DRAINED JUICES	COOL.
1 C	STRAWBERRIES	PUREE THESE, ADD GELATIN MIX
2 C	COTTAGE CREAM (p 392)	& CHILL.

Fill 8 parfait glasses alternately with cream puree & berries. Chill 4 hours.

MOM'S GOLDEN CAKE

 easy   SERVES 12   FAT = TR EA

1 C	SUGAR	WHIP THESE 5 MINUTES.
3/4 C	APPLESAUCE	
3/4 C	EGG BEATERS	
1 T	REAL VANILLA EXTRACT	
3-4 DROPS	YELLOW FOOD COLORING	
2 1/4 C	CAKE FLOUR	SIFT THESE & FOLD INTO THE ABOVE.
5 T	BUTTER BUDS	
4 t	BAKING POWDER	
1/2 t	SALT	
6	EGG WHITES, BEATEN TO MEDIUM PEAKS	BEAT THESE TO SOFT PEAKS.
1/2 C	POWDERED SUGAR	FOLD INTO THE ABOVE.

Pour into 2 lined & sprayed 9" cake pans. Bake in pre-heated oven at 350 for 25-30 minutes or until pick comes clean. Cool well.
(For Tiramisu or other dessert bases, I make this in 3 layers in springform pans)

CHOCOLATE FROSTING

easy   SERVES 12   FAT = 1 GM EA

1 t	KNOX GELATIN (SPRINKLED OVER THE MILK)	LET SIT FOR 2 MINUTES.
2 1/3 C	SKIM MILK	SIMMER ALL UNTIL THICK.
1/2 C	NON-FAT MILK POWDER	
1 C	COCOA POWDER	
1 C	POWDERED SUGAR	
1/4 C	CORNSTARCH	COOL, THEN FOLD IN THE EGG
1 t	BUTTER BUDS	WHITES WELL.
1 t	REAL VANILLA EXTRACT	
		REFRIGERATE AFTER ICING THE
3	EGG WHITES, BEATEN STIFF, NOT DRY	CAKE.

ANGEL CAKE

 easy   SERVES 8   FAT = TR EA

24	EGG WHITES, BEATEN TO MEDIUM PEAKS	WHIP THESE TO STIFF PEAKS, NOT DRY.
3 C	POWDERED SUGAR	
3 C	CAKE FLOUR	COMBINE & FOLD INTO ABOVE.
2 T	LEMON ZEST, MINCED (OPTIONAL)	
1/4 C	BUTTER BUDS	POUR INTO A SPRAYED & LINED
2 T	REAL VANILLA EXTRACT	TUBE PAN. BAKE IN PRE-HEATED
4 t	BAKING POWDER	OVEN AT 300 FOR 45 MINUTES OR UNTIL PICK COMES CLEAN.

CHOCOLATE RASPBERRY DREAM CAKE   SERVES 16   FAT = 2 GM EA

Make the Double Chocolate Cake (only use 2 of the 3 layers). Cool well. Puree 1 Cup Seedless Raspberry
Jam. Spread on the tops of 2 layers & stack. Make White Cream Frosting & pipe vertically onto sides.
Pipe rosettes on the outside edge of the top. Fill the center space with fresh raspberries.

WHITE CREAM FROSTING   *quick*   SERVES 16   FAT = 1.5 GM EA

2	1.3 OZ ENVELOPES DREAM WHIP	BEAT THESE TO STIFF PEAKS.
3/4 C	ICE COLD SKIM MILK	
2 t	REAL VANILLA EXTRACT	

DAD'S CHOCOLATE LACE CAKE   SERVES 12   FAT = 1 GM EA

Make the Double Chocolate Cake (only use 2 of the 3 layers). Cool well. Make the 7-Minute Icing (p 363) &
ice the cake. Place in the refrigerator. Make the Bitter-Chocolate Drizzle, cool slightly & drizzle in a lacy
pattern around the top edges & sides of the cake. Refrigerate.

BITTER CHOCOLATE DRIZZLE   THIS ADDS A TOTAL OF 5 GM OF FAT

1/2 t	KNOX GELATIN (SPRINKLED OVER THE WATER)	LET SIT FOR 2 MINUTES.
1/2 C	WATER	THEN, SIMMER OVER BOILING
1/2 C	COCOA POWDER	WATER UNTIL THE GELATIN IS
1/2 C	POWDERED SUGAR	DISSOLVED.
1/2 t	REAL VANILLA EXTRACT	

WHISK TO COOL AND THICKEN
BEFORE DRIZZLING OVER.

QUICK CHOCOLATE ICING   *quick*   SERVES 12   FAT = 1 GM EA

2 1/2 C	SKIM MILK	WHISK THESE IN THE TOP OF A
2 PKG	CHOCOLATE PUDDING(3.9 OZ EA)	DOUBLE BOILER UNTIL THICK.
3/4 C	COCOA	
1/2 C	SUGAR	COOL.
2 T	CORNSTARCH	
1 t	BUTTER FLAVORING	

DOUBLE CHOCOLATE CAKE

SERVES 12   FAT = 1 GM EA

2 1/2 C	CAKE FLOUR	SIFT THESE INGREDIENTS.
1 C	COCOA POWDER	
4 t	BAKING POWDER	
2 T	BUTTER BUDS	
1/2 t	SALT	

3/4 C	APPLESAUCE	WHIP THESE FOR 5 MINUTES.
3 T	INSTANT COFFEE	
2 C	SUGAR	
3/4 C	EGG BEATERS	

2 C	SKIM MILK	COMBINE THESE & ADD TO THE
1 T	REAL VANILLA EXTRACT	EGG MIX, ALTERNATELY WITH
2 T	WHITE VINEGAR	DRY INGREDIENTS.

| 3 | EGG WHITES, BEATEN TO MEDIUM PEAKS | FOLD INTO THE BATTER. |

Pour into 3 (never use just 2) lined & sprayed 9" cake pans. Bake at 350 for 25-30 minutes or pick comes out clean. Cool.
This is a very dense, heavy cake. If you'd like it a little lighter, fold in 4 to 6 egg whites, beaten stiff but not dry. It's always better to under cook cakes rather than over cook. Otherwise they tend to be tough or chewy.

CHOCOLATE CREAM FROSTING

SERVES 12   FAT = 3 GM EA

3	1.3 OZ ENVELOPES DREAM WHIP	BEAT THESE AT HIGH SPEED TO
1 1/4 C	ICE COLD SKIM MILK	STIFF PEAKS.
6 T	COCOA POWDER	
1 T	REAL VANILLA EXTRACT	SPREAD ON CAKE. KEEP CAKE REFRIGERATED.

7-MINUTE ICING

SERVES 12   FAT = TR EA

3	EGG WHITES	HEAT THESE IN THE TOP OF A
1 1/2 C	SUGAR	DOUBLE BOILER. BEAT AT HIGH
5 T	COLD WATER	SPEAD CONSTANTLY FOR 7 MIN.
1 T	BUTTER BUDS	OR UNTIL SOFT PEAKS FORM.
1/4 t	CREAM OF TARTAR	
		REMOVE FROM HEAT.
1/2 t	REAL VANILLA EXTRACT	ADD.
		BEAT UNTIL COOL. REFRIGERATE ICED CAKE.

BRANDY ALEXANDER CAKE

easy   SERVES 12   FAT = TR EA

3/4 C	APPLESAUCE	WHIP THESE FOR 5 MINUTES.
2 C	POWDERED SUGAR	
1 t	FRESH LEMON JUICE	
1 t	REAL VANILLA EXTRACT	
1 1/4 C	EGG BEATERS	
1 3/4 C	FLOUR	SIFT THESE & FOLD INTO ABOVE.
4 t	BAKING POWDER	
1/4 t	NUTMEG	
------	SALT	
		ADD BRANDY.
1/2 C	BRANDY	
		FOLD IN WHITES & POUR INTO 2
6	EGG WHITES, BEATEN STIFF, NOT DRY	LINED & SPRAYED 9" CAKE PANS.

Bake in a pre-heated oven at 325 for 25 minutes or until knife comes out clean.

BRANDY ALEXANDER FROSTING

SERVES 12   FAT = TR EA

Make 7-Minute Icing and add 3 T of Brandy, & a dash of Nutmeg to taste.
Keep refrigerated after icing the cake.

WHITE SPONGE CAKE

easy   SERVES 12   FAT = TR EA

3 1/2 C	CAKE FLOUR	SIFT THESE INGREDIENTS.
2 T	BAKING POWDER	
1/4 C	BUTTER BUDS	
3/4 t	SALT	
3/4 C	APPLESAUCE	WHIP THESE 5 MINUTES & FOLD
2 1/2 C	SUGAR	INTO THE FLOUR MIX.
1 C	SKIM MILK	
2 T	REAL VANILLA EXTRACT	
8	EGG WHITES, BEATEN TO MEDIUM PEAKS	FOLD INTO THE BATTER.

Pour into 2 sprayed & lined, 9" pans & bake in pre-heated oven at 325 for 25-30 minutes or until pick comes out clean. Cool.

BERRY-BERRY FROSTING

SERVES 12   FAT = TR EA

Make 7-Minute Icing & add 3/4 C Seedless Raspberrry Jam (or your favorite) while beating.

FROZEN PARTY ROLL CAKE   SERVES 12   FAT = 1 GM EA

3/4 C	EGG BEATERS	WHIP THESE 5 MINUTES.
1 C	SUGAR	
1/3 C	SKIM MILK	COMBINE & FOLD INTO THE EGG
2 t	REAL VANILLA EXTRACT	MIXTURE.
1 C	CAKE FLOUR	DO NOT STIR TOO MUCH.
2 T	BUTTER BUDS	
1 T	BAKING POWDER	SPREAD ON A SPRAYED & LINED
1/4 t	SALT	JELLY ROLL PAN.

Bake in pre-heated oven at 350 for 12-15 minutes or until pick comes out clean. Roll up (including liner) & let sit 20 minutes. Unroll, remove liner, spread icing (below) & roll up again. Freeze for 6 hours. Remove 30 minutes before serving.

2 C	PREPARED DREAM WHIP	COMBINE & SPREAD OVER THE
1/2 C	FAT-FREE CAKE DECORATIONS	CAKE.

If you'd like a chocolate roll, add to batter: 1/4 C   COCOA POWDER,

                                                1/4 C   POWDERED SUGAR

(This adds 2 1/4 GM Fat to total cake)   1 t   VANILLA EXTRACT

INSTANT DESSERT CAKE   *quick*   SERVES 6   FAT = 1 GM EA

1	ENTENMANN'S FAT-FREE LOAF CAKE	SLICE IN 3 HORIZONTAL SLICES.
1 C	COTTAGE CREAM (p 392)	PUREE THESE & SPREAD ON THE
1 C	POWDERED SUGAR (OR TO TASTE)	3 CAKE SLICES & STACK.
1/2 C	COCOA (OR TO TASTE)	
1/4 C	NON-FAT MILK POWDER	
1 1/2 T	REAL VANILLA EXTRACT	TO SERVE, HEAT JAM & BRANDY
1 T	BUTTER BUDS	FOR SAUCE TO TO SERVE UNDER
		EACH PIECE OF CAKE.
3/4 C	CHERRY PRESERVES (OR YOUR FAVORITE)	
1/4 C	BRANDY	

Even easier: Spread slices with lots of jam, using the same jam for the brandy sauce.

CARROT CAKE

SERVES 8   FAT = TR EA

1 1/4 C	BROWN SUGAR	WHIP THESE FOR 5 MINUTES.
1/4 C	APPLESAUCE	
1/2 C	EGG BEATERS	
1/2 C	NON-FAT YOGURT	
1 t	REAL VANILLA EXTRACT	
1 LB	CARROTS, GRATED (3 CUPS)	STIR INTO ABOVE.
2 1/2 C	FLOUR	SIFT THESE & ADD TO ABOVE.
4 t	BAKING POWDER	(EXCEPT THE RAISINS---
2 t	CINNAMON	DUSTING RAISINS KEEPS THEM
1 t	ALLSPICE	FROM SINKING TO THE BOTTOM
1 t	GROUND GINGER	OF THE BATTER)
1 t	BUTTER BUDS	
1/2 t	SALT	ADD RAISINS LAST.
1/2 C	RAISINS !!!DO NOT OVER MIX!!!	

Bake in sprayed & lined 9" x 9" pan in pre-heated oven at 350 for 40 minutes.

CREAM CHEESE FROSTING

quick   SERVES 8   FAT = TR EA

1/2 C	FAT-FREE CREAM CHEESE	WHISK THESE & SPREAD ON THE
2 C	POWDERED SUGAR (MORE IF NEEDED)	COOLED CAKE.
1/2 C	NON-FAT MILK POWDER	
2 T	ORANGE ZEST, MINCED	

APPLESAUCE CAKE

SERVES 12   FAT = TR EA

1 C	APPLESAUCE	WHIP THESE FOR 5 MINUTES.
2 C	SUGAR	
3/4 C	EGG BEATERS	
2 1/2 C	CAKE FLOUR	COMBINE THESE & ADD TO THE
1 C	RAISINS	ABOVE, ALTERNATELY WITH THE
4 t	BAKING POWDER	BUTTERMILK.
1/2 t	SALT	
1/2 t	CINNAMON !!!DO NOT OVER MIX!!!	
1/2 t	ALLSPICE	
1/2 t	GROUND CLOVES	POUR INTO A SPRAYED & LINED
		9" x 9" PAN.
1/2 C	1% BUTTERMILK	BAKE IN A PRE-HEATED OVEN AT
		325 FOR 35-40 MINUTES OR PICK
		COMES CLEAN.

Try serving this with Non-Fat Vanilla Yogurt.

EASY LEMON CAKE

SERVES 12   FAT = 4 GM EA

1 PKG	DUNCAN HINES LEMON CAKE MIX	
1 PKG	INSTANT LEMON PUDDING MIX	
1 C	EGG BEATERS	!!!DO NOT OVER MIX!!!
3/4 C	SKIM MILK	
3/4 C	APPLESAUCE	
2 T	BUTTER BUDS	

COMBINE ALL & POUR INTO A SPRAYED BUNDT PAN.

BAKE IN PRE-HEATED OVEN AT 350 FOR 55 MINUTES OR PICK COMES CLEAN.

EASY LEMON ICING

FAT = TR

2 C	POWDERED SUGAR
1/4 C	FRESH LEMON JUICE

COMBINE THESE.

Poke holes in Easy Lemon Cake while still warm & drizzle this over.

OATMEAL CAKE

SERVES 12   FAT = TR EA

1 C	QUAKER OATS
1 1/4 C	BOILING WATER

COMBINE & COOL 10 MINUTES.

3/4 C	APPLESAUCE
1 C	SUGAR
1 C	BROWN SUGAR
3/4 C	EGG BEATERS

WHIP THESE FOR 5 MINUTES.

ADD OAT MIXTURE.

2 C	CAKE FLOUR
1 1/2 t	CINNAMON
4 t	BAKING SODA
1 t	NUTMEG
1/2 t	SALT
1 C	RAISINS

FOLD THESE INTO ABOVE & ADD RAISINS. POUR INTO A SPRAYED & LINED 9" x 9" PAN.

BAKE IN PRE-HEATED OVEN AT 350 FOR 40-45 MINUTES.

OATMEAL CAKE ICING

SERVES 12   FAT = TR EA

1/2 C	BROWN SUGAR
1/2 C	NON-FAT MILK POWDER
1/2 C	NO-FAT SOUR CREAM
1/4 C	SKIM MILK
2 t	CORNSTARCH

SIMMER THESE, WHILE STIRRING CONSTANTLY UNTIL THICK.

1 t	REAL VANILLA EXTRACT
1/2 t	COCONUT FLAVORING (OR TO TASTE)
1/3 C	GRAPE-NUTS

ADD THESE & SPREAD ON THE COOLED CAKE.

GINGERBREAD CAKE

SERVES 12   FAT = TR EA

1 C	APPLESAUCE	WHIP THESE FOR 5 MINUTES.
2 C	BROWN SUGAR, PACKED	
1 1/2 C	EGG BEATERS	
2 C	DARK MOLASSES	COMBINE & FOLD INTO ABOVE.
2 C	STRONG DECAF COFFEE	
4 C	CAKE FLOUR	SIFT THESE & ADD TO ABOVE.
2 T	BAKING SODA	
1 T	GROUND GINGER	MIXTURE WILL BE THIN.
2 t	GROUND CLOVES	
2 t	CINNAMON	POUR INTO A SPRAYED & LINED
1 t	PEPPER	9" x 13" PAN.

Bake in pre-heated oven at 350 for 45 minutes or until pick comes out clean. Serve w Fat-Free Frozen Yogurt & Fruit Compote (p 381) or use icing below.

SUGAR GLAZE ICING

(quick)   FAT = TR

2 C	POWDERED SUGAR	SIMMER ALL FOR 2 MINUTES.
3 T	SKIM MILK	
1 t	REAL VANILLA EXTRACT	

GINGERBREAD

SERVES 9   FAT = TR EA

1/2 C	APPLESAUCE	WHIP THESE FOR 5 MINUTES.
1 C	BROWN SUGAR	
3/4 C	EGG BEATERS	
3/4 C	SKIM MILK, SCALDED	COMBINE THESE & ADD TO THE
1/2 C	MOLASSES	ABOVE ALTERNATELY WITH THE
		DRY INGREDIENTS.
2 1/4 C	CAKE FLOUR	
1 T	BAKING POWDER	COMBINE THESE.
2 t	GROUND GINGER	
1 t	CINNAMON	
1/2 t	ALLSPICE	POUR INTO A 9" x 9" LINED &
1/4 t	NUTMEG	SPRAYED PAN.
1/4 t	SALT	PRE-HEAT OVEN TO 350.

Bake for 35-40 minutes or until pick comes out clean. Serve with pumpkin custard or use icing above.

PINEAPPLE CAKE

 SERVES 9   FAT = TR EA

2 1/2 C	CAKE FLOUR	
2 C	SUGAR	
2 C	CRUSHED PINEAPPLE & JUICE	
3/4 C	EGG BEATERS	
4 t	BAKING POWDER	
2 t	REAL VANILLA EXTRACT	
1/4 t	ALMOND FLAVORING	
1/4 t	SALT	

COMBINE ALL & POUR INTO A SPRAYED & LINED 9" x 9" PAN.

BAKE IN A PRE-HEATED OVEN AT 350 FOR 30 MIN. OR UNTIL PICK COMES CLEAN.

PINEAPPLE GLAZE

FOR 1 LARGE CAKE   FAT = TR

3 C	POWDERED SUGAR	
2 T	FROZEN PINEAPPLE CONCENTRATE (OR AS NEEDED)	

DISSOLVE THESE WELL.

You could make almost any flavor glaze, using your favorite frozen juice.

PINA COLADA CAKE

 SERVES 9   FAT = TR EA

3 C	FLOUR	
2 C	SUGAR	
4 t	BAKING SODA	
1/2 t	SALT	

SIFT THESE INGREDIENTS.

2 C	CRUSHED PINEAPPLE & JUICE	
1 C	CORN SYRUP	
1/2 C	EGG BEATERS	
2 t	RUM EXTRACT	
2 t	COCONUT FLAVORING	
1/4 C	SKIM MILK	
8	EGG WHITES, BEATEN STIFF, NOT DRY	

COMBINE & ADD TO ABOVE.

FOLD IN WHITES & POUR IN A SPRAYED & LINED LARGE BUNDT PAN OR A 9" x 13" PAN.

Bake in pre-heated oven at 350 for 45 minutes or until pick comes out clean.

BUTTER RUM GLAZE

FAT = TR

2 C	POWDERED SUGAR	
1/4 C	BUTTER BUDS	
6 T	RUM	
6 T	WATER	
1 T	CORNSTARCH	

SIMMER THESE FOR 3 MINUTES.

IF GLAZING A WARM CAKE, POKE TINY HOLES IN CAKE FIRST.

BASIC CREPES

12 CREPES   FAT = TR EA

1/2 C	EGG BEATERS	
1 1/2 C	SKIM MILK	
1 1/2 C	FLOUR (OR AS NEEDED)	
1 T	BUTTER BUDS	
1/2 t	BAKING POWDER	

WHISK ALL & CHILL 30 MINUTES OR MORE.

TO MAKE SWEET CREPES:
ADD 1 T POWDERED SUGAR.

Spray hot pan with Pam Butter Spray, swirl in small amount of batter to cover bottom. Turn when golden & fry other side. Stack between was paper.

These freeze well & they're great to have on hand. Freeze in boxes so that the edges don't get damaged.

Crepes can be rolled or folded in different ways, some of which are:

Rolled like a burrito
Folded in half
Folded in half, then in half again (these are usually not stuffed)

CHOCOLATE CREPES

12 CREPES   FAT = 1 GM EA

1 C	HONEYDEW MELON BALLS	
1 C	STRAWBERRIES	
1 C	BLUEBERRIES	
6	KIWI, PEELED & SLICED	
1/2 C	KIRSCHWASSER	
1 T	HONEY	

MARINATE THESE 8 HOURS OR AS LONG AS POSSIBLE.

DRAIN.

1 C	EGG BEATERS	
3/4 C	POWDERED SUGAR	
1 1/2 C	CAKE FLOUR	
3/4 C	COCOA POWDER	
3/4 C	SKIM MILK (OR AS NEEDED)	

WHISK THESE & LET SIT 1 HOUR.

FRY AS ABOVE, PLACING EACH COMPLETED CREPE OVER A TEA-CUP TO COOL.

After crepes are cool & will hold the cup shape, fill w fruit, place on dessert plates & top with Kahlua Cream (below).

KAHLUA CREAM

2 CUPS   FAT = TR EA

2 C	FAT-FREE VANILLA YOGURT	
3 T	KAHLUA (OR TO TASTE)	
1 T	POWDERED SUGAR (OR TO TASTE)	

WHISK THESE TOGETHER.

STRAWBERRY CREPES   6 CREPES   FAT = TR EA

1/2 C	SUGAR	COMBINE THESE & LET SIT 30
3 C	STRAWBERRIES, SLICED	MINUTES.
		DRAIN, SAVING LIQUID.
1 T	KIRSCHWASSER OR ARMAGNAC	
1/2 T	CORNSTARCH	COMBINE THESE WITH BERRIES.
1/2 t	REAL VANILLA EXTRACT	FILL CREPES, ROLL UP & BAKE AT 350 FOR 10 MINUTES.
2 C	STRAWBERRIES, SLICED	COMBINE THESE AND PROCESS
1 C	NON-FAT VANILLA YOGURT	CHOP-CHOP.

Spoon sauce over crepes (previous page) & drizzle with reserved liquid. Garnish with any berries not used in stuffing the crepes. This works well with almost any fruit.

APPLE CREPES   *easy*   6 CREPES   FAT = TR EA

4	APPLES, PEELED (SAVE PEELS), SLICED THIN	SIMMER THESE FOR 15 MINUTES.
1/2 C	BROWN SUGAR	
1/2 C	DARK RUM	
1/8 t	CINNAMON	
1/8 t	FRESH NUTMEG	
6	CREPES FROM PREVIOUS PAGE	FILL CREPES, ROLL UP & BAKE AT 350 FOR 10 MINUTES.

APPLE CREAM SAUCE   *quick*   1 CUP   FAT = TR EA

	PEELS FROM APPLES ABOVE, DICED	BOIL FOR 10 MINUTES & DRAIN.
1/2 C	WATER	PUREE, ADDING BACK ENOUGH
1/2 C	SUGAR	OF THE BOILED JUICES TO MAKE A SMOOTH SAUCE.
1/4 C	APPLESAUCE	ADD THESE & SPOON OVER THE
1/4 C	BRANDY	CREPES. SERVE WITH FAT-FREE
1/2 C	FAT-FREE VANILLA YOGURT	FROZEN YOGURT.

CHERRIES JUBILEE   *easy*   SERVES 6   FAT = TR EA

16 OZ CAN	DARK CHERRIES, DRAIN & SAVE JUICE	SIMMER THESE 3 MINUTES AND
1 T	CORNSTARCH	SPOON OVER CREPES (p 370) AND
1 T	ORANGE JUICE	FAT-FREE FROZEN YOGURT.
1/8 t	CINNAMON (OPTIONAL)	
1/2 C	BRANDY, VERY HOT	SPOON OVER FRUIT & FLAME.

GRAHAM CRACKER CRUST

1 CRUST   FAT = 10 GM

1 PKG	GRAHAM CRACKERS (10 ONLY), CRUSHED	
3 T	SUGAR	
2 T	BUTTER BUDS	
2 T	EGG BEATERS (+ OR -)	
	(OR SUBSTITUTE LIQUID BUTTER BUDS)	

WHIRL IN FOOD PROCESSOR. ADD ENOUGH EGG BEATERS TO HOLD TOGETHER WHEN PRESSED INTO A PIE PAN.

Use as is or bake at 350 for 7 minutes.

CHOCOLATE GRAHAM CRACKER CRUST

1 CRUST   FAT = 14 GM

Make plain Graham Cracker Crust & add 2 T COCOA, 2 T POWDERED SUGAR.

CINNAMON GRAHAM CRACKER CRUST

1 CRUST   FAT = 10 GM

Make Plain Graham Cracker Crust & add 1/4 t CINNAMON.

APPLE GRAHAM CRACKER CRUST

1 CRUST   FAT = 10 GM

1 PKG	GRAHAM CRACKERS (10 ONLY), CRUSHED	
3 T	SUGAR	
2 T	BUTTER BUDS	
2 T	APPLESAUCE (+ OR -)	

WHIRL IN FOOD PROCESSOR. ADD ENOUGH APPLESAUCE TO HOLD TOGETHER WHEN PRESSED INTO PIE PAN.

PHYLLO PIE CRUST

1 CRUST   FAT = 4 GM

Lay out a sheet of Phyllo Dough, spray with Pam Butter Spray. Repeat 3 times. Press in a sprayed pie plate, bringing edges up high. Trim edges & spray.

PHYLLO LATTICE (or cut outs)

Lay out Phyllo as above, 4 times. Cut into strips for lattice or shapes.

CRUMBLE (OR STREUSEL) TOPPING

1 TOPPING   FAT = TR

1 C	BROWN SUGAR	
1/4 C	SOFT BREAD CRUMBS	
2 T	APPLESAUCE	
2 T	CINNAMON	

COMBINE & SPRINKLE OVER THE BASE RECIPE.

1 T	BUTTER BUDS	
3 T	HOT WATER	

COMBINE & DRIZZLE OVER. BAKE AS DIRECTED.

BLACK BOTTOM PIE   SERVES 8   FAT = 4 GM EA

BASE:

2 PKG	KNOX GELATIN (SPRINKLED OVER THE MILK)	LET SIT 2 MINUTES, THEN WHISK THESE IN A DOUBLE BOILER TO THICKEN.
4 C	SKIM MILK	
3 C	SUGAR	
1/4 C	NON-FAT MILK POWDER	
1/4 C	BUTTER BUDS	REMOVE FROM HEAT.
1/2 C	CORNSTARCH	
1 1/2 C	EGG BEATERS	TEMPER THESE, RETURN AND HEAT JUST TO THICKEN.
1 T	REAL VANILLA EXTRACT	

!!!DO NOT OVER COOK!!!

BLACK BOTTOM:

6 T	COCOA POWDER	ADD 2/3 OF BASE TO THESE AND POUR IN A CHOCOLATE GRAHAM CRACKER CRUST. CHILL.
1/4 C	HOT WATER	

CREAM TOP:

1/2 C	SKIM MILK	ADD THESE TO THE REST OF THE BASE.
1 C	COTTAGE CREAM (p 392)	
1/2 C	DARK RUM	FOLD IN THE EGG WHITE & POUR ONTO THE COOLED 'BLACK' BOTTOM. CHILL.
1	EGG WHITE, BEATEN STIFF	

CHOCOLATE DRIZZLE:

1/2 t	KNOX GELATIN (SPRINKLED OVER THE MILK)	LET SIT FOR 2 MINUTES.
1/2 C	SKIM MILK	
		ADD & SIMMER OVER BOILING WATER TO DISSOLVE GELATIN.
1/2 C	COCOA POWDER	
3/4 C	HONEY (OR TO TASTE)	
1 t	REAL VANILLA EXTRACT	COOL. DRIZZLE A LACY PATTERN OVER THE TOP. CHILL OVERNIGHT.

KEY LIME PIE   *easy*   SERVES 8   FAT = 2 GM EA

2 PKG	KNOX GELATIN (SPRINKLED OVER THE MILK)	LET SIT 2 MINUTES, THEN HEAT TO DISSOLVE.
1 1/4 C	SKIM MILK	
2 C	SUGAR	
4 T	BUTTER BUDS	
1/4 C	LIME ZEST, MINCED	ADD, COOL TO ROOM TEMP.
4 C	NO-FAT SOUR CREAM (OR YOGURT CHEESE)	WHISK THESE INTO ABOVE AND POUR ALL IN A BAKED GRAHAM CRACKER CRUST.
2 C	FRESH LIME JUICE (OR TO TASTE)	
2-3 DROPS	YELLOW FOOD COLORING	GARNISH WITH KIWI OR LIMES.
1-2 DROPS	GREEN FOOD COLORING	

LEMON MERINGUE PIE

SERVES 8   FAT = 1 GM EA

1 1/4 C	SUGAR	
2 C	SKIM MILK	
1/4 C	NON-FAT MILK POWDER	
6 T	CORNSTARCH	
1 T	LEMON ZEST, MINCED	
1 T	BUTTER BUDS	
1/2 C	EGG BEATERS	
1/2 C	FRESH LEMON JUICE	

!!!DO NOT OVER COOK!!!

WHISK THESE IN THE TOP OF DOUBLE BOILER UNTIL THICK.

CONTINUE TO HEAT FOR 1 MORE MINUTE.

TEMPER THESE & HEAT JUST TO THICKEN. POUR INTO A BAKED PHYLLO CRUST.

4	EGG WHITES, WHIPPED TO MEDIUM PEAKS	
6 T	POWDERED SUGAR	
1/2 t	FRESH LEMON JUICE	

COMBINE THESE AND WHIP TO STIFF PEAKS, NOT DRY.

Spread on pie completely to edges. Bake at 375 for 5 minutes or until golden.

CHOCOLATE CREAM PIE

SERVES 8   FAT = 1 GM EA

3 C	SKIM MILK	
6 T	CORNSTARCH	
2 C	SUGAR	
6 T	COCOA	
1/4 C	NON-FAT MILK POWDER	
1 T	BUTTER BUDS	

WHISK THESE IN THE TOP OF A DOUBLE BOILER UNTIL THICK. CONTINUE TO HEAT FOR 1 MORE MINUTE.

1 1/4 C	EGG BEATERS	
1 T	REAL VANILLA EXTRACT	

TEMPER THESE & HEAT JUST TO THICKEN. POUR IN A BAKED PHYLLO PIE CRUST.

4	EGG WHITES, WHIPPED TO MEDIUM PEAKS	
6 T	POWDERED SUGAR	

COMBINE AND WHIP TO STIFF PEAKS.

Spread on pie completely to edges. Bake at 375 for 5 minutes or until golden.

PEACH PIE

easy   SERVES 8   FAT = 1 GM EA

6 C	PEACHES, PEELED & SLICED	
1/3 C	BOYSENBERRY JAM (OR YOUR FAVORITE)	
1/2 C	SUGAR	
2 T	BUTTER BUDS	
1 T	CORNSTARCH	
1/8 t	NUTMEG	

TOSS THESE INGREDIENTS.

FILL A PHYLLO PIE CRUST. TOP WITH PHYLLO LATTICE. BAKE AT 375 FOR 45 MINUTES.

EASY FRUIT TART

 SERVES 12   FAT = .5 GM EA

1	PHYLLO CRUST, BAKED OR 1 LAYER OF WHITE SPONGE CAKE IN SPRINGFORM	
1 PKG	KNOX GELATIN (SPRINKLED OVER THE MILK)	LET THESE SIT IN THE TOP OF A
1 C	SKIM MILK	DOUBLE BOILER FOR 2 MINUTES.
1 1/2 C	EGG BEATERS	ADD AND HEAT UNTIL SLIGHTLY
1 C	SUGAR	THICKENED.
3 T	BUTTER BUDS	!!!DO NOT OVER COOK!!!
1 t	REAL VANILLA EXTRACT	COOL.
2-3 DROPS	YELLOW FOOD COLORING	
1 C	FAT-FREE VANILLA YOGURT	WHISK THESE IN & POUR INTO A
2 C	FAT-FREE CREAM CHEESE	CRUST OR ONTO THE CAKE IN
2 C	COTTAGE CREAM (p 392)	THE SPRINGFORM PAN.

Arrange 3 types of fruit in large, medium & small circles on top of the pie.
(Peaches, Strawberries, Kiwi, Blueberries, Raspberries or Pineapple work well)

1/2 C	APRICOT JAM, HEATED, PUREED	BRUSH OVER FRUIT & CHILL

APPLE PIE

 SERVES 8   FAT = 1 GM EA

6	GRANNY SMITH APPLES, PEELED & SLICED	COMBINE THESE AND PILE IN A
1 t	FRESH LEMON JUICE (TOSS w APPLES)	PHYLLO PIE CRUST.
1 C	SUGAR	
1 T	FLOUR	
1 T	CINNAMON	
1/2 t	MACE	
1/4 t	NUTMEG	
1/4 C	BUTTER BUDS	COMBINE & DRIZZLE OVER THE
1/4 C	HOT WATER	APPLES.

Top with Phyllo Lattice & bake at 375 for 45 minutes.

SOUR CREAM APPLE PIE

 SERVES 8   FAT = 1 GM EA

Follow the apple pie recipe above, but add the following when tossing apples:

3/4 C NO-FAT SOUR CREAM
1/4 C EGG BEATERS
1 t   REAL VANILLA EXTRACT

MR. MAC'S FROZEN LEMON PIE

SERVES 10   FAT = 1 GM EA

1 1/2 C	SUGAR
2 C	SKIM MILK
1/2 C	NON-FAT MILK POWDER
7 T	CORNSTARCH
2 T	LEMON ZEST, MINCED
2 T	BUTTER BUDS
1 1/2 C	EGG BEATERS
3/4 C	FRESH LEMON JUICE
	!!!DO NOT OVER COOK!!!
------	DREAM WHIP

WHISK THESE IN THE TOP OF A DOUBLE BOILER UNTIL THICK.

CONTINUE TO WHISK, HEAT FOR 1 MORE MINUTE.

TEMPER THESE & HEAT JUST TO THICKEN. POUR IN A GRAHAM CRACKER CRUST. CHILL 6 HOURS, THEN FREEZE OVERNIGHT.

Remove from freezer 15 minutes prior to serving. Pipe Dream Whip around edge.

CHOCOLATE FUDGESCICLE PIE

SERVES 10   FAT = 3 GM EA

3 C	SKIM MILK
6 T	CORNSTARCH
2 C	SUGAR
6 T	COCOA
1/4 C	NON-FAT MILK POWDER
2 T	BUTTER BUDS
1 3/4 C	EGG BEATERS
1 T	REAL VANILLA EXTRACT !!!DO NOT OVER COOK!!!

WHISK THESE IN THE TOP OF A DOUBLE BOILER UNTIL THICK. CONTINUE TO HEAT FOR 1 MORE MINUTE.

TEMPER THESE AND HEAT JUST UNTIL THICKENED.

Pour into a Chocolate Graham Cracker Crust & chill 6 hours, then freeze 6 hours. Remove from freezer 15 minutes before serving. Pipe Dream Whip around edge.

CHERRY (or Blueberry) PIE

easy   SERVES 8   FAT = .5 GM EA

1/4 C	WATER OF FRUIT JUICE
1 C	SUGAR
1 T	CORNSTARCH
4 C	PITTED CHERRIES (OR BLUEBERRIES)
1/2 t	ALMOND FLAVORING

COMBINE & HEAT TO THICKEN.

ADD AND POUR INTO A PHYLLO CRUST. TOP WITH PHYLLO CUT OUTS (p 372).

Bake at 375 for 30 minutes.

MOM'S APPLE BETTY

SERVES 6   FAT = TR EA

6 C	APPLES, CHOPPED	PUT IN A SPRAYED CASSEROLE.
2 C	SOFT BREAD CRUMBS	SPRINKLE OVER APPLES.
1/2 C	BROWN SUGAR	COMBINE & SPRINKLE OVER.
1/2 t	CINNAMON	
1/4 t	NUTMEG	
2 T	BUTTER BUDS	COMBINE & DRIZZLE OVER.
3 T	HOT WATER	BAKE AT 350 FOR 35 MINUTES.

Serve with Heavenly Clafouti Sauce (p 358).

CHERRY CRISP

SERVES 6   FAT = TR EA

6 C	PITTED CHERRIES	COMBINE & TOSS THESE INTO A
1/2 C	POWDERED SUGAR	SPRAYED, 3 QUART DISH.
1 T	BUTTER BUDS	
2 t	CORNSTARCH	
2 t	FRESH LEMON JUICE	
1 T	BUTTER BUDS	COMBINE THESE
1 1/2 C	SOFT BREAD CRUMBS (p 391)	
1 C	SUGAR	ADD BUTTER BUDS MIXTURE
1/4 C	APPLESAUCE (OR AS NEEDED)	BELOW & SPRINKLE OVER.
2 T	BUTTER BUDS	BAKE AT 350 FOR 45 MINUTES
3 T	HOT WATER	

BLUEBERRY CRISP

SERVES 6   FAT = TR EA

6 C	BLUEBERRIES	COMBINE & POUR IN A SPRAYED
2 T	CORNSTARCH	3 QUART DISH.
1 1/2 C	SOFT BREAD CRUMBS	COMBINE THESE.
1 C	SUGAR	ADD THE BUTTER BUDS MIXTURE
1/4 C	APPLESAUCE (OR AS NEEDED)	BELOW & SPRINKLE OVER.
2 T	BUTTER BUDS	BAKE AT 350 FOR 30 MINUTES.
3 T	HOT WATER	

PEACH CRUMBLE

easy   SERVES 6   FAT = TR EA

6 C	PEACHES, PEELED & SLICED	COMBINE, TOSS AND PLACE IN A
1	LEMON, JUICED	SPRAYED DISH.
1/2 C	SUGAR	
1 t	CINNAMON	
1/4 t	NUTMEG	
1 C	SOFT BREAD CRUMBS	TOSS THESE & ADD THE BUTTER
1/2 C	BROWN SUGAR	BUDS MISTURE.
1/4 C	APPLESAUCE (OR AS NEEDED)	
1/4 C	QUICK COOKING OATS	SPRINKLE OVER THE PEACHES.
2 T	BUTTER BUDS	BAKE AT 350 FOR 30 MINUTES.
3 T	HOT WATER	SERVE WITH VANILLA FAT-FREE FROZEN YOGURT OR HEAVENLY CLAFOUTI SAUCE (p 358).

PLUM PHYLLO TURNOVERS

SERVES 8   FAT = 1 GM EA

2 LBS	BLACK PLUMS, PITTED, QUARTERED	COMBINE THESE & SIMMER FOR 1
1/2 C	HONEY	HOUR.
1/3 C	WATER	
2 SL	LEMON PEEL	REMOVE LEMON PEEL.
1	CINNAMON STICK	
1/4 t	GROUND CLOVES	
2 T	CORNSTARCH	COMBINE & ADD TO ABOVE TO
3 T	WATER	THICKEN. COOL WELL.

Layer 2 sheets of Phyllo Dough with Pam Butter sprayed in between, trim into a square. Place 3 spoons of plums in each near a corner. Roll once, tuck ends in, & finish rolling up like an eggroll.

Repeat 7 times, place on a lined pan & spray each.. Bake at 375 for 25 minutes. Serve with Vanilla or Blueberry Fat-Free Frozen Yogurt.

EASIER FRUIT TURNOVERS

SERVES 8   FAT = TR EA

Just use canned pie fillings & finish as above.

SOUFFLE WHITES

BASE FOR SOUFFLE'S   FAT = TR EA

8		EGG WHITES, BEATEN TO MEDIUM PEAKS
1/4 C		SUGAR
1 t		CREAM OF TARTAR

COMBINE AND BEAT TO MOIST, STIFF PEAKS. FOLD 1/4 INTO THE BASE VERY WELL. THEN FOLD IN THE REST.

Spray 8 ramekins with Pam Butter Spray & sprinkle well with sugar. Bake in a pre-heated 350 oven as directed.

BANANA SOUFFLE w CHOCOLATE RUM SAUCE

SERVES 8   FAT = 1 GM EA

1 C	MASHED BANANAS
1/2 C	POWDERED SUGAR
1 T	FRESH LEMON JUICE
1 T	EGG BEATERS
1 BATCH	SOUFFLE WHITES (ABOVE)

WHISK THESE VERY WELL.

FOLD IN SOUFFLE WHITES AND BAKE AS ABOVE FOR 13 MIN.

CHOCOLATE RUM SAUCE

1 CUP   FAT = 8 GM EA

3/4 C	SKIM MILK
3/4 C	COCOA POWDER
3/4 C	POWDERED SUGAR
1/2 C	NON-FAT MILK POWDER (OR MORE)
1/4 C	DARK RUM (OR TO TASTE)

SIMMER THESE TO MELT.

SPLIT SOUFFLE'S & SPOON IN THIS SAUCE. SERVE IMMEDIATELY.

GRAND MARNIER SOUFFLE

SERVES 8   FAT = TR EA

1/2 C	POWDERED SUGAR
1/4 C	CAKE FLOUR
1/4 C	SKIM MILK
1/4 C	GRAND MARNIER
1 BATCH	SOUFFLE WHITES (ABOVE)

WHISK THESE VERY WELL.

FOLD IN SOUFFLE WHITES AND BAKE AS ABOVE FOR 12 MIN.

SERVE IMMEDIATELY.

CHOCOLATE SOUFFLE

SERVES 8   FAT = .5 GM EA

1/2 C	POWDERED SUGAR
1/4 C	COCOA POWDER
1/4 C	SKIM MILK
2 T	EGG BEATERS
1 t	REAL VANILLA EXTRACT
1 BATCH	SOUFFLE WHITES (ABOVE)

WHISK THESE VERY WELL.

FOLD IN SOUFFLE WHITES AND BAKE AS ABOVE FOR 13 MIN.

SERVE w HEAVENLY CLAFOUTI SAUCE.

EASY FRUIT SOUFFLE

SERVES 8   FAT = TR EA

1/2 C	SUGAR	
1/2 C	APRICOT JAM (OR YOUR FAVORITE)	
1/4 C	GRAND MARNIER	
1 BATCH	SOUFFLE WHITES (PREVIOUS PAGE)	

WHISK THESE VERY WELL.

FOLD IN SOUFFLE WHITES AND BAKE AS DIRECTED FOR 12 MIN.

SERVE IMMEDIATELY.

This works with any seedless jam or marmalade. Try experimenting with Brandy, Rum, Chambord or your favorite liqueur.

FRUIT SOUFFLE SAUCE

easy

2 CUPS   FAT = TR EA

1 C	NO-FAT SOUR CREAM
1/2 C	POWDERED SUGAR
1/2 C	EGG BEATERS
1/2 C	JAM (TO MATCH THE SOUFFLE')
1/4 C	LIQUEUR

WHISK THESE IN THE TOP OF A DOUBLE BOILER UNTIL THICK.

SPOON OVER HOT SOUFFLE'S & & SERVE IMMEDIATELY.

COLD LEMON SOUFFLE

SERVES 8   FAT = TR EA

2 PKG	KNOX GELATIN (SPRINKLED OVER THE MILK)
2 C	SKIM MILK
1 C	SUGAR
3/4 C	EGG BEATERS
1/2 C	NON-FAT MILK POWDER
1 C	FRESH LEMON JUICE
1 T	LEMON ZEST, MINCED
1 BATCH	SOUFFLE WHITES (PREVIOUS PAGE)

LET SIT FOR 2 MINUTES.
WHISK ALL IN THE TOP OF A DOUBLE BOILER & HEAT UNTIL THICK.
!!!DO NOT OVER COOK!!!

ADD THESE & COOL 30 MINUTES OR UNTIL ROOM TEMPERATURE.

FOLD IN 1/3 & THEN THE 2/3 LEFT. BLEND VERY WELL.

Pour into 8 sprayed & sugared ramekins with 2" collars (p 396). Do not bake. Chill 6 hours. Remove collars to serve. Garnish with mint leaves.

CREPE SOUFFLE'S

SERVES 12   FAT DEPENDS ON THE RECIPE USED

12	CREPES (p 120, 122, 370)
1 BATCH	SOUFFLE RECIPE (YOUR CHOICE)

PLACE IN SPRAYED MUFFIN TINS. FILL WITH SOUFFLE   MIX & FOLD IN THE EDGES OF CREPES TO COVER.

Bake in pre-heated 375 oven for 15 minutes. Serve with the souffle's matching sauce under the crepe 'Bundle' & also spoon some sauce over each.

THESE ARE GREAT OVER FAT-FREE ICE CREAM OR FROZEN YOGURT!

APPLE COMPOTE

 easy   SERVES 8   FAT = TR EA

8	APPLES, PEELED, SLICED IN EIGHTHS	SIMMER THESE 20 MINUTES OR
1 C	SUGAR	UNTIL TENDER.
1/2 C	APPLE JUICE (& WATER AS NEEDED)	
ZEST OF 1	LEMON, MINCED	
1	LEMON, JUICED	
2 T	BUTTER BUDS	SERVE OVER GINGERBREAD w
2 T	APPLE JELLY	FAT-FREE FROZEN YOGURT.
2 T	DRY SHERRY	

PINEAPPLE COMPOTE

 easy   SERVES 4   FAT = TR EA

1 C	DRY WHITE WINE	SIMMER THESE 15-20 MINUTES.
1/2 C	WATER (OR AS NEEDED)	
1/4 C	SUGAR	
4	DRIED APRICOTS, HALVED	
4	DRIED FIGS, HALVED	
2	DRIED PRUNES, HALVED	
2 T	BUTTER BUDS	ADD THESE & SIMMER 10 MIN.
2 T	CRYSTALLIZED GINGER, CRUSHED	
1	PINEAPPLE, WEDGED	SERVE WARM OR COLD.
1 t	REAL VANILLA EXTRACT	

BRANDIED FRUIT COMPOTE

easy   SERVES 8   FAT = TR EA

1 C	FROZEN PINEAPPLE JUICE CONCENTRATE	SIMMER THESE 20 MINUTES.
4 C	STRAWBERRIES, STEMMED & HALVED	
8	PEACHES, PEELED & SLICED	
1 C	BLUEBERRIES	
2	BANANAS	PUREE THESE & ADD TO ABOVE.
1/2 C	BRANDY	

If you have an ice cream maker, great! Have fun with these recipes!!

If you don't have one, don't worry, there are now very good commercial Fat-Free Frozen Yogurts & Low-Fat Ice Creams.

In other words...these recipes are designed to work with an ice cream maker.

ICE CREAM BASE I   SERVES 12   FAT = TR EA

1 PKG	KNOX GELATIN (SPRINKLED ON VANILLA)	LET SIT FOR 2 MINUTES.
2 T	REAL VANILLA EXTRACT	
4 C	COTTAGE CREAM (p 392)	COMBINE ALL & PROCESS IN ICE
2 C	YOGURT CHEESE (p 393)	CREAM MAKER.
2 C	NON-FAT VANILLA YOGURT	
1 C	HONEY	
1 t	BUTTER FLAVORING	

OPTION: Add fruits or other flavorings during final minutes of processing.

ICE CREAM BASE II   SERVES 8   FAT = TR EA

1 PKG	KNOX GELATIN (SPRINKLED ON VANILLA)	LET SIT FOR 2 MINUTES.
2 T	REAL VANILLA EXTRACT	MICROWAVE FOR 30 SECONDS TO
		DISSOLVE THE GELATIN.
3 C	NON-FAT YOGURT CHEESE	ADD & PROCESS IN ICE CREAM
2 C	COTTAGE CREAM (p 392)	MAKER.
3/4 C	MAPLE SYRUP OR OTHER FLAVORS	
1 t	BUTTER FLAVORING	

ORANGE BUTTERMILK ICE CREAM   SERVES 12   FAT = 2 GM EA

4 C	1% BUTTERMILK	COMBINE & PROCESS IN AN ICE
4 C	NON-FAT VANILLA YOGURT	CREAM MAKER.
1 1/2 C	SUGAR	
1/2 C	GRAND MARNIER	
1/3 C	ORANGE ZEST, MINCED	
1 t	BUTTER FLAVORING	
1 t	ALMOND FLAVORING	
1/2 t	REAL VANILLA EXTRACT	

APRICOT SHERBET

easy　　SERVES 4　　FAT = TR EA

2 C	APRICOT OR PEACH NECTAR
2 T	FRESH LIME JUICE
3/4 C	SUGAR
3/4 C	1% BUTTERMILK

PROCESS IN AN ICE CREAM MAKER.

COFFEE SHERBET

easy　　SERVES 6　　FAT = TR EA

4 C	BREWED STRONG DECAF COFFEE, CHILLED
1 C	SUGAR
1/2 C	1% BUTTERMILK
1 t	BUTTER FLAVORING
1 t	REAL VANILLA EXTRACT

PROCESS IN AN ICE CREAM MAKER.

FRUIT SHERBET

easy　　SERVES 10　　FAT = TR EA

4 C	SKIM MILK
2 C	SUGAR
1 t	BUTTER BUDS
1 1/2 C	STRAWBERRIES, DICED
2	BANANAS, DICED
1/4 C	FRESH LEMON JUICE
1/4 C	FRESH LIME JUICE
1 t	REAL VANILLA EXTRACT
1 t	LEMON ZEST, MINCED
1 t	LIME ZEST, MINCED

PROCESS IN AN ICE CREAM MAKER.

APPLE SORBET

easy   SERVES 4   FAT = TR EA

1 C	APPLE JUICE	HEAT THESE TO DISSOLVE.
1 C	SUGAR	COOL.

2 C	COLD APPLE JUICE	ADD & PROCESS IN ICE CREAM
1 t	FRESH LEMON JUICE	MAKER.
1/2 t	REAL VANILLA EXTRACT	

BLACKBERRY SORBET

easy   SERVES 6   FAT = TR EA

4 C	BLACKBERRIES	HEAT THESE TO DISSOLVE.
1 C	WATER	COOL.
1/2 C	SUGAR	PUREE, STRAIN OUT SEEDS & CHILL.
2 T	BLACKBERRY LIQUEUR	ADD & PROCESS IN ICE CREAM MAKER.

BLUEBERRY SORBET

easy   SERVES 4   FAT = TR EA

1 C	JUICE FROM BERRIES (& WATER IF NEEDED)	HEAT THESE TO DISSOLVE.
1/2 C	SUGAR	COOL.

15 OZ	CANNED WILD BLUEBERRIES	ADD & PROCESS IN ICE CREAM MAKER.

GRAPEFRUIT SORBET

easy   SERVES 6   FAT = TR EA

1 C	FRESH RUBY GRAPEFRUIT JUICE	HEAT THESE TO DISSOLVE.
1 C	SUGAR	COOL.

3 C	FRESH RUBY GRAPEFRUIT JUICE	ADD & PROCESS IN ICE CREAM
1	GRAPEFRUIT, ZESTED	MAKER.
1/4 C	PINK COLD DUCK	

LIME SORBET

easy   SERVES 6   FAT = TR EA

1 C	WATER	HEAT THESE TO DISSOLVE.
1 C	SUGAR	COOL.

2 C	WATER	ADD & PROCESS IN ICE CREAM
1 C	FRESH LIME JUICE	MAKER.
1	LIME, ZESTED, MINCED	
1 DROP	GREEN FOOD COLORING	

MANGO SORBET

easy   SERVES 12   FAT = TR EA

4 C	WATER	HEAT THESE TO DISSOLVE.
2 C	SUGAR	COOL.
4 C	MANGO PUREE	ADD & PROCESS IN ICE CREAM
1 C	MANGO SLICED	MAKER.
1/2 C	FRESH LEMON JUICE	
2 T	GRAND MARNIER	

CHOCOLATE ORANGE SORBET

easy   SERVES 6   FAT = 3 GM EA

2 C	SUGAR	HEAT THESE TO DISSOLVE.
2 C	COCOA	COOL.
3 1/2 C	WATER	
1 T	HONEY	
1/2 C	FRESH ORANGE JUICE	ADD & PROCESS IN ICE CREAM
3 T	ORANGE ZEST, MINCED	MAKER.

ORANGE JUICE SORBET

easy   SERVES 8   FAT = TR EA

7 C	FRESH ORANGE JUICE	PROCESS IN ICE CREAM MAKER.
1/2 C	SUGAR	
3 T	ORANGE ZEST, MINCED	
2 T	CONTREAU	
1 t	VANILLA NUT BUTTER EXTRACT	

PINEAPPLE SORBET

easy   SERVES 4   FAT = TR EA

4 C	PINEAPPLE JUICE	PROCESS IN ICE CREAM MAKER.
2 T	COCONUT FLAVORING	
ZEST OF 1	LIME & JUICE	

TANGERINE SORBET

easy   SERVES 6   FAT = TR EA

4 C	FRESH TANGERINE JUICE	HEAT THESE TO DISSOLVE.
1 1/2 C	SUGAR	COOL.
2 T	TANGERINE ZEST, MINCED	PROCESS IN ICE CREAM MAKER.
3 T	GRAND MARNIER	

TROPICAL SORBET

easy   SERVES 10   FAT = TR EA

1 C	WATER	
1/2 C	SUGAR	

HEAT THESE TO DISSOLVE.
COOL.

4 C	FRESH ORANGE JUICE
2 C	CRUSHED PINEAPPLE
1 C	BANANA, MASHED
1/2 C	FRESH LEMON JUICE
1 T	COCONUT FLAVORING

ADD & PROCESS IN ICE CREAM
MAKER.

WATERMELON SORBET

easy   SERVES 4   FAT = TR EA

4 C	WATERMELON JUICE
1/2 C	SUGAR

HEAT THESE TO DISSOLVE.
COOL.

2 T	MADORI LIQUEUR

ADD & PROCESS IN ICE CREAM
MAKER.

GRAPE WINE SORBET

easy   SERVES 4   FAT = TR EA

1 C	WATER
1 C	SUGAR
1 C	WHITE GRAPE JUICE
1 C	RED GRAPE JUICE
1/2 C	SWEET WHITE WINE

HEAT THESE TO DISSOLVE.
COOL.
ADD & PROCESS IN ICE CREAM
MAKER.

SPARKLING WINE SORBET

easy   SERVES 6   FAT = TR EA

1 C	WATER
1 C	SUGAR

HEAT THESE TO DISSOLVE.
COOL.

2 C	ASTI SPUMANTE
1/4 C	WATER
2 T	FRESH LEEMON JUICE
1 t	REAL VANILLA EXTRACT

ADD & PROCESS IN ICE CREAM
MAKER.

ICED FRUIT SALAD

SERVES 12   FAT = TR EA

| 1 C | LIQUID FROM APPRICOTS BELOW | HEAT TO DISSOLVE. |
| 1 C | SUGAR | COOL. |

1 C	COTTAGE CREAM (p 392)	PUREE THESE INGREDIENTS.
1/4 C	NON-FAT MILK POWDER	
3	BANANAS, MASHED	
3 T	FRESH LEMON JUICE	
3/4 C	FROZEN ORANGE JUICE CONCENTRATE	

2 LBS	FROZEN STRAWBERRIES	COMBINE ALL AND POUR INTO LINED MUFFIN TINS.
2 C	CRUSHED PINEAPPLE	FREEZE, THEN POP OUT & STORE
2 C	CANNED APRICOTS, SLICED	IN A ZIPLOC BAG.

To serve, thaw 15 minutes, turn upside down on lettuce lined plates. Remove liners, surround with Creme Anglaise (p 354) or Sauce Ambrosia below.

SAUCE AMBROSIA   (CUSTARD SAUCE)

3 CUPS   FAT = TR EA

1 C	EGG BEATERS	WHISK THESE IN THE TOP OF A DOUBLE BOILER UNTIL IT STARTS
1/2 C	SUGAR	TO THICKEN.
3/4 C	SKIM MILK	REMOVE FROM HEAT
3 T	GRAND MARNIER	

!!!DO NOT OVER COOK!!!

| 1 C | NO-FAT SOUR CREAM | FOLD IN THESE. |
| 1/4 C | POWDERED SUGAR | |

CHOCOLATE APRICOT SAUCE

4 CUPS   FAT = 2 GM EA

| 2 C | SKIM MILK | COMBINE THESE WELL. |
| 2 T | CORNSTARCH | |

2 C	BROWN SUGAR	ADD REMAINING ITEMS.
1/2 C	COCOA	
2 C	NON-FAT MILK POWDER	HEAT & WHISK CONSTANTLY TO THICKEN.
1/2 C	APRICOT JAM	
1/4 C	APRICOT BRANDY	
1 T	BUTTER BUDS	

CARAMEL SAUCE

1 1/2 CUPS   AT = TR EA 1/2 CUP

1 C	BROWN SUGAR	COMBINE THESE IN THE TOP OF A
1/2 C	CORN SYRUP	DOUBLE BOILER.
1/2 C	SKIM MILK	HEAT, WHISKING CONSTANTLY
1 T	CORNSTARCH	UNTIL THICKENED.
1/4 C	NON-FAT MILK POWDER	
2 T	BUTTER BUDS	REMOVE FROM HEAT.
		TEMPER AND RETURN TO HEAT
1/4 C	EGG BEATERS	BRIEFLY TO THICKEN.
1 t	REAL VANILLA EXTRACT	REMOVE & ADD VANILLA.

!!!DO NOT OVER COOK!!!

CHERRY SAUCE

quick   4 CUPS   FAT = TR EA

2 C	CHERRY PIE FILLING	PUREE THESE INGREDIENTS.
1 C	SUGAR	
1/4 C	KIRSCHWASSER	SERVE WARM OR COLD.

For a change, you might like to add 1/8 t of cinnamon.

CHOCOLATE SAUCE

2 1/2 CUPS   FAT = 3 GM EA

2 C	SKIM MILK	COMBINE THESE IN THE TOP OF A
3 T	CORNSTARCH	DOUBLE BOILER & HEAT UNTIL
1 1/2 C	SUGAR	THICKENED.
3/4 C	COCOA	
1/2 C	NON-FAT MILK POWDER	REMOVE FROM HEAT.
3 T	BUTTER BUDS	WHISK IN EGG BEATERS & HEAT

!!!DO NOT OVER COOK!!! JUST TO THICKEN.

| 1/2 C | EGG BEATERS | |
| 2 t | REAL VANILLA EXTRACT | ADD LAST. |

PEACH SAUCE

quick   4 CUPS   FAT = TR EA

1 C	PEACH SYRUP	PUREE AND HEAT TO THICKEN.
1 T	CORNSTARCH	
3 C	CANNED PEACHES, DRAINED	
2 T	SUGAR (OR TO TASTE)	

DRUNKEN RAISIN SAUCE

easy   4 CUPS   FAT = TR EA

3 C	RAISINS	SIMMER THESE FOR 30 MINUTES.
2 C	SKIM MILK	
1 C	BRANDY	
1 C	BROWN SUGAR	REMOVE FROM HEAT.
1/4 C	BUTTER BUDS	
1/2 t	CINNAMON (OR TO TASTE)	
3 T	CORNSTARCH (SLIGHTLY ROUNDED)	COMBINE THESE, ADD, & HEAT
1 C	SKIM MILK	UNTIL THICKENED.

HOLIDAY SAUCE

quick   1 1/2 CUP   FAT = TR EA 1/2 CUP

1/2 C	ORANGE JUICE (OR YOUR FAVORITE)	WHISK THESE WELL AND HEAT
1/2 C	WATER	UNTIL THICKENED.
1 T	CORNSTARCH, SLIGHTLY ROUNDED	
1/2 C	CURRANT JAM (OR YOUR FAVORITE)	
1/2 C	RAISINS, CHERRIES OR DATES, CHOPPED	
1/4 C	BROWN SUGAR	
1/4 t	ALLSPICE, MACE, CINNAMON OR NUTMEG	

CRANBERRY BOURBON SAUCE

easy   3 CUPS   FAT = TR EA

1 LB	CRANBERRIES	TOSS THESE AND POUR INTO A
2 C	SUGAR	SPRAYED 9" x 13" BAKING DISH.
1 T	LEMON ZEST, MINCED	
1/4 t	CINNAMON	BAKE AT 350 FOR 1 HOUR.
1/4 C	BOURBON	ADD BOURBON & PROCESS CHOP-CHOP. CHILL.

RASPBERRY SAUCE

quick   1 CUP   FAT = TR EA

12 OZ	FROZEN RASPBERRIES	PROCESS IN A FOOD MILL TO REMOVE SEEDS. (OR USE SEEDLESS JAM & USE LESS HONEY)
1/4 C	HONEY	
3 T	KIRSCHWASSER OR BRANDY (OR TO TASTE)	COMBINE ALL.

You could substitute strawberries & you wouldn't have to remove the seeds.

WHIP CREAM TOPPING

easy   2 CUPS   FAT = TR EA

1 t	KNOX GELATIN (SPRINKLED OVER THE MILK)	LET SIT 2 MINUTES.
1/2 C	SKIM MILK	
1/2 C	EVAPORATED SKIM MILK	ADD THESE & SIMMER JUST TO DISSOLVE GELATIN & SUGAR.
1/4 C	NON-FAT MILK POWDER	
1/4 C	SUGAR	
1/4 t	REAL VANILLA EXTRACT	ADD VANILLA & FREEZE FOR 30 MINUTES. BEAT AT HIGH SPEED TO STIFF PEAKS.

BANANA SAUCE I OR II

quick   2 CUPS   FAT = TR EA

I			**II**	
2	BANANAS		2	BANANAS
1/2 C	NON-FAT YOGURT		1 C	NO-FAT SOUR CREAM
1/2 C	NO-FAT SOUR CREAM		4 T	BROWN SUGAR
1/2 C	FRESH ORANGE JUICE		1 t	LEMON JUICE
1 T	FRESH LEMON JUICE			(OR TO TASTE)
1 T	HONEY			
1/2 t	POPPY SEEDS (OPTIONAL)		PUREE EITHER RECIPE.	

FRUIT SAUCE

quick   3 CUPS   FAT = TR EA

3 C	MANGO (OR BLUEBERRIES OR APRICOTS OR PAPAYAS OR PLUMS ETC.)	
1/4 C	FRESH ORANGE JUICE	
2 T	SUGAR OR HONEY	PUREE ALL INGREDIENTS.
1 T	FRESH LEMON JUICE	
1/4 C	FRUIT LIQUEUR (OPTIONAL-TRY TO MATCH THE FRUIT YOU'RE USING)	

OPTIONS: MINCED GINGER, MAPLE SYRUP, MINCED GARLIC, MINCED CITRUS ZEST, CURRY, SHERRY VINEGAR, MATCHING JAMS OR PRESERVES, NO-FAT CREAM CHEESE.

QUICK FRUIT SAUCE

quick   2 CUPS   FAT = TR EA

1 C	NON-FAT YOGURT (FRUIT FLAVOR OF YOUR CHOICE)	
1 C	MATCHING FRUIT, PEELED, PITTED, DICED	PUREE ALL INGREDIENTS.
1/4 C	MATCHING FRUIT JAM OR PRESERVES	SEASON WITH CINNAMON OR NUTMEG OR ALLSPICE.

QUICK LEMON SAUCE

quick   1 3/4 CUPS   FAT = TR EA

1 1/2 C	LEMON CURD
3 T	FROZEN LEMONADE CONCENTRATE
1 T	LEMON ZEST

Base Recipes

Don't throw away any Fat-Free Bread. Just make Soft Bread Crumbs by tearing it in small pieces & process in a food processor to fine crumbs. Store in an air tight container.

COTTAGE CREAM
quick   1 CUP   FAT = TR EA 1/2 CUP

| 8 OZ | NON-FAT COTTAGE CHEESE | PUREE THESE VERY, VERY WELL. |
| 3 T | NON-FAT MILK POWDER | |

TANGY COTTAGE CREAM
1 CUP   FAT = TR EA 1/2 CUP

Make Cottage Cream & add 1-2 T Fresh Lemon Juice while pureeing.

SOUR COTTAGE CREAM
1 CUP   FAT = TR EA 1/2 CUP

Make Cottage Cream, add 1/2 C 1% Buttermilk or Non-Fat Yogurt while pureeing.

MOCK SOUR CREAM
quick   2 CUPS   FAT = TR EA 1/2 CUP

2 C	COTTAGE CREAM (ABOVE)	PUREE THESE. ADD THE LEMON
1/2 C	1% BUTTERMILK	LAST WHILE PROCESSING.
1 T	FRESH LEMON JUICE	

OPTIONS: CHIVES, GARLIC, GINGER, CUMIN, CURRY, HERBS, TABASCO, CURRY
BASIL, CHILI POWDER, WORCESTERSHIRE, CAVENDER'S GREEK SEASONING.

SWEET COTTAGE CREAM
1 CUP   FAT = TR EA 1/2 CUP

Make Cottage Cream, add these ingredients while pureeing:

| 1 t | REAL VANILLA EXTRACT |
| 1/2 C | POWDERED SUGAR (OR TO TASTE) |

LIGHT CHEESE I
3 CUPS   FAT = 10 GM EA

1 C	NON-FAT YOGURT CHEESE (p 393)	PUREE THESE INGREDIENTS.
2 C	PART SKIM RICOTTA CHEESE	
1/4 C	NON-FAT MILK POWDER	OPTIONS: GARLIC, HERBS, ETC.
1 T	BUTTER BUDS	
1/4 t	SALT	

LIGHT CHEESE II
2 CUPS   FAT = 10 GM EA

1 C	NON-FAT COTTAGE CHEESE	PUREE THESE INGREDIENTS.
1 C	NON-FAT YOGURT CHEESE (p 393)	
1/2 C	PARMESAN CHEESE	
2 T	BUTTER BUDS (DISSOLVED IN 2 T HOT WATER)	

HOT FUDGE SAUCE

1 1/2 CUPS   AT = .25 GM EA T

1/2 C	COLD WATER	COMBINE THESE IN THE TOP OF A
2 T	CORNSTARCH	DOUBLE BOILER.
2 C	POWDERED SUGAR	ADD & HEAT UNTIL THICKENED.
1/2 C	COCOA	REMOVE FROM HEAT.
6 T	BUTTER BUDS	
1/2 C	EGG BEATERS	TEMPER EGGS AND HEAT AGAIN
	!!!DO NOT OVER COOK!!!	WHISKING CONSTANTLY.
		(JUST UNTIL THICKENED)
1/2 t	REAL VANILLA EXTRACT	ADD LAST.

When serving over Fat-Free Frozen Yogurt or Ice Cream, it works better if the sauce is warm, not hot. Fat-Free melts more easily than the fatty ice creams.

CHOCOLATE CHIPS SUBSTITUTE REPLACES 1 OZ MELTED CHIPS   FAT = 1.2 GM

2 T	UNSWEETENED COCOA POWDER	BLEND THESE TOGETHER.
2 T	HOT WATER	
2 T	HONEY	
2 t	BUTTER BUDS	
1/2 t	REAL VANILLA EXTRACT	

SUGAR SYRUP (SIMPLE SYRUP)

1 CUP   FAT = TR

2 C	SUGAR	BOIL THESE TO DISSOLVE.
1 C	WATER	

MOCK SWEETENED CONDENSED MILK

2 1/4 C   FAT = 4 GM EA

1 C	SKIM MILK, SCALDED (OR AS NEEDED FOR CONSISTENCY)	
4 C	NON-FAT MILK POWDER	
1/4 C	BUTTER BUDS	PUREE ALL INGREDIENTS.
2 C	POWDERED SUGAR	

YOGURT CHEESE

2 CUPS   FAT = 1 GM EA

32 OZ	NON-FAT YOGURT (MADE WITHOUT GELATIN)

Place in a yogurt funnel or a strainer lined w paper towels or coffee filter. Let sit over a bowl for 24 hours in the refrigerator. Do not let the strainer touch the liquid that gathers in the bottom of the bowl.

COULIS   FAT = TR EA

A Coulis is simply a puree of vegetables or fruits (either raw or cooked) with or without various additions:

VEGETABLES	& HERBS	FRUITS	& SPICES
"	& WINE	"	& SWEETENERS
"	& SKIM MILK	"	& SKIM MILK
"	& FAT-FREE STOCK	"	& FRUIT JUICES
"	& NO-FAT SOUR CREAM	"	& LIQUEURS
"	& VINEGAR	"	& FAT-FREE SOUR
		"	& CREAM

These are used as sauces, to decorate plates & other sauces, as well as food. See p 261, 263, 265.

APRICOT GLAZE   1 CUP   FAT = TR EA

1 C	APRICOT PRESERVES (OR YOUR FAVORITE)	COMBINE & HEAT THESE.
2 T	RUM, ORANGE JUICE OR GRAND MARNIER	

BUTTERMILK GLAZE   1 CUP   FAT = 2 GM EA

1 C	1% BUTTERMILK	COMBINE & HEAT THESE.
1 C	SUGAR	
3 T	BUTTER BUDS	
1/4 C	SKIM MILK	COMBINE WELL, WHISK IN AND
1 T	CORNSTARCH	HEAT TO THICKEN.
1/4 t	BAKING SODA	REMOVE FROM HEAT.
1 T	REAL VANILLA EXTRACT	ADD LAST.

SUGAR GLAZE   1/2 CUP   FAT = TR EA

1 C	POWDERED SUGAR	HEAT TO DISSOLVE.
1 T	SKIM MILK	
1/2 t	REAL VANILLA EXTRACT	

BROWN SUGAR GLAZE   1 CUP   FAT = TR EA

1 C	SKIM MILK	COMBINE THESE & THEN BOIL
1 T	CORNSTARCH	FOR 2 MINUTES.
1/2 C	BROWN SUGAR	
1/4 C	BUTTER BUDS	

CHEESE SAUCE

SEE ALSO MOCK HOLLANDAISE (p 257)

32 OZ   FAT = 1 GM EA

1 C	SKIM MILK	COMBINE THESE IN THE TOP OF A DOUBLE BOILER AND HEAT TO THICKEN.
1 T	CORNSTARCH (SLIGHTLY ROUNDED)	
1 C	NO-FAT SOUR CREAM	ADD THESE TO MELT CHEESE.
1/2 C	PARMESAN CHEESE	
1/4 C	FAT-FREE PARMESAN CHEESE	
2 T	BUTTER BUDS	

You might like to try thinning with a little white wine or adding herbs.

MAYONNAISE

8 OZ   FAT = TR EA

1/2 C	NON-FAT YOGURT CHEESE	PUREE ALL & LET SIT 1 HOUR.
1/2 C	COTTAGE CREAM (p 392)	
2 T	BUTTER BUDS	
1 t	FRESH LEMON JUICE (OR TO TASTE)	
1 t	DRY MUSTARD (OR TO TASTE)	
1 t	SALT (OR TO TASTE)	
1/2 t	CAYENNE PEPPER (OR TO TASTE)	

MOCK OIL

 easy   2 CUPS   FAT = TR EA

2 C	WATER OR SKIM MILK	SIMMER THESE & REMOVE FROM HEAT.
2	KNORR CHICKEN BOUILLON CUBE	
2	KNORR VEGGIE BOUILLON CUBE	
1 C	COLD WATER OR SKIM MILK	COMBINE WELL, WHISK IN AND HEAT TO THICKEN. CHILL.
1/2 C	ARROWROOT OR CORNSTARCH	

Whether you use water or milk depends on how you plan to use the Mock Oil.

This is to be used to thicken recipes. You cannot fry with this!!
It works best when it is pureed with other ingredients.

NON-FAT YOGURT

easy   4 CUPS   FAT = TR EA

Heat oven to 200 & turn off, or if your oven has a light, leave on while making.

4 C	SKIM MILK, HEATED TO 115 DEGREES	COMBINE & PLACE IN STERILE CONTAINER(S).
1/2 C	NON-FAT MILK POWDER	
2 T	YOGURT, UNPASTEURIZED, WITH LIVE CULTURE	
1/3 C	HONEY (OPTIONAL)	COVER & LET SIT IN A WARM OVEN FOR 24 HOURS.
1 t	REAL VANILLA EXTRACT (OPTIONAL)	

GLOSSARY

FAT CONTENTS LISTED:

The fat content given for each recipe is for the unit of measure it makes. For example, if a recipe states...

MAKES 20 OZ The fat content given as .5 GM EA means .5 GM PER OZ

SERVES 8   The fat content given as 1 GM EA means 1 GM PER SERVING

MAKES 2 CUPS The fat content given as TR EA   means TRACE PER CUP

------	Dash of an ingredient or as needed
'TIL	Until
BNCH	Bunch
C	Cup
CH	Chopped
CHIFFONADE	Leafy vegetable, rolled up & sliced thin
CL	Clove
CONCASSE	Peeled, seeded & chopped tomatoes
CR	Crushed
EA	Each
FR	Fresh
GM	Gram
GR	Ground
KNOX	Knox Gelatin
LB	Pound
LGE	Large
MIN	Minute
OZ	Ounce
PDR	Powder
PKG	Package
QT	Quart
S & P	Salt & pepper
SEA LEGS	Imitation crab meat
SL	Slice
STKS	Sticks
TT	To taste
T	Tablespoon
t	Teaspoon
TR	Trace

BLANCH

Submerge in boiling liquid for a brief time (usually 30-60 seconds).

COLLAR

A band of foil or parchment, usually 3" or more, surrounding a cake or pan to give extra height the dish needs to finish off properly.

DE-FAT

Add 3 ice cubes to stock or pan juices. Pour into a Ziploc Freezer Bag, press out the air & place in freezer for 10 minutes. When you are ready, hold the bag over a clean pan, cut a small slit (do not cut off the corner or you'll lose it in the stock), in a bottom corner & drain juice. When the fat level gets close to the slit, pinch it closed & discard.

DEGLAZE

To add wine, stock, vinegar or any liquid to a hot pan after removing the item that has been cooked, (usually meats). This loosens the bits & pieces stuck to the pan & creates a rich flavorful base for a sauce.

DRY-FRY

To fry in a hot non-stick pan that has been heated, then lightly sprayed with Pam or other vegetable oil spray. (The item may or may not have been first salted, peppered & floured—be sure to shake off **ALL** extra flour).

FLAG FOLD

Usually with Phyllo Dough. Take top left corner of an narrow strip, bring down to right edge of strip & below (= to the width of strip). Now fold this top right peak down the right side (= to the width of strip). Repeat (Starting with the top right corner, folding to left side).
Keep repeating the folding procedure until you use up the strip.

KNIFE (OR PICK) COMES CLEAN

Insert a toothpick or knife into center. Item is done if nothing is stuck to it when it is withdrawn.

LET RISE

Place dough in warm place, usually in a sprayed container, covered 'til either doubled or tripled in volume.

MAKING CREPES

Heat non-stick pan & spray with Pam Butter Spray. Pour 2-3 T of batter into pan, swirling to coat entire bottom. Turn when golden brown. Don't worry if the first one is not great, they'll get better.

MAKING OMELETS

Heat non-stick pan, spray with Pam Butter Spray. Pour in 6 oz. of Egg Beater mixture. With plastic spatula, draw cooked edges toward the center, allowing uncooked egg to escape to outside edges. This will prevent your omelet from turning out "flat". When almost set, spoon 2-3 spoons of mixture down the center. Fold one side over. Shake omelet to edge of pan, roll over and out of the pan onto a warm plate.
Repeat for other omelets.

PROCESS CHOP-CHOP

Place ingredients in food processor & process in on-off motions.

SEAR

Used to sear flavor & moisture in meats. To fry in a very hot pan that has been sprayed with Pam, turning to brown all sides.

SHOCK

Usually with vegetables, after blanching, dip in ice water until cool.

SLURRY

A combination of cold water & cornstarch to use as a thickening agent. Be sure to dissolve **all** of the corn starch. Add this to boiling liquid (off the heat) & bring to a boil, whisking constantly, to thicken.

SPRAY & LINE PAN

Spray pan with Pam & cut either parchment or wax paper to fit bottom of pan, then spray the paper lightly. Use wax paper only if it will be completely covered by ingredients (cake batters etc., not drop cookies).

TEMPER

Slowly whisk a little of the hot part of the recipe into the cold part until the cold part is warm. Then return all back to the hot part.

WATER BATH

Place container(s) of food to be cooked in a large dish & fill half way up with hot water.

BOVRIL

This is a concentrated beef flavoring. It is a paste that comes in a jar and is similar to Vegimate, Marmite or Kitchen Bouquet.

CAVENDER'S GREEK SEASONING

My favorite seasoning & almost impossible to explain the ingredients. It's worth asking your grocer. I had to write for it, but it's in more stores now. Or write: S. C. Seasoning Co., PO# 1296, Harrison, AR   72601.

PICKLED RED BELL PEPPERS

Roasted red bell peppers preserved in a vinegar & sugar solution. Usually kept chilled in the grocery store, near the chilled pickles.

MY ALL-TIME FAVORITE, TIME SAVING DEVICE!!!

I don't go anywhere without my trusty SLICE & DICER. It's the only one that I've found that really works. I always tell people to save time whenever & wherever possible. To me, it's truly **'WORTH IT'S WEIGHT IN GOLD'**. I've added it onto the order form because so many people have asked for it.

PLEASE SEND ME THE FOLLOWING:

____Copies GUILT FREE GOURMET   @ \$49.95 ea   \$ _____
                                                                                   plus 4.95 S & H ea

                                                                                   _____

____Copies 70-DAY MENU PLANNER   @ 4.95 ea   _____
                                          (plus 1.00 S & H if not ordering
                                                2 or more books)
                                                                                   _____

____GUILT FREE GOURMET APRON   @ 19.95 ea   _____
      70 DAY MENUE PLANNER   (plus 3.95 S & H)

                                                                                   _____

____My all-time favorite SLICE & DICER   @ 39.95 ea   _____
                                          (plus 4.95 S & H)

                                                                                   _____

____GUILT FREE GOURMET CREW SHIRTS   @39.95 ea   _____
                                          (plus 3.95 S & H)

                                                                                   _____

                                                        SUB TOTAL   _____

                        Florida residents add 6 % sales tax   _____

I am enclosing a check or money order for   TOTAL   _____

Name_____Street_____Apt/Box_____

City_____State_____Zip_____

Allow 4-6 weeks for delivery or add \$15.00 for Express Service & circle this..

MAKE CHECKS OR MONEY ORDERS PAYABLE TO:

WWW.GUILTFREETV.COM
954-462-4239
WELLNESS PUBLISHING
PO #460682
FT LAUDERDALE, FL 33346-0682

Even though GUILT FREE GOURMET is not connected with GUILT FREE NONFAT ICE CREAM, I would like to recommend it highly, VERY HIGHLY. I tried it because it's name is so similar to my book & I love it. It's great! If you haven't tried it yet, you'll really be surprised. If you can't find it, ask for it. This does two things: it lets the stores know that the demand for Fat Free Foods is still growing & lets them know which brands we want. And we want the best, right? So I called Dean Foods & asked if they would offer my readers a coupon & they were delighted to help.

Guilt Free® Ice Cream is unbelievably rich and absolutely delicious—without any fat or sugar! Enjoy the great taste of Guilt Free® in seven scrumptious flavors—Vanilla, Chocolate, Strawberry Delicious, Banana Nut Crunch, Vanilla Fudge, Praline Pecan Crunch and Triple Chocolate. And, Guilt Free® makes a nonfat frozen yogurt, too! Flavors include Vanilla, Peach, Black Cherry, Strawberry Swirl and Chocolate Fudge.

After you've tasted rich and creamy Guilt Free®, you'll know why it's a winner in taste tests. Guilt Free® is great tasting—without any guilt!

NutraSweet®   All Natural Simplesse® Fat Substitute

Guilt Free is a registered trademark of Yarnell Ice Cream Company, Inc.